Soviet Policy and Practice toward Third World Conflicts

Soviet Policy and Practice toward Third World Conflicts

Stephen T. Hosmer
Thomas W. Wolfe
The Rand Corporation

LexingtonBooks
D.C. Heath and Company
Lexington, Massachusetts
Toronto

The authors are grateful to the following publishers for permission to quote from previously published materials:

Bobbs-Merrill Co., Inc., for Donald S. Zagoria, *Vietnam Triangle: Moscow, Peking, Hanoi.* Copyright 1967 by Western Publishing Company, Inc. Reprinted by permission.

Foreign Affairs for Donald S. Zagoria, "Into the Breach: New Soviet Alliances in the Third World," Spring 1979; and William M. LeoGrande, "The Revolution in Nicaragua: Another Cuba?" Fall 1979. Copyright 1979 by the Council on Foreign Relations, Inc. Reprinted by permission.

Times Books, a division of Quadrangle/The New York Times Book Co., Inc., for excerpts from *The Road to Ramadan* by Mohamed Heikal. Copyright © 1975 by Times Newspapers Ltd. and Mohamed Heikal. Reprinted by permission.

Library of Congress Cataloging in Publication Data

Hosmer, Stephen T.
    Soviet policy and practice toward Third World conflicts.

    Bibliography: p.
    Includes index.
    1. Soviet Union—Foreign relations—1945-   . 2. Underdeveloped areas—Foreign relations. 3. Soviet Union—Military relations—Foreign countries. I. Wolfe, Thomas W. II. Title.
DK274.H67   1982   327.47   82-16194
ISBN 0-669-06054-2

Published simultaneously in Canada

Printed in the United States of America

International Standard Book Number: 0-669-06054-2

Library of Congress Catalog Card Number: 82-16194

Contents

Maps

Tables

Glossary

ANC	African National Congress (South Africa)
ASEAN	Association of Southeast Asian Nations (Indonesia, Malaysia, the Philippines, Singapore, and Thailand)
C³	Command, control, and communications
CEMA (CMEA)	Council of Mutual Economic Assistance (USSR, Bulgaria, Czechoslovakia, East Germany, Hungary, Poland, and Romania)
CPSU	Communist Party of the Soviet Union
DRV	Democratic Republic of Vietnam (North Vietnam)
ELF	Eritrean Liberation Front (Ethiopia)
EPLF	Eritrean Liberation Front/Popular Liberation Forces (Ethiopia)
FLNC	Congolese National Liberation Front
FNLA	National Liberation Front of Angola
Frelimo	Front for the Liberation of Mozambique
Frolinat	Front for the National Liberation of Chad
FSLN	Sandinista National Liberation Front (Nicaragua)
GDR	German Democratic Republic (East Germany)
KGB	Committee of State Security (USSR)
LDCs	Less-developed countries
LSD	Landing ship, dock
LSM	Landing ship, medium
LST	Landing ship, tank
MFA	Armed Forces Movement (Portugal)
MPLA	Popular Movement for the Liberation of Angola
MRBM	Medium-range ballistic missile
MVD	Ministry of Internal Affairs (USSR)
NVA	North Vietnamese Army
OAS	Organization of American States
OAU	Organization of African Unity
PAIGC	Party for Independence of Guinea-Bissau and Cape Verde
PDPA	People's Democratic Party of Afghanistan
PDRY	People's Democratic Republic of Yemen (South Yemen)
PF	Patriotic Front (Zimbabwe)
PFLO	Popular Front for the Liberation of Oman
PLO	Palestine Liberation Organization

PMAC	Provisional Military Administrative Council, or Dergue (Ethiopia)
Polisario	Sahara Liberation Movement (Morocco)
PRC	People's Republic of China
PVO	Air defense (USSR)
SEATO	Southeast Asia Treaty Organization
SWAPO	South-West Africa People's Organization (Namibia)
UAR	United Arab Republic (Egypt and Syria)
UNITA	National Union for the Total Independence of Angola
VTA	Military Transport Aviation (USSR)
WSLF	Western Somali Liberation Front (Ogaden)
YAR	Yemen Arab Republic (North Yemen)
ZANLA	Zimbabwe African National Liberation Army
ZANU	Zimbabwe African National Union
ZAPU	Zimbabwe African People's Union

Acknowledgments

The research leading to this book was conducted at The Rand Corporation and sponsored by the U.S. Air Force. The authors thank the officials of the U.S. Air Force and other government agencies who provided information and valuable help during the course of this study. They also thank The Rand Corporation for its support in enabling them to reach a wider audience through this book.

The authors express their indebtedness and gratitude to Rand colleagues who contributed to this study: Rose E. Gottemoeller, who provided valuable research assistance; Susanna W. Purnell, who assembled useful case studies on past Soviet Third World conflict behavior; and John K. Walker, Jr., who surveyed developments in Soviet force-projection capabilities. They also thank Francis Fukuyama, Harry Gelman, and Paul M. Kozar for their careful reading of the manuscript and thoughtful comments, criticisms, and suggestions. The authors acknowledge their debt to Erma Packman for her invaluable help in editing the manuscript, to Eleanor Wainstein, who prepared the index, and to Joan Allen and Rosalie Fonoroff for their able secretarial assistance throughout the preparation of this book.

Any views presented in this book are the responsibility of the authors and do not necessarily reflect the opinions or policies of the U.S. Air Force.

Introduction

The Soviet invasion of Afghanistan in late 1979, following closely on the Soviet-Cuban intervention in Angola and Ethiopia, and the concomitant improvements in Soviet power-projection capabilities underline the importance of Third World contingencies for U.S. policy and defense planning. Such planning requires an understanding of Soviet policy and practice toward Third World conflicts.

This book examines the patterns of past Soviet involvement in Third World conflicts, illuminates the political-military conditions that encourage such intervention, and explores the possible thrust of Soviet behavior that may be expected in the future.

Part I traces the evolution of post-World War II Soviet policy and practice toward the Third World from the standpoint of salient characteristics and instrumentalities (including military- and economic-assistance programs), shifting strategic focus and geographic emphasis, and adjustment to opportunities and constraints. Soviet military involvements and threatened interventions in a variety of Third World conflicts and crises are examined. Special attention is given to the motivations and military-political circumstances leading to the more-recent Soviet-Cuban interventions in Angola and Ethiopia and the USSR's invasion of Afghanistan. The Part I narrative is constructed to convey a sense of the historical development and chronological relationships of the various aspects of Soviet Third World policy and practice upon which the book focuses. The analysis takes account of the effects of the impressive growth of the USSR's force-projection capabilities during the past two decades. It does not examine Soviet force structure and capabilities in detail since such information is available in studies devoted to that purpose.

Part II presents a distillation of the authors' findings concerning the principal attributes and patterns of Soviet Third World conflict behavior. Particular emphasis is given to how Soviet policy and operations have been tailored to accommodate the requirements and risks of differing situations, the dominant considerations that seem to condition Soviet intervention decisions, and the effectiveness and responsiveness of Soviet military-support operations. Trends that may increase future Soviet activism in the Third World are identified along with the potential constraints that may limit future Soviet freedom of action and influence in the Third World. The book speculates on the patterns of Soviet Third World activity that might be anticipated in the future and, finally, addresses some of the implications of past Soviet behavior for the design and conduct of U.S. policy.

In brief, the book finds that Soviet Third World policy during the past thirty years has combined assertiveness with caution. The assertive tendency, evident since the mid-1950s, seeks to exploit instabilities arising from indigenous Third World political upheavals and conflicts. The cautious side of Soviet policy aims at avoiding unmanageable risks, as manifest, for example, in the Soviet tendency to intervene in conflict situations primarily where opportunity has arisen through some combination of local requests for support and the reluctance or inability of other potential great-power patrons, especially the United States, to become engaged. Indeed, Soviet military-political successes in the Third World usually have come where the Soviets or their surrogates essentially have been unopposed by outside powers.

The experience suggests that future Soviet behavior in the Third World will depend importantly on the extent to which Moscow may perceive the United States as resolved to commit and capable of committing its power to check further Soviet expansion. The experience also underlines the importance of preventive measures aimed at reducing the vulnerability of Third World states to the types of internal instability and adverse political change that invite Soviet exploitation. For this reason, the United States should pursue a policy of anticipatory involvement. Such a policy might include, among other things, strengthening the capability, competence, and reliability of Third World military establishments, which, more often than not, are the final arbiters of their countries' domestic- and foreign-policy orientations.

To the extent that Soviet policy in the Third World remains opportunistic, the United States will continue to be challenged to find ways to foreclose Soviet opportunities.

Part I
Evolution of Soviet Third World Policy and Practice

The notion that the USSR—impelled by reasons of ideology, history, and realpolitik—would seek opportunistically to "fill every nook and cranny available to it in the world basin of power" was one of the key premises underlying the post-World War II Western policy of containment of the USSR. (The words are George Kennan's, in his famous "X" article on "The Source of Soviet Conduct," *Foreign Affairs*, July 1947, p. 575.) Although containment in the context of East-West relations today appears defunct, much the same premise concerning the expansionist proclivities of the Soviet system is usually taken to apply to contemporary Soviet behavior in the Third World where, in a sense, containment of the USSR gradually met its demise, beginning about the mid-1950s.

A combination of factors has made Soviet Third World policy particularly disturbing to many observers toward the beginning of the 1980s. The USSR appears to possess an untiring urge to expand its influence and to reduce that of its rivals in the Third World. In addition, the changing and troubled international environment has become increasingly vulnerable to Soviet opportunism at a time when the USSR's capabilities to project power into the Third World have increased.

Part I offers a broad overview of Soviet Third World policy and practice as they have evolved in the post-World War II period, from Stalin's last years to the beginning of the 1980s, three decades later. Some earlier phases of Soviet experience also are relevant to the subject but cannot be taken up here without exceeding the scope of the book. However, a brief survey of pre-World War II Soviet attitudes toward the revolutionary potential of the colonial world and of Soviet military aid and intervention during the first thirty years of Soviet history may be found in appendixes A and B.

The pattern of Soviet military and economic assistance to the less-developed countries is traced over time. Statistical data on Soviet aid to three Third World communist states—North Korea, Vietnam, and Cuba—are treated separately and not always in the same detail.

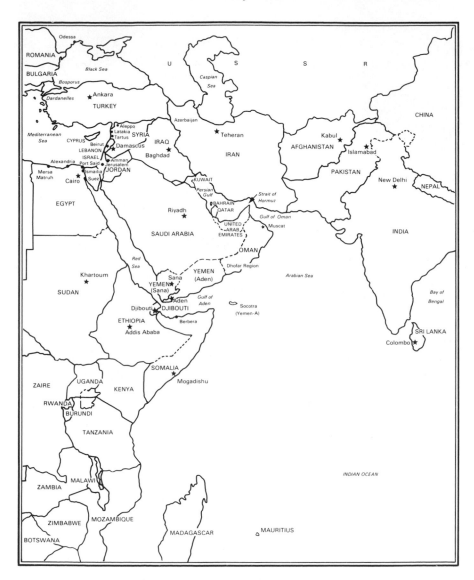

Middle East and Southwest Asia

1

Soviet Third World Policy under Stalin, 1946-1953

Secondary Interest Shown Third World Potential

Despite the postwar disintegration of colonial empires and a long-standing Marxist-Leninist tenet that colonial revolution would weaken Western imperialism and hasten the demise of the capitalist system,[1] Soviet foreign policy paid only secondary attention to Third World developments in Stalin's later years. Observers typically hold that Stalin was slow to recognize the postwar revolutionary potential of the Third World because in the early postwar years he was engrossed with the economic reconstruction of the USSR, with consolidation of the USSR's position in Eastern Europe and elsewhere around its borders, and with intrabloc communist power relationships growing out of the rapid rise to power of communist China.[2]

Postwar Soviet policy under Stalin was not, however, altogether passive with respect to the Third World. Immediately after the war, for example, the USSR sought to establish a presence in Africa and the Mediterranean by demanding a trusteeship over one or more of the former Italian colonies in Africa and by pressing Turkey for revision of the Montreux Convention and for a Soviet base in the Dardanelles.[3] None of these demands was met. In Soviet-occupied areas of northern Iran, meanwhile, support of local rebellions in 1945 went as far as helping to establish "autonomous" Azerbaijanian and Kurdish republics.[4] However, this effort too proved abortive; after the situation was taken up in the United Nations (UN) and the United States threatened to intervene, Soviet troops were withdrawn in March 1946, and the two puppet regimes fell, as had the Soviet Republic of Gilan of 1920-1921.[5]

The Soviets also showed some interest in postwar Third World situations more distant from the USSR. At the September 1947 founding of the Cominform, for example, Andrey Zhdanov had noted that the Vietminh conflict with the French in Indochina exemplified "a powerful movement for national liberation in the colonies and dependencies."[6] Thereafter, the Soviets began to give some propaganda encouragement to the Vietminh, although rendering little material support, which came mainly in the early 1950s from the Chinese communists after their accession to power in Peking in October 1949.[7]

Elsewhere in Asia in the late 1940s, local communists fomented armed insurrections in India, Malaya, the Philippines, Burma, and Indonesia,

3

presumably in accordance with a revolutionary strategy set forth by Zhdanov at the Cominform founding meeting in 1947.[8] This strategy, an accompaniment of Zhdanov's two-camp thesis, called for abandoning an earlier postwar approach that permitted cooperation between local communist parties and what the Soviets called bourgeois-nationalist groups seeking independence in the underdeveloped world.[9] The new strategy, however, more or less backfired. Not only were the several attempts at armed uprisings poorly organized and soon suppressed but also, since they took place in Asian countries where nationalist regimes already had been established or were on the verge of gaining independence, Soviet stock in the formerly colonial world suffered an appreciable decline.

In effect, by pursuing the dogmatic line that "the solution of colonial slavery is impossible without a proletarian revolution,"[10] and by asserting that nationalist leaders of the period such as Gandhi, Nehru, and Sukarno were merely imperialist "lackeys,"[11] the USSR left itself little room for effective courtship of potential anti-Western allies in the nonaligned formerly colonial states. Stalin was later criticized inside the USSR because even though he had belatedly recognized the collapse of the colonial system, he had underestimated the potential of the "national bourgeoisie" in the developing countries as an ally of the "world proletariat" in the "struggle against imperialism."[12]

Military Aid and Interventions in the Third World

Soviet military-aid programs in the postwar Stalinist period were largely confined to Moscow's Eastern European satellites, communist China, and North Korea; virtually no military aid was proffered to any of the noncommunist countries then emerging in the Third World. Likewise, the several Soviet political-military interventions of the period occurred only in contiguous areas and were mostly attempts to help communist-oriented movements to secure a foothold in regions bordering the USSR.

Proving more successful than the abortive attempt mentioned earlier to set up puppet regimes in northern Iran, a brief postwar presence of Soviet troops in Manchuria and Inner Mongolia facilitated the lodgement of Chinese communist elements in those areas, to the ultimate detriment of the nationalist government in the Chinese civil war.[13] (The Soviet military presence in Manchuria, incidentally, also facilitated the dismantling of former Japanese industrial installations there for shipment to the USSR prior to Soviet withdrawal in May 1946.) In neighboring North Korea, where the postwar Soviet presence ensured the establishment of a communist regime, Soviet troops were not withdrawn until 1949, by which time a strong North Korean army had been created.

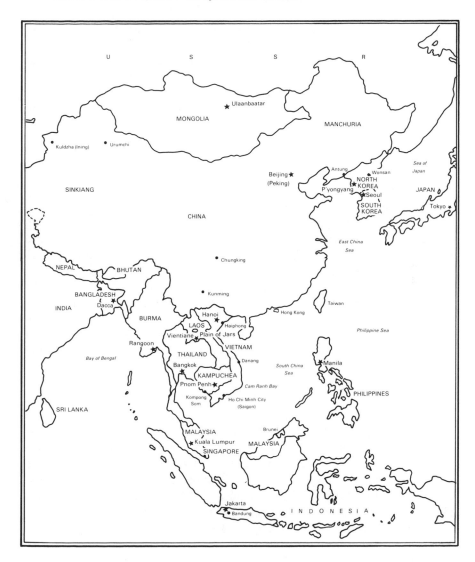

Far East

Another political-military intervention of the immediate postwar period—also in Asia—took place in 1946, when Soviet and Outer Mongolian troops crossed into the Kuldzha-Ili and Altay regions of Sinkiang to support a recently organized East Turkestan Republic, opposed by Chinese nationalist authorities. Within some months, however, local Kazakh and Uighur groups turned against the Soviets, who withdrew in 1947, leaving the Chinese communists eventually to secure control of Sinkiang in 1949.[14]

In contrast to their activities in their Asian borderlands, the Soviets did not intervene militarily in postwar situations arising on their European fringes, except, of course, for the massive occupation of Eastern Europe. Some indirect support was given the guerrilla uprising in Greece in 1945-1946, but following proclamation of the Truman Doctrine in March 1947, Stalin grew alarmed, as disclosed by Milovan Djilas, lest the uprising "endanger his already won positions," leading him to insist in early 1948 that it be called off.[15]

The prime example of what might be considered a major proxy intervention came in 1950, in Stalin's last years, when the U.S. withdrawal from the Asian mainland apparently led Stalin, Mao Tse-tung, and Kim Il-sung (at a series of meetings in Moscow between December 16, 1949, and February 18, 1950) to conclude that the time was ripe for a relatively risk-free operation to extend communist control over all of the Korean peninsula. These expectations, of course, were upset by the U.S. (and UN) response to the invasion of South Korea, providing a lesson in the unpredictability of U.S. decisions—a lesson that was to color Soviet risk perceptions for many years to come. During the war itself, it eventually became necessary to save North Korea by massive direct Chinese intervention and large-scale but mainly indirect Soviet intervention in the form of arms and military advisers.

In place of the earlier, widely held view that the Korean war was launched at Soviet initiative, it is now thought that the attack was proposed by Kim Il-sung and agreed to by Stalin and Mao in the expectation that the Syngman Rhee regime would quickly collapse from within and that U.S. intervention could be ruled out, thus permitting a virtually risk-free operation to unify the divided peninsula under communist rule. This is essentially the version given by Khrushchev in his memoirs, although he did not participate directly in Stalin's preinvasion meetings with Kim and Mao.[16]

In preparation for and during the Korean conflict of 1950-1953, the USSR furnished substantial amounts of materiel to its North Korean and Chinese partners, together with up to 3,000 military advisory and training personnel and some combat-air backup. The materiel supplied to communist China during the active phase of the war included some 2,400 aircraft (MIG-15 fighters, TU-2 piston bombers, IL-28 jet bombers, and other types) and sizable numbers of tanks and artillery.[17]

According to several sources, including Khrushchev, at the start of the war Stalin had called back all of the Soviet advisers in North Korea as a precaution against their being captured and thus implicating the USSR in the invasion. However, Soviet advisers and some combat personnel soon returned when Kim Il-sung's forces encountered adversity. Most of the

Soviet combat personnel are thought to have been MIG pilots. Khrushchev's memoirs, for example, note that Soviet fighter planes were stationed in North Korea for the defense of Pyongyang, and Marshal Ivan Kozhedub of the Soviet air force in 1956 told one of the authors of this book that he had commanded air-defense fighter units in the Korean war. Other Soviet sources have also mentioned Soviet air-combat activity in Korea.[18]

2 Revived Soviet Interest in the Third World, 1954-1957

Soviet Third World Policy Lines after Stalin

Following Stalin's death in March 1953, his successors renewed Soviet interest in the revolutionary potential of the African and Asian colonial world. Khrushchev, in particular, became an exuberant exponent of extending support to new regimes in the Third World, viewing the Bandung Conference of April 1955—the first major gathering of African and Asian leaders—as a sign that trends were favorable for advance toward communism in countries passing from colonial status to independence.[1] Khrushchev's early efforts to promote an image of the USSR as the friend and benefactor of the newly emerging Third World states included his offers of lavish developmental aid during a much publicized journey with Marshal Bulganin to India, Burma, and Afghanistan in late 1955, the same year in which Soviet arms began appearing in the Middle East.[2]

Although some of Khrushchev's colleagues, including Molotov, apparently argued that it was preferable to pursue Soviet interests through patient organizational activities by African and Asian communist parties rather than counting on bourgeois national leaders to advance the cause of national liberation, Khrushchev's approach won out.[3]

At the Twentieth CPSU (Communist Party of the Soviet Union) Congress in February 1956, perhaps best remembered for Khrushchev's anti-Stalin secret speech, Khrushchev noted that the "disintegration of the imperialist colonial system" was of "world-historical significance."[4] Also at the Twentieth CPSU Congress, the zone-of-peace concept was introduced to amend the Zhdanov two-camp thesis of 1947 and to give Soviet diplomacy greater flexibility. According to Khrushchev's definition, the zone of peace embraced the communist camp and the so-called nonaligned states of the Third World, with both opposing Western "imperialism."[5]

Other doctrinal expressions of the period, such as those by Evgeniy Zhukov in 1956 and Evgeniy Varga in 1957, also emphasized the new post-Stalin view that the national-liberation movement in the colonies was an important part of the world revolutionary process, even where the national bourgeoisie rather than a local communist party might be playing the main role in the "struggle for independence."[6]

Interestingly enough, neither Khrushchev's zone-of-peace formulation nor most of Soviet theoretical writing of the 1950s included Latin America

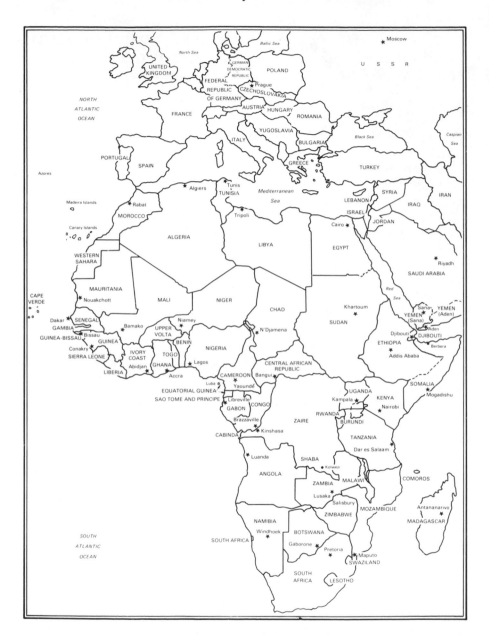

Africa and Europe

as a promising Third World target area—a status it was to acquire only in the next decade after Castro had come to power in Cuba and had successfully defied the United States.

**Beginning of Military- and Economic-Aid
Programs in the Third World**

In terms of Soviet practice, the mid-1950s marked the beginning of military-
and economic-aid programs to selected noncommunist countries of the
Third World. The initial Soviet arms-aid program in the mid-1950s coincided
with both the Soviet discovery of political opportunities in the Third World
and Soviet efforts to offset the system of Western-sponsored alliances such as
the Baghdad Pact and the Southeast Asia Treaty Organization (SEATO),
which were being forged to contain Soviet expansionism.[7]

Egypt was the first arms-aid recipient, under a $250 million agreement
announced in September 1955 after Nasser some months earlier had taken
the initiative in seeking military aid from Moscow. The USSR initially (in
1954) had taken a negative attitude toward Nasser and his accession to
power by a military coup d'etat but, by 1955, had evidently begun to see the
potential advantages of arranging an arms deal with him. The circumstances and date of the first arms agreement with Egypt have been
reported variously. The most recent account, by Mohamed Heikal, an in-
sider, indicates that Nasser relayed his initial request for Soviet arms to
Moscow in April 1955 through Chou En-lai. According to Heikal, the
Soviet arms shipment was already on the way when Nasser announced the
deal in September 1955.[8]

The initial shipment of arms to Egypt included about 100 MIG-15
fighters, 45 IL-28 jet bombers, 150 T-34 tanks, and several surface naval units
and submarines. This ice-breaking arms deal in the Middle East was followed
in early 1956 by arms-aid agreements with Syria (then in a military alliance
with Egypt) and Afghanistan. Czechoslovakia served as the nominal supplier
in these first military-aid transactions. Again according to Heikal, the arms
negotiations with Egypt in summer 1955 were carried out with the Soviet
military attaché in Cairo and other high-ranking Soviet officers sent from
Moscow, but in order not to prejudice the spirit of Geneva that ensued from
the four-power summit of July 1955, Moscow decided that the initial arms
transfers should be nominally concluded through Czechoslovakia.[9] However,
after the Suez crisis of November 1956 and a step-up of Soviet-bloc military
assistance, the USSR became a direct arms provider.

The introduction of Soviet arms into the Middle East was in part
facilitated by Western reluctance to supply arms, at least on terms acceptable
to nonaligned leaders like Nasser. In the mid-1950s, Nasser's rise to promi-
nence in Egypt and Syria was in full swing. Because he regarded the Baghdad
Pact as Western interference with his plans for Arab unity, and because the
Tripartite Declaration of May 1950 had made it difficult for him to obtain
arms in the West, the time proved ripe for him to engineer the first purchase
of Soviet arms by a middle-eastern country. Similarly, Afghanistan had
tried and failed to get Western (U.S.) arms to buttress itself against

Pakistan and hence was receptive to Soviet military-aid offers by Khrushchev and Bulganin during their 1955 tour of southern Asia.[10]

Other early requests for Soviet military aid came from Yemen (under the imamate) in 1956[11] and from Indonesia in 1957-1958. The Indonesians sought arms aid from the USSR, after requests to the United States had been turned down, both to help deal with domestic rebellion and to contest Dutch control of western New Guinea.[12]

In the economic sphere, where political objectives were clearly the dominant factor behind the initial Soviet program, the Soviets tended, as one observer put it, to place "blind trust in the efficacy of the state sector," emphasizing that the expansion of public ownership—especially of a few large heavy-industry projects such as steel mills and machine-building plants—would lead the recipient countries speedily to prosperity and economic independence.[13] Afghanistan in 1954 and India in 1955 were the first recipients of Soviet economic and trade agreements.

Soviet Threats to Intervene in the Middle East

The Suez crisis, which grew out of Nasser's July 1956 takeover of the Suez Canal, found the USSR proffering support of various kinds to Egypt. During the first week after Israel, France, and the United Kingdom began military operations against Egypt on October 29, 1956, Soviet support consisted mainly of seconding U.S. efforts in the UN to obtain a ceasefire and withdrawal resolution. Only after eight days did the Soviets take a more-assertive initiative on behalf of Egypt.

On November 5, 1956, the USSR threatened to intervene militarily in the Suez conflict, hinting that Soviet rockets might be used against the United Kingdom and France unless they ceased operations against Egypt. This was Khrushchev's initial resort to "missile diplomacy."[14]

On the same day, in what Khrushchev later conceded to have been merely a ploy, Bulganin proposed to President Eisenhower that joint Soviet-U.S. intervention be carried out if the U.K., French, and Israeli forces did not halt in twelve hours.[15] The United States rejected the joint-intervention proposal on November 6 and warned that a Soviet rocket attack would provoke U.S. retaliation.[16] The Suez crisis also saw Khrushchev's first threats to send Soviet volunteers to oppose what he called aggression—on August 23, before the fighting began, and on November 6, the day of the ceasefire.[17]

According to the historical consensus, Khrushchev was probably bluffing when he threatened to use strategic rockets and send volunteer troops. Sadat, for example, called the Soviet ultimatums "nothing but muscle-flexing" to make it appear that the USSR had saved the situation, and he credits Eisenhower with having gotten the United Kingdom, France, and Israel to call off the hostilities against Egypt.[18]

Soviet and Czechoslovak military advisers and technicians in Egypt at the time of the Suez affair were ordered to avoid taking part in the fighting. Some of them flew Soviet-built aircraft out of the country, while others put to sea in Soviet-supplied submarines.[19]

During the Syrian-Turkish crisis of September-October 1957, when Khrushchev accused the United States of inciting Turkey to attack Syria, the USSR threatened to help "crush aggression with its military forces."[20] Accompanying these threats were announcements of combined military and naval exercises by Soviet forces in areas bordering Turkey and of Marshal Rokossovskiy's appointment to command the Transcaucasus Military District. During the initial phase of the crisis in September, a small Soviet naval contingent had been sent to visit Latakia, Syria, but it was withdrawn as the crisis developed further.

3 Khrushchev's Forward Strategy, 1958-1960

Growing Soviet Optimism Regarding
Third World Prospects

On the heels of Soviet missile and space achievements of 1957, a more-forward strategy toward the Third World unfolded in 1958-1960. This strategy coincided with Khrushchev's increasing use of missile diplomacy in dealing with the Western powers.[1]

Khrushchev seemed confidently optimistic during this period about the prospects for projecting Soviet power and influence globally, thanks both to the deterrent effect on the West of impressive Soviet strides in strategic technology and to what was seen in somewhat oversimplified fashion as a largely self-sustaining revolutionary tide in the Third World, a tide that would move newly independent states along the "socialist path of development" with the help of political guidance and some economic and military aid from Moscow.[2]

The doctrine of national democracy as a stage, preferably a nonviolent one, in the transition to Soviet-style socialism now came to provide the main theoretical basis for Soviet Third World policy. The adoption of the new doctrine allowed for a shortcut to socialism by newly independent states of Asia and Africa along a "noncapitalist path of development," provided the national leadership of these states maintained political and economic independence of the West and refrained from suppressing local communist parties. In essence, national democracy was defined as the stage when a "liberated" people had broken away from "imperialist oppression" and had been taken under the wing of the Soviet bloc (initially, this bloc included China) but when the new nation was still engaged in carrying out "bourgeois reforms" and had not yet embarked on the "building of socialism."[3]

This doctrine was enunciated at the World Conference of Eight-one Communist Parties in Moscow in November 1960 and elaborated on by Khrushchev a couple of months later.[4] Khrushchev also stressed both the possibility of national-liberation conflicts, which Moscow was obligated to support, and the danger of their escalation if the nuclear powers became involved. Western opinion widely interpreted Khrushchev's report as the prelude to a wave of Soviet-backed violence in the Third World. In practice, however, Khrushchev proved cautious in supporting revolutionary wars

15

and insurgencies, a factor that became a major point of contention in the emerging polemics between Moscow and Peking after 1960.[5]

Castro's coming to power in Cuba in January 1959 was taken by the Soviets as a demonstration of the concept of national democracy, in which national-bourgeois leaders could in fact play a positive revolutionary role.[6] However, the Soviets were cautious for at least a year about accepting the Cuban windfall because of fear that Castro might turn out to be a revolutionary backslider.[7] Perhaps they were also concerned that his brand of revolution might prove a more-attractive alternative in Latin America than the orthodox communist model.

Extension of Third World Military- and Economic-Aid Programs

The Soviet military-aid diplomacy, which had begun in the Middle East in 1955 with sending arms to Nasser, was widened somewhat geographically in this period. In November 1958, the USSR made its first military-aid agreement with Iraq, following the overthrow of the pro-West monarchy in July 1958 by General Abdul Kassem.

The first military-aid agreement with India was signed in November 1960, after the USSR offered to meet Indian requirements at less cost than the United States, and to allow commodity repayment as well. Indian receptivity to aid overtures, which apparently had originated from the Soviet side, was heightened by concern over Pakistan's defense buildup.[8] The initial agreement, however, was of relatively minor scope, covering about thirty-two transport aircraft and ten helicopters together with crew training.[9]

In late 1959 and early 1960, sub-Saharan Africa began to receive modest amounts of Soviet military aid, beginning with Guinea, followed in 1961 by agreements with Ghana and Mali.[10] Each of these countries had adopted a radical pan-African, anti-Western posture. Also, in July-August 1960, the USSR began to supply the Lumumba faction in the Congolese civil war, but Soviet aid in this instance was cut off by UN action, as noted in the following section.

In late 1960, during the last stages of the French-Algerian war, the USSR started to furnish arms aid to the Algerian rebels but kept it quite limited so as not to jeopardize Soviet relations with France.[11] A small amount of arms aid, beginning in 1960, also was furnished to Morocco over the next two years.

Altogether, during the first six years of Soviet military aid to less-developed countries (LDCs) of the Third World, the value of arms deliveries—either by the USSR directly or through other Warsaw Pact members—has been estimated at an average of about $300 million per year, or close to $1.8 billion for the period.[12] Aid deliveries represented perhaps about 85 percent of commitments made during the period.

The eleven nominally nonaligned Third World recipients of Soviet military aid during the 1955-1960 period are listed in table 3-1. The table does not include Third World countries such as North Korea, North Vietnam, and Cuba; while also recipients of Soviet military aid during this period,[13] these countries—categorized as belonging to the Soviet bloc—customarily have been excluded from most of the statistical data published by U.S. government agencies on Soviet arms transfers to nonaligned LDCs.[14] Similarly, these statistical data omit estimates of aid to national-liberation or insurgent movements not holding formal governing power.

By far the principal beneficiaries of Soviet military aid in this period were Egypt and Indonesia, the two accounting for more than half the aid dispensed by Moscow. Roughly another third of the total went to Syria, Iraq, and Afghanistan, and the remainder to the other recipients shown in the table.

Most of the Soviet arms delivered to the Third World between 1955 and 1960 came from surplus stocks of older equipment made available by the USSR's own postwar modernization programs, although after 1961 Mos-

Table 3-1
Nonaligned Third World Recipients of Soviet Military Aid, 1955-1960
($US millions)

Major Recipients	Amount	Other Recipients	Amount
Egypt	More than 500	North Yemen	Less than 30
Indonesia	More than 500	India	Less than 30
Syria	More than 200	Guinea	Less than 10
Iraq	More than 200	Morocco	Less than 10
Afghanistan	More than 200	Congo	Less than 10
		Algeria	Less than 10

Sources: Precise figures for Soviet military aid to individual Third World countries during the 1955-1960 period are lacking. The sources from which the table has been compiled include the following: Roger E. Kanet, "Soviet Policy toward the Developing World: The Role of Economic Assistance and Trade," in *The Soviet Union in the Third World: Successes and Failures,* ed. Robert H. Donaldson (Boulder, Colo.: Westview Press, 1981), pp. 343-347; Wynfred Joshua and Stephen P. Gibert, *Arms for the Third World: Soviet Military Aid Diplomacy* (Baltimore: Johns Hopkins University Press, 1969), pp. 101-103; Stockholm International Peace Research Institute, *The Arms Trade with the Third World* (New York: Humanities Press, 1971), pp. 188-191, 823-870; Marshall I. Goldman, *Soviet Foreign Aid* (New York: Frederick A. Praeger, Inc., 1967), pp. 73-182; U.S. Department of State, Bureau of Intelligence and Research, *Communist States and Developing Countries: Aid and Trade in 1970,* RECS-15 (Washington, D.C., September 22, 1971), pp. 17-18; and Central Intelligence Agency, *Communist Aid to Less Developed Countries of the Free World, 1975,* ER 76-10372U (Washington, D.C., July 1976), p. 1.

cow began to furnish more-modern, first-line weapons systems to certain Third World clients.[15] On the whole, comparatively low prices and favorable repayment terms tended to characterize the Soviet military-aid programs from the start, doubtless increasing their attractiveness to Third World countries.

Along with provision of military equipment, the USSR also furnished technical assistance in training recipient personnel to operate and maintain it. This aspect of the Soviet aid programs evolved along two lines: the sending of Soviet instructors and technicians to countries receiving arms aid and of Third World military personnel to the USSR for training.

Soviet commitments of economic aid to nonaligned Third World countries in the 1954-1960 period paralleled rather closely the pattern of military aid, being concentrated mainly in the Middle East and southern Asia. Altogether, in this seven-year period, economic-aid commitments by the USSR and its Eastern European allies came to more than $2 billion, slightly exceeding the amount devoted to military-aid programs, which had begun a year later.[16] Actual deliveries of economic aid, however, lagged considerably behind the rate of military-aid deliveries, coming to about 45 percent during the period.[17]

More than 90 percent of Soviet-bloc economic-aid commitments went to six countries: Egypt, India, Indonesia, Iraq, Afghanistan, and Syria, with the first two topping the list with commitments of more than half a billion each. The Aswan Dam project in the case of Egypt and the Bhilai steel mill in India were major factors in boosting the economic-aid levels committed to these two countries.[18]

Notably, Soviet economic assistance also embraced projects for harbor, airport, and road construction that held potential strategic interest for the USSR.[19] An example was the project initiated in 1956 to build a sixty-seven-mile highway and two-mile tunnel through the forbidding Hindu Kush Mountains in northern Afghanistan. Completed in 1964, the highway was to serve as an invasion route for Soviet troops fifteen years later.

Soviet Intervention and Threats to Intervene in Third Area Conflicts

In July-August 1958, following the overthrow of the pro-Western monarchy of King Faisal II in Iraq and the establishment, under Abdul Kassem, of a new regime friendly to the USSR, Lebanon and Jordan appealed to the United States and the United Kingdom for armed help against expected pressure from Egypt and Syria, then conjoined in the United Arab Republic (UAR), and from revolutionary Iraq. The quick dispatch of U.S. and U.K. troops elicited a propaganda campaign and announcements from Moscow to the effect that maneuvers of Soviet forces were taking place in the Trans-caucasus and Turkestan military districts, with participation of air force and airborne units under Marshal Skripko.[20]

As one analyst wrote, the Soviets on this occasion had again displayed a characteristic crisis-reaction pattern, combining verbal threats with military caution.[21] According to Sadat, the USSR declined to give a commitment to Nasser to aid the UAR militarily in the event of war arising from the coup in Iraq.[22] Khrushchev reportedly told Nasser on this occasion that he "was not prepared to take any risks that could lead to war" and that the best he could do was to declare maneuvers in the border areas, admonishing Nasser to "please keep in mind that it is nothing more than maneuvers."[23]

During the Quemoy Strait crisis of August-September 1958, Khrush-chev warned Eisenhower that the USSR would retaliate with nuclear weapons in the event of a U.S. nuclear attack on China. Subsequently, the Chinese communists charged that Khrushchev's threat was an empty bluff, coming only on September 18 after it was already clear "that there was no possibility that a nuclear war would break out."[24]

In July 1960, after Katanga's secession from Congo-Leopoldville, the Lumumba government requested Soviet military aid, in addition to its prior request for UN help. The Soviets responded by first arranging an airlift of Ghanaian troops and supplies in five IL-18s and, in August, began sending in additional Soviet aircraft and equipment. In September, however, when the Mobutu-Kasavubu faction ousted Lumumba, Congo's airports were closed to the Soviets, diplomatic relations were broken, and the initial Soviet military intervention in sub-Saharan Africa ended in a setback.[25]

A substantial Soviet airlift, amounting to some 1,000 IL-14 flights, was carried out in late 1960 and early 1961 between North Vietnam and Laos. This delivery of military equipment and supplies followed a Soviet decision to furnish direct and open support to a Kong Le-Pathet Lao coalition fighting against the U.S.-backed forces of General Phoumi.

The Soviet motive for this open intervention in the Laotian civil war has been ascribed by some analysts to Moscow's need to retain the allegiance of North Vietnam in the then unfolding quarrel with China.[26] In any event, the outcome of the intervention was distinctly favorable from the Soviet and North Vietnamese viewpoint, for it led the United States to drop support of Phoumi and enabled Pathet Lao and North Vietnamese forces to remain in effective control of eastern Laos, assuring Hanoi's future logistic access to South Vietnam via the Ho Chi Minh Trail complex.

In the western hemisphere, the Soviets reacted initially with hesitancy and caution to Fidel Castro's 1959 ascent to power in Cuba since Moscow was uncertain about both the eventual political orientation and the staying power of the new regime.[27] While these uncertainties persisted in some degree for a year or so, the communist bloc nevertheless began to provide economic and military assistance to the Castro government as Cuban-U.S. relations deteriorated during 1959-1960. Arms agreements with the Czechoslovak and Soviet governments were negotiated by Raul Castro during his visit to Eastern Europe in summer 1960, and by the end of that year an estimated $50 million worth of arms and munitions had been delivered to Cuba.[28] Additional deliveries arrived in early 1961,[29] and Cuban forces used some of these weapons (for example, Soviet field artillery and Czechoslovak antiaircraft guns) to defeat the landing at the Bay of Pigs in April 1961.[30]

The prospect of more-encompassing Soviet support was raised when Khrushchev, in a July 1960 speech, promised the Castro regime the "protection" of Soviet-based intercontinental ballistic missiles (ICBMs).[31] Several months later, however, Khrushchev backed away from this rash promise, declaring that he had meant it only symbolically.[32]

4 Peaking of Khrushchev's Third World Expectations, 1961-1964

Soviet Policy Lines in the Early 1960s

During this period, Khrushchev's expectations remained high concerning the prospects of revolutionary advance in the Third World, and the national-liberation movement there was now ranked as "second in historical importance only to the formation of the world socialist system."[1] In accordance with the national-democracy formula, Moscow courted anti-Western regimes in the Third World with political flattery and military and economic aid and encouraged local communists to cooperate with and to help radicalize such regimes further rather than to try to develop their own bases of power.[2]

Castro, who began to describe the Cuban revolution as socialist in early 1961 and who declared himself a Marxist-Leninist for the first time in December 1961, was accepted early in this period by the Soviets. Indeed, he served as a shining example of the process by which, according to some Soviet theoreticians, it was possible for a leader from the national bourgeoisie in a Third World country to metamorphose into a "revolutionary democrat" and, in turn, to "come over to the positions of scientific socialism."[3]

In the early 1960s, Africa became defined as the focal point of the historical struggle between capitalism and "scientific socialism."[4] Soviet hopes for a fairly quick leap by the formerly colonial countries of Africa from tribally oriented communities to some form of sociopolitical and economic organization along Marxist-Leninist lines probably peaked in October 1961, when delegates from Guinea, Ghana, and Mali attended the Twenty-second CPSU Congress in Moscow.

These countries, together with Egypt, Algeria, and Morocco, were members of the so-called Casablanca bloc. They were especially favored by the USSR for their leftist, anti-Western leaning and were believed to have "genuine revolutionary potential."[5] The Casablanca bloc itself was disbanded when the Organization of African Unity (OAU) was formed in 1963, but Khrushchev's endorsement of its members continued throughout his remaining tenure, as attested by his bestowal of Hero of the Soviet Union awards on Ben Bella of Algeria and Nasser of Egypt in May 1964. After Khrushchev's ouster, one of the criticisms heard was that this decoration was not supposed to be awarded to noncommunist leaders.[6]

21

Although Soviet optimism about revolutionary prospects in Africa characterized the first half of the 1960s, the first doubts and a new appreciation of African reality probably also had been born after the failure in 1960-1961 of the Soviet plunge into the former Belgian Congo in support of Lumumba.[7] Séko Touré's expulsion from Guinea of the Soviet ambassador in 1962 for meddling in the country's internal affairs was another sign that even in the radical African states, pro-Soviet attitudes would not necessarily always prevail.[8]

It is not at all clear whether Soviet Third World policy of the Khrushchev period grew essentially out of antecedent theoretical formulations such as those concerning the revolutionary potential of the national-liberation movement and the transitional functions of national democracy or whether the theories were largely contrived to fit a policy line that Khrushchev more or less improvised as he went along, with an eye to exploiting opportunities to outflank the Western network of alliances and to implant a lasting Soviet presence in the Third World.

Soviet policy in conflict situations clearly was constrained, however, by the danger of escalation. Khrushchev talked a strong line of support for national-liberation struggles,[9] but when concrete cases arose that might have involved the USSR in direct confrontation with U.S. military power, he was quite cautious about tendering Soviet aid in any form that might have entailed the unpredictable danger of a widening war.[10] In this connection, the risk of confrontation with the United States and other Western countries doubtless appeared greater in the Middle East, Asia, and Latin America than in the bulk of Africa. The fact that this risk appeared to be smaller in Africa may have been one reason why that continent was regarded by Khrushchev as an especially promising national-liberation arena.

Rising Military- and Economic-Aid Levels

During the period 1961-1964, Soviet military-aid agreements signed with nonaligned Third World countries rose in value about 20 percent over the preceding six years, coming to an estimated total of slightly more than $2.5 billion.[11] At the same time, the number of recipients grew from eleven to sixteen, with most of the new ones in sub-Saharan Africa. Actual deliveries during this period, however, fell somewhat below the earlier rate.

Military aid to Algeria, which gained independence in July 1962, was increased greatly in October 1963 after the border conflict between Morocco and Algeria broke out and after Ben Bella's basically anti-Western posture became apparent to the USSR.[12] Competition with the Chinese for political influence in Algeria also figured in the upping of Soviet aid in 1963, as it was to do again in 1965.

Military aid to India was increased steeply in 1962, when the border conflict between India and China, as well as the prospect of an India-Pakistan war, served to heighten India's reliance on Soviet weapons. The 1962 agreements included provisions for Soviet construction of two aircraft plants in India: one to produce MIG-21 fighters, the other to manufacture jet engines.[13]

In connection with the 1964 Cyprus crisis, Archbishop Makarios appealed to the USSR for arms aid following Turkish air strikes in August. Though the Soviets responded in late September with a pledge of air-defense weapons and other equipment, the situation presented certain difficulties for Moscow, which did not want to alienate the Turks. According to unconfirmed reports, the Soviets may have given Ankara some form of assurance that the arms supplied to Makarios would not be used offensively against Turkey.[14]

As indicated in table 4-1, three countries received by far the greatest share of Soviet military-aid commitments between 1961 and 1964: again Egypt and Indonesia, joined in this period by India. The three together accounted for more than 70 percent of the total. The other four major recipients accounted for about 20 percent.

Between 1961 and 1964, Soviet and Eastern European commitments of economic aid to Third World countries together came to about $2.5

Table 4-1
Third World Recipients of Soviet Military Aid, 1961-1964
($US millions)

Major Recipients	Amount	Other Recipients	Amount
Egypt	More than 700	North Yemen	More than 30
Indonesia	More than 500	Somalia	More than 30
India	More than 500	Cyprus	Less than 20
Iraq	More than 100	Morocco	Less than 10
Syria	More than 100	Ghana	Less than 10
Afghanistan	More than 100	Cambodia	Less than 10
Algeria	More than 100	Laos	Less than 10
		Mali	Less than 10
		Tanzania	Less than 10

Sources: Roger E. Kanet, "Soviet Policy toward the Developing World: The Role of Economic Assistance and Trade," in *The Soviet Union in the Third World: Successes and Failures,* ed. Robert H. Donaldson (Boulder, Colo.: Westview Press, 1981), pp. 343-347; Wynfred Joshua and Stephen P. Gibert, *Arms for the Third World: Soviet Military Aid Diplomacy* (Baltimore: Johns Hopkins University Press, 1969), pp. 101-103; Stockholm International Peace Research Institute, *The Arms Trade with the Third World* (New York: Humanities Press, 1971), pp. 188-191, 823-870; Marshall I. Goldman, *Soviet Foreign Aid* (New York: Frederick A. Praeger, Inc., 1967), pp. 73-182; U.S. Department of State, Bureau of Intelligence and Research, *Communist States and Developing Countries: Aid and Trade in 1970,* RECS-15 (Washington: September 22, 1971), pp. 17-18; and Central Intelligence Agency, *Communist Aid to Less Developed Countries of the Free World, 1975,* ER 76-10372U (Washington: July 1976), p. 1.

billion,[15] approximately the same amount as was extended in military aid. The delivery of economic assistance, however, continued to lag behind that of military aid, with only about 40 percent being drawn.[16]

Partly as a consequence of intensified competition with China during this period for influence over Third World LDCs,[17] the number of recipients of Soviet economic assistance increased, especially in sub-Saharan Africa where the Khrushchev regime's theoreticians saw hopeful prospects of leading newly independent states along a "noncapitalist path of development."[18] However, even though the Khrushchev regime committed about 20 percent of Soviet aid to Africa, no sub-Saharan countries were among the principal aid recipients.[19] Of the thirty-one LDCs receiving Soviet-bloc economic aid during the period, the main recipients by far (accounting for some 70 percent of the total) continued to be Egypt, India, Indonesia, Afghanistan, Iraq, and Syria, joined in 1963 by Algeria.[20]

As was the case earlier under the Khrushchev regime, a major proportion of Soviet economic assistance was earmarked for the development in the recipient countries of an industrial base focused on large projects in the state sector.[21]

The Cuban Missile Episode and Other Projections of Soviet Military Power

In Khrushchev's time, the major projection of Soviet military forces abroad on behalf of a Third World client—and, of course, in the service of other Soviet political and strategic interests as well—came in connection with the 1962 Cuban missile episode. Available accounts differ as to where the missile-deployment idea originated. Khrushchev indicated a couple of months after the October showdown that the Cubans had asked for additional assistance, including missiles,[22] but he later claimed that he had originated "the idea of installing missiles with nuclear warheads in Cuba."[23] Castro at various times has also given contradictory accounts, saying both that the missiles were sent at Cuban request and that Khrushchev suggested the idea.[24]

In any event, the Strategic Rocket Forces units deployed to Cuba in September-October 1962, along with forty-two IL-28 jet bombers, would have had sixty-four to seventy-two missiles (SS-4 medium-range and SS-5 intermediate-range ballistic missiles) when fully operational. Together with Soviet personnel in Cuba to install and help operate air-defense SA-2 missile sites, MIG-21 interceptors, and other equipment, the strategic offensive-force deployment—plus a little-remarked combat force estimated at about 5,000 tank-equipped ground troops—brought the total number of Soviet soldiers and technicians in Cuba in October 1962 to more than 22,000 by

U.S. reckoning, or about twice that number according to a statement by Castro seventeen years later.[25] By either count, this represented the largest overseas deployment of Soviet military personnel before or since, approached only by the Soviet military presence in Egypt in 1970-1972.

Relatively little public attention during the Cuban missile crisis was given the Soviet ground-combat formations equipped with T-54 tanks, anti-tank missiles, and Frog tactical rockets that had also been dispatched to Cuba, ostensibly to protect the strategic-missile force. This inattention has been explained by the fact that the ground-combat troops had not been clearly identified until low-level photographic coverage began late in the crisis, and hence, these troops were not included in the removal demands voiced by President Kennedy on October 22, 1962.[26] Seventeen years afterward, of course, the issue of Soviet ground-combat troops in Cuba was to become the center of a controversy that strained U.S.-Soviet relations, as is discussed in chapter 8.

During the dispute in 1962 between Indonesia and the Dutch over West Irian, New Guinea, Soviet training personnel were prepared to play a combat role had the issue not been settled, according to a public statement by Mikoyan two years later. In the second volume of his memoirs, Khrushchev also indicated that he had pledged, in event of a war against the Dutch, to allow participation by "Russian pilots who were flying Indonesian planes and Russian officers who were commanding Indonesian submarines."[27] According to Khrushchev, Indonesian Foreign Minister Subandrio then leaked this information to the Americans in the belief that the United States would try to persuade the Dutch to accept a negotiated settlement rather than fight.

The beginning of a Cuban military presence in Africa, which was to lead about fifteen years later to Soviet-Cuban cooperative intervention in various African countries, came a year before the Cuban missile crisis, when Cubans in 1961 set up a guerrilla training camp in Ghana that functioned until Nkrumah's overthrow in 1966. In the mid-1960s, the Cubans also formed presidential guards to help protect ruling regimes in Guinea and Congo-Brazzaville from counterrevolutionary activity.[28]

The first Cuban arms shipments and dispatch of combat troops to an African country came in October 1963 to aid Ben Bella's Algeria in its border conflict with Morocco. The Cuban contingent, which apparently did not see much combat action, consisted of about 400 tank troops, with tanks.[29] Trips by Ché Guevara to Africa in 1964 and 1965 were followed by the sending of arms and Cuban advisers to several countries. From about this time to the end of the 1960s, Castro's ties with Moscow were to become somewhat strained, but activities in Africa do not appear to have been a particular source of friction between Moscow and Havana.

In the Middle East, the early 1960s found the USSR taking sides in the Yemeni civil war, which began in September 1962 after a military coup overthrew the new imam. Soviet military aid to the new Yemen Arab Republic (YAR), in its protracted struggle with the royalist side, was funneled through Egypt, which sent an intervention force of 70,000 to back the republican government.[30] Eventually, after the 1967 Arab-Israeli war and Egypt's withdrawal from Yemen, the Soviets provided limited air combat and other support that enabled the republicans to defeat the royalists and to end the civil war.[31]

The USSR's military involvement in southeast Asia between 1961 and 1964 was fairly modest in scale. It consisted partly of transport aircraft flights in Laos and Vietnam to ferry military supplies for Pathet Lao and Viet Cong groups. Some Democratic Republic of Vietnam (DRV) requests for increased military assistance apparently were turned down after inspection visits to Vietnam in late 1962 by Soviet General Pavel Batov and in early 1963 by Yuriy V. Andropov, head of the USSR Committee of State Security (KGB).[32] On the whole, however, the USSR met most of the DRV's requirements for support in the struggle against South Vietnam during the period.[33] The real surge in Soviet support of Hanoi was to begin, of course, in 1965.

5 Setbacks and Reappraisal of Third World Policy, 1965-1969

**Less-Optimistic Soviet View of
Third World Developments**

Following Khrushchev's ouster in 1964, Soviet Third World policy suffered two setbacks. In June 1965, Colonel Houari Boumédienne overthrew the Ben Bella regime in Algeria. Also in 1965, an abortive communist coup attempt in Indonesia (apparently encouraged by China) and a successful countercoup by Indonesian military leaders brought about the fall of Sukarno and the establishment of the anticommunist Suharto government.[1] The Indonesian case was a particularly rude blow in light of the more than $1 billion worth of military aid and $600 million of economic assistance that the Soviet bloc had extended by 1965.

Military coups also removed from office two other leading revolutionary democrats—Kwame Nkrumah in Ghana (February 1966) and Modibo Keita in Mali (November 1968).[2] Since both these former Casablanca-bloc countries had also been among the prized Soviet candidates for transition to genuine socialism, the replacement of their leaders by military-led regimes less radical and less anti-Western in outlook was hardly a welcome trend. These setbacks evidently helped to spur a searching reappraisal by Soviet analysts and policymakers of the USSR's approach to the Third World.[3]

Among the points to emerge from this reappraisal in the late 1960s was a more-realistic view of the limitations of economic assistance as a policy tool in the Third World and the acknowledgment that earlier hopes of telescoping the Third World's transition to socialism into a relatively brief process led by radical nationalist leaders had been misplaced.[4] According to Soviet commentary, factors such as the "toppling of colonial regimes" by the national-liberation movement in the late 1950s and early 1960s; the coming into being of "dozens of new national states," some of which "rejected the capitalist way"; and the "rapid growth of the economic might and authority of world socialism, especially after the USSR's launching of the world's first sputnik," had led to the assumption "that all, or almost all, the developing countries would opt for the noncapitalist way without much delay" and had "tended to create the erroneous impression that the struggle was almost at an end . . . that the forces of imperialism were played out."[5]

However, as one Soviet scholar put it, these earlier expectations had then undergone a "cooling off, especially after the events in Indonesia,

27

Ghana and Mali.''[6] Soviet researchers, evidently encouraged by the authorities, now offered more ''sober'' and ''realistic'' analyses of the Third World situation than those common in the Khrushchev period.[7] They suggested that in light of the relatively backward political and economic conditions prevailing in most Third World countries, the skipping of stages and premature radical steps in the transition to scientific socialism were inadvisable, and that the revolutionary process in the Third World would therefore probably turn out to be much slower than once thought, perhaps spanning ''an entire historical epoch.''[8]

In particular, the transitional potential of national bourgeois leaders came under increasing question. A high-ranking Central Committee official, Professor R. Ulyanovskiy, wrote in 1968: ''During the period of struggle against colonial regimes, the national bourgeoisie often led the struggle. At the present stage of the national liberation struggle, the national bourgeoisie already has demonstrated its inability to continue playing such a role.''[9] Negative appraisals of this sort, it may be noted, foreshadowed subsequent shifts in Soviet theory and practice away from the courting of national democratic elements in the Third World and toward greater reliance on Marxist parties and other left-wing revolutionary groups with pro-Soviet leanings.[10]

Declining optimism with regard to rapid evolution toward socialism under conditions prevailing in the Third World was reflected in figures cited by a Soviet analyst in 1966 to the effect that of sixty-six liberated countries in Asia and Africa, only seven had chosen the noncapitalist path of development.[11] With regard to communist prospects in Africa, particularly, where nationalism and other internal conditions had proved much more resistant than originally assumed, the earlier Soviet optimism waned markedly in the late 1960s, although it was to revive again after the mid-1970s.[12]

Renewed Attention to the Role of the Military

In the Soviet reassessment of Third World developments, the role of the military in the developing countries of Asia, Africa, and Latin America came in for renewed attention. As noted in 1970 by G.I. Mirskiy, perhaps the leading Soviet authority on the subject, there had been successful military coups in thirty of these countries in the preceding ten years, so that in the Third World the ''transfer of power to the military is no longer an exception, but almost the rule.''[13]

Earlier, during the Khrushchev period, the Soviets had taken a positive view of the military's political role, crediting Third World military officers with often having ''formed the backbone of revolutionary democratic forces'' and with having played ''an outstanding part in laying the basis of a new life'' in a number of developing countries.[14]

After several of the early nationalist leaders upon whom the Soviets had staked their bets became the victims rather than the beneficiaries of military coups, however, a more-mixed view of the military's political potential emerged. There was a fair measure of agreement that the military in the developing countries could exert decisive influence on the national direction taken because of factors such as the tentative shape of the political structure and the low socioeconomic level of recently liberated states, along with the army's position in many cases as the "symbol of independence" and "the most organized force of society."[15]

However, while recognizing that "in some countries the army has long been functioning as the only effective political force,"[16] Soviet analysts were now more wary concerning the military's potential for what they called a progressive role. As one writer put it: "The lesson of military upheavals in several countries of Asia and Africa shows that although the army can play a progressive role in the national-liberation movement, it can also easily turn into a tool of reactionary forces."[17]

Which role the army might play at a particular historical stage would depend on many factors, including which segment of the military might manage to gain the upper hand in a given country—those officers wishing to "accelerate progressive development" toward socialism, or those "influenced by imperialist internal reaction" and prepared to "use the army against the revolution."[18] Indeed, the danger that even revolutionary-democratic- and socialist-oriented Third World states were vulnerable to being reversed was probably one of the more-sober lessons drawn from the military coups of the latter 1960s.

This lesson, in turn, led various Soviet analysts to the conclusion that it would be necessary to develop a well-organized vanguard party in each socialist-oriented country in order to institutionalize the policies of a progressive leadership stratum, even if an individual leader should be overthrown.[19] As Mirskiy wrote in 1970 and reiterated six years later, to count on the army as "the motive force of anticapitalist revolution and leader of society in countries of socialist orientation would be a serious mistake . . . the only condition guaranteeing genuine progressive development of countries of Asia, Africa and Latin America is the formation of a vanguard party, occupying the positions of scientific socialism."[20] One of the important tasks of such a party, according to Mirskiy, would be to transform the existing army into a reliable "people's army," for which the Soviet armed forces provided an "unsurpassed example."

In addition to the need to shore up progressive regimes from within by the creation of vanguard parties, the potential reversibility of such regimes also prompted expressions of concern about their vulnerability to intervention from the outside. Thus, according to one Soviet expert on the Third World, the "most important and difficult task of the revolution there is to prevent imperialist intervention."[21]

While the Soviets were reappraising their Third World policy and keeping a relatively low profile in sub-Saharan Africa in the late 1960s, they were also deeply preoccupied with supporting Egypt and Syria in the Middle East in and after the 1967 Arab-Israeli conflict and with continuing support of Vietnam in southeast Asia. At the same time, both U.S. and Chinese competition with the USSR in most of the Third World tended to decline during this period—in the U.S. case because of the Vietnam priority and in the Chinese case perhaps because of the turmoil of the Cultural Revolution.[22] In a sense, therefore, Moscow could be said to have had its Third World reverses of the period in Africa and Indonesia cushioned by problems then distracting its competitors.

Military- and Economic-Aid Programs after Khrushchev's Ouster

Between 1965 and 1969, a period when Soviet support of Hanoi in the Vietnam war was increasing substantially,[23] Soviet-bloc military-aid commitments to nonaligned Third World countries elsewhere continued at approximately the same level as before. New commitments amounted to an estimated total of about $2.5 billion, of which the Eastern Europeans contributed around $300 million.[24] Deliveries during this period for the first time slightly exceeded the amount of new commitments, partly as a consequence of the major effort made to replace promptly Arab materiel losses in the Arab-Israeli six-day war of June 1967.

To resupply Egyptian and Syrian forces, the USSR mounted a large airlift (some 100 aircraft, 350 flights) immediately after the war, followed by further arms shipments and an increase of training personnel. More than 80 percent of Egypt's losses of aircraft, armor, and other equipment reportedly was replaced within a few months after the June war. The number of Soviet advisers and technicians rose from about 500 to between 2,000 and 3,000 by the end of 1967.[25]

According to Sadat, the Egyptians assimilated the new weapons in five months, rather than three years, as the Soviets had expected. Sadat also said that the Soviets undertook the replacement program to "secure their presence" in the region but that they did not intend the new weapons to be used in another war.[26]

The principal Soviet military-aid programs in sub-Saharan Africa in the period were extended to Nigeria and the Sudan. Both countries were divided between a Moslem north and a non-Moslem south, with the central government in the north facing a separatist liberation movement in the south. Despite an ideological obligation to side with the latter, the Soviets sent military aid to the former.

In Nigeria, following the outbreak of civil war over regional and ethnic issues in June 1967, the central government under Colonel Yakubu Gowon turned to the USSR for military assistance after having failed to obtain the kinds of arms it wanted from the United States and the United Kingdom. Of the twenty countries supplying arms to Nigeria prior to the civil war, the United Kingdom had been the principal supplier. Although London continued to support Gowon's government during the war, U.K. refusal to furnish air-force equipment has been singled out as a major factor in opening the door to introduction of Soviet arms into Nigeria.[27]

The USSR gave very selected aid, including a small amount of ground armaments and about fifty MIG-17 and MIG-19 fighters and four IL-28 bombers flown by Egyptian and possibly East German pilots.[28] Some of the fighters reportedly were delivered by air in Antonov transports via Algeria, demonstrating a Soviet potential for distant airlift operations involving route cooperation from other Third World clients.[29]

The Soviet aid contributed to the defeat of the Biafra secessionists by the end of 1969. Although the USSR received in return no special privileges in Nigeria, Soviet involvement in the civil war was by no means a wasted effort because it not only swung Nigeria out of its former unwavering pro-Western orbit but also helped to reverse the trend toward diminished Soviet influence in West Africa, a trend that had been evident following the setbacks in Ghana and Mali.[30]

In Sudan, the Soviets signed a substantial aid agreement in 1968 with the incumbent civilian government of Mohammed Ahmed Mahgoub. The agreement covered fighters, transport aircraft, tanks, and other ground-forces equipment. By the time deliveries began in 1969, a military overthrow had brought to power a new radical Arab nationalist government, under Jaafar el-Nimeiry, with which the USSR would enjoy improved relations until an abortive communist-led coup was attempted against the Sudanese leader in 1971.

According to Mohamed Heikal, however, Soviet relations with Sudan improved only marginally after the military coup that brought Nimeiry to power in May 1969, partly because the Soviets resisted Nimeiry's request for a large cash loan to buy additional arms.[31] The Soviets did actively assist Nimeiry in quelling the Anya-Nya rebellion during the 1969-1971 civil war in Sudan by providing it in-country logistic support and possibly even some direct-combat air support.[32]

To sum up the military-aid picture in the 1965-1969 period, the number of Third World recipients grew from sixteen to twenty-one, with the bulk of the arms transfers going to countries in the Middle East. As indicated in table 5-1, India was by far the largest single recipient in this period outside the Middle East.

Cumulatively, by the end of 1969, the total of Soviet-bloc military aid extended to the nonaligned Third World came to around $6.5 billion, of

Table 5-1
Third World Recipients of Soviet Military Aid, 1965-1969
($US millions)

Major Recipients	Amount	Other Recipients	Amount
India	More than 400	Nigeria	More than 30
Egypt	More than 300	Pakistan	More than 30
Iraq	More than 200	Morocco	Less than 20
Syria	More than 200	North Yemen	Less than 20
Iran	More than 150	South Yemen	Less than 20
Algeria	More than 150	Uganda	Less than 20
Afghanistan	More than 80	Indonesia	Less than 10
Sudan	More than 80	Somalia	Less than 10
		Cambodia	Less than 10
		Congo-Brazzaville	Less than 5
		Guinea	Less than 5
		Tanzania	Less than 5
		Cyprus	Less than 5

Sources: Roger E. Kanet, "Soviet Policy toward the Developing World: The Role of Economic Assistance and Trade," in *The Soviet Union in the Third World: Successes and Failures,* ed. Robert H. Donaldson (Boulder, Colo.: Westview Press, 1981), pp. 343-347; Wynfred Joshua and Stephen P. Gibert, *Arms for the Third World: Soviet Military Aid Diplomacy* (Baltimore: Johns Hopkins University Press, 1969), pp. 101-103; Stockholm International Peace Research Institute, *The Arms Trade with the Third World* (New York: Humanities Press, 1971), pp. 188-191, 823-870; Marshall I. Goldman, *Soviet Foreign Aid* (New York: Frederick A. Praeger, Inc., 1967), pp. 73-182; U.S. Department of State, Bureau of Intelligence and Research, *Communist States and Developing Countries: Aid and Trade in 1970,* RECS-15 (Washington: September 22, 1971), pp. 17-18; and Central Intelligence Agency, *Communist Aid to Less Developed Countries of the Free World, 1975,* ER 76-10372U (Washington: July 1976), p. 1.

which more than 70 percent had gone to three countries—Egypt, India, and Indonesia.[33] However, after the overthrow of Sukarno in 1965, Indonesia ceased to receive large-scale Soviet aid, and almost half of the aid extended by Moscow in the 1965-1969 period went to three Middle Eastern countries: Egypt, Syria, and Iraq.

In the sphere of economic aid to the Third World, overall commitments for the years 1965-1969 were greater than for any earlier comparable time span, despite the reassessment and reorientation of Soviet economic-assistance policy that began around the middle of the period. Commitments approached $4 billion,[34] partly as a result of greater participation by Eastern European countries that accounted for more than 30 percent of the total. The year 1966 saw a record annual commitment of more than $1 billion for the first time, most of which went to four Third World countries: India, Pakistan, Syria, and Iran.[35]

In 1964, the last year of Khrushchev's tenure, aid extensions of some $800 million included a sizable agreement with a new client, Turkey, whose acceptance of Soviet aid offers reflected in part resentment toward the United States and other NATO powers for having failed to support Turkey on the Cyprus issue.[36] In 1967, a year when new aid undertakings in the Middle East, Asia, and Africa dropped off sharply after the record $1.2 billion in 1966, some Soviet interest in expanding trade and aid in Latin America was manifested in offers to several countries. Part of the reported total of about $200 million was accepted by Chile; Brazil had accepted an aid offer of $85 million the previous year.[37]

From 1967 through the rest of the period, new aid extensions remained relatively low, apparently as attempts were made to catch up with lagging deliveries and as trade and aid programs in the Third World were being brought under closer scrutiny and reassessment.[38] The rapid extension of industrial-development aid and concentration on large prestige projects in the Khrushchev era were criticized as a costly failure, and economists like V.G. Solodovnikov of the African Institute urged careful advance study of feasibility and costs and a lower development rate for new projects.[39] Third World countries were also advised that hasty nationalization was counter-productive and that some features of capitalism should be "permitted to exist alongside the state economic sector," not only to help create a proletarian class with a revolutionary potential but also to shift some of the burden to economic assistance to the West.[40]

According to Alexander Kaznacheev, a former Soviet diplomat, the reassessment of Soviet economic strategy in the Third World under Khrushchev's successors led, after 1967, to a definite shift in policy. Among its features, he said, were to avoid heavy-industry development in Third World countries, to channel aid investments primarily into mining and materials export activities, to reorient the economies of the LDCs toward the Council for Mutual Economic Assistance (CEMA) according to a division-of-labor principle giving the LDCs a guaranteed market in return for being raw-materials suppliers, and to require the Eastern European members of CEMA to put up more of the capital investment needed for raw materials and processing facilities in the LDCs.[41] One of the objectives of the new policy, according to Kaznacheev, was to take some of the burden of raw-material supply to Eastern Europe off Soviet shoulders, while at the same time ensuring that the Eastern European countries would remain cooperative with Moscow so as to protect their growing investment in the LDCs.

In any event, from around 1967 on, Soviet economic relations with the Third World underwent a change from the pattern set under the Khrushchev regime. While economic-aid programs continued to serve objectives such as establishing a Soviet presence and increasing Soviet influence in Third World countries, they now also were aimed at becoming economically more effective abroad, commercially more beneficial to the USSR, and more carefully integrated with strategic considerations serving Soviet objectives.[42]

**Shift of Doctrine and Military Posture Relevant to
Intervention**

Early in the 1965–1969 period, following decisions taken by Khrushchev's
successors in connection with the planning cycle for the Eighth Five-Year
Plan,[43] a definite shift in Soviet policy evidently occurred, denoting a
greater readiness than before to employ limited force for political purposes
in the Third World, even in situations where less than vital Soviet interests
might be involved.[44] The shift became manifest at roughly the same time
that Soviet disenchantment with nationalist-bourgeois leaders in the Third
World began to set in, along with expressions of a need to nurture left-wing
vanguard parties as forerunners of future full-fledged communist parties.

Evidence for the argument that the 1965–1969 period marks the beginning of a greater Soviet readiness to contemplate interventionary force in
Third World conflict situations includes Soviet doctrinal and declaratory
statements, improvements in Soviet capabilities for projecting a military
presence into the Third World, and a tendency to exercise such capabilities
more frequently and over a wider geographic range than had been the case
in previous years.

Among pertinent doctrinal signs was the explicit addition of military
support to the other kinds of support to the Third World that it was the pro-
fessed duty of the USSR to render. For example, the listing of "ideological,
political, and material" categories of aid in the 1963 edition of
Sokolovskiy's *Military Strategy* was expanded in the 1968 edition to include
the statement: "The USSR will, when necessary, also render military support to peoples subjected to imperialist aggression."[45]

Renewed emphasis also was placed on the international mission of the
armed forces in the service of the world socialist revolution. In discussing
the "international tasks" of the armed forces under "new historical conditions when the military might of socialism has become a direct factor
in . . . safeguarding the world revolutionary process," one Soviet writer
pointed out, with specific examples, that even in earlier "hardship years"
the USSR "lent military help to weaker countries struggling for independence."[46] In his Central Committee report at the Twenty-third CPSU
Congress in 1966, Brezhnev made it explicit that in fulfilling "its internationalist duty," the USSR would "extend all possible support" to the
national-liberation movement, including "political, economic, and, where
necessary, military support."[47]

A 1972 Soviet study on military force and international relations provided another relevant doctrinal note. The study stated in much more-
explicit terms than previously customary that "greater importance is being
attached to Soviet military presence in various regions throughout the
world" and that "in cases where the need arises to give military support to

peoples fighting . . . against the forces of internal reaction and imperialist intervention, the Soviet Union requires mobile armed forces that are suitably trained and equipped." In some situations, the authors of this work observed, "the very fact of a Soviet military presence in the area of an imminent or developing conflict could exert a restraining influence upon the imperialists and local reaction."[48]

A visible improvement in Soviet military capabilities applicable to intervention in Third World situations, particularly growth in naval forces and airlift potential, paralleled the emergence in the latter 1960s of more-doctrinal emphasis on a Soviet military presence abroad. It is worth noting here that steps to extend the global reach of Soviet forces and to create a supporting infrastructure of ports, airfields, access routes, and communications in the Third World had been initiated for the most part in the Khrushchev period. Earlier Soviet steps toward becoming a more globally mobile military power included blue-water naval deployments, development of a capacity for long-range airlift and of better amphibious and airborne landing capabilities, reactivation of naval infantry, and buildup of merchant shipping and airline operations overseas.[49]

In essence, Khrushchev's successors simply continued what appeared to be a determined Soviet effort to alter a power relationship in which the United States enjoyed not only strategic superiority over the USSR but also went virtually unchallenged in its capacity to intervene locally in troubled situations around the globe.

While the USSR was in the process of improving its Third World intervention capacities in the 1965–1969 period, it also began to display a military presence in wider areas of the Third World than previously. With regard to instances of actual intervention or threats to intervene in conflict situations with a substantial risk of Soviet-U.S. confrontation, however, the Soviet leadership appeared to remain essentially as conservative as before.

In April 1965, the Brezhnev-Kosygin leadership, in a gesture recalling Khrushchev's 1956 threats to send Soviet volunteers to the Middle East during the Suez crisis, announced that the USSR would permit volunteers to fight in Vietnam if U.S. "aggression" against the DRV were intensified. The 1965 Soviet threats came after the U.S. bombing of North Vietnam in February of that year; the U.S. bombing had, in turn, come after the Vietnamese attack on Pleiku earlier the same month, while Kosygin was in Hanoi.[50] When Kosygin visited Cairo in May 1966, incidentally, he told Nasser that the USSR had "offered to send military contingents" to North Vietnam but that Hanoi had turned down the offer.[51]

Though volunteer combat contingents did not materialize, the USSR furnished large amounts of materiel, together with military advisers and technicians, in support of the DRV. The number of Soviet military advisers and technicians in Vietnam was estimated at somewhat less than 3,000, some of whom helped operate Hanoi's air-defense system for brief periods during the mid-1960s.[52] The military materiel furnished to the DRV in the 1965–1969 period included surface-to-air-missile batteries, antiaircraft artillery, radars, fighter aircraft, and a wide array of infantry weapons, with a value estimated at about $1.5 billion. The military-aid figure for the next five years would come close to another $1.8 billion, making almost $3.3 billion worth of weaponry to North Vietnam in what can be described as the USSR's largest and eventually one of its most successful attempts to bring about a local war outcome favorable to its own and its client's interests.[53]

During the 1967 six-day war in the Middle East, when it appeared on June 10 that the Israelis might continue their swift advance into Syria and go on to Damascus, Kosygin called President Johnson on the hot line and warned that unless Israeli forces halted within the next few hours, the USSR would take "necessary actions, including military."[54]

Johnson's firm response included instructions to the Sixth Fleet to move toward Syria, as he put it, to convey a deliberate message to the Soviet leadership.[55] However, since the United States shared with the USSR an interest in bringing a quick end to the fighting, Johnson also applied pressure on the Israelis to accept an immediate ceasefire, which they did—thus satisfying Moscow's objective of rescuing its imperiled clients.

Among other developments associated with the 1967 Arab-Israeli war was an augmentation of the Soviet naval squadron, the Fifth *Eskadra*, in the Mediterranean. The squadron later was credited by Soviet spokesmen with having played a "decisive role in frustrating the adventurous plans of the Israeli aggressors."[56] The appearance of the squadron, which displayed for the first time a small amphibious capability (two LSMs, one LST) well away from Soviet home waters, also marked the establishment of a permanent Soviet naval presence in the Mediterranean. With the apparent purpose of deterring the resumption of Israeli attacks, Soviet warships paid conspicuous visits to Egyptian and Syrian ports after the war. Similarly, in December 1967, a group of ten TU-16 bombers made a publicized visit to Egypt.

Beginning in November 1967, apparently after consultation with Nasser and perhaps at his urging, the Soviets intervened directly in the Yemeni civil war with both an airlift and sealift of military supplies along with military advisers and some Soviet-manned combat aircraft, to prop up the republican regime against the royalists. According to Sadat, consultation between Nasser and King Faisal of Saudi Arabia, which had supported the royalist side in the Yemeni civil war, also preceded the decision for Egyptian withdrawal from Yemen, where five years of involvement had been for Egypt a "military failure" and heavy economic burden.[57]

The Soviets intervened just as the last Egyptian troops were being withdrawn from Yemen and the British had pulled out of Aden in neighboring South Arabia. Soviet combat support of the republican regime in Yemen, as previously pointed out, helped to break the siege of Sana and to insure final defeat of the royalists in 1970. Meanwhile, besides supporting the YAR, the USSR signed a military-aid agreement in 1968 with the new left-oriented South Yemen government in Aden, demonstrating a strong interest in expanding a Soviet foothold on the Arabian peninsula.

A possible example of the kind of interpositioning tactics that might be used by naval forces in some Third World conflict situations was provided by the USSR in January 1968, after the *Pueblo* incident. In response to the dispatch of a U.S. task force to the Sea of Japan, the Soviet Pacific Fleet staged a show of force by deploying a group of sixteen ships in waters between the U.S. task force and the coast of North Korea.[58] However, this episode also seemed to illustrate characteristic caution in crisis situations, in view of the fact that the Soviet force appeared on the scene after the peak of crisis had passed and that its major anticarrier elements (Kynda-class missile cruisers) took care not to approach the U.S. force closely.[59]

Following a visit to India by Admiral Gorshkov in spring 1968, a group of five Soviet warships made the first extended goodwill cruise through the northern Indian Ocean and Persian Gulf, calling at various ports. This cruise marked the beginning of a recurrent Soviet naval presence in these waters.[60] The USSR first deployed amphibious ships to the Indian Ocean in 1969.

The first visit of Soviet naval combatants in a coercive-diplomacy role along the west coast of Africa came in February-March 1969, after Ghana had seized two Soviet fishing trawlers the previous October on charges of aiding pro-Nkrumah dissidents. The Soviet naval contingent, dispatched to Ghana following several months of diplomatic and economic pressure on the Ghanaian government, consisted of two missile destroyers, one submarine, and one oiler. The visit brought release of the trawlers and crews. The extent to which the Soviet trawlers may have engaged in a covert operation to smuggle arms and exiles into Ghana for an attempt to restore Nkrumah, as charged by the Ghanaian government, is not clear.[61]

Other Soviet naval activity in the Third World included the initiation in 1969 of periodic visits to the Caribbean, providing the first opportunity since 1962 to test U.S. reaction to the presence of Soviet armed forces in the western hemisphere, and a first visit in December 1969 by a Soviet naval group to Somali ports. The latter visit was intended to show support for the new Siad Barre regime then threatened by internal instability. The visit was repeated in April 1970.

A shift in Soviet attitude toward the Palestine guerrilla movements took place in this period. The Soviets had initially regarded the Palestine Liberation Organization (PLO) as a troublesome group of little significance and apparently had made contact with it only at Nasser's insistence. By March

1968, however, after Palestinian guerrillas had fought off Israeli armor at Karameh, according to Heikal, the Soviets began to recognize their potential, and in February 1970, they invited Arafat to Moscow for the first time.[62]

6 Furthering of Soviet Strategic Interests in the Third World, 1970–1974

Soviet Persistence Despite Third World Policy Disappointments

The somewhat revised Soviet approach toward the Third World, an approach that emerged from the policy reappraisal of the late 1960s, continued under Brezhnev in the 1970–1974 period with its basic features largely unchanged. Principal emphasis was placed on improving the USSR's relations with and furthering its strategic interests in a broad arc of Third World countries stretching south of the USSR from Morocco to India. In this period, therefore, the high-priority targets for Soviet diplomatic, economic, and military aid in the Third World lay in the Arab Middle East and southern Asia; sub-Saharan Africa, Southeast Asia, and Latin America were accorded a lower priority.[1] The last, however, received somewhat more attention than had been the case earlier, as noted later.

In the Middle East, where the establishment of a Soviet foothold had centered on Egypt for the preceding fifteen years, the net Soviet position suffered serious depreciation in this period, as underscored by the mass expulsion from Egypt in mid-1972 of Soviet military advisers and operational troops, along with the restriction of Soviet basing privileges in that country.

The number of Soviet military personnel expelled from Egypt in July 1972 has varied in accounts by Sadat, Heikal, and others from 15,000 to 21,000.[2] A somewhat lower figure has been given in U.S. estimates, placing the number of operational troops withdrawn at about 7,500 and the number of advisers and technicians at about 5,000.[3] These troops were evacuated largely by air in seven days, in what the Egyptians described as an orderly and efficient operation run by General V.V. Okunev, an air-defense expert and head of the Soviet military mission in Egypt. Some Soviet personnel were also evacuated by sea. Several hundred Soviet military instructors remained in the country.[4]

The Soviets were obliged by the expulsion order to give up the seven airfields from which they had been operating in Egypt, but they were allowed naval visits to Egyptian ports (a right that also would be withdrawn four years later). According to Heikal, when arrangements had originally been made by Nasser for military cooperation with the USSR and on various subsequent occasions, including a visit by Grechko and Gorshkov in May 1972, the Soviets had asked for more than Nasser and Sadat were prepared to grant, such as permanent naval-base facilities at Mersa Matruh on the Mediterranean and Bernis on the Red Sea and port-visiting, overflight, and landing rights with minimal or no prior notice.[5]

The Soviet setback in Egypt at the hands of Sadat came despite massive arms transfers and unprecedented Soviet participation in 1970 in the active defense of Egyptian territory against Israeli air attacks—attacks that at the time had threatened the viability of Nasser's regime.

According to Sadat, he ordered the expulsion because the USSR "had begun to feel it enjoyed a privileged position in Egypt" and because of the constraints it sought to impose upon Egypt's freedom to wage another war against Israel, including Soviet refusal to provide offensive weapons.[6] As Sadat saw it, according to Heikal, it was not the USSR alone but "the two superpowers [who] had agreed that there was to be no war in the Middle East area."[7]

The Soviets were said by the Egyptians to have been "shocked" and "deeply annoyed" by Sadat's order to leave, but their "reaction was very restrained."[8] According to some non-Egyptian sources, the Soviet leadership chose to make the exodus from Egypt even more complete than Sadat had actually wanted, for example, by withdrawal of certain equipment and personnel from the integrated air-defense system.[9]

On a conceptual plane, no new ground was broken by Soviet theorists in this period regarding the developmental process for transition of relatively backward Third World societies, especially in Africa, to scientific socialism. It was acknowledged that "serious obstacles of an objective and sometimes subjective nature" stood in the way of such a transition even in "countries of socialist orientation"[10] and that some of these countries had unfortunately either "turned aside from a progressive course or slowed their advance."[11]

Given what was described as the "political passivity of a significant part of the population" in many developing countries, some Soviet analysts reiterated the need to create vanguard parties made up of "representatives of the proletariat, the peasantry, the progressive intelligentsia, and the radical portion of the military."[12] However, it was also asserted that there were "no grounds for skepticism about the future prospects for non-capitalist development," since in a stubborn struggle one must expect "along with victories also isolated defeats."[13]

Seen in policy terms, the Soviet Third World approach of the 1970-1974 period seemed to call for persisting despite disappointments and to count on the efficacy of Soviet power—as brought to bear through fraternal political guidance, economic aid, and arms transfers—to help set Third World countries on a "progressive" course. At the same time, Soviet policy during this period still appeared to be more a matter of responding to local demands for Soviet aid and involvement—and of exploiting the opportunities offered —than one of contriving or creating fresh opportunities.[14] In this connection, two of the major opportunities that were to help refocus Soviet interest in Africa in the second half of the 1970s grew out of events in 1974 that the Soviets had done little or nothing to bring about: the collapse of Portugal's African empire and the overthrow of Emperor Haile Selassie in Ethiopia.

Despite, or perhaps because of, lowered Soviet expectations of gains in radical Third World states early in the 1970-1974 period, clandestine Soviet support of promising guerrilla liberation movements in sub-Saharan Africa and the Middle East began to increase after 1971.[15] Among the insurgency movements—in addition to the PLO in the Middle East—to receive Soviet, and in some cases Chinese, support were the following:

ANC (African National Congress), external element of the South African Communist Party;

Frelimo (Front for the Liberation of Mozambique), headed by Machel;

Frolinat (Front for the National Liberation of Chad);

MPLA (Popular Movement for the Liberation of Angola), headed by Neto;

PAIGC (Party for the Independence of Guinea-Bissau and Cape Verde);

PFLO (Popular Front for the Liberation of Oman);

Polisario (Sahara Liberation Movement), versus Morocco and Mauretania;

SWAPO (South-West Africa People's Organization), headed by Nugoma;

ZANLA (Zimbabwe African National Liberation Army), split from ZANU;

ZANU (Zimbabwe African National Union), headed by Mugabe, originally backed by China;

ZAPU (Zimbabwe African People's Union), headed by Nkomo, later joined with Mugabe's organization to form the PF (Patriotic Front).

Renewed competition from China for influence in the Third World appears to have been another factor in the step-up of Soviet backing for guerrilla movements at this time.[16] Also around 1971, Soviet interest in access to naval-support facilities on both sides of Africa—Guinea, Equatorial Guinea, and Congo-Brazzaville on the west side, Somalia on the east side—seemed to crystallize.[17]

By contrast with the somewhat lowered Soviet expectation of further Third World advances in Africa and the Middle East in the early 1970s, Soviet

recognition of the supposed anti-imperialist and national-liberation potential of Latin America increased significantly. Two factors in particular accounted for this increase. First, at the close of the 1960s, what were regarded
as progressive military regimes—that is, regimes displaying an anti-U.S.
orientation combined with sufficient leftist domestic measures to enable
Soviet spokesmen to identify them with a new "revolutionary process" in
Latin America—seized power in Peru, Panama, and Bolivia.[18]

Second, in September 1970, a communist-socialist united-front regime
under Salvador Allende was elected in Chile. Soviet Politburo member B.N.
Ponomarev described Allende's election as "second only to the victory of
the Cuban revolution . . . in its significance as a revolutionary blow to the
imperialist system in Latin America."[19] The Chilean armed forces were at
first considered protectors of the Allende regime "against foreign and
domestic reaction,"[20] but this assessment eventually proved wrong when,
after the retirement of a sympathetic minister of defense in August 1973, a
military coup engineered by General Augusto Pinochet overthrew the
Allende government.[21]

While welcoming the election of Allende in Chile, the Soviets were
cautious about embracing him ideologically and were apparently unwilling
to provide him with more than marginal economic assistance, even though
his government urgently needed massive credits to meet Chile's outstanding
foreign debts. This Soviet failure to underwrite Allende may have reflected
uncertainties on the part of Moscow about his survivability over the longer
term, as well as a probable Soviet reluctance to assume another economic
burden in Latin America like the USSR's already costly relationship with
Cuba.[22]

Expansion of Soviet Military-Aid Programs

In the five years between 1970 and 1974, Soviet-bloc military-aid commitments to Third World countries rose steeply to about $14 billion, of
which more than half was extended in 1973 and 1974, largely in support of
the Arab side during and in the aftermath of the October 1973 Yom Kippur
war. About 10 percent of the total was furnished by Moscow's Eastern
European allies.[23]

Although the number of countries receiving Soviet military aid grew to
about thirty in the 1970-1974 period, as indicated in table 6-1, the main flow
of arms was concentrated in the three Middle East Arab states of Syria,
Iraq, and Egypt. The arms-aid relationship with these countries, particularly
with Egypt, was, however, far from harmonious. According to the Egyptians, "arguments about arms supply" were the dominant theme of
Nasser's last two visits to Moscow in 1970 and of Sadat's four visits between

Table 6-1
Third World Recipients of Soviet Military Aid, 1970-1974
($US millions)

Major Recipients	Amount	Other Recipients	Amount
Syria	More than 2,500	South Yemen	More than 150
Egypt	More than 2,500	Afghanistan	More than 150
Iraq	More than 2,000	Peru	More than 150
Libya	More than 2,000	Tanzania	More than 75
India	More than 600	Somalia	More than 75
Iran	More than 600	Nigeria	More than 75
		Uganda	More than 50
		Bangladesh	More than 50
		Algeria	More than 50
		Guinea	More than 50
		Mali	More than 25
		Morocco	More than 25
		Pakistan	More than 25
		Congo-Brazzaville	More than 10
		Lebanon	More than 10
		Sri Lanka	More than 10
		Zambia	More than 5
		Equatorial Guinea	More than 5
		Central African Republic	More than 5
		Burundi	Less than 5
		Ethiopia	Less than 5
		Sierra Leone	Less than 5

Sources: U.S. Department of State, Bureau of Intelligence and Research, *Communist States and Developing Countries: Aid and Trade in 1970,* RECS-15 (Washington, D.C., September 22, 1971), pp. 18-19; U.S. Department of State, Bureau of Intelligence and Research, *Communist States and Developing Countries: Aid and Trade in 1972,* RECS-10 (Washington, D.C., June 15, 1973), appendix tables 9, 10; U.S. Department of State, Bureau of Intelligence and Research, *Communist States and Developing Countries: Aid and Trade in 1973,* INR RS-20 (Washington, D.C., October 10, 1974), appendix table 9; and U.S. Department of State, Bureau of Intelligence and Research, *Communist States and Developing Countries: Aid and Trade in 1974,* Report no. 298 (Washington, D.C., January 27, 1976), appendix table 9.

the time he took over in October 1970 after Nasser's death to the expulsion of Soviet military advisers two years later.[24]

By and large, Egyptian requests for defensive arms between 1970 and 1972 fared better than requests for aircraft and missiles that fell in the offensive category.[25] Despite Egyptian complaints, the USSR refused to fulfill Sadat's persistent request for weapons that, by posing the threat of retaliation "in kind," would deter the Israelis "from hitting Egyptian targets far inland."[26] One may conjecture that the Egyptians wanted TU-22 (Blinder) supersonic-dash bombers equipped with air-to-surface missiles for attacking Israel.[27] In addition, the Egyptians probably also pressed the Soviets for Scud surface-to-surface high-explosive missiles, a weapon system the USSR eventually provided in 1973.[28]

Aside from offensive systems, Moscow also reneged on its promise to provide more-advanced MIG-23 fighter-interceptor aircraft, which the Egyptians believed they needed to cope with the formidable Israeli air force,[29] and there were repeated delays in other Soviet-promised arms deliveries.[30] Sadat complains in his memoirs about the Soviet failure prior to the Yom Kippur war to replenish fully the Egyptian artillery-ammunition stocks consumed during the war of attrition. According to him, Moscow curtailed ammunition replacement until the Soviet airlift of the October 1973 war as punishment of the Egyptian leadership "for starting and continuing the war of attrition against the wishes of the Soviet Union."[31]

Despite the evident Egyptian dissatisfaction with aspects of the nature and pace of the arms assistance it was receiving from the USSR from 1970 to 1972, the overall level of Soviet assistance, stemming in part from new agreements made in conjunction with a friendship and cooperation treaty signed in May 1971, was nevertheless substantial. In addition to the Soviet-manned air-defense forces sent to Egypt in 1970 (see pp. 46-47), the delivery in 1970-1972 of some 120 MIG-21 interceptors and around 700 SA-2, SA-3, and SA-6 air-defense missiles resulted in doubling Cairo's MIG-21 inventory and more than trebling its surface-to-air-missile stocks.[32] At the same time, the Egyptians received further shipments of ground-attack aircraft, tanks, and artillery—increasing their stocks of these weapons by about 50, 100, and 200 percent respectively. Included in these deliveries were a number of front-line T-62 tanks and some 20 SU-7 fighter-bombers.[33]

From an Egyptian viewpoint, however, the flow of arms and spare parts remained unsatisfactory until after a series of consultations between Moscow and Cairo had taken place in late 1972 and early 1973 to patch up various differences. Thereafter, the USSR substantially accelerated arms deliveries to both Egypt and Syria, enabling the two countries to complete their preparations for the Yom Kippur war of October 1973. According to Heikal, the Soviets seemed to be trying to "recover lost ground" in Soviet-Egyptian relations "by speeding up the flow of arms."[34]

Although the Egyptians still did not receive the MIG-23 interceptors and TU-22 bombers they had sought, the equipment furnished at this time included more SA-3 and SA-6 missile systems; tanks with infrared ranging devices; large numbers of portable, infantry-operated antiaircraft and anti-tank weapons; and bridging equipment— all of which fitted into the war plans that the Egyptians say were drawn up without Soviet participation.[35] From about the mid-1970s on, the USSR reportedly began to seek hard-currency cash payments for arms deliveries to the Middle East,[36] although the ability of Egypt and Syria to meet such a requirement appeared to be questionable.

Apart from the major role played by Soviet arms transfers in Moscow's relations with Egypt and Syria in the early 1970s, Soviet military-aid programs proved instrumental in opening up access to strategically located territory in the Horn of Africa in this period. When Somalia turned to Moscow for economic and military aid after General Siad Barre seized power in a 1969 military coup, the Soviets took advantage of the opportunity by way of a quid pro quo to begin the buildup in 1972 of a naval-support complex at Berbera, near the mouth of the Red Sea, and an airfield for TU-95 reconnaissance use at Mogadishu, on the Indian Ocean. A communications facility set up at Berbera linked navy headquarters in Moscow with the Soviet Indian Ocean squadron.[37]

After Allende's election in 1970, the USSR denied rumors that it intended to establish a military base in Chile. It was reported in 1971, but never confirmed, that the USSR had offered to supply Chile with from $50 million to $300 million worth of military equipment. In September 1972, a Soviet military delegation, headed by the chief of the air force, Marshal P.S. Kutakhov, visited Chile for the independence celebrations. No known Soviet military-aid or base programs had been set up prior to Allende's overthrow by a military coup in September 1973.[38] However, the first transfer of Soviet arms to Peru took place in 1973.

In 1974, Soviet competition with the Chinese sharpened in supplying military aid to rival factions in Angola in anticipation of impending independence from Portugal. The Soviet aid went to the MPLA, which the USSR had supported since the early 1960s, although Soviet support was reduced temporarily in 1973 during an MPLA leadership split. The level of Soviet military aid furnished the MPLA through 1974 is obscure but has been estimated at upward of $60 million.[39]

Toward the end of the 1970-1974 period, Libya became a major recipient of Soviet military aid, acquiring a large modern arsenal of Soviet arms that might allow it to serve, in the words of one report, as a possible "warehouse for equipment needed by other Arab nations."[40]

In the field of economic aid, even though Soviet-bloc commitments between 1970 and 1974 increased some 30 percent to about $6.5 billion, economic assistance to Third World countries for the first time lagged far behind military aid.[41] Some 40 percent of the economic aid in this period was pledged by the USSR's Warsaw Pact allies. Delivery of economic aid amounted to slightly more than half of that pledged. In 1970, the first year of the period, the combined total of Soviet and Eastern European economic credits and grants to the Third World, $395 million, fell for once substantially below the economic aid tendered by China, $780 million.[42] Well over half of the Chinese commitment in 1970 went to Tanzania and Zambia for the construction of the TanZam railroad.

India, Pakistan, and Iraq were the three top recipients of economic aid in this period, out of some forty Third World recipients altogether. They were followed by Argentina, Egypt, Algeria, Iran, Syria, Turkey, Chile, and Afghanistan, in that order.[43] The relatively light economic burden of its aid program to Moscow, estimated at around 0.03 percent of Soviet GNP annually, eased somewhat more in this period as repayments of aid principal and interest began to narrow the net Soviet aid outflow. By the end of the period, about 40 percent of economic-aid obligations incurred by LDCs had been repaid, and some recipients—notably, Egypt and India—were approaching the point at which servicing their aid debt to Moscow would cost more than they received annually in aid.[44]

Soviet Intervention in the Middle East and Africa

In late January 1970, after Israel had responded to Nasser's war of attrition along the Suez Canal by mounting low-altitude air strikes deep into Egypt, Nasser urgently asked the Soviets (during a secret four-day visit to Moscow) for advanced interceptor aircraft and low-altitude SA-3 air-defense missiles, to be operated temporarily by Soviet crews.[45] Nasser also requested, according to Sadat, that a Soviet air commander head up Egypt's air defenses and that the USSR send "deterrent" offensive weapons like bomber aircraft.[46]

Nasser's request for what amounted to direct Soviet intervention in the air defense of Egypt probably did not take the Soviet leadership entirely by surprise because most of the hardware requested—including the SA-3 missiles—had already been promised for delivery in mid-1970 under a deal negotiated the previous month in Moscow.[47] What may have given the Kremlin leaders some pause was the need to commit substantial numbers of Soviet personnel in a combat role to cope with Nasser's air-defense emergency, since suitably trained Egyptians were not at hand.[48]

According to Heikal, who had accompanied Nasser to Moscow, the Politburo decided to commit Soviet personnel in organized units to the air defense of Egypt only after Nasser dramatically had threatened to resign in favor of a pro-American Egyptian president. How much credibility the Soviet leadership attached to Nasser's threat to resign and the degree to which this threat weighed in the Soviet decision to deploy combat personnel to Egypt are, of course, a matter of conjecture.

Undoubtedly, other key considerations helped to shape the Soviet decision to intervene—considerations like the large Soviet investment of prestige that was at stake in the USSR's role as the great-power patron of Egypt. However, Heikal reports that Nasser's resignation threat (which "electrified the room" and produced "outcries on the Russian side") prompted the calling of a Politburo meeting to decide whether to deploy Soviet pilots and missile crews to Egypt. According to Heikal, Nasser warned that if Soviet assistance was not forthcoming, "I shall go back to Egypt and I shall tell the people the truth. I shall tell them that the time has come for me to step down and hand over to a pro-American President. If I cannot save them, somebody else will have to do it. That is my final word.''[49]

An affirmative decision was reached, in any case, while Nasser was still in Moscow,[50] as a result of which the USSR took the unprecedented step of dispatching SA-3 missile units and MIG-21 interceptor forces, under the command of General V.V. Okunev, to engage directly in the air defense of Egypt. No bomber aircraft, however, were furnished.

The Soviets did not begin to send air-defense forces to Egypt until March 1970. In the meantime, on January 31, Kosygin had sent a personal note to President Nixon warning that if the United States could not restrain Israel, the USSR would have no alternative but to send new arms to Nasser. The Soviets also may have informed the United States that introduction of Soviet fighting personnel would be essential to defend Egypt,[51] but according to Kissinger, this was not spelled out.[52] For the delivery of the SA-3 missile and MIG-21 units and supporting air-defense (PVO) elements, the Soviets used approximately ninety AN-12 flights plus sealift.[53]

In the ensuing air-defense operations, several Soviet MIG-21 pilots were shot down by Israeli F-4 Phantoms in July 1970.[54] Nevertheless, the Soviet air-defense intervention deterred further penetration by the Israeli air force over Egypt's heartland and helped to bring about the August 7, 1970, ceasefire (Secretary of State William P. Rogers's initiative) along the Suez Canal.[55]

Described as a disturbing new factor in the Middle East by Henry Kissinger,[56] the decision of the Soviet leaders "to inject their own combat forces into the area" in March 1970 was followed in September by several developments that were interpreted at the time to portend a hardening of Soviet policy in the Third World. One was the prompt and virtually open Egyptian violation of the August ceasefire by setting up new antiaircraft-missile sites within the canal zone, which presumably required some Soviet cooperation.[57] Another development was Syrian intervention in the Jordanian civil war on the side of the Palestinian guerrilla groups on September 18.

The extent of Soviet backing of the Syrian move, which took place in an atmosphere of internal rivalry between Syrian leadership factions, has never been established fully. The Syrian government, then headed by Salah Jedid, had dispatched several hundred tanks to northwestern Jordan to bolster the Palestinian guerrillas, but the tanks had no air cover because Jedid's rival, General Assad, who controlled the Syrian air force, refused to provide it.[58] Soviet advisers accompanied the invading Syrian tanks to the Jordanian border but did not cross it.[59]

In any event, the USSR apparently pressed Syria to withdraw from Jordan to avert a major showdown after having observed the movement of the U.S. Sixth Fleet and selective alert of other U.S. forces,[60] together with visible Israeli preparations to intervene with air strikes at the behest of King Hussein of Jordan.[61] Emboldened by this strong backing from the United States and Israel, Hussein finally committed his small air force against the invading Syrian armor, and shortly thereafter the Syrian forces withdrew, defusing the crisis before active U.S.-Israeli intervention was needed.[62] The threat of Israeli intervention was no doubt a key factor motivating the Syrian withdrawal, as was probably General Assad's refusal to provide any air cover for the invading forces.

A third development in September 1970, which could be taken as Soviet probing for advantage, came when U.S. photoreconnaissance detected Soviet preparations in progress at Cienfuegos, Cuba, for what appeared to be a facility for servicing missile-firing nuclear submarines. After a series of U.S. diplomatic warnings that the Cienfuegos activity would be a violation of the agreement that had resolved the 1962 Cuban missile crisis, the USSR denied that it was building its own base in Cuba, and Foreign Minister Gromyko privately assured President Nixon that the 1962 understanding would be upheld.

Shortly after Gromyko's private chat with the president at which this assurance was given, the construction at Cienfuegos reportedly came to a halt.[63] According to Kissinger's account of the Cienfuegos episode, however, the Soviets had tried out various combinations of visiting submarines and supporting vessels over a five-month period in an apparent effort to test the U.S. level of toleration before finally halting construction of support facilities.[64] The reported resumption in 1979 of pier construction at Cienfuegos, where two Soviet submarines were then temporarily based, suggested that another round of Soviet probing like that of 1970 might be in the offing.[65]

Two noteworthy Soviet airlifts to Third World countries for nonmilitary purposes were mounted in 1970. A long-range operation to Peru for earthquake disaster relief proved not very effective, with only twenty-two of sixty-five scheduled flights being completed and one AN-22 aircraft lost. The second airlift, amounting to about twenty-five flights, carried flood disaster supplies to Bangladesh in late 1970 and early 1971. An AN-22 was also lost in this operation.[66]

In December 1970, in response to requests from Sékou Touré for a show of military force against Portuguese Guinea after Portuguese-led commando attacks on Conakry in November had alarmed him, the Soviets sent three warships on a brief visit to the area from the Mediterranean.[67] In 1971, they followed up this initial patrol off Guinea with a semipermanent naval-patrol presence, which in the early years usually consisted of two destroyers, an LSD, and an oiler.

The November 1970 attacks on Guinea-Conakry represented both a domestic challenge to Touré from exiles within the commando ranks and Portuguese reprisal for his sheltering of the PAIGC—a national-liberation group directed against Portuguese rule in Guinea-Bissau and Cape Verde. Touré called on both the United States and the USSR for military help. In early December, the United States joined the UN condemnation of Portuguese "aggression" against Guinea but offered Touré no military support. The USSR, however, provided naval patrols and additional arms for Touré's army, and Cuba sent several hundred technical advisers to the PAIGC's guerrilla units.[68]

The Soviets hesitated, according to some analyses, to commit naval forces to the Guinea area until international reaction to the situation clarified what risks might be involved.[69] Whatever the case, the USSR apparently exploited Touré's dependence on a Soviet presence for protection against external and domestic threats to obtain access to operational facilities. The latter included the use of Conakry airport for naval TU-95D reconnaissance flights over the Atlantic, beginning in 1973. Four years later, in September 1977, Touré terminated the TU-95 reconnaissance flights from Guinea.[70]

On the other side of Africa, the Soviets verbally supported a communist-led anti-Nimeiry coup in Sudan in July 1971 but apparently had no direct hand in arranging it. According to Ilya Dzhirkvelov, a Soviet defector who was a KGB officer in Sudan in 1971, Soviet authorities had mistakenly believed that Sudan was ripe for a pro-Soviet coup and had therefore supported the conspirators.[71] The July coup occurred two months after Nimeiry had cracked down on the Sudanese communist party, the largest such party in Africa, for opposing his plans to join the Arab Federation.

Nimeiry was deposed briefly but regained power in a few days with the aid of Libya and Egypt. At that point, the USSR asked Egypt to intervene on behalf of the now imprisoned coup leaders, who were then promptly executed by Nimeiry. Soviet diplomatic relations with Sudan became strained but were not completely broken off.[72]

In the Persian Gulf area, Soviet support of the Dhofar insurgency against the Oman sultanate picked up in 1972, after having been rendered on essentially a token basis for several years previously. Soviet aid was channeled largely through the new People's Democratic Republic of Yemen (PDRY), along with some support from Iraq.[73]

In summer 1973, the USSR contributed more directly to the support of the Dhofar liberation campaign by transporting some PDRY troops and equipment from Aden to the Dhofar area in an amphibious vessel.[74] Despite this intervention, Iranian assistance to the other side in 1973-1975 helped the sultanate to survive.

The Soviet navy intervened in support of Soviet Third World interests on other occasions between late 1971 and early 1973. During the second Indo-Pakistani war in December 1971, several days after the United States had sent a Seventh Fleet carrier task force into the Bay of Bengal, the USSR dispatched units of the Soviet Pacific Fleet to the same waters in what was purportedly described by the Soviet ambassador to India as a move intended to show tht the USSR would "not allow the Seventh Fleet to intervene" in Bangladesh.[75]

In another instance, in April 1973, two Soviet ships (again, Alligator-class LSTs), escorted by naval combatants, transported a contingent of Moroccan armored troops and their equipment through the Mediterranean to Syria. King Hassan had promised these troops in February for deployment against Israel on the Golan Heights sector of the Syrian front. A second, similar sealift may have been carried out in July to move the remainder of the Moroccan expeditionary force of around 2,000 tank troops, who were subsequently to see action in the October 1973 war.[76]

Soviet Role in the October War

The Arab-Israeli Yom Kippur war of October 1973 was one that the USSR apparently had neither sought to forestall nor deliberately encouraged. Although the war could not have been planned or initiated without the arms supplied by the USSR, it seems clear, as argued by William Quandt, that the initiative for the October 6 attack against Israel lay with Egypt and Syria. Egyptian testimony as to where the Soviets stood is somewhat contradictory. Sadat claimed that the Soviets were uncooperative, despite the resumption of major arms shipments in early 1973, and that they consistently sought to discourage a resort to arms by making the Egyptians feel "not capable of waging any kind of war." Soviet lack of confidence in Egyptian fighting ability was reflected, according to Sadat, in the hasty Soviet request on October 4 to fly out Soviet civilians after he had informed the Soviet ambassador the day before of impending military action.[77]

Heikal suggests, conversely, that the Soviets regarded a new round of warfare as offering an opportunity to restore the Soviet position in the Middle East or, at least, to prevent the Arabs from turning away from the USSR to deal directly with the United States. The probable Soviet rationale, according to Heikal, was to "let the Arabs have sufficient arms to enable them to risk a battle." Had the Egyptians won, the USSR would have gotten the credit; if they had lost or been stalemated, they again would have had to depend on the USSR for help.[78]

When war came, the Soviet leaders intervened both diplomatically and militarily to preserve their credibility as superpower patron of Egypt and Syria and to prevent an Arab defeat, while at the same time keeping their intervention from developing into a direct military confrontation with the United States.

Soviet diplomatic intervention began at the very outset of the war with efforts to obtain a ceasefire that would protect the initial gains unexpectedly scored by the coordinated Arab attacks of October 6, before the Israelis could mount effective counterattacks.[79] Soviet military intervention in the form of a major arms-resupply effort by air and sea began several days later, October 9 or 10, after the high rate of arms and equipment consumed in the early fighting had led to Arab requests for immediate replenishment.[80] Similar Israeli pleas had gone out to Washington.[81]

During the course of the fighting, the Soviet airlift, for which some contingency planning and prepositioning evidently had been done, flew mainly over Hungary and Yugoslavia, although some aircraft overflew Iran and Turkey.[82] After a brief standdown in October, the Soviet airlift to the Middle East resumed at a reduced rate. By early November, an estimated 950 to 1,000 flights had been made to the region.[83] Estimates of tonnage lifted over this period vary from 12,500 to 14,000 tons; at the same time, beginning on October 13, the United States airlifted some 22,000 tons to Israel over a much longer distance. The Soviet sealift, mainly from Odessa through the Bosporus to Alexandria or Latakia, with naval escort, delivered about 63,000 tons during the conflict.[84]

In addition to the support by airlift and sealift, Soviet technical and advisory personnel also apparently participated in a broad range of noncombat operations during the war. These included advising Syrian air-defense and ground forces, driving tanks from Syrian ports to Damascus, assembling crated aircraft, and operating air-traffic-control and air-defense electronics equipment. Soviet personnel probably also participated in the firing from Egypt of two Scud short-range (150-mile) missiles near the end of the war.[85]

After the military situation had begun to change in Israel's favor around October 14 or 15, Soviet diplomatic intervention steadily intensified. The Brezhnev-Kissinger negotiations in Moscow five days later led to the ceasefire of October 22.[86] When this ceasefire promptly broke down, placing the encircled Egyptian Third Army in peril, Brezhnev sent an urgent message to Nixon on October 24, urging joint U.S.-Soviet intervention to enforce the ceasefire and—if the United States declined the invitation—threatening to "consider the question of taking appropriate steps unilaterally."[87]

Brezhnev's urgent message to Nixon, delivered by Ambassador Dobrynin at 9:25 P.M., October 24, had been preceded earlier in the day by a public appeal from Sadat for a joint Soviet-U.S. force to police the ceasefire. The Soviet proposal for joint intervention brought to mind the somewhat similar Soviet proposal in November 1956 during the Suez conflict. However, the pressures on the USSR to act unilaterally and its capability to do so were much greater in October 1973, thus rendering the two situations hardly comparable. Certainly, Brezhnev's threat to act unilaterally was much more credible, given the change in Soviet capabilities, than earlier Soviet interventionary threats.

Precisely what unilateral steps the Soviet leadership was considering during the closing stages of the Yom Kippur war remains an unanswered question. The Soviet military measures known to have been under way would have been compatible with sending a small Soviet peacekeeping force to Egypt and, beyond that, signaling possible Soviet commitment to a larger-scale military intervention. The military measures in question, which went far beyond those taken by the USSR in the June war six years earlier, included increasing the size of the Fifth *Eskadra* from sixty to ninety-six ships and assigning anticarrier groups to trail U.S. carriers in the Mediterranean; dispatching a small naval combat force of about eight ships, including two amphibious landing craft, toward the Egyptian coast on October 25; placing seven airborne divisions on increased alert and standing down the cargo airlift to make transport aircraft available; and establishing an airborne command post in southern Russia.[88]

The placing of U.S. forces on a worldwide DefCon 3 alert in the early hours of October 25, together with other U.S. military moves and a presidential response to Brezhnev that unilateral action would not only jeopardize detente but also would be unacceptable to the United States, had the effect of speeding agreement later that day on another ceasefire resolution to be policed by a UN emergency force that excluded both Soviet and U.S. troops.[89] The prospect of a direct Soviet military intervention that could have led to a Soviet-U.S. confrontation thus came to an end.

7 Increased Soviet Third World Involvement, 1975-1980

Soviet Third World Policy Lines

Increasingly active Soviet involvement in volatile situations arising in the Third World characterized the second half of the 1970s. Continuing a trend in evidence earlier in the decade, the USSR displayed a readiness to furnish new and more-visible backing to Third World clients, particularly Marxist-oriented regimes, and to a variety of guerrilla movements. This trend was especially evident in Africa, where significant interventions in Angola and Ethiopia were carried out between 1975 and 1978 through the newly applied technique of combining Soviet military-logistic capabilities with large-scale use of Cuban combat troops.

What remained a matter of controversy among some observers by the close of the 1970s was the extent to which the Soviet leadership had, on the one hand, merely responded opportunistically to events (and to U.S. reluctance to become actively involved in most areas of Third World instability) or, on the other hand, deliberately set out to shape Third World developments directly by means of a muscular and well-contrived strategy of intervention.

The Soviet leadership, a gerontocracy on the verge of replacement by a younger generation,[1] had long tended, out of necessity, to pursue a rather cautious foreign policy. By the second half of the 1970s, however, it had taken up in a sense a new vocation—that of deciding how the growing power of the USSR might be managed so as to yield greater advantages abroad.

Whether the generation of leaders coming up in the 1980s will prove bolder and more capable than the incumbent gerontocracy remains to be seen. At any rate, the results of the period in terms of improving the Soviet position in the Third World can best be described as mixed—with both substantial gains and notable losses having been registered.

New Soviet Gains in the Third World

High on the favorable side of the ledger was the outcome of the Angolan and Ethiopian interventions, which could be said to have validated the USSR's credentials as a major actor in the Third World and as a superpower patron capable of resolving local and regional struggles for political power in favor of its clients.[2] These two major examples of the cooperative-intervention technique are examined separately later. A side effect of the Angola conflict, incidentally, was the furnishing of fresh momentum to guerrilla movements active in the southern part of the African continent, thanks partly to what one Soviet analyst in early 1979 called "the more effective help" to these armed movements made possible by access through the "frontline states" of "independent Africa . . . right up to the very borders of South Africa and Rhodesia."[3]

Another side benefit of Angola, from the Soviet viewpoint, was that it enabled the USSR to reduce China's influence as a patron and arms supplier to African guerrilla movements, including some of those seeking to end white rule in Rhodesia and Namibia. Subsequent developments in Rhodesia, which became the new nation of Zimbabwe in 1980, probably proved at least temporarily disappointing to the Soviets,[4] although Angola-based guerrilla activities against Namibia and other Soviet-supported movements against South Africa continued to yield politically useful returns.[5]

Besides Angola and Ethiopia, two other takeovers of power in the Third World in the late 1970s provided particularly favorable political outcomes at the time for the USSR. First, in April 1978 a coup led by Nur Mohammad Taraki and Hafizullah Amin in Afghanistan ousted the Daoud regime and brought to power a pro-Soviet "people's democratic" regime. This coup and subsequent developments in Afghanistan are taken up at length later.

Second, in June 1978, a radical pro-Soviet leadership faction in South Yemen headed by Abdel Fattah Ismail and Ali Nasir Muhammad al-Hasani overthrew the Rubai Ali regime.[6] Subsequently, Ismail was himself ousted as the PDRY's top leader and replaced by Hasani.[7] Precisely what brought about Ismail's resignation on April 21, 1980, as president of the PDRY and head of South Yemen's Marxist party was not clear, since he was a radical, pro-Soviet Marxist. Speculation had it that the resignation was the consequence of an internal power struggle between the northern faction, led by the North Yemen-born Ismail, and a faction of indigenous South Yemeni, headed by Hasani.[8] While probably reducing Aden's desire for unification with North Yemen, the apparent emergence into power of the southern faction did not cause any fundamental change in the Marxist orientation of the government of South Yemen.

In both the Afghanistan and South Yemen cases, it may be noted, an already Soviet-leaning leftist but noncommunist regime had found itself ousted by a still more-radical, pro-Soviet one dominated by local communists. In Ethiopia also, the strongly pro-Soviet alignment that emerged in February 1977, after a series of purges and executions had eliminated the Dergue rivals of Lt. Col. Mengistu Haile-Mariam and his supporters, replaced a regime that had already set Ethiopia on a "socialist, anti-imperialist path."[9]

To these four cases in which pro-Soviet communist elements had forcibly seized power in Third World countries in the latter half of the 1970s might be added three others in southeast Asia where pro-Soviet changes of regime were engineered by North Vietnam. Two of these occurred in 1975—North Vietnam's imposition of communist control over South Vietnam and seizure of power in Laos by the Pathet Lao; the third was the replacement in January 1979 of the pro-Chinese Pol Pot government in Cambodia by a pro-Soviet, Vietnamese-dominated regime as a result of Hanoi's invasion of Cambodia.

It remains debatable among some observers whether these seven takeovers of power by local communist leadership elements came as an unexpected political windfall for Moscow, or whether—along with other locally led conspiracies that suffered suppression in Iraq, Sudan, and Somalia—they had been engineered from Moscow in line with a major shift of Soviet Third World strategy. The question of such a shift is taken up later. Windfall or otherwise, the coming to power of communist-oriented Third World regimes willing to cooperate more closely with the USSR was doubtless regarded in Moscow as a positive trend.

Another plus for Soviet Third World interests was the emergence of strains in Turkish-U.S. ties in mid-1975 and an accompanying improvement in Soviet-Turkish relations, manifested among other things in a cooperative Turkish attitude toward Soviet airlift operations in Ethiopia. The USSR had begun the process of mending relations with Turkey in the mid-1960s with the extension of substantial economic aid to Ankara. The Turks held back from close relations with the USSR, however, until the cutting off of U.S. arms aid over the Cyprus issue brought about the suspension of U.S. activities at Turkish bases and a rise in anti-Americanism in July 1975.

Soviet-Turkish relations grew closer over the next few years, although Ankara continued to turn down Soviet suggestions that Turkey should drop out of NATO entirely.[10] Following the election of the relatively pro-Western government of Suleyman Demirel in December 1979, however, Turkey's relations with the USSR again began to deteriorate, and by August 1980 Ankara was accusing the Soviets of subsidizing terrorist organizations in Turkey and of "an unprecedented military buildup" along Turkey's northern border.[11] Soviet influence in Turkey declined further following the September 1980 coup against Demirel that brought a group of Western-oriented military leaders to power.

The overthrow of the shah of Iran in January 1979, though not necessarily an immediate and undiluted gain for the USSR, was at least a serious setback for U.S. interests in the Middle East. Opportunism appeared to characterize Soviet policy in Iran as the temptation for Moscow to exploit the troubled Iranian situation was partly offset by potential dangers inherent in it.

On the one hand, internal unrest and disorder arising under the Moslem fundamentalist rule of the Ayatollah Khomeini and the mullahs gave promise of creating the preconditions for seizure of power by the left. On the other hand, Iranian developments also had some adverse implications for the USSR, such as interruption of oil and gas deliveries and potentially destabilizing ethnic-religious perturbations if Islamic fundamentalism should spread across the border among the central Asian peoples of the USSR.

By September 1979, Khomeini's suppression of leftist groups, and other aspects of the theocratic revolution in Iran, had prompted Moscow to express its first open reservations about developments there.[12] After the seizure of the U.S. embassy and hostages in early November 1979, however, the Soviets moved swiftly to take advantage of the political situation. Although joining in formal disapproval of Iran's "encroachment on diplomatic norms," the USSR promptly began to give vociferous backing to Khomeini's demands on the United States and to condemn what it called U.S. attempts "to blackmail Iran" by threats of force.[13] Besides its rather transparent currying of favor with Iran, Moscow's stance may also have reflected some concern about the escalatory potential of any U.S. resort to forceful measures.

Meanwhile, in return for the USSR's tilt toward Khomeini, the ayatollah and his followers softened their own previous castigation of the "godless" USSR and in early December 1979 lifted some of the restrictions on the pro-Soviet Tudeh party.[14] The Soviet invasion of Afghanistan a few weeks later, however, evoked harsh Iranian criticism and contributed to another abrasive phase in Soviet-Iranian relations, marked among other things by Iran's expulsion of a Soviet diplomat on espionage charges and a threat to recall the Iranian ambassador in Moscow.[15]

Although the emergence of a pro-Soviet regime in Teheran might seem for the time being quite unlikely, the Soviet leadership could doubtless derive considerable satisfaction not only from the virtual elimination of U.S. influence in Iran but also from the geopolitical leverage on Iran and other regional actors that might be expected to accrue from the lodgement of Soviet military power in neighboring Afghanistan.

In Southeast Asia, the signing of a friendship and cooperation treaty between the USSR and Vietnam in November 1978 was followed by the Vietnamese invasion of Cambodia and China's retaliatory foray against Vietnam in early 1979.[16] The USSR's support of Vietnam boosted its stock in Hanoi and earned it access to bases helpful to Soviet naval and maritime activity in the Third World.[17] For example, Soviet access to Vietnamese naval facilities greatly shortened the crisis response time for Soviet forces

home-based in Vladivostok. It also helped to offset one of the negative consequences of the Afghanistan invasion—namely, the denial of port facilities
to Soviet naval combatants at Singapore in early 1980. Besides extending
the reach of Soviet naval and naval air patrols in the region of the South
China Sea and the Indian Ocean, the post-1978 relationship with Vietnam
also helped the USSR in its drive to forge a ring of containment around
China.

Latin America

From Moscow's viewpoint, the growth in the latter 1970s of domestic unrest, rebellion, and anti-U.S. sentiment in Central America and the Caribbean, reflected by the leftist coup in Grenada in March 1979 and climaxed by the July 1979 Sandinista overthrow of the Somoza regime in Nicaragua, represented positive Third World trends with further revolutionary potential.

While Havana may have had foreknowledge of the March 13, 1979, coup that brought Maurice Bishop and the New Jewel Movement to power in the small Caribbean island state of Grenada, the Cubans apparently did not engineer it.[18] The coup occurred the day after Prime Minister Eric Gairy had ordered the arrest of forty-four members of the New Jewel Movement as he departed on a trip to the United States. Before Gairy's orders could be carried out, a small group of New Jewel members, reportedly "with 25 guns, a small truck, and two cars, one of which was rented," seized control of the airport and radio station, routing Gairy's 200-man army. Following the coup, Havana moved quickly to establish its influence in Grenada and to help the new regime consolidate its power.[19] Among other actions, Cuba dispatched arms and military advisers to train the new Grenadian army and reportedly set up antiaircraft guns at the island's airport, presumably to forestall any attempt at a countercoup. Economic assistance has been provided in the form of a loan, construction equipment, and some 250 Cuban technicians to build an international-class airport in Grenada.[20]

Although neither the USSR nor Cuba could take major credit for the Sandinista National Liberation Front (FSLN) victory in Nicaragua, Havana's support was important to the success of that revolution. Aside from assisting the FSLN with training, asylum, and money during its organizational phase, Havana provided significant arms and advisory support to the Sandinistas as their prospects brightened in the final months prior to Somoza's overthrow.[21] Working in collaboration with Panama and Costa Rica, Cuba clandestinely provided the FSLN with a variety of Soviet-made arms including machine guns, recoilless rifles, and mortars. Several hundred Cuban military advisers were reportedly flown to Costa Rica toward the end of 1978 to train and equip Sandinista troops near the Nicaraguan border with additional arms sent directly from Cuba. In early 1979, according to the U.S. State Department, Cuba also helped to "organize, arm and transport an 'internationalist brigade'," drawn from several Central and South American extremist groups, to fight alongside the Sandinistas. When the FSLN launched its final offensive in mid-1979, Cuban military advisers, in direct radio communication with Havana, entered Nicaragua to work with Sandinista columns. A number of these Cubans were reportedly wounded in the fighting.[22]

As in Grenada, the Cubans moved expeditiously to strengthen and extend FSLN control in Nicaragua once victory was achieved. In April 1980, about 200 Cubans were advising Sandinista military and security forces, and some 1,800 other Cuban personnel (including 1,200 teachers) were engaged in a variety of social-service programs. By the beginning of 1982, the Cuban presence in Nicaragua had grown to some 5,000 advisers including, according to U.S. government sources, 1,500 to 2,000 military and security personnel. East Germans also were reported to be involved in the training of internal-security forces. The major buildup of communist-supplied weapons in Nicaragua that accompanied this influx of advisers led Secretary of State Haig to charge at the OAS general assembly in December 1981 that under the Sandinista regime, Nicaragua was working to establish the largest military force in Central American history.[23]

Both Moscow and Havana appeared to have found cause for considerable encouragement as a result of the Nicaraguan revolution. Soviet spokesmen asserted that the "revolutionary changes in Nicaragua" would "undoubtedly exert a tremendous influence on the development of events throughout Latin America."[24] The Cubans also, according to a U.S. intelligence report made public in July 1979, had concluded that "prospects for revolutionary upheaval in Central America over the next decade or so had markedly improved."[25]

An example of the rhetoric inspired in the USSR by the Nicaraguan revolution was the following:

> The feat accomplished in Nicaragua reflected the intensification of revolutionary processes on the Latin American continent and the steadfast striving of its peoples for genuine independence. It is significant that the triumph of the righteous cause of the Nicaraguans was preceded by the victory of progressive forces in Grenada, Dominica, and Saint Lucia. In turn, the events in Nicaragua doubtless will be an inspirational stimulus in the struggle of Latin American peoples against imperialism and its henchmen.[26]

The Cubans seem to consider El Salvador the most promising target in the region for such an intensification of the revolutionary processes. Salvadoran guerrillas trained in Cuba have been infiltrated back into El Salvador through neighboring Honduras, which along with Nicaragua, has served as a major transshipment point for the clandestine flow of the arms that Havana has helped to organize for the leftist insurgents seeking to overthrow the current government in San Salvador.

According to the U.S. State Department, documents captured from Salvadoran guerrillas and other corroborative intelligence sources revealed the central role played by Cuba in the "political unification, military direction, and arming of insurgent forces in El Salvador."[27] In late 1979 and 1980, Havana helped to coordinate the previously fragmented factions of the extreme left in El Salvador and assisted the insurgents with the planning of their military operations. In addition, Cuba served as a transshipment point for much of the arms and munitions that Salvadoran guerrilla leaders had solicited from a number of communist and radical countries and facilitated the subsequent ground-, sea-, and airlift of these weapons to El Salvador from Nicaragua. Weapon deliveries were timed to enable the guerrillas to launch their general offensive in January 1981. The campaign aborted, however, because of a lack of popular support for the revolutionary camp and the insurgents' inability to sustain heavy casualties.

Despite this initial setback, the insurgency in El Salvador grew during 1981. The Salvadoran guerrillas continued to be nourished by a flow of arms transshipped through Cuba and Nicaragua, weapons and munitions transported in part aboard the network of small ships the Cubans had specially organized in 1981 for clandestine arms deliveries to El Salvador. In addition to aiding the Salvadoran insurgents, the Cubans have also been active in assisting other Central American insurgent groups, particularly those in Guatemala. Following the pattern set earlier in Nicaragua and El Salvador, Havana used its influence to promote the unification of the previously divided Guatemalan insurgent groups in 1980 and reportedly conditioned increased Cuban aid to the Guatemalans on a "commitment to armed struggle and a unified strategy." A large number of the estimated 2,000 or so guerrillas now operating in Guatemala have trained in Cuba.[28]

While Central America remains the principal immediate target of Cuban subversive activity, Havana has also supported revolutionary movements elsewhere in the Americas. For example, Cuba trained a number of guerrillas for insurgent operations against the government of Colombia. Some 100 to 200 Cuban-trained M-19 guerrillas infiltrated into Colombia from Panama by boat along the Pacific coast to help launch coordinated attacks against government outposts in rural areas of Colombia in March 1981. Vigorous countermeasures by Colombian army and police units rapidly quashed the M-19 offensive, and over ninety guerrillas were killed or captured.[29]

Finally, also on the plus side of the ledger was Castro's skillful manipulation of the nonaligned movement at its September 1979 summit conference in Havana. There, despite resistance from Tito and a few other Third World leaders, Castro succeeded in swinging a majority of the ninety-two so-called nonaligned countries to a more-pro-Soviet stance than before.[30] He also emerged as chairman of the nonaligned movement for the next three years, a position giving him further opportunity to wield his influence in the Third World. Subsequently, Castro's unquestioning support of the Soviet invasion of Afghanistan apparently tarnished his unaligned credentials in the eyes of some Third World countries.

Some Soviet Setbacks in the Third World

High on the less-favorable side of the USSR's Third World balance sheet in the 1975-1980 period was the further deterioration of the Soviet position in Egypt. In March 1976, Sadat abrogated the five-year-old Soviet-Egyptian treaty of friendship and cooperation. Sadat, said to believe that "the Russians had nothing to offer" any longer toward solving the political deadlock in the Middle East,[31] set in motion a process of negotiation involving the United States and Israel from which the USSR was to find itself increasingly shut out. This process included the dramatic initiative that produced Sadat's precedent-shattering visit to Israel in November 1977 and led to the Egyptian-Israeli agreement at Camp David in September of the following year. Although the USSR had just got a foot back in the Middle East negotiating process as a result of the joint U.S.-Soviet statement of October 1, 1977, calling for prompt resumption of the Geneva peace conference with the United States and USSR as cochairmen, Sadat's initiative had the effect of relegating the Soviets to the sidelines again.[32]

The expulsion of some 2,500 Soviet advisers and loss of base rights in Somalia in November 1977 represented another serious setback to the USSR's position in the Horn of Africa and the Indian Ocean. This reverse came after the USSR had unsuccessfully sought—in part through visits to the area in spring 1977 by both Soviet President Nikolay Podgorny and Fidel Castro—to halt an Ethiopian-Somali conflict over the Ogaden by suggesting a federation of the two countries.[33] Presumably, it was hoped that such a federation would relieve the Soviet leadership of having to decide which side to support in a conflict where important Soviet interests were at stake on both sides. An influx of Soviet and Cuban military aid to Ethiopia in subsequent months of 1977, however, coupled with a cutback of arms deliveries to Somalia, gave evidence of a definite Soviet tilt toward the Mengistu regime in Ethiopia. Although thus jeopardizing its position in Somalia, Moscow may have felt that the Somalis had nowhere else to turn, inasmuch as their efforts to solicit military aid from the United States and France had proved fruitless. Thus, the Soviets may have counted on preserving relations with both parties.

One analysis has suggested that the Soviets probably regarded Ethiopia as more suitably located than Somalia both strategically and in terms of "a position from which to influence future events in the area—in Sudan, Kenya, Egypt, the two Yemens, Saudi Arabia."[34] The facts that Ethiopia has a population of 30 million and Somalia has only 3 million and that Ethiopia's movement into the Soviet orbit would be a distinct loss both politically and strategically to the West and the conservative Arab states, among other reasons, may have accounted for the Soviet gamble on Ethiopia. Ideologically, though both Ethiopia and Somalia were self-declared Marxist states, the Soviets were said to feel that the Ethiopian revolution was "the more genuine," hence meriting preferential support on this count also.[35]

Conversely, several considerations may have given the Soviets pause about siding with Ethiopia. To discriminate against predominantly Moslem Somalia might cost the Soviets something in the Moslem world. Perhaps more to the point, an already sizable investment in Somalia might be jeopardized, and Moscow might be risking immediate loss of naval and air operating facilities on the Indian Ocean littoral as a trade-off against future access to Eritrean facilities on the Red Sea.

Whatever Moscow's calculations may have been, in November 1977 Somali leader Siad Barre, in reaction to the Soviet tilt in Ethiopia's favor, renounced the Soviet-Somali friendship treaty of July 1974 and deprived the Soviets of their military-base privileges in strategically located Somalia.[36] At the same time, Siad broke diplomatic relations with Cuba.

How permanent the Somalia setback might be remained problematical. Second thoughts reportedly began to be aired within the Somali leadership in early 1978 to the effect that the country had broken too precipitately with the USSR,[37] and in April 1978, according to Siad, a coup was attempted by Somali military officers allegedly sympathetic to Soviet interests. Although the coup failed, it posed the possibility that some way might yet be found to restore the Soviet position in Somalia.

The prospect of restoring a Soviet foothold there appeared to recede once more, however, when in August 1980 Somalia reached an agreement allowing the United States the use of the Soviet-built naval base at Berbera and other facilities. This development came about following the taking of U.S. hostages in Iran in November and the Soviet invasion of Afghanistan in December 1979, events that led the United States to seek the use of base facilities in Somalia and elsewhere in the area of the Persian Gulf.[38]

Another country in the Horn of Africa where Soviet influence also suffered a setback in the latter 1970s was Sudan. Soviet relations with Sudan, which had remained somewhat strained following a communist-supported coup attempt in 1971, worsened still further after another abortive coup supported by Libya and Ethiopia in July 1976. At that point, Sudan's leader Nimeiry took the offensive against what he called "Soviet imperialism" in Africa, entering during the next few months into mutual defense arrangements with Egypt and Saudi Arabia and, in May 1977, expelling some ninety Soviet military advisers from Sudan.[39]

Also on the debit side of the Soviet balance sheet in Africa was an August 1979 coup in Equatorial Guinea, bringing a pro-Western government to power in that former Spanish colony. Besides costing the USSR lucrative fishing rights, the coup ended Soviet access to a small base at Luba on the Gulf of Biafra, which then served as a communications-intelligence post and which had been used previously as a staging area for the Soviet-Cuban intervention in Angola.[40]

Soviet relations with Syria and Iraq, two of the Arab states on which Moscow counted to compensate for its declining position in Egypt, fell subject to recurrent tension in the 1975-1980 period. In the case of Syria, the USSR found cause for what was described by a visiting PLO leader as "deep regret and bewilderment" over Syria's 1976 armed intervention in Lebanon and military action against Palestinian groups there.[41] To show its disapproval, Moscow temporarily withheld arms transfers to Syria. Again in November 1978 and early 1979, disputes were said to have arisen between Moscow and Damascus over Soviet arms deliveries,[42] although these problems subsequently were worked out.

For its part, Syria, in September 1976, reportedly rejected a note from Brezhnev requesting withdrawal of its forces from Lebanon[43] and the following year turned down Soviet requests for additional access to military bases in Syria.[44] President Assad also reportedly declined to go along with Soviet propaganda backing of the attempted invasions of Zaire by Katangan (Shaba) exiles from Angola in April 1977 and June 1978.[45]

The chill in Soviet-Syrian relations that persisted in some degree into early 1979 began to dissipate later in the year, however, when in November the Soviets were said to have canceled Syrian debts amounting to $500 million, in addition to furnishing more-advanced types of aircraft and armor. This Soviet largesse came in response to a reported claim by Assad that Syria needed to modernize its forces because it had become the principal Arab country confronting Israel following the Egyptian-Israeli peace treaty of March 26, 1979.[46]

A further Syrian alignment with Moscow became apparent in October 1980, when Assad signed a formal treaty of friendship and cooperation with the USSR, a commitment that he had been resisting for a decade. The treaty was thought to involve a new arms deal under which Syria would receive more than $1 billion worth of new military aid, to be paid for by Libya as part of the Syrian-Libyan unity agreement of September 10, 1980.[47]

Despite the close military and economic relationship between the USSR and Iraq, frictions continued into the late 1970s over a number of matters. For one thing, the Baghdad government cracked down on the Communist Party of Iraq for political activity in the army and civil service and executed about forty communists in May and December 1978.[48] Again in the summer of 1979, shortly after Saddam Hussein replaced Ahmed Hassan al-Bakr as president of Iraq, another crackdown for an alleged coup attempt took place, though it was not clear what part communists had played, if any, in the conspiracy.[49]

On several Third World issues, Iraq adopted differing positions from those of the Soviets—for example, supporting the Eritrean rebellion in

Ethiopia (though Baghdad permitted the Soviets to transit Iraqi territory for their airlift to Ethiopia),[50] discontinuing help to the Dhofar insurgency against Oman, and cooperating with Saudi Arabia to halt South Yemen's invasion of North Yemen in 1979. Behind these surface differences, in the view of many observers, lay an underlying Iraqi drive for greater independence from Moscow, which in its turn displayed resentment for oil-rich Iraq's shopping in the West from 1974 on for some major economic-development projects and even weapon procurement.[51]

France, on the one hand, proved interested in competing head-on with the USSR for influence in Iraq, selling Baghdad substantial quantities of aircraft, armored vehicles, and missiles in 1978 and 1979, in return for oil. Although these transactions were not without benefit to France, they also had the effect of reducing Iraq's dependence on the USSR as armorer and trading partner.[52] The USSR, on the other hand, was prompted to boost its own arms commitments to Iraq in 1979, perhaps in an effort to offset Western influence.

The case of Iraq, indeed, illustrated a significant change in the environment in which Soviet military- and economic-aid penetration of the Middle East had been launched two decades earlier. Oil money had weakened Moscow's leverage over both old and potential new clients, and an increasing number of countries in the Middle East now had the wherewithal to make their own purchases of arms, technology, and services in the West.

The outbreak of war between Iraq and Iran in September 1980 gave the USSR another opportunity to regain some of its waning influence over Iraq, in view of the latter's need for replacement of equipment and ammunition for its largely Soviet-equipped forces. However, to avoid a break with Iran, Moscow reportedly refrained from large-scale shipment of military supplies to Iraq, although some indirect resupply of arms from Eastern European sources was carried out with Moscow's approval.[53] The USSR appeared to be seeking to mediate the war, trying both to keep in Iraq's good graces and to avoid a split with Iran.

Strategy Shift to More-Forceful Backing
of Pro-Soviet Marxist Regimes

Changes of regime in several Third World countries in the second half of the 1970s, as mentioned earlier, suggest a shift of Soviet strategy toward giving more-forceful support to Moscow-oriented Marxist regimes that were taking power. One astute observer, Donald Zagoria, described the shift in the following terms:

> Having realized the error of excessive cooperation with unreliable "bourgeois nationalist" leaders in the 1950s and 1960s, the Soviets have

come up with a new strategy for the 1970s and 1980s. They continue, in some cases, such as Iraq, Syria and Algeria, for example, to support noncommunist "socialists" of one kind or another. But now that more orthodox Marxist-Leninist groups and parties have proliferated in many parts of Asia and Africa, the new element in the Soviet strategy is to help communist parties gain state power. Then, via friendship treaties, arms aid, and Soviet, Cuban or East European advisers, the Soviets will help the local communists hold onto and consolidate power. Ultimately, the aim of this strategy is to establish a new alliance system for the Russians in Africa and Asia, a looser eastern version of the Warsaw Pact.[54]

Additional factors helping to account for a shift of Soviet strategy in the 1970s are cited by other analysts. According to Hannah Negaran, for example, it reflects not only Soviet disappointment over the results of dealing with non-Marxist regimes but also a heightened willingness to seize opportunities to damage Western interests in the Third World, with the latter attitude growing out of both confidence in improved Soviet power-projection capabilities and the belief that the United States finds itself unable or unwilling to respond in timely fashion.[55]

Another analyst, Francis Fukuyama, contends that although Moscow's Third World objectives in the 1970s remained essentially unchanged, the strategy for achieving them began to change significantly as the result of considerations such as the following:

Soviet concern—based on experience of the late 1960s and early 1970s—that even left-oriented regimes, if not communist dominated, may backslide;

Moscow's dissatisfaction with simple nonalignment or even pro-Soviet neutralism among its Third World clients, wanting active collaboration instead; hence, narrowing of permissible deviation by Third World clients from Soviet foreign-policy objectives;

Soviet awareness that influence without political control may be inadequate to permit Soviet manipulation of local politics in the face of nationalism and other aberrant tendencies; hence, greater Soviet willingness to interfere in the internal affairs of client states to achieve political control;

Appreciation by the Soviet leadership of the USSR's growing capabilities for power projection in the Third World, permitting the USSR to supplement the sometimes ineffective bartering of arms for influence with the application of direct military pressure;

Soviet recognition that an effective international infrastructure for Soviet-bloc military intervention in critical Third World areas requires mutual support and cooperation of the kind best assured among states led by Soviet-dominated communist regimes.[56]

While the several foregoing explanations of a shift in Soviet Third World strategy cover a broad range of factors, at least one pertinent issue previously mentioned appears to be left unresolved by the evidence at hand. Have the Soviets primarily been profiting from windfalls and responding to opportunities created by more or less spontaneous developments in the Third World, or have they been engineering forcible communist seizure of power actively, perhaps in accordance with some sort of master plan or Third World target list?

Certainly, the available evidence offers little support for the thesis that takeovers in cases such as Angola, Ethiopia, and Afghanistan were staged at Soviet initiative in accordance with a preplanned hit list. The pattern of Soviet intervention in these situations, to be examined presently, suggests that local initiative and exigencies tended to pave the way for Soviet involvement, rather than the other way around.

This is not to argue, on the one hand, that because they may have done little more than take advantage of opportunities that came their way in the later 1970s, the Soviets will necessarily eschew future initiatives to expedite seizure of power by local communists. At the least, in situations where the interplay of indigenous political forces may bring pro-Soviet communist elements to the top or close to it, the USSR appears to be prepared to help them dispose of their remaining opposition and to consolidate their power.

On the other hand, although Soviet preference for communist-led Third World regimes under Moscow's control would seem almost axiomatic, other considerations could temper actual Soviet initiatives in this direction. These include the claim on Soviet resources and protection of such regimes, the conflicting regional interests of some clients, and the degree to which a new series of attempted takeovers of power in the Third World might provoke a damaging response from the United States. Furthermore, Third World countries—in a majority of which power is held by strongly nationalist regimes—have proved relatively resistant to direct communist takeovers and may continue to do so. The Third World, therefore, may not provide a particularly favorable environment for frequent use of a direct takeover strategy.

Theoretical Guidelines for Third World Strategy

In the latter 1970s, as during earlier periods, Soviet theoreticians disagreed among themselves on an appropriate strategy for the transition of Third World countries to "scientific socialism." One school of thought, centering around a group of younger scholars at the Institute of Oriental Studies, argued essentially that Third World countries at very diverse stages of development were not ripe to be pressed into a single communist ideological mold. Rather, a more-elastic strategy, which might encourage a fairly lengthy transitional phase—including even a mixed socialist-private arrangement like the NEP (New Economic Policy) of Lenin's time—was more likely to advance the revolutionary process than a strategy of trying to hasten it by premature communist seizure of power.[57]

Other, more-orthodox scholars disagreed with this analysis. Some found fault with it for downplaying the applicability of Marxist-Leninist theories of class struggle and class domination to liberated countries that were still struggling against imperialism.[58] Others implicitly dismissed it by asserting that the revolutionary process, especially in some African countries, had by the second half of the 1970s acquired an "important new political feature," precisely what had been prescribed earlier: "vanguard parties" of a "genuinely revolutionary" type, armed with "the ideas of scientific socialism" and actively pursuing "the goal of creating a socialist society."[59] Although such parties had made headway in only a few countries, according to this group of scholars, they offered an example for others to follow.

According to still another viewpoint, expounded by a Soviet expert on Third World affairs, many contradictions characterized the development process, and no single community of interests bound the liberation movement in the Third World and socialism together automatically. Hence, as Lenin had stressed, what was needed was a flexible approach to liberation movements, an approach that would take into account factors such as the national attitudes influencing a given country, its social heterogeneity, and the psychological motivations of its various classes. The same author also insisted that there was "no contradiction whatsoever" between the "Soviet Union's line on détente and its support of national-liberation movements."[60] This approach thus appeared to endorse Soviet persistence in the Third World but with due regard for what the traffic would bear. Since its author was K.N. Brutents, a deputy chief of the Central Committee's International Department dealing with Third World policy, the formula might be thought to reflect authoritative policy thinking in Moscow.

Another similarly placed official and author of many previous Third World analyses, R.A. Ulyanovskiy, likewise noted that, given the "contradictory conditions" being encountered by developing countries, including "nationalistic rebirth" of their leadership, transition to a genuine socialist society might be difficult and long in coming even for countries now at the stage of "socialist orientation." This appraisal of the situation, he wrote, was one "combining historical optimism with healthy realism."[61]

Reflected in Soviet theoretical discourse on Third World questions toward the end of the 1970s and the beginning of the 1980s was an apparently growing concern about the long-term stability of "progressive" socialist-oriented regimes. This concern, perhaps stimulated by setbacks in Egypt and Somalia, led Soviet leaders to propose guidelines to keep such regimes from regressing. Politburo member Boris Ponomarev, after urging Soviet scholars in October 1980 to analyze the causes of "the regression in the sociopolitical development of Egypt, Somalia and several other countries,"[62] a few days later at a conference in East Berlin laid down some guidelines to prevent just that.

In his address, published in the CPSU's theoretical journal, *Kommunist,* in November 1980, Ponomarev emphasized seven factors important to the preservation of "progressive positions": (1) the creation of a revolutionary vanguard party guided by the principles of scientific socialism, (2) strong democratic organs of power from top to bottom throughout the country (meaning a powerful state apparatus under party control), (3) the training of party and state cadres dedicated to socialism, (4) strong national armed forces, (5) the broadening of ties between the party-state apparatus and the masses, (6) the development of close ties to socialist countries, and (7) an economic and social policy designed to strengthen the country's independence, raise production, and improve the conditions of daily life.[63] According to a Foreign Broadcast Information Service (FBIS) analysis of the subject, Brezhnev seemed to have endorsed Ponomarev's guidelines—"if only in general terms"—in his report to the Twenty-sixth CPSU Congress in February 1981.[64]

Other Soviet discourse on preserving progressive positions in the Third World stressed the point that local military and security forces must be reorganized and purged of unreliable social-class elements so as to minimize the risks of "internal and foreign counterrevolution." A Soviet political-military commentator, writing in spring 1980, called for the organization of politically and socially reliable officer corps in the armies and security agencies of socialist-oriented countries building new societies. The writer attributed the socialist setbacks in Ghana and Egypt to the failure of those countries to reorganize their armed forces on the class principle. After Ghana gained independence in 1957, he noted, the reorganization of the former colonial army was cosmetic only, with indigenous personnel, mainly from "well-to-do families," replacing the U.K. officers. Consequently, according to the commentator, Ghana's army was not brought under the control of the country's "ruling national-democratic party" and remained virtually without "connections with the masses." Similarly, according to the commentator, the aftermath of the 1952 revolution in Egypt saw no "breakup of the old state machinery" or real democratization of the armed forces, in which the "sons of rich families" continued to retain key positions. This failure to purge and recast the Egyptian military establishment, he continued, "fostered its transformation into a repressive force protecting the interests of the exploiter classes."[65]

Twenty-Five Years of Soviet Third World Aid Programs

Soviet-bloc arms supply to Third World countries in 1979, the twenty-fifth year of Soviet arms aid to noncommunist LDCs, came to about $8.6 billion, almost all of which was furnished by the USSR. This amount was nearly three times greater than that for 1978 but slightly less than the $9.2 billion reached in 1977, which represented the largest total of new agreements in any single year in the twenty-five-year history of Soviet Third World military-aid programs.[66]

For the five-year period 1975-1979, the total of new commitments came to more than $30 billion, of which slightly over $2 billion was furnished by the Eastern European countries, as shown in table 7-1. This five-year total was more than double that of the previous five-year period, although part of the increase probably stemmed from factors such as higher prices for equipment and ruble-exchange adjustments rather than from a commensurate hike in the level of aid extended.[67] Actual deliveries of weapons between 1975 and 1979 were at about 75 percent of cumulative commitments. In 1978, deliveries exceeded new commitments by a substantial margin.

Some Changes in the Pattern of Military Aid

Although most of the major recipients of Soviet-Third World arms transfers were again to be found in the arc of countries extending from North Africa through the Middle East to southern Asia, a number of notable changes occurred in the pattern of Soviet military aid in the 1975-1979 period. One of these was a pronounced shift in the distribution of Soviet arms aid within the Middle East to the more-radical Arab states.

Table 7-1
Soviet-Bloc Military-Aid Commitments, 1975-1979
($US billions)

Year	USSR	Eastern Europe	Total
1975	3.3	0.64	3.94
1976	5.5	0.34	5.84
1977	8.7	0.47	9.17
1978	2.5	0.55	3.05
1979	8.4	0.25	8.65
Total	28.4	2.25	30.65

Source: Central Intelligence Agency, *Communist Aid Activities in Non-Communist Less Developed Countries, 1979 and 1954-79,* ER 80-10318U (Washington, D.C., October 1980), table A-1, p. 13.

After cutting off aid to Egypt (which had been perennially among the leading recipients) in 1975, the USSR increased the supply of modern Soviet arms to Iraq, Libya, and Algeria.[68] Thanks to an agreement in 1976 for more than $1 billion worth of arms, and even larger commitments in subsequent years, Iraq moved to the top of the list of Third World recipients of Soviet-bloc arms. Syria, which temporarily suffered a sharp reduction of arms aid in 1976 during a cooling of relations with Moscow,[69] regained a place among the top Middle East recipients later in the period. Syria, however, lacked one of the advantages that Moscow derived from arms transactions with Iraq, Libya, and Algeria—namely, the ability of these oil-rich states to make hard-currency repayments for Soviet aid.[70]

Reflecting support given new clients in Angola and Ethiopia in active-conflict situations, the last half of the 1970s was marked by the largest Soviet commitments of military aid ever made to black Africa. From 1975 through 1979, the value of Soviet military-aid programs in sub-Saharan Africa increased to about $3.9 billion, while about half of Eastern Europe's aid extensions went to this region also, bringing the Soviet-bloc total to about $4.9 billion.[71]

A substantial share of this was accounted for by the aid programs to Angola and Ethiopia. In the case of the former, an estimated $450 million had been furnished through 1978 and, in the case of the latter, about $1.8 billion.[72] Although available estimates do not provide figures after 1978, it is probably a conservative assumption that ongoing Soviet-bloc military-support activities in both places would have boosted the aid totals to well over a half billion for Angola and perhaps to $2.5 billion for Ethiopia by the end of 1980. Prior to the USSR's 1977 break with Somalia, the latter had been an important recipient of Soviet aid, amounting to some $300 million. Other sub-Saharan countries receiving sizable amounts of arms aid were Mozambique, $135 million; Mali, $100 million; and Nigeria, $80 million.[73] Nigeria represented an oil-endowed customer able to pay for arms with hard currency.

Hard-currency sales of arms to petrodollar countries in Africa and the Middle East tended during the latter 1970s to supplant the earlier Soviet practice of providing arms at attractive discounts and terms of payment, or in exchange for commodities, although there were a few exceptions where political expediency so dictated—India and Afghanistan being cases in point. By 1978, arms transfers had not only come to supplement Moscow's hard-currency earnings significantly but also regularly helped to cover the large annual deficits in Soviet nonmilitary trade with LDCs.[74]

In 1977, the USSR broke the West's monopoly as arms supplier to conservative Persian Gulf oil states with a $50 million cash sale of rockets and missiles to Kuwait.[75] In 1978, however, the USSR temporarily lost its own virtual monopoly of seventeen years as India's arms supplier, when India turned to the West (the United Kingdom) for a major $1.7 billion purchase of aircraft. In May 1980, however, with Indira Gandhi back in office in New Delhi, Moscow regained its preeminent role, concluding a $1.6 billion arms deal on terms very favorable to India.[76]

During the 1975-1979 period, some other LDCs formerly dependent almost entirely on the USSR for arms also began to diversify their buying of weapons, technology, and services by making deals with the West. These included Iraq and Syria, which turned especially to France for arms purchases.[77] Again, however, both Middle East countries in 1979 found it expedient to negotiate new large-scale arms agreements with Moscow for aircraft, tanks, and air-defense equipment.[78]

In the western hemisphere, along with significant arms modernization and training programs for Castro's Cuban forces, Moscow established itself as Peru's principal arms supplier with substantial sales in 1976 and 1977 of Soviet jet fighter/bombers (SU-22s) and land armaments. No new agreements were made with Peru in 1978, however, as friction arose over rescheduling of Peru's heavy military debt (more than $600 million in 1978) to the USSR.[79]

Elsewhere in Latin America, political ferment in 1979 and 1980 opened some opportunities for using communist military aid as an entering wedge, but Cuba rather than the USSR took the lead in furnishing a combination of military and economic aid to several countries in the Caribbean basin, including Grenada, Nicaragua, and Jamaica.[80]

Continuing a trend set earlier in the 1970s, the USSR demonstrated both the capacity and willingness to furnish sizable quantities of modern aircraft and ground armaments to selected Third World clients, sometimes in advance of furnishing particular items to Warsaw Pact countries.[81] In the latter 1970s, late-model equipment sold to LDCs included MIG-25 and MIG-27 jet fighters, IL-76 transports, SA-9 surface-to-air missile systems, and T-72 tanks. In 1979, MI-24 assault helicopters also were introduced into Afghanistan.

Support of guerrilla insurgency movements, a facet of Soviet Third World policy that had been given increased attention in the early 1970s, continued to receive emphasis in the latter 1970s, particularly in Africa and the Middle East. This included military aid channeled through the front-line states of Mozambique, Zambia, and Tanzania to guerrilla forces of the Zimbabwe Patriotic Front operating against Rhodesia until the new state of Zimbabwe came into being, and to the South-West Africa People's Organization in Nimibia,[82] as well as some support to the African National Congress in South Africa.[83]

Soviet aid also included cooperation with Cubans in training guerrillas of the Popular Front for the Liberation of Oman for operations from South Yemen, as well as some indirect backing of the Polisario Front operating with Algerian and Libyan support against Morocco's interests in Western Sahara.[84] Aid to the Polisario began in late 1975, at about the time Boumédienne made Algeria airport available to the USSR for the airlift to Angola. Some observers argued, however, that up to mid-1979 at least the Polisario had been trying to maintain its political distance from the communist states, which was why it had refrained from seeking direct Soviet military support.[85]

Cumulative Dimensions of Military Aid since the Mid-1950s

For the entire twenty-five-year period from 1955, when the USSR first began to supply arms to Third World countries, to the beginning of 1980, the value of the military aid extended came to slightly more than $51 billion, of which about $4.3 billion was furnished by other Soviet-bloc countries.[86] China contributed another $1.1 billion to Third World recipients.

In addition to these figures, Soviet arms transfers to Cuba, North Korea, and Vietnam during the period can be estimated to have been at least $7 billion (of which Vietnam received more than one-half), bringing the grand total to at least $58 billion of military aid to Third World countries.[87]

On a regional basis, the Middle East was by far the priority area for the distribution of Soviet military aid, receiving more than 50 percent over the whole period. Table 7-2 shows the regional breakdown of the USSR's military-aid commitments. The additional $4 billion furnished by the Eastern European members of the Soviet bloc followed roughly the same distribution pattern.

Under the Soviet-bloc military-assistance effort up to 1980, some 52,000 Third World military personnel had received advanced training of one sort

Table 7-2
Regional Distribution of Soviet Military Aid, 1955-1979

Region	Amount ($US million)	Percent
Middle East	24,445	52
North Africa	10,960	23
South Asia	5,410	11
Sub-Saharan Africa	4,635	10
Latin America	970	2
East Asia	890	2
Total	47,310	100

Source: Central Intelligence Agency, *Communist Aid Activities in Non-Communist Less Developed Countries, 1979 and 1954-79,* ER 80-10318U (Washington, D.C., October 1980), p. 14.

or another in the USSR and other communist countries, in addition to on-site training for many thousands more, conducted in their own countries by Soviet, Eastern European, and Cuban instructors from abroad. In 1979, the number of Soviet and Eastern European military instructors and advisers present in some twenty-seven Third World countries was around 16,000—plus some 34,300 Cuban military personnel, the majority of whom doubled as combat troops.[88]

Over the twenty-five-year period beginning in 1955, some forty-five Third World countries received military aid from the Soviet bloc. Not included in this total are three communist countries—Cuba, North Korea, and North Vietnam—that, as noted earlier, have received substantial military aid from Moscow. Table 7-3 lists recipients and a rough approximation of the value of the aid extended to them up to 1980.

The fifteen major recipients (Iraq through South Yemen) in table 7-3 received almost 95 percent of the military aid furnished to the Third World, while the top six countries—Iraq, Syria, Libya, India, Egypt, and Algeria—received about three-fourths of the total. In terms of the correlation between arms exports and political influence, it is a point of some interest that these data suggest something less than a fully satisfactory rating for the Soviet arms-transfer effort.

Of the top six recipients, none has embraced the communist system nor can be said to follow a foreign-policy line dictated in Moscow, although at least four of the group tend to exhibit an anti-U.S. attitude more or less consistently. Of the entire top fifteen recipients, only four—Ethiopia, Angola, South Yemen, and Afghanistan—might be considered to be, for the time being, politically in the Soviet orbit, while at least two—Egypt and Indonesia—have moved out of the Soviet orbit. The remainder tend to follow a relatively autonomous, though frequently anti-U.S., course that may be as much a product of their Third World outlook as of the exercise of Soviet influence through military- and economic-aid programs.

In this connection, the tendency of many Third World countries to use anti-Americanism as a common rallying point has been increasingly demonstrated over the past decade or so—for example, in the UN. This attitude does not necessarily equate with a pro-Soviet stance, although the USSR certainly has sought to cultivate the Third World as its natural constituency.[89]

Notwithstanding the rather poor correlation of major Soviet arms transfers with ongoing political influence as suggested earlier, this is not to say that Moscow's twenty-five-year investment in Third World military-aid programs has failed to improve the USSR's overall international position. On the contrary, it should not be overlooked that military aid has provided the USSR access to most Third World countries more readily than any other avenue. As one analyst remarked, an arms agreement with a developing

Table 7-3

Third World Recipients of Soviet-Bloc Military Aid, 1955-1980

($US millions)

Major Recipients	Amount	Other Recipients	Amount
Iraq	More than 7,000	Mozambique	More than 300
Syria	More than 7,000	Tanzania	More than 300
Libya	More than 7,000	Nigeria	More than 100
Algeria	More than 4,000	Zambia	More than 100
India	More than 4,000	Uganda	More than 100
Egypt	More than 4,000	Guinea	More than 100
Ethiopia	More than 2,000	Mali	More than 100
Afghanistan	More than 1,000	Sudan	More than 100
Indonesia	More than 1,000	Morocco	More than 70
Iran	More than 500	Pakistan	More than 70
North Yemen	More than 500	Madagascar	More than 70
Angola	More than 500	Bangladesh	More than 70
Peru	More than 500	Congo	More than 70
Somalia	More than 400	Kuwait	More than 25
South Yemen	More than 400	Cape Verde	More than 25
		Cyprus	More than 25
		Benin	More than 25
		Guinea-Bissau	More than 15
		Ghana	More than 15
		Equatorial Guinea	More than 15
		Lebanon	More than 15
		Kampuchea	10 or less
		Sri Lanka	10 or less
		Central African Republic	10 or less
		Burundi	5 or less
		Mauritania	5 or less
		Burma	5 or less
		Chad	5 or less
		Sierra Leone	5 or less
		Nepal	5 or less
		Maldives	5 or less

Sources: U.S. Department of State, Bureau of Intelligence and Research, *Communist States and Developing Countries: Aid and Trade in 1970,* RECS-15 (Washington, D.C., September 22, 1971), p. 18; U.S. Department of State, Bureau of Intelligence and Research, *Communist States and Developing Countries: Aid and Trade in 1971,* RECS-3 (Washington, D.C., July 10, 1972), p. 18; U.S. Department of State, Bureau of Intelligence and Research, *Communist States and Developing Countries: Aid and Trade in 1972,* RECS-10 (Washington, D.C., June 15, 1973), appendix table 10; U.S. Department of State, Bureau of Intelligence and Research, *Communist States and Developing Countries: Aid and Trade in 1974,* Report no. 298 (Washington, D.C., January 27, 1976), appendix table 8; U.S. Arms Control and Disarmament Agency, *World Military Expenditures and Arms Transfers 1967-1976* (Washington, D.C., July 1978), pp. 157-160; U.S. Arms Control and Disarmament Agency, *World Military Expenditures and Arms Transfers 1968-1977* (Washington, D.C., October 1979), pp. 155-158; U.S. Arms Control and Disarmament Agency, *World Military Expenditures and Arms Transfers 1969-1978* (Washington, D.C., December 1980), pp. 159-162; Roger F. Pajak, "The Effectiveness of Soviet Arms Aid Diplomacy in the Third World," in *The Soviet Union in the Third World: Successes and Failures,* ed. Robert H. Donaldson (Boulder, Colo.: Westview Press, 1981), pp. 404-408; and Stockholm International Peace Research Institute, *The Arms Trade with the Third World* (New York: Humanities Press, 1971).

country has been the opening wedge for nearly every major Soviet advance in the Third World.[90] In the 1970s especially, military aid enabled the USSR to insert itself into several pivotal local conflicts and led to significant gains in Soviet prestige and influence, as well as to the weakening of Western influence in some parts of the Third World.

Among other benefits of the military-aid effort that doubtless justify it in Soviet eyes has been the creation of an infrastructure for the projection of Soviet power abroad and the experience that Soviet personnel have acquired over a wide range of political-military situations in the Third World. Moreover, in recent years, as previously noted, Moscow has found its arms sales profitable economically, accounting not only for an important boost in Soviet hard-currency receipts but also making up a significant share of Soviet export trade with LDCs. In 1977, for example, Soviet delivery of around $4.7 billion in arms amounted to more than half of Soviet exports of about $8 billion to LDCs.[91]

Soviet Economic Aid

Soviet-bloc economic-aid extensions to the Third World in the second half of the 1970s rose substantially, reaching slightly more than $12 billion for the 1975-1979 period, compared with about $6.5 billion for the 1970-1974 period. Despite this rise (which included a record economic-aid commitment for a single year in 1978), the trend of the early 1970s toward some decline in economic commitments relative to military aid continued. The economic aid pledged in 1975-1979, for example, came to about 40 percent of the military aid for that period, while in the preceding five-year period it had come to 46 percent.[92]

The Eastern European share of the economic aid tendered by the Soviet bloc also declined somewhat, from 47 percent of the total in the 1970-1974 period to 34 percent in 1975-1979.[93] As usual, the delivery of economic aid lagged well behind commitments, amounting to about one-third of new extensions during the period.

Overall, for the entire twenty-five-year period up to 1980, Soviet-bloc economic aid to the Third World (excluding Cuba, North Korea, and Vietnam) ran well behind military-aid commitments. Economic aid for the period came to about $28 billion; military aid, to about $51 billion. Of the economic-aid total, about $9.8 billion, or 35 percent, was furnished by Eastern European members of the Soviet bloc.

Major recipients of Soviet-bloc economic aid were ten countries in the Middle East and southern Asia, which together received more than 65 percent of the $28 billion total, of which about $12 billion had been drawn at the end of 1979. Turkey, a country strongly wooed but not won by Moscow, was the single largest recipient of Soviet-bloc economic assistance. A breakdown of amounts received by the ten top recipients, out of some eighty countries, is shown in table 7-4.

As in the case of military aid, the immediate correlation between political success and economic aid is not impressive. Only one country— Afghanistan—of the top ten has acquired a communist regime. However, Soviet influence need not be measured by conversions to communism; the political leverage attained by the USSR in the countries concerned is probably felt by Moscow to be well worth the cost of economic-aid disbursements—running at less than 0.1 percent of the Soviet GNP. Moreover, repayments in recent years have begun to catch up with disbursements, pointing toward a net inflow of resources.[94]

In 1978, as mentioned previously, the Soviet bloc pledged the largest single year's worth of economic aid to the Third World, amounting to $4.6 billion, of which the Soviet share was a little more than $3 billion. Virtually all of this went to only two countries—Turkey and Morocco—both traditionally oriented toward the West. Much of a $1.2 billion credit for Turkey was earmarked for the expansion of steel, aluminum, and oil-refining capacity, while Morocco got $2 billion for phosphate exploitation intended to provide the Soviet bloc with up to 5 million tons of phosphate yearly.[95]

The large phosphate project underscored a trend set earlier in the 1970s of Soviet-sponsored programs aimed at developing sources of raw materials for the Soviet bloc. One example of such programs was a bauxite-mining

Table 7-4
Major Recipients of Soviet-Bloc Economic Aid, 1955-1980
($US millions)

Recipients	From USSR	From Eastern Europe	Total
Turkey	3,330	395	3,725
India	2,280	455	2,735
Egypt	1,440	890	2,330
Morocco	2,100	170	2,270
Iran	1,165	685	1,850
Syria	770	955	1,725
Afghanistan	1,290	135	1,425
Algeria	715	525	1,240
Iraq	705	495	1,200
Pakistan	920	215	1,135
Total	14,715	4,920	19,635

Source: Central Intelligence Agency, *Communist Aid Activities in Non-Communist Less Developed Countries, 1979 and 1954-79,* ER 80-10318U (Washington, D.C., October 1980), pp. 18-20.

project in Guinea, designed to supply 2.5 million tons annually to meet about half of the Soviet requirements for this important mineral.[96] Other examples included aid to national oil industries in Iraq, Syria, and Iran, to be repaid in oil and gas. These projects illustrated not only a trend toward open-ended development programs aimed at long-term supply of materials needed by the Soviet economy but also a growth of commercial ventures meant to support Soviet economic plans.[97]

During the past several decades, the USSR also has provided substantial economic aid to its Third World communist allies, North Korea, Vietnam, and Cuba, with the last two receiving the bulk of such support. Moscow probably provided more than $3 billion in economic assistance to North Vietnam between 1955 and 1974.[98] According to Vietnamese government sources, economic aid from Moscow averaged about $750 million a year from 1976 through 1980.[99] However, the level of Soviet economic assistance seems to have increased somewhat following Hanoi's association with CEMA, its 1978 friendship treaty with the USSR, and the Sino-Vietnamese conflict in early 1979 and reached an estimated $850 million to $900 million in 1980.[100] Cuba has been by far the single greatest recipient of Soviet economic support. Between 1960 and 1979, Soviet assistance to Havana amounted to some $16.7 billion, the largest share of which ($9.6 billion) was provided in the post-Angolan period from 1976-1979.[101]

Soviet Economic Strategy in the Third World

The emergence of a situation in which the USSR and its CEMA partners are seen to be facing growing shortages of some basic raw materials such as oil and alumina has drawn new attention to the question of Soviet economic strategy in the Third World. The traditional Leninist injunction to cut off the capitalist countries from the raw materials and cheap labor of the colonial world has found expression in more-recent times in Soviet attempts to persuade the LDCs to deny their raw-materials resources to the West to the extent feasible, or at least to offer them only at exorbitant prices. Moscow's 1973 advice to Middle East countries to use the oil weapon against the West was an example.

During the latter 1970s, however, the supposition grew that Soviet interest in Middle East oil resources might go beyond encouraging the producing countries to boost the price of oil in order to disrupt dependent Western economies while, incidentally, increasing the hard-currency earnings of Soviet oil exports. The argument then arose that as the USSR began to lose its self-sufficiency in oil (expected by the mid-1980s), it would be driven to adopt an access strategy of its own, either to bid for Middle Eastern oil at OPEC prices or to obtain control over it by some combination of force, blackmail, and political maneuver.[102]

A resource war—involving denial of critical resources to the West per classic Leninist advice, plus the new necessity of meeting the Soviet bloc's impending energy crunch and shortages of some strategic raw materials—thus was said by some observers to be likely to become the centerpiece of Soviet economic strategy in the Third World.[103]

As other observers see it, however, neither the objective of impeding Western access to Third World resources nor that of diverting them to the Soviet bloc on concessionary terms of some kind can be considered realistic or realizable. On economic grounds, one of the reasons cited is what Elizabeth Valkenier describes as a shift of Soviet aid and trade policies in the latter 1970s away from the conception of unremitting competition between the socialist and capitalist camps for exclusive control of Third World resources toward a more broadly and pragmatically conceived international division of labor and a more-interdependent world economy.[104]

Some rather unorthodox ideas have been advanced in the specialized Soviet theoretical literature of the past few years on economic development in the Third World. It has been acknowledged, for example, that private enterprise and foreign investment make important contributions to Third World economic development and that integration into the world market may better serve the developmental needs of even "progressive" Third World countries than being tied exclusively to the economies of the socialist bloc.[105]

How much weight such somewhat heretical economic ideas may carry in the overall conduct of Soviet Third World policy is not easy to determine. Such ideas certainly are at considerable variance with orthodox Soviet prescriptions for moving the developing countries along the path to communism and for exploiting the so-called weak link of heavy Western dependence on strategic materials in the Third World. Soviet military writers are still to be found saying, for example, that from "a military-strategic viewpoint," one of the achievements of the national-liberation movement is that "it is depriving [the capitalist countries] of many bridgeheads, sources of raw materials, and manpower reserves which up to now have been actively used for aggressive purposes."[106]

The economic literature pointing to the developmental advantages of steps like integrating Third World countries into the world market also appears somewhat incompatible with the previously noted Soviet tendency of the latter 1970s to favor the takeover of power by strongly pro-Soviet elements in already left-oriented Third World countries. While there may be no inherent reason against proceeding with economic development along nonorthodox lines while pressing for closer conformity along political lines in client Third World countries, the odds do seem to be against this combination's becoming a dominant Soviet policy pattern in the Third World.

8

The Introduction of Cooperative Intervention

Several congruous factors came together in the last half of the 1970s to help make this a period of notably active Soviet intervention in Third World conflict situations.[1] Among these factors were the following:

The collapse of Portugal's African empire accompanying the Portuguese revolution after Salazar's death and the ensuing struggle in Angola among rival factions seeking outside support;

The overthrow of Haile Selassie, which left Ethiopia in the hands of a radical regime antipathetic toward the United States and in desperate need of support against external and internal armed threats;

The post-Vietnam trauma to which the United States fell victim and which, despite presidential warnings to the Soviets not to fish in troubled waters,[2] apparently persuaded Moscow that the risk of U.S. opposition was low;

The longer reach of the USSR's power-projection capacity, attributable to the improvement of Soviet air- and sealift and related logistic capabilities;

The introduction of the technique of cooperative intervention, combining Soviet logistics and command contributions with the Cuban potential to provide combat troops, making for a militarily effective and politically serviceable new instrument of Third World policy, at least in Africa.

Two major Soviet interventions in the last half of the 1970s—those in Angola and Ethiopia—employed the technique of *cooperative intervention.* Both involved close cooperation with Cuban combat troops, and neither was opposed more than peripherally by an external military power. These interventions are examined in the following sections.

Angola

The Angola intervention in 1975-1976 took place in several stages. As noted earlier, competition between Moscow and Peking in supplying military aid

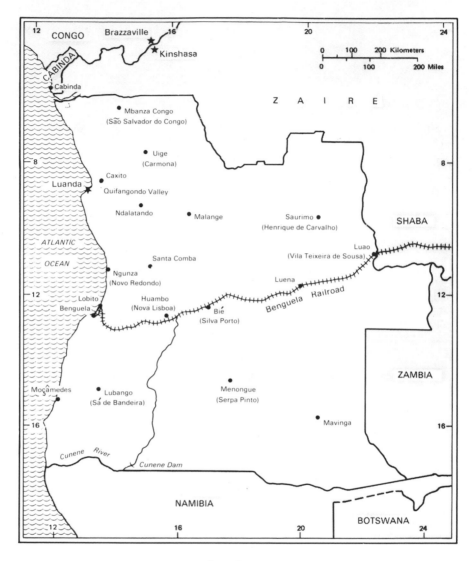

Angola

to rival revolutionary factions in Angola had increased after the collapse of the Portuguese government in April 1974.[3] By early spring 1975, the January 1975 Alvor agreement, under which transitional arrangements for Angolan independence were to be carried out, had begun to break down.[4] Up to that point, at least, Moscow apparently seemed willing to accept some sort of coalition among the competing liberation movements.

The External Intervention and Marxist Takeover in Angola

Beginning in March 1975, however, the USSR substantially boosted arms shipments to its chosen contender among the Angolan factions—Agostinho Neto's Marxist-oriented MPLA. The MPLA, led largely by mulatto, urban intellectuals, was supported by the USSR and the radical Portuguese armed-forces movement (MFA), as well as by Cuba. Cuban ties with the MPLA revert to the mid-1960s. Jonas Savimbi's National Union for the Total Independence of Angola (UNITA), with black leadership and a strong Ovimbundu tribal base, was at first supported by China, later by South Africa. Holden Roberto's National Liberation Front of Angola (FNLA), black led and with a Bakongo tribal base, had varied support from Zaire, China, and the United States.[5]

The arms deliveries to the MPLA, which were mostly transshipped through the Congo, markedly changed the internal military balance among the three liberation movements maneuvering for power in anticipation of Angola's scheduled independence from Portugal in November 1975. Bolstered by this influx of Soviet arms, the MPLA went on the offensive and by mid-July had taken control of the capital city of Luanda and the oil-rich enclave of Cabinda.

Despite this initial success and the fact that it had by now become the dominant military faction in Angola, by mid-1975 the MPLA found itself stretched thin and with insufficient forces to guarantee the complete victory that Neto now sought. In particular, the MPLA required trained personnel capable of handling the Soviet-supplied armor and artillery, a large part of which remained in storage because MPLA forces could not operate or maintain these more-sophisticated weapons. Moreover, the prospect of increased outside assistance—from Zaire, South Africa, and the United States—to the two other Angolan liberation movements, the FNLA and UNITA, threatened to swing the balance the other way. In July 1975, Zaire began to commit troops to help the FNLA, and in early August, a small South African contingent entered southern Angola in a show of force intended to demonstrate South African resolve to protect hydroelectric projects on the Cunene River. The first U.S. aid of $300,000 to the FNLA, in January 1975, did not include arms supply. The initial increment of a $32 million U.S. program of covert arms support for the FNLA and UNITA, approved after the MPLA captured Luanda in mid-July, did not arrive in Angola until the beginning of August 1975.[6]

In view of the situation its forces faced by mid-1975, the MPLA reportedly requested Moscow to send Soviet combat troops to Angola but was turned down apparently because of concern over a possible U.S. reaction and told to ask the Cubans instead.[7] Precisely when Castro agreed to furnish Cuban troops, how large an initial commitment was made and the extent to which the intervention decision may have been taken at Havana's rather than Moscow's initiative are somewhat contentious questions.[8] In any event, presumably with assurances that Moscow would help defray the costs of the undertaking, Castro began a progressively expanding military intervention in the Angolan civil war. In July, some 50 Cuban military advisory personnel arrived in Angola.[9] By late September, a more-sizable contingent of Cuban combat troops—numbering from 1,500 to perhaps twice that figure and described by some sources as Castro's reserves—began to arrive in Angola aboard Cuban merchant ships.[10] Coincidentally with deciding to commit troops, Castro dispatched a senior military mission to oversee the Cuban effort and to provide high-level advisory support to the MPLA command in Angola. This mission was composed of some of Cuba's most senior officers, including among others "the chairman of the joint chiefs of staff, the chiefs of three armies and the air force," all of whom relinquished their commands in Cuba between August 20 and September 5.[11] Along with the Cuban buildup, Soviet advisers and technicians also began to appear in Angola, and by the end of the year they numbered several hundred.[12]

Although the MPLA was able to extend its control over most of Angola's provincial centers by late summer, the military situation began to take an unfavorable turn in October 1975, when an FNLA-Zairian task force threatened Luanda from the north and South African troops, operating jointly with FNLA-UNITA in the south, began a rapid advance against Cuban-MPLA forces.[13]

With defeat of their client in Angola now a distinct possibility, the USSR and Cuba faced another key decision toward the end of October. The options were to (1) seek a compromise solution per the Alvor agreement, (2) withdraw Cuban troops and accept defeat, or (3) up the ante. The last option was chosen, resulting in a major new deployment of Cuban troops and Soviet arms by air and sea over the next four months, beginning at the end of October.

In early November, Cuba began to airlift troops to Angola aboard aircraft from its government airline, *Cubana de Aviación,* making refueling stops at Barbados and Guinea-Bissau. When U.S. diplomatic pressure persuaded the Barbadian government in mid-December to deny Havana refueling privileges, the Cubans rerouted their airlift first through the Azores, where refueling rights also were soon denied because of U.S. objections, and finally through the newly independent Cape Verde. However, the last proved to be a marginal route since it stretched the Cuban Bristol Britannia aircraft's range limits. As a result of these problems, the Soviets, in early January, provided the Cubans two longer-range IL-62 aircraft on charter from Aeroflot, which alone carried about 2,800 Cuban troops to Angola between January 8 and 21.[14] The Soviets began to airlift arms and ammunition to the Angolan theater at the end of October. Using Military Transport

Aviation (VTA) AN-22 and AN-12 aircraft, the Soviet airlift flew from the USSR via Yugoslavia, Algeria, Mali, Guinea, and Congo-Brazzaville, with refueling stops in Algiers and Conakry. When the Soviet airlift terminated in March 1976, about 3,000 tons of military cargo had been ferried to Angola aboard seventy flights.[15]

The bulk of arms and ammunition was delivered to Angola by sealift, mostly in Soviet bottoms. All told, the USSR is estimated to have provided nearly $200 million worth of military assistance to Angola in 1975 alone—equaling "the entire amount of all military aid from all sources to sub-Saharan Africa in 1974." Among the Soviet arms brought into Angola were infantry weapons and machine guns, bazookas, mortar and recoilless rifles, helicopters and MIG aircraft, armored personnel carriers, heavy artillery, light and medium tanks, and truck-mounted 122-mm multitube rocket launchers.[16] These weapons gave the Cuban and MPLA forces a decisive firepower advantage on the battlefield, and the tanks and truck-mounted rocket launchers had a particularly devastating effect on the morale of the MPLA's Angolan adversaries.

By the end of February 1976, when the conventional fighting ended in Angola, some forty-five Soviet and Eastern European arms deliveries had also been made by sea to the Angolan theater. An additional thirty-four troop and arms deliveries had also been made in Cuban-owned bottoms by that date.[17] Altogether, the combined air- and sealift brought the number of Cuban troops to over 11,000 by mid-January 1976 and to around 20,000 during the next few months when the Cuban buildup reached its peak.[18]

It should be noted that the foregoing figures on Cuban troop deployments to Angola, including the peak figure of 20,000 in 1976, reflect the best Western estimates. Castro, however, in a speech in December 1979, gave the number of Cuban soldiers in Angola in 1976 as 36,000.[19]

During the Angolan operations in late 1975 and early 1976, the USSR deployed a small contingency naval force off West Africa. At its height in February, the naval force included a cruiser, a guided-missile destroyer, an amphibious landing ship with some naval infantry reportedly aboard, and a cruise-missile submarine.[20]

With the exception of the amphibious landing ship that moved to a holding area off northern Angola in early December, presumably to help evacuate Soviet personnel from Luanda should that have become necessary, these Soviet naval combatants did not arrive in Angolan waters until after the peak of the Angolan crisis had passed and after U.S. intervention had been ruled out.[21] Among other purposes, these Soviet naval deployments may have been intended to deter Zairian military actions against the sealift to Angola, to discourage any possible U.S. naval exercises in the area, and to support the Soviet IL-62 airlift from Cuba.[22] They also may have been simply a show of the flag after the fact. In mid-January 1976, again after the threat of further U.S. intervention had been ruled out by congressional action, the Soviets also deployed TU-95 reconnaissance aircraft to Conakry and Cuba for surveillance operations over the South Atlantic.[23]

As it turned out, despite a bad scare in mid-December after MPLA and Cuban forces had lost a three-day pitched battle to South African troops about 150 miles from Luanda, no need arose to pull out of Angola.[24] Rather, the South Africans chose on January 23 to disengage from the conflict following the U.S. Senate action on December 19 that ruled out further aid to FNLA-UNITA.[25]

Thereafter, thanks both to the South African withdrawal and the buildup of Cuban troops, which did the bulk of the fighting, the MPLA managed to prevail on the battlefield in February 1976, while in the same month a parallel diplomatic offensive paid off with recognition of the MPLA as the legitimate government of Angola by the OAU, soon followed by the majority of West European governments.[26]

Factors Contributing to Success of the
Angola Intervention

While it would be imprudent to denigrate the efficacy of Soviet and Cuban operations in Angola, it is nevertheless important to recognize some of the unique attributes of the Angola situation and other advantageous factors that facilitated the successful communist intervention of 1975-1976.

First, Angola was, in many respects, a political and military vacuum in 1975. As the only Portuguese territory in Africa without a unified liberation movement in a position to receive the transfer of power, Angola presented a unique opportunity to outside forces to influence the succession to Portuguese rule. This opportunity was improved by the fact that African opinion was divided over which movement should assume authority in Angola and the Portuguese colonial authorities, preoccupied with the political struggle at home and encumbered by a military establishment no longer disposed to fight in Angola, were themselves unwilling and unable to impose a solution.

Second, the character of the Angolan conflict was such that even modest amounts of external aid and intervention could produce great leverage on the battlefield. The indigenous forces contending for power had only marginal military capabilities, and as a result, a few heavier weapons or reasonably disciplined, well-led troops could determine decisively the outcome of a given engagement. This was demonstrated by the devastating effect of Soviet-supplied 122-mm rockets and T-34 tanks against FNLA and Zairian forces in the north or, conversely, by the striking success of battle groups spearheaded by the South Africans in the south. Thus, when unopposed by the more-capable South Africans, superior Soviet weaponry and disciplined Cuban forces were able to dominate a conflict marked by little hard or sustained combat.[27]

Third, while none of the Angolan liberation movements possessed good combat capabilities, the MPLA was clearly the best of the lot. In comparative terms, Neto's forces were superior in leadership, discipline, and organizational abilities; thus the Soviets and Cubans enjoyed the advantage of working with the most capable of the indigenous groups.

Fourth, the MPLA benefited greatly, particularly in the earlier stages of the conflict, from the support and protection of local Portuguese military personnel sympathetic to their movement. It may well have been the threat of Portuguese counteraction that deterred the FNLA from crushing the MPLA during the latter's time of greatest weakness in early 1975. At any rate, there is no question that Portuguese military personnel assisted the infiltration of Soviet arms into Angola and on occasion helped MPLA military operations in the capital.[28] Not all Portuguese aid was directed to the MPLA—some went to the FNLA and UNITA as well—but on balance Neto's forces benefited most from Lisbon's policy of active neutrality in Angola.

Fifth, external Soviet and Cuban support of their Angolan client was made possible because several key African states permitted their territory to be used as staging areas for the airlift and other arms-supply operations. These included Algeria, Guinea (Conakry), Mali, and the People's Republic of the Congo. The last was by far the most important, providing a secure rear base for training, troop assembly, and logistic transfers. Staging facilities were made available ad hoc by governments that both politically supported MPLA objectives in Angola and received Soviet military assistance. Indeed, all the mentioned African countries involved in supporting the Soviet airlift apparently received commitments for increased military assistance from the USSR in return for the use of their facilities.

Sixth, while the United States had some limited success in obtaining the denial of landing rights to the transatlantic airlift of Cubans to Angola, it was unable to close down this operation entirely; moreover, it failed completely to impede the airlift from the USSR, despite vigorous protests to Yugoslavia.[29] In short, U.S. diplomatic leverage proved marginal in affecting external communist support operations even to a rather remote area.

Finally, while not decisive, standardized communist weaponry of Soviet origin provided inherent advantages. The Cuban expeditionary force could operate with equal facility with weapons brought from Cuba, delivered directly from the USSR, or previously stockpiled in Angola for MPLA use. The FNLA and UNITA, conversely, were forced to operate with weapons of diverse origin and vintage, a situation that compounded their logistical problems and that served, along with the other factors mentioned, to give their communist-supported opponents in Angola an important edge throughout the conflict.

Continuing Cuban Presence in Angola

Following the successful collaborative Soviet-Cuban intervention of the mid-1970s, a substantial Cuban military presence remained in Angola, seemingly on a semipermanent basis. The number of troops fluctuated some, but apparently the level was maintained at around 19,000, along with some 8,500 civilian technicians.[30] Cuban advisers and technicians are found at all levels of the Angolan infrastructure, in some respects filling the role of the former Portuguese colonials. Among other things, the Cubans helped to put down an attempted coup against Neto in May 1977.

The coup attempt was staged by an extremist MPLA faction led by Nito Alves, known for his strong pro-Soviet leanings, thus feeding speculation at the time of possible Soviet-Cuban differences over internal Angolan political alignments and perhaps even Soviet backing of the coup. Another supposition was that a basic grievance behind this attempted coup was resentment by blacks against the preponderance of mulattoes and whites in the MPLA leadership.[31]

Cuban troops were also employed on behalf of the Angolan government to complete the "pacification" of the country. This they failed to accomplish, and by 1981 the best the Cubans apparently could do was to keep under some semblance of control a continuing guerrilla campaign carried on in southern Angola by Jonas Savimbi's UNITA, whose forces to date have prevented the reopening of Angola's vital Benguela railroad.

In addition to combating the UNITA insurgents and training the 30,000-man Angolan armed forces, a slow process, the Cubans, with Soviet assistance, also used Angola as a base for training and equipping other southern African liberation movements, particularly the SWAPO forces operating in Namibia. Concerns that Angola would become a staging area for further communist-backed probes into neighboring states were intensified by the March 1977 and May 1978 Katangan incursions into Zaire's mineral-rich Shaba province (formerly Katanga). In both years, Angola-based Katangan separatist forces invaded Shaba to some distance (capturing the key mining center of Kolwezi in 1978) and were expelled only after the intervention of outside forces—namely, Moroccan units in 1977 and Belgian and French troops airlifted by the United States in 1978.

The incursions were mounted by the Congolese National Liberation Front (FLNC), composed of former Katangan gendarmes who had fled to eastern Angola from Zaire after the collapse of Moise Tshombe's secessionist movement. During the 1975-1976 Angolan conflict, about 4,000 of these former gendarmes were armed with Soviet weapons and fought alongside the MPLA and Cubans. Being comparatively well trained, the Katangans were considered the MPLA's most effective African combat force.

In March 1977, some 1,500 to 2,000 Katangans invaded Shaba from Angola and occupied about one-third of the province, meeting little if any resistance from the poorly trained and motivated Zairian forces in the area. The May 1978 incursion, mounted from Angola through Zambian territory by a larger (5,000 by some accounts) and better-equipped Katangan force, also met little opposition from regular Zairian units and penetrated even deeper. After French and Belgian forces had intervened and recaptured Kolwezi, evacuating about 2,000 Europeans, the Katangans melted into the bush. The European troops eventually were replaced by an African peacekeeping force, made up mainly of Moroccans and Senegalese, with smaller contingents from Togo, Gabon, and the Ivory Coast.[32]

The degree of Soviet and Cuban involvement in the Katangan incursions remains a matter of some controversy. Castro has claimed that Cuba's association with the Katangans ended with the MPLA victory in early 1976 and that he had unsuccessfully attempted to stop the 1978 invasion.[33] However, U.S. intelligence sources reported that the Katangan insurgents had been trained and armed by the Cubans, with "indirect Soviet involvement," well into spring 1978 and that both the 1977 and 1978 attacks "took place with the cooperation of the Angolan government and the Cubans."[34] While the precise motives of the incursions were obscure (the Katangans claimed that the objective was the overthrow of Zaire's President Mobutu), one of Neto's purposes seems to have been to bring pressure on Zaire to halt its support of the FNLA remnants operating in northern Angola. This objective was realized in mid-1978, when in return for restraining further Katangan forays into Zaire, Neto apparently secured agreement from Mobutu to cut off aid to the FNLA insurgents.

Having provided the Angolans with more than $500 million worth of military supplies since 1974, the Soviets seem also to be strongly entrenched in that country. On October 8, 1976, Neto signed a friendship and cooperation treaty with the USSR that committed both countries to "further broaden and deepen their cooperation" in a number of areas and that alluded to unspecified "corresponding agreements in the military sphere." Soviet advisers were emplaced in every government ministry and assumed virtual control of Angola's police, railroads, aviation, and fishing. An estimated 1,000 Soviet officers also occupy key positions in the Angolan military command and control structure.[35] While the Angolans apparently have resisted Soviet attempts to gain formal base rights on their territory, the USSR continues to have "limited use of naval maintenance facilities in Luanda" and Soviet naval ships call at that port. In addition, the Soviets have been permitted the use of Angolan facilities to stage occasional TU-95 reconnaissance flights over the Atlantic.[36]

Neto's death in September 1979, after an operation in Moscow, brought no apparent change in the Luanda leadership's need for Cuban personnel in both military- and civilian-aid categories. However, Neto had been making indirect contacts with Savimbi's UNITA, looking toward cessation of guerrilla warfare and reconciliation—for which part of the price probably would be Cuban withdrawal. If a strongly nationalist-minded faction should become dominant within the succession leadership, it might pursue such a reconciliation policy.[37]

Neto's immediate successor, José Eduardo dos Santos, while not identified with any internal group in the ruling MPLA party favoring a purely Angolan system free of dependence on Cuba and the USSR, has at the same time been continuing the process begun by Neto of gradually establishing economic contacts with Western countries.[38]

Ethiopia

Coming less than two years after Angola, the Ethiopian intervention confounded those who had suggested that another Soviet-Cuban adventure on the scale of Angola was unlikely for a variety of reasons, including a probable Cuban desire to "quit while ahead."[39] Other analysts, however, believed that the very success of Soviet-Cuban collaborative intervention in Angola had probably helped to persuade the Soviet leadership to apply a similar technique when the opportunity presented itself in Ethiopia.[40]

Soviet interest in Ethiopia had perked up with the dethronement of Haile Selassie in September 1974 and the pronouncement three months later by the Dergue (Provisional Military Administrative Council, or PMAC) that Ethiopia was to be a socialist state. According to some accounts, the Soviets had even made a tentative proposal at that time to replace the United States as Ethiopia's arms supplier.[41] However, the immediate initiatives leading to direct Soviet involvement three years later apparently came from the Ethiopian leftist military regime, which found itself in an increasingly difficult situation in 1975 and early 1976 as it sought to cope not only with domestic turmoil but also with guerrilla activity against the Ogaden in support of Soviet-armed Somalia's irredentist claims and a growing Arab-backed rebellion in Eritrea.[42]

Although the United States was still furnishing some arms aid to Ethiopia under agreements scheduled to run until 1978, relations between the two countries had deteriorated greatly in the post-Haile Selassie period. It was not surprising, therefore, that the Dergue should explore the possibility of obtaining military support from the USSR.

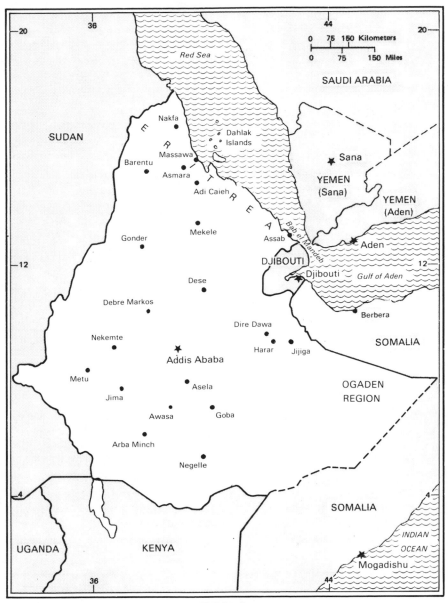

Ethiopia

According to some reports, the USSR was not forthcoming when first approached in spring 1975. The Soviets told the Ethiopians that it would be difficult to provide them arms in light of the strong Ethiopian ties with the United States and the problems that would be created if Soviet arms were used against Somalia.[43] As the power struggle within the Dergue moved Ethiopia increasingly leftward and in a direction favoring Mengistu and a policy of closer bonds with the USSR, however, the Soviets became more receptive to arms requests from Addis Ababa. Indeed, the Soviets seem to have suggested on several occasions that it was the obstructing presence of pro-Western elements in the Dergue that stood in the way of reaching an arms agreement.[44]

In any event, following PMAC-delegation visits to Moscow in July 1976 and again six months later, an initial arms deal was concluded in December 1976.[45] Later this agreement was expanded greatly. The delivery of weapons under the initial agreement, however, did not begin for several months, reflecting possible Soviet uncertainty about Mengistu's staying power and perhaps the hope of reconciling the conflict between their established client, Somalia, and their new one in Addis Ababa in a way that would allow them to keep a foot in both camps.[46]

When, as mentioned previously, Somalia balked at efforts by the USSR and Castro in early 1977 to resolve this dilemma through the device of a federation of Soviet-aligned states in the Horn of Africa,[47] and as the Ethiopian military situation worsened, Moscow decided to increase the supply of arms. This decision, it may be observed, coincided also with Mengistu's assumption of control in February 1977.

Whether the final purging of Western elements in the Dergue that marked Mengistu's seizure of power had been a condition linked to the actual delivery of Soviet arms is somewhat obscure, as is the question of what help Mengistu may have received during the power struggle that eliminated his rivals within the Dergue. It is quite possible that the Soviets had some foreknowledge of Mengistu's plan to seize power in early February 1977 and had provided the Ethiopian leader with assurances of immediate recognition and backing in the event of a takeover.[48] According to Soviet accounts, Mengistu's takeover of power was meant to preserve the country's unity in the face of many separatist "national liberation fronts" that "sprang up like mushrooms" and that were threatening the Ethiopian revolution to which the USSR lent "powerful moral-political support."[49]

Whatever the degree of direct Soviet complicity in Mengistu's elimination of his pro-Western rivals, the outcome certainly did not displease Moscow and seems to have been a factor in opening up the flow of Soviet arms to Ethiopia. A consignment of tanks and other items reportedly arrived in Ethiopia via South Yemen by May 1977,[50] the same month in which the United States cut off its military aid after the Dergue had expelled all U.S. military advisers a few weeks earlier. Also in May, the first contingent of about 50 Cubans arrived in Ethiopia to join a few Soviet military personnel in initial aid undertakings such as training the Ethiopians in the use of Soviet armor and helping to organize an expanded militia.[51] By November, the number of Cuban military advisers in Ethiopia reportedly had risen to more than 400.[52]

During Mengistu's first trip to Moscow in May 1977, a major new aid agreement was negotiated. This addition to the initial aid agreement of December 1966 brought the amount of aid pledged by the Soviet bloc to an estimated figure of more than $500 million,[53] more military aid than the United States had provided in three decades. The items to be furnished included modern fighters and tanks, armored personnel carriers, artillery, and other equipment.[54]

In midsummer 1977, when regular Somali forces began to take part in the Ogaden fighting, the USSR temporarily shut off arms supplies to Somalia. The flow of arms resumed briefly in August while the USSR sought to persuade Siad Barre to accept a negotiated settlement and to dissuade him from turning for support to the West and the Arab League states. These negotiations in Moscow in late August came after the United States, the United Kingdom, and France had announced on July 26, 1977, their readiness in principle to provide Somalia with defensive arms. This promise proved short lived, however, being reversed the following month by Washington on the grounds that aid to Somalia "would add fuel to a fire we are more interested in putting out."[55]

By early October, after a stepped-up Somali campaign in the Ogaden had sent the Ethiopians into disorderly retreat,[56] Moscow apparently abandoned the idea of a negotiated solution of the conflict and came down squarely on the Ethiopian side, announcing on October 19 that it "formally and officially" had ended arms aid to Somalia.[57] As previously observed, this was followed in November 1977 by Somalia's renunciation of its treaty with the USSR and expulsion of Soviet and Cuban military personnel, many of whom were transferred to Addis Ababa.[58]

Meanwhile, the pace of Soviet arms shipments in support of what were described as Ethiopia's "beleaguered and semimutinous troops" in the Ogaden picked up considerably with the advent of a sealift through Suez in October and of an airlift from the USSR in late November.[59] This acceleration of arms supplies came on the heels of Mengistu's clandestine trip to both Moscow and Havana in October to seek a speedup of military aid.[60] A Soviet on-the-spot survey of Ethiopian needs was also made at this time. Somewhat as in Angola, the inability of Ethiopian troops by themselves to man the arriving equipment and otherwise to cope with a worsening military situation posed the need for intervention by outside combat forces—a role that again fell to the Cubans.

Precisely when the decision was made to bring in combat Cubans is not known, but they began to arrive in growing numbers in late 1977 and early 1978. Some came by air (both from Angola and Havana), and others came by sea aboard Soviet vessels along with further shipments of war materiel.[61]

In its first two months, the Soviet airlift, according to the International Institute for Strategic Studies, involved some fifty transport flights—considerably fewer than indicated by other reports at the time.[62] Another fifty to sixty transport flights were made in the next six months. A noteworthy aspect of the airlift in its first and subsequent phases was the variety of routes used.[63] Some difficulties with overflight arrangements encountered in early phases of the airlift subsequently were worked out.

The parallel sealift, mainly from the Black Sea through Suez to Aden and thence to the Eritrean ports of Massawa and Assab, reportedly engaged from thirty to fifty Soviet merchant cargo ships.[64] In some cases, Soviet amphibious landing craft were used for off-loading or ferrying cargoes from Aden, which served as a valuable transshipment link in the Ethiopian intervention.[65] To protect the sea- and air-arms-resupply effort, the Soviets established a sizable naval presence off the Ethiopian coast in the Massawa-southern Red Sea area. More than twenty Soviet naval vessels reportedly were concentrated in this area.[66] By the third week of February 1978, Ethiopia had received an estimated $850 million worth of Soviet arms, including about 400 tanks and 50 MIG jet fighters.[67] The Soviets continued to supply arms to Ethiopia at a high rate in succeeding months, delivering some 61,000 tons of military equipment during the first half of 1978 alone.[68]

By March 1978, the Cuban military force in Ethiopia, some of which had been transferred from other locations, including Somalia, Angola, and South Yemen, and some of which came from Cuba by various circuitous routes, had been built to a level variously estimated at from 11,000 to 17,000 troops.[69] Again furnishing a retrospective figure, Castro placed the Cuban troop level in Ethiopia at 12,000, near the lower range of the Western estimates.[70] In command of the Cuban combat contingent in Ethiopia was Division General Arnaldo Ochoa, who had been one of the Cuban commanders in Angola.

The Cuban air and ground forces, together with a Soviet command and staff element of from 1,000 to 1,500, headed by four general officers, including Vasily I. Petrov and Grigoriy Barisov,[71] turned the tide against the Somalis, who in early March broke off the battle in the Ogaden and withdrew to their side of the border. Cuban mechanized elements contributed importantly to the victory by successfully outflanking the Somali positions in the Ogaden and threatening their already tenuous lines of communication.

Even before the campaign in the Ogaden was completed, the Soviets and Cubans began in February 1978 to help out the Mengistu regime in Eritrea, where their presence not only was incompatible with the claim of being in Ethiopia to defend it against border-crossing aggression but also contributed to suppression of guerrilla liberation groups that they had previously supported. The two principal Eritrean liberation groups that had received support not only from the USSR and Cuba but also from the pan-Islamic Arab states were the Eritrean Liberation Front (ELF) and the more-militant Eritrean Liberation Front/Popular Liberation Forces (EPLF). As in the case of the Ethiopian-Somali conflict, in the Mengistu regime's campaign against Eritrea, Soviet arms were used extensively by both sides.

Although it appears that both the Soviets and the Cubans would have preferred to find a workable political solution to the Eritrean secession problem,[72] they nevertheless went along with Mengistu's resolve to settle it by a military offensive, partly perhaps to ensure access to the Red Sea ports of Massawa and Assab, without which Ethiopia's strategic value would be much diminished. Their intervention took the form of substantial logistic backup, command assistance to Ethiopian field units, some air and naval support, but apparently only limited ground-combat use of Cuban troops.[73]

As a result of Cuban and Soviet help, the Ethiopian army in summer 1978 succeeded in reopening communications and driving Eritrean forces away from the province's ports and most of its towns, although some continuing guerrilla resistance could not be stamped out readily. In July 1979, for example, unsuccessful attempts by some 50,000 Ethiopian government troops to take the town of Nakfa, still held by Eritrean secessionist forces, reportedly cost the Ethiopians about 6,000 casualties.[74] A year later, after a second Ethiopian attack in December 1979 against the Eritrean stronghold at Nakfa also failed, the Mengistu regime reportedly solicited additional Soviet advisers and arms, including helicopter gunships, to help crush the insurgency in Eritrea.[75]

Meanwhile, the conflict in the Ogaden, which had subsided in March 1978, revived on a somewhat less-intense scale within a year. In summer 1980, Ethiopian troops, with Cuban assistance, were still seeking unsuccessfully to subdue guerrilla forces of the Western Somali Liberation Front (WSLF).[76]

One novel aspect of the Soviet-Cuban division of labor in Africa during the Ethiopian intervention was the reported sending of about thirty Soviet pilots to Cuba to replace temporarily Cubans brought to Africa to fly combat missions.[77] A similar switch of pilots had been made during the Angola conflict.[78] The Ethiopian intervention also found the USSR bringing in some hundreds of East European military advisers and technicians to lend a helping hand, along with South Yemenis, some of whom reportedly flew combat missions.[79]

The Soviets and Cubans remain heavily entrenched in Ethiopia, as in Angola. In addition to the some 13,000 Cuban troops still in Ethiopia, about 1,000 Soviet military personnel also remain to provide instruction and to help maintain equipment. In return for some $2 billion worth of Soviet military aid extended since December 1976, the Ethiopians have signed a twenty-year friendship treaty with Moscow and granted the USSR virtually exclusive rights to a naval facility being built at the Dahlak Islands, off Massawa on the Red Sea Strait.[80] The Dahlak facility, which includes a floating dry dock that was towed from the port of Berbera in Somalia,[81] evidently is to serve as a support and replenishment base for Soviet naval forces.

In retrospect, the following were probably the main features of the Soviet-Cuban intervention in Ethiopia:

> An invitation to intervene from a local party portrayable as the victim of aggression (an intervention made awkward for the Soviets by the Ethiopian suppression of the rebels in Eritrea);

> The availability of Cuban combat troops amenable to Soviet strategic direction, permitting the USSR to bring military force to bear directly with minimal censure from black Africa and low risk of a regional or global confrontation with the United States, and even with little apparent concern for Western counteraction;[82]

> Soviet capability for prompt arms delivery to the scene of conflict and to arrange for the air- and sealift of Cuban forces;

> The availability of key transit and staging areas in Iraq, South Yemen, and Angola, which were available because of previous Soviet investments in those countries;

> Apparent inability of the joint intervention forces to provide the kind of assistance required to wipe out resistance in Eritrea and the Ogaden conclusively;

> Notwithstanding the difficulty of bringing about a conclusive resolution of Ethiopia's problems with Eritrea and Somalia, the winning by Moscow of an important strategic foothold in the Horn of Africa from which it can exert strong political-military influence on an area that includes Egypt, Saudi Arabia, the Yemens, Sudan, Kenya, and Somalia.

Other Interventions in the Third World

Although the USSR did not participate directly in either the invasion of Cambodia by Vietnam in late December 1978 or the attack on North Yemen by South Yemen two months later, both situations involved some Soviet backing of the invading parties. In the first case, as noted previously, the Vietnamese assault on Cambodia (Kampuchea) followed the signing of a USSR-Vietnam treaty of cooperation, strongly suggesting that the treaty was intended to abet Hanoi's plans and to discourage China from interfering.[83]

During the invasion, Moscow gave diplomatic and some logistic support to Hanoi and to the Heng Samrin Cambodian faction opposing the Pol Pot regime. Another Soviet action supportive of Vietnam during the invasion was the deployment of a fourteen-ship naval task force in the South China Sea and off the Vietnamese coast. This was assumed to be a warning move in reaction to the buildup of Chinese military forces facing Vietnam,[84] although when China attacked in mid-February to "teach Vietnam a lesson," the USSR attempted no direct military intervention, perhaps in view of the clearly limited nature of the Chinese foray into Vietnam.[85]

The USSR did, however, assist in the redeployment of Vietnamese troops from southern to northern Vietnam and promptly increased deliveries of Soviet arms and other materiel to Vietnam.[86] The Soviets mounted an airlift of critical war materials to the Indochina theater (sometimes overflying Thai territory without Bangkok's permission) and dramatically stepped up sea deliveries to Vietnam.[87] During the first six months of 1979, Hanoi is believed to have received about 90,000 tons of materiel from the USSR, and by the end of 1979, Soviet military shipments were estimated to have more than quadrupled over the previous year.[88] Most of this war materiel was primarily for the "replacement and resupply of existing weapons," but some new sophisticated military weapons (for example, tanks and MIG-21 aircraft) were delivered as well.[89] Soviet military aid continued at a high rate through 1980, amounting to slightly more than $1 billion for the year.[90]

In addition to providing Hanoi with vital economic aid, the USSR also continued to support the attempts of Hanoi and its puppet government to suppress continuing opposition from Khmer Rouge insurgents in the western part of Vietnamese-dominated Cambodia by air delivery of supplies, ammunition, and troops to Vietnamese forces in Cambodia.[91] By 1980, about 5,000 Soviet military and civilian advisers were stationed in Vietnam.[92] Aside from manning some twelve AN-12 aircraft providing shuttle logistic support to the Vietnamese forces in Laos and Cambodia, a substantial number of these Soviet advisers were also training Vietnamese air-force personnel.[93] Soviet technicians and dockworkers also play a vital role in operating the port of Haiphong.[94]

In return for this support, the USSR, as previously noted, received access to naval and air facilities in Vietnam. The USSR had long coveted such facilities for projecting its military presence farther into Southeast Asia and for supporting its naval deployments in the southwest Pacific and Indian Oceans. Soviet submarines and naval ships frequently use port facilities at Haiphong, Danang, and Cam Ranh Bay, and Soviet long-range TU-95 reconnaissance aircraft operate out of Danang on an increasingly regular basis.[95] The Soviets also built a large communications-monitoring station in Vietnam, presumably targeted primarily at China.[96]

In the case of the South Yemen (PDRY) attack on North Yemen (YAR) in late February 1979, it is not altogether clear whether the attack was a premeditated probe or a defensive move that grew out of border clashes between the two Yemens.[97] Neither is it clear to what extent the USSR might have encouraged the invasion. According to some accounts, Moscow had not approved of the PDRY's campaign against North Yemen for fear the PDRY might lose. Such a loss might have jeopardized Soviet access to Aden—then of increasing importance to the Soviets because of their expulsion from Somalia on the other side of the Gulf of Aden.[98] Given the presence of Soviet and Cuban advisers throughout the PDRY's military structure and Aden's manifest dependence on the USSR for weapons and munitions, however, it is difficult to believe that the Soviets and Cubans were not consulted beforehand about the operation into North Yemen or that they did not give the invasion their tacit support.

Once the fighting began, the USSR stood publicly behind the PDRY, asserting that the latter had been attacked by North Yemen.[99] Perhaps more to the point, Soviet and Cuban advisers apparently provided PDRY forces some limited logistic and communication support for the operation, and probably some artillery backup as well.[100] There were also unconfirmed reports that some external communist pilots participated in air operations during the invasion.[101] No communist advisers, however, are reported to have accompanied PDRY troops across the border into North Yemen. At the beginning of 1979, there were estimated to be about 550 Soviet and Eastern European and 1,000 Cuban military advisers and technicians in South Yemen.[102]

During the early days of March, following the alert and partial mobilization of Saudi military forces and the announcement of new U.S. support measures for North Yemen, including the dispatch of a U.S. carrier task force to the region, steps were taken to provide additional outside combat support to the PDRY. Cuban troop reinforcements, along with additional Soviet advisers, reportedly were airlifted from Ethiopia to Aden purportedly to ward off any attack on South Yemen.[103]

In retrospect, the Yemen border war did not constitute much of a conflict. The PDRY committed only limited forces (around 3,000 by some accounts) to the invasion and did not penetrate North Yemen's territory beyond the immediate border region.[104] Little if any serious fighting took place between PDRY and North Yemeni forces.[105] The Yemen border war came to an inconclusive end in mid-March, after Arab League diplomatic pressure, especially from Syria and Iraq, along with the dispatch of a U.S. carrier task force to the Arabian Sea and other U.S. aid measures on behalf of North Yemen,[106] had persuaded both belligerents to accept an Arab League peace plan.

The Soviet position in South Yemen did not suffer following the hostilities. Port and air facilities at Aden and at South Yemen's Socotra Island, 600 miles to the southeast, not only remained at Soviet disposal but also new construction and renovation of naval and air facilities were reported.[107] The USSR also stepped up its naval deployments to the area, and a large Soviet task force visited in June 1979. While in waters off Aden, the task force—which included the carrier *Minsk*, a Kara-class cruiser, and an Ivan Rogov amphibious ship with air-cushion landing vehicles—gave an operational demonstration for South Yemeni officials.[108] Aside from providing support to the Soviet Indian Ocean squadron in an area proximate to Western oil routes, the Aden base also serves as a transit point for Soviet logistic support to Ethiopia and is used by Soviet aircraft, including IL-38s, conducting surveillance missions over U.S. warships in the Indian Ocean.[109] According to Central Intelligence Agency (CIA) estimates, the number of Soviet and Eastern European military and security advisers in South Yemen doubled to around 1,100 after the 1979 border conflict.[110] Soviet advisers reportedly were assigned to almost every South Yemeni ministry, and virtually all major decisions had to be cleared with them. East German advisers were said to run the PDRY's internal-security system, external intelligence network, and immigration section, while Cuban military advisers worked primarily with South Yemen's militia and air force. Soviet and Cuban pilots in MIG aircraft were also reported to be flying daily patrols over the Red Sea and the Gulf of Aden.[111]

Meanwhile, in the wake of the brief border war, the Soviets also began to improve their position with respect to North Yemen. Delivery of the U.S. arms aid earmarked for North Yemen in March had been held up by Saudi Arabia, acting as middleman in the transfer. The Saudis, who had offered to pay for the arms, evidently had second thoughts about strengthening North Yemen's forces and therefore delayed releasing the twelve F-5E fighters and sixty-four M-60 tanks provided by the United States.[112]

Irritated by both the delay and what he considered to be the insufficient amount of the U.S. aid package, President Ali Abdullah Saleh of North Yemen turned in September to Moscow, which promptly dispatched a shipment of aircraft, tanks, and other equipment that eclipsed the modest U.S. offering in numbers and variety.[113] The Soviet move, which reintroduced some additional military advisers into North Yemen along with the weapons,[114] marked renewal of an earlier military-aid relationship with Sana.[115]

The Soviet-Cuban Connection in the Third World

The nature of Cuba's relationship with the USSR and Cuba's contribution to Soviet policy aims in the Third World became matters both of keen interest and of some controversy after the two countries began to exhibit a new form of cooperative intervention in Third World conflict situations in the last half of the 1970s. Applied first in Angola and then in Ethiopia, as discussed earlier, cooperative intervention found the Soviets providing most of the military materiel, mobility, planning, communications, and command functions, with Cuba furnishing the combat forces.

Although the combat use of Cuban troops on a substantial scale was an innovative aspect of the new intervention technique, some precedent had already been set for the deployment of Cuban combat elements abroad. As previously noted, some 400 Cuban tank troops had been sent to Algeria in 1963 to help Ben Bella in a conflict with Morocco,[116] and small numbers of Cuban military personnel also had been involved in the 1960s in guerrilla fighting in Zaire, Tanzania, and Portuguese Guinea.[117]

Ten years later, a Cuban contingent including more than 500 tank troops and some pilots was sent to the Middle East to furnish combat support to Syria after the outbreak of the Arab-Israeli war in October 1973.[118]

In these instances, in contrast to the later Angolan and Ethiopian cases, the Cuban contingents were small and saw only limited combat action; moreover, extensive military cooperation with the Soviets was not involved. The deployments in Algeria and Syria in particular were probably meant mainly to symbolize revolutionary Cuba's devotion to its "international duty."

Subsequent to the interventions in Angola and Ethiopia, no large-scale Cuban combat involvement occurred in other Third World countries; Cuban military personnel did, however, to a limited extent, assist guerrilla campaigning from bases in Mozambique and possibly the other front-line states in the latter 1970s. Cuban pilots probably also backed up the South Yemen invasion forces against North Yemen in 1979.[119]

Besides the several combat interventions in which Cubans have participated, Cuban military advisers and technicians also have furnished military training and security assistance of various kinds to a number of "progressive" regimes and national-liberation movements in the Third World, mostly in Africa. Cuban assistance has included training of both regular and guerrilla forces, organization and training of popular militia forces to offset regular army units, and in some cases (for example, Guinea, Congo-Brazzaville, and Equatorial Guinea), setting up and manning of special security formations to serve as a kind of praetorian guard for the host-country leadership.

The countries in which Cuban military and paramilitary personnel have made their services available at one time or another, and the estimated numbers of personnel present in 1978 and early 1981, are shown in table 8-1. Cuban military and paramilitary personnel were to be found in more than thirty Third World countries at some time during the twenty-year

Table 8-1
Cuban Military and Paramilitary Personnel in Third World Countries

Countries in which Formerly Present	Countries in which Present, 1978-1981	Approximate Number of Personnel	
		1978	1981[a]
	Algeria	15	15
	Angola	20,000	19,000
	Benin	10	10
Bolivia			
Colombia			
	Congo-Brazzaville	400	500
	El Salvador	Few	Few
	Equatorial Guinea	150	200
	Ethiopia	15,000	13,000
Ghana			
	Grenada	150	Few
	Guatemala	Few	Few
	Guinea	200	50
	Guinea-Bissau	140	50
	Guyana	10	5
	Iraq	150	Few
	Jamaica	Few	
	Libya	200	200
	Madagascar	Few	
Mali			
	Mozambique	800	300
	Nicaragua	Few	1,500
North Vietnam			
	Panama		30
Peru			
	Sao Tome	Few	Few
	Sierra Leone	100	100
Somalia			
	South Yemen	1,000	1,000
Syria			
	Tanzania	Few	Few
Venezuela			
Zaire			
	Zambia	75	100
Total		38,400[b]	36,060[c]

Sources: Central Intelligence Agency, *Communist Aid Activities in Non-Communist Less Developed Countries, 1978,* ER 79-10412U (Washington, D.C., September 1979), p. 4; Central Intelligence Agency, *Communist Aid Activities in Non-Communist Less Developed Countries, 1979 and 1954-79,* ER 80-10318U (Washington, D.C., October 1980), p. 15; Hedrick Smith, "Cuban Military and Advisory Presence in Africa," *The New York Times,* November 17, 1977; William J. Durch, "The Cuban Military in Africa and the Middle East: From Algeria to Angola," *Studies in Comparative Communism,* Spring-Summer 1978, pp. 43-51; International Institute for Strategic Studies, *Strategic Survey 1977* (London, 1978), p. 14; Robert Kaylor, "Cuba's Africa Role Said Growing," *Washington Post,* January 21, 1979; John M. Goshko and Walter Pincus, "Sense of Duty behind Cuba's Global Role," *Washington Post,* September 21, 1979; John Darnton, "Mozambique, with Cuban Help, Is Shoring up Its Internal Security," *The New York Times,* June 24, 1979; U.S. Department of State, *Department of State Bulletin,* December 1979, p. 30; U.S. Department of State, *Department of State Bulletin,* July 1980, pp. 77-78; Department of Defense, *Annual Report, Fiscal Year 1981,* January 29,

Table 8-1 *(continued)*

1980, pp. 55-58; Edward Gonzalez, "Cuban Policy toward Africa: Activities, Motivations, and Outcomes," in *The Communist States in Africa,* eds. David Albright and Jiri Valenta (Bloomington: Indiana University Press, forthcoming); and Don Oberdorfer, "Haig Asks Joint Action on Cuba," *Washington Post,* December 2, 1981.
[a]In some cases, figures in this table for 1981 are extrapolated from the last published data available.
[b]Includes about 27,500 combat troops in Angola, Ethiopia, Mozambique, and South Yemen.
[c]Includes about 23,000 combat troops in Angola, Ethiopia, Mozambique, and South Yemen.

period from 1961, when the first training mission went to Ghana, until 1981. Seventeen of these countries were in sub-Saharan Africa; five were Arab countries in the Middle East and North Africa. Not usually known is that small numbers of Cubans were sent to North Vietnam in the mid-1960s to serve as antiaircraft and construction crews.[120] Eight countries in Latin America and the Caribbean received Cuban revolutionary assistance, mostly training of rural guerrilla movements. This activity was carried out largely in the 1960s but was revived to some extent in the latter 1970s.[121]

During 1981, the Cuban military presence in the Third World was distributed among twenty-five countries, the majority of which were in Africa. The total number of personnel declined by about 2,300 during the 1978-1981 period, mostly resulting from the partial withdrawal of Cuban combat personnel from Ethiopia.[122] Some transient traffic of Cuban military and paramilitary advisers to several countries in Central America and the Caribbean also took place from 1978-1981.

Differing Views of the Soviet-Cuban Relationship

The extent of Soviet control over Cuban political-military activities on the African continent and elsewhere in the Third World has been interpreted variously. According to one influential school of thought, Cuba has been little more than a Soviet pawn, compelled because of heavy dependence on the USSR—at least from the early 1970s on—to dance to the latter's tune. Thus, even though Cuba went through a period in the middle 1960s of defying Moscow on some issues and flirting with Peking, this school argues that between 1968 and 1970 the Cubans began to accommodate themselves fully to Soviet policy under economic duress like that arising from the sugar disaster of 1970.[123] Among implications of the Soviet-pawn thesis is not only that Havana takes its orders from Moscow regardless of what Cuba's own interests may be but also that the USSR can be held accountable for Cuban conduct in the Third World.[124]

As seen by another school of thought, Cuba has been not a subservient tool of Soviet interests but essentially an autonomous actor in the Third

World, pursuing its own self-generated policies responsive to ideology, internal Cuban needs, and Castro's ambition to play the role of revolutionary paladin on a global stage.[125] One implication of this view is that Soviet control over Cuban conduct in the Third World is quite limited and that parallel policies are more the result of a temporary convergence of interests than of Soviet dictation.

A variant of this view holds that a major motivation for Cuban involvement abroad has been the need to mobilize Cuban society periodically to sustain revolutionary élan.[126] Partly because of Cuba's revolutionary failures in Latin America in the 1960s, Castro found it expedient to switch to the more-promising African arena. An implication of this thesis is that a shrinking of opportunities in Africa and readier prospects of revolutionary successes in the western hemisphere might bring Castro to refocus Cuba's revolutionary energies more toward Latin America and the Caribbean basin, particularly if Cuba lacks the resources to maintain elsewhere large standing commitments that have begun to lose their pristine revolutionary luster.

A third interpretation between the pawn and independent-actor hypotheses suggests that elements of both dependent and autonomous Cuban behavior have characterized the Soviet-Cuban relationship, which can perhaps best be described as a complex partnership arrangement involving mutual interests and dependencies, as well as frictions—but withal, a partnership in which Soviet seniority and power also count.[127] In this relationship, the USSR is not seen as the party that always initiates Third World actions and drags the other along; rather the Cubans may sometimes get out ahead, making it necessary for the Soviets either to follow suit or put on the brakes.[128]

Here the implication is that while Cuban activities in the Third World are not necessarily Moscow dictated, the Cubans nevertheless are obliged, in William Durch's words, to "operate within the parameters set by the Kremlin."[129] An exception may pertain with respect to Cuban support of revolutionary activity in the western hemisphere, where Havana's revolutionary writ probably runs stronger than Moscow's.

Although these examples do not exhaust the possible forms of the Soviet-Cuban relationship, the third seems best to reflect the available evidence. Whether Cuba properly can be termed a surrogate or proxy of the USSR—if at the same time conceived to be a kind of junior partner in Third World activities—is probably open to argument, at least in the strict sense of these terms—that is, a surrogate or proxy would act only on authority delegated by the principal and for the principal's purposes only.

The Cubans appear to enjoy more leeway than this strict construction allows. For all practical purposes, however, the terms appropriately apply to Cuba and to other countries of the Soviet sphere that serve Soviet purposes while sparing the USSR direct involvement in some particular Third World activity.

Although Cuba has been the principal Soviet surrogate in the Third World since the mid-1970s, several other countries also have furnished services. North Koreans, Yemenis, Ethiopians, and Egyptians are among those who reportedly have played combat roles at least partly on Soviet behalf in the Third World, mostly as pilots. Syria, Iraq, Algeria, Libya, North Korea, and several members of the Warsaw Pact also have provided assistance in the training of guerrillas in various parts of the Third World.[130]

The Eastern European members of the Warsaw Pact are not known to have served to any appreciable extent in surrogate combat roles, but East Germany, Czechoslovakia, Hungary, Poland, and Bulgaria have rendered support in the form of arms supply, training, transport, and internal security. East Germany has made a particularly strong contribution in the latter field. Among countries in which East Germans have been active as police and security advisers are South Yemen, Angola, Ethiopia, Mozambique, and Libya.[131] In the course of helping to shape local police and intelligence organizations, the East Germans may be assumed at the same time to be recruiting their own informant networks and developing reliable indigenous security assets that can be counted on to help assure the favorable longer-term political orientation of these regimes. East German advisory personnel in Africa reportedly also have helped in training guerrillas and planning guerrilla operations against Zimbabwe-Rhodesia and South-West Africa.[132]

Several other Eastern European countries maintain small military-advisory missions in a few Middle Eastern and African countries including Libya, Iraq, Syria, Angola, and Ethiopia. Eastern European flag vessels also have delivered arms to Soviet clients in Third World conflict situations—for example, during the Angolan conflict.[133] Eastern European countries furthermore have provided economic and military assistance to Third World allies engaged in ongoing conflicts (for example, to North Vietnam between 1965 and 1975) and to revolutionary movements fighting so-called wars of national liberation.

The cooperation between members of the Soviet bloc and other radical states to aid the revolutionary forces in El Salvador, discussed previously, is an example of a coordinated communist effort to bring about the overthrow of an established government. According to captured documents, in 1980 the Salvadoran guerrillas successfully solicited extensive military-supply, training, and logistic-support commitments from several Eastern European states, Vietnam, Cuba, Ethiopia, Nicaragua, and Iraq.

The captured documents indicate that particular care was taken to disguise the origins of this military aid. Czechoslovakia offered the Salvadoran guerrillas nontraceable Czechoslovak arms, circulating in the world market, to be transported in coordination with East Germany.

Bulgaria promised German weapons, "rebuilt from World War II," and East Germany was to donate medicines and "combat kits," seek sources of Western-made weapons, and provide military training, especially for clandestine operations. Ethiopia offered "several thousand weapons" of Western origin, and Vietnam some 60 tons of U.S.-made rifles, machine guns, mortars, rocket launchers, and ammunition. Nicaragua considered giving Western-manufactured arms in exchange for the communist-made weapons that had been promised the guerrillas. Iraq made a $500,000 "logistic donation" for use in Nicaragua and El Salvador. While agreeing to consider assisting with the transport of arms from Vietnam and to provide limited training, the USSR apparently decided to allow other bloc members to shoulder the major burden, thus minimizing direct Soviet involvement with the Salvadoran guerrillas. [134]

The trend of recent years points toward the wider use of Eastern Europeans for logistic, security, and various training functions but does not necessarily suggest that they will furnish combat units for intervention in Third World conflict situations. If such be the case, then this aspect of cooperative intervention presumably will continue to be largely a Cuban monopoly, although other pro-Soviet Third World countries (for example, Ethiopia) may provide combat assistance on occasion.

Boundary Conditions Affecting Cooperative Intervention

The instrument of cooperative intervention, combining essentially Soviet logistic and C^3 capabilities with Cuban combat contributions, as applied in Angola and Ethiopia, answers to various interests of both parties. However, in addition to its mutual benefits, it also has some liabilities and limitations.

The benefits, from the Soviet standpoint, appear to be severalfold. For one thing, the experience to date in Africa indicates that the Cuban military input can be a decisive factor in determining the outcome of political-military struggles in favor of Soviet clients and in helping to assure consolidation of power by pro-Soviet Marxist regimes.

Second, the availability in Africa of Cuban troops as a surrogate combat force has put at Soviet disposal an instrument of active intervention employable with relatively low risk of superpower confrontation. At the least, the presence of readily redeployable Cuban combat forces on or close to the scene of potential intervention situations tends to put the burden of initiating a great-power confrontation on the United States.

Finally, cooperative Cuban surrogates help to minimize Soviet visibility and to make the Soviet presence politically and culturally more acceptable to black African states.

From the Cuban viewpoint, though the original combat commitment envisaged in Angola apparently was a good deal smaller than subsequently proved necessary, the opportunity to deploy a substantial intervention force to Africa probably was welcomed by influential institutional constituencies in Cuba looking for an international revolutionary mission for the armed forces.[135] The Cuban combat contribution in Angola and perhaps even more so in Ethiopia also provided a considerable measure of leverage on the USSR.[136] How much influence its combat contributions might continue to give Havana in its relationship with Moscow would depend, however, on a number of boundary conditions and limitations affecting the cooperative-intervention technique.

One condition would be a continuing reluctance on the part of the USSR to commit its own combat forces in the Third World, particularly in cases involving direct Soviet participation in offensive military operations. The greater such reluctance, the stronger Havana's leverage on Moscow. However, should Soviet inhibitions to participate in combat diminish in the future, as the Afghanistan case might presage, then Cuba's leverage in the partnership presumably would decline.

A second condition would be the availability of invitations to intervene from local parties with ostensible claims to internal legitimacy or need for help against external threats. While some departure from this condition for intervention has been seen, as in Eritrea, if the Soviet-Cuban partners were to run out of suitable invitations in the future, the resort to combat intervention would at least become more complicated, in some circumstances riskier, and thus perhaps less likely.

A third condition bearing on cooperative intervention would be the Cuban capability to deal successfully with the expected opposition. In Angola and Ethiopia, better-organized, -trained, and -equipped Cuban units were pitted against local opposition of lower quality, under which circumstances even relatively small Cuban forces proved effective—except in encounters with South African units.[137] However, unless the Soviets were to feel more confident than they probably are concerning Cuban capability to handle South African or outside Western opposition in the future, the combat use of Cubans for any cooperative interventions against such opposition would not appear to recommend itself to Moscow. Among other things, this also would tend to reduce Cuba's leverage in the partnership.

Conversely, should Cuba, through its own or Soviet decision, become involved militarily against strong opposition forces, the effort to prevail might put a greater strain on Cuban resources and domestic morale than the country could sustain without a considerable boost in Soviet material aid, which at an estimated $2.4 billion a year from 1976 to 1979,[138] is probably at a level already causing some concern in Moscow.[139] Incidentally, the steep rise in Soviet economic support to Cuba, paralleling the latter's combat contributions to Third World interventions (the pre-Angola level of Soviet support over a fifteen-year period had averaged only about $470 million a year), would suggest that Cuba's efforts indeed enabled Castro to extract an increasing price from Moscow for services rendered.

Whether Cubans have been performing in a combat role as partners or paid mercenaries of the USSR, another factor to which the relationship might become vulnerable would be the unequal distribution of casualties. Estimates are sketchy, but Cuban combat losses are certainly far heavier than Soviet. Cuban casualties in Angola and Ethiopia up to mid-1978 were estimated by some analysts at about 1,800[140]; Jonas Savimbi has claimed that his UNITA guerrillas killed at least 3,000 Cubans in Angola alone between 1976 and 1979.[141] The total of Cubans killed in African campaigns up to mid-1980, although uncertain, is at least several thousand. By contrast, the toll of Soviet military casualties in all Third World conflicts since the mid-1950s (excluding the Afghanistan intervention) has been estimated at no more than several hundred.[142]

Domestic complaints about casualties reportedly have been dealt with severely by Cuban authorities,[143] but if it were to become felt within the country or by some elements of the leadership that Cuba was bearing more than its fair share of the fighting, then this could act as a constraint upon future Cuban combat commitments.

Soviet leaders may show an increased willingness to risk the commitment of their own combat forces in Third World conflicts because of the built-in limitations of the cooperative-intervention technique. Such limitations include the possibility that the Cubans or other surrogates may find the opposition too tough to handle or the unsuitability in some areas of using proxy or allied forces in combat. In the latter context, a case in point is Afghanistan, where the USSR slipped gradually into a pattern of increased combat involvement and eventually found itself obliged to commit by far the largest combat force that it had ever committed in the Third World.

Apart from combat intervention in active conflict situations in some Third World areas, Cuban military personnel already deployed abroad have also intervened in the internal-leadership power struggles of Marxist regimes. Relatively small numbers of Cuban military and security personnel seem to have influenced significantly the outcomes of such struggles— whether a coup failed to displace the incumbent leadership, as in Angola in May 1977, or succeeded, as in June 1978 in South Yemen. The extent of cooperation between the Soviets and Cubans in the Angola case is not clear. However, there would seem to be a future potential for discord here over which local Marxist contender for power should be supported in a given instance.

Soviet-Cuban Military Cooperation in the Caribbean

In addition to Cuban forces deployed abroad, Soviet-Cuban military cooperation also has involved both temporary and semipermanent manifestations of a Soviet military presence in Cuba. In the first category are periodic visits, usually several times annually, of Soviet naval forces and long-range reconnaissance aircraft.[144] The second category takes in up to 5,000 Soviet military personnel in Cuba, some acting in the standard capacity of military advisers and others manning what was labeled by the U.S. government in September 1979 a combined-arms combat brigade of 2,000 to 3,000 men.[145]

As brought out during the controversy over unmet U.S. demands for removal of the brigade,[146] the unit, or a precursor, may have been in Cuba since the 1962 missile crisis.[147] What its current mission might be was in dispute. According to Moscow and Havana, the unit in question was not a combat brigade but a training-base organization with the mission of training Cuban troops. Therefore, it had every right to be in Cuba; making an issue of it, they said, had been timed by so-called hostile circles to undermine Cuba's status in the nonaligned movement and to block ratification of the SALT II treaty.[148]

On the U.S. side, apart from domestic political and SALT considerations that helped to inflame the combat brigade issue but that need not be gone into here, there were also other concerns related to the growing Soviet-Cuban military connection. As put by Zbigniew Brzezinski, President Carter's national-security adviser, these concerns included the problem of Soviet-Cuban military cooperation in the Third World being used "directly, or indirectly, against our interests," as well as how "to compete effectively" with Moscow's use of Cuban troops as "a proxy force" in Third World conflicts.[149]

Another set of concerns grew out of the new buildup of Cuba's military capabilities, a buildup that had been in progress with Soviet help since the 1975 Cuban combat intervention in Angola. By 1979, cumulative Soviet military aid to Cuba amounted to more than $1.6 billion, and by the end of 1981, the total of Soviet assistance since 1960 had grown to $2.5 billion. Some 63,000 metric tons of Soviet arms reportedly were shipped to Cuba in 1981 alone, more than in any year since the 1962 Cuban missile crisis. While portions of these arms deliveries served to replace equipment used by the Cuban forces deployed to Africa, they also clearly were designed to upgrade Cuban military capabilities with more-modern Soviet arms. Included in the military-aid packages furnished by the USSR in recent years were MIG-23 fighter-bombers, MI-8 helicopter gunships, AN-26 medium-range transports, Foxtrot diesel-powered attack submarines, and hydrofoil patrol boats, as well as assistance for the expansion of naval facilities at Cienfuegos Bay.[150]

Acquisition of new capabilities that could be used to intervene in small-scale conflict situations in the Caribbean and Central America came at a time when endemic unrest and revolutionary activities in the region were on the rise.[151] The potential thus seemed to be opening up for greater Cuban activism in the western hemisphere, where the Soviet contribution might include the maintenance of a Soviet trip-wire military presence in Cuba to deter a direct U.S. attack on Castro's power base, much as the small Western garrisons in Berlin have long been intended to deter greatly superior Soviet forces nearby.

Thus, it might be speculated that the design for a new phase of Soviet-Cuban cooperative intervention in the western hemisphere was gradually maturing.

9

The Soviet Intervention in Afghanistan

In Afghanistan, where the USSR was unable to use proxy combat forces, the Soviet leaders chose in the closing days of December 1979 to intervene with their own combat forces on a scale unprecedented in any previous Third World conflict situation. There is some question as to whether this resort to the raw use of Soviet military power opened up an entirely new chapter in Soviet Third World policy and practice or essentially escalated already established trends. In either case, the Soviet invasion of Afghanistan—the ultimate outcome of which at this writing remains to be seen—is in many ways a watershed event with major geopolitical and strategic implications.

Background of the Soviet Invasion

As noted, Afghanistan was one of the first Third World recipients of Soviet economic and military aid in the mid-1950s,[1] attesting to Moscow's long-standing interest in bringing Afghanistan—once a neutral buffer state between imperial Russia and British India—clearly into the Soviet sphere of influence.[2]

The Coup of April 27, 1978

For background purposes here, perhaps the best starting point is the pro-Soviet coup of April 1978, staged by two rival Marxist-Leninist factions—the Khalq and Parcham groups.[3] The April coup ended the regime of Mohammed Daoud, who had unseated the parliamentary monarchy of King Mohammed Zahir (his brother-in-law) in July 1973 with some help from these same pro-Soviet leftist groups.[4]

How large a role the USSR played in the violent overthrow of the Daoud government has not been clearly established. Although Daoud initially had proclaimed his government socialist and followed an essentially pro-Soviet line, by mid-1976 he had begun to take steps to reduce Afghanistan's dependence on the USSR, reportedly looking toward a posture of "true nonalignment."[5] In view of this, it seems not unlikely, as U.S. Ambassador Theodore Eliot suggested, that Moscow gave some encouragement

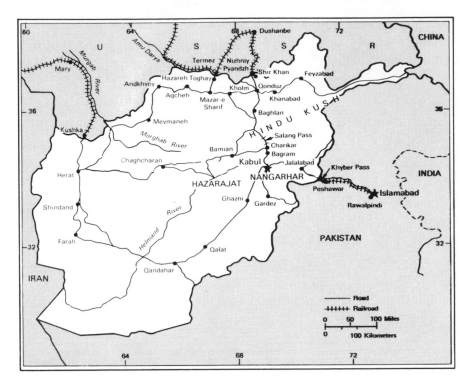

Afghanistan

and guidance to the Khalq-Parcham leaders, at least to the extent of having persuaded the two factions to join in a coalition in 1977 in order to offer more-effective opposition to Daoud.[6] The Soviets also may have lent covert assistance in preparing for a coup, especially in organizational work within the armed forces, as some analysts believe.[7]

The Soviets, however, apparently had no hand in the immediate circumstances that triggered the April 27 coup. These included the assassination of a well-known Parcham leader, Mir Akbar Khyber, on April 17; an unexpectedly massive communist-led demonstration at his funeral on April 19; in response, the arrest a few days later of several top civilian leaders of the Khalq-Parcham coalition; and the fear of the latter, in turn, that an anticommunist purge would shortly engulf their supporters in the Afghan military as well.[8]

Coup plotting had been under way for some time within the Afghan armed forces (with or without direct Soviet participation), but the communist organizational work was still far from complete, so the coup had to be put together hastily at the last minute on a makeshift basis. According to the account by Louis Dupree, the coup was set in motion by Hafizullah Amin after he had been placed under house arrest on the night of April 26. Amin used his teenage sons as couriers to deliver handwritten instructions to various conspirators. Through a combination of the Daoud government's incompetence, accident, and the support of several key army and air force officers who had been trained in the USSR, the coup proved successful after two days of fighting in which Daoud, his family, and perhaps 1,000 to 2,000 others died.[9]

Despite the unsubstantiated charges that Soviet pilots may have been flying Afghan planes in support of the rebellion (based on the alleged accuracy of their bombing),[10] the coup appears to have been a purely Afghan affair. While the Soviets were no doubt aware that coup plotting was under way, no credible evidence shows that they played a direct role in the coup itself.[11] In this sense, the observation may be justified that the coup had "dumped an obviously Moscow-leaning government into their laps, ready or not."[12]

The Taraki Government and Its Problems

Whatever may have been the Soviet role in the April 1978 coup, the Soviets were quick to recognize the new Democratic Republic of Afghanistan and to assist the Khalq-Parcham coalition in consolidating its power. Hundreds of additional Soviet civilian advisers took up posts throughout the Afghan government, and the number of military advisers assigned to Afghan military units doubled to around 700.[13] A direct communication link between Moscow and the Soviet military advisory group in Kabul also was set up.[14] In the new regime, Nur Mohammed Taraki, the Khalq head of the People's Democratic Party of Afghanistan (PDPA), became prime minister; Hafizullah Amin, the reputed strongman of the revolutionists, became deputy premier and foreign minister; and Babrak Karmal, the head of Parcham, was made a deputy premier without any specific governmental authority.

Despite early public denials to the contrary, it became evident within a few months after the April coup that the new regime was moving deeper into the Soviet orbit, a trend underscored in December 1978 by the signing of a twenty-year treaty of friendship and cooperation with the USSR.[15] It also soon became evident that the new regime suffered from a number of fundamental weaknesses. It lacked legitimacy and a broad popular following; it was short of competent cadres; and most important, it had only a narrow base of support within the Afghan military. Aware of its fragile hold on power, the regime began to purge Afghan military and civilian agencies of all unreliable elements, removing most of the senior officer corps and experienced government functionaries.

By late 1978, serious problems had begun to emerge. The Kabul government was riven by a series of behind-the-scenes power struggles that produced further purges—including the ousting in July of Babrak Karmal and many of his Parcham associates—and resulted in further narrowing of the regime's political base.[16] More important, Taraki, with prodding from the harder-line Amin, had embarked on a number of radical socialist reforms—reforms that alienated the country's strongly Islamic tribal groups and gradually aroused their opposition.

Although early resistance to the government's land-redistribution, antireligious, and educational programs was scattered and sporadic, by late 1978 the scope of opposition began to spread.[17] Concurrently, the USSR increased its economic and military support of the Kabul regime, flying in both supplies and personnel. By March 1979, a series of largely spontaneous and uncoordinated tribal revolts had spread to more than half of Afghanistan's twenty-eight provinces.[18] As efforts of the Afghan army to stamp out their growing opposition met with scant success, Soviet military involvement also began to grow.

Admonishment from Washington at this time against Soviet military intervention in Afghanistan's civil strife had no perceptible restraining effect.[19] Rather, in March and April the USSR accelerated military hardware deliveries, including helicopters for gunship and trooplift missions,[20] and Soviet advisory personnel for the first time played a combat role against insurgent forces, piloting helicopters and other aircraft with Afghan insignia and directing artillery fire.[21]

By May, the number of Soviet military advisers in the country, assigned down to battalion level, had risen to about 1,000.[22] Some of these Soviet military personnel were said to have lost their lives in the fighting in spring 1979, while in March a number of other Soviet advisers reportedly were beaten to death in a local insurrection in the city of Herat in northwestern Afghanistan.[23] The Herat unrest also involved the first known mutiny of Afghan government troops, followed by another mutiny at Jalalabad near the Pakistan border in April.[24]

Growing Soviet Involvement
Paralleling Spread of Insurgency

Attempts to impose radical revolutionary changes too rapidly on traditional societies, as by the Khalq faction of local communists in Afghanistan, manifestly can produce unwelcome results. An appreciation of this erroneous approach (left-wing infantilism in the Bolshevik vocabulary of an earlier day[25]) seems to have been reflected in Moscow's apparent effort in 1979 to slow down the Khalq's radical revolutionary course in Afghanistan. In turn, this would suggest that a pragmatic sense of what the traffic would bear in terms of retaining control of the situation rather than any preoccupation with rapid revolutionary advance prevailed in Soviet decision-making councils.

Concern about the inability of the Taraki government to deal with its insurgency problems prompted the Soviets to send General Aleksey A. Yepishev, chief of the main political administration of the Soviet armed forces, to Kabul in April 1979. Yepishev's mission probably included evaluating the political reliability and morale of the 100,000-man Afghan armed forces. Soviet accounts of the Yepishev visit noted that his delegation had "meaningful conversations with the organizers of party work and political education in units of the armed forces."[26] However, there was no public suggestion that Yepishev may have been dissatisfied with what he found.

Another Soviet official who also turned up in Kabul in April was Vasiliy S. Safronchuk, a diplomat reportedly sent to recommend a political solution to Afghanistan's troubles.[27] In part, he apparently urged the Kabul regime to back off from the radical policies that had been fueling the tribal revolts and to broaden the base of its government, but as the summer passed, it became evident that this advice was being ignored.

By September 1979, the insurgency had intensified, with guerrilla groups now controlling much of the country's mountainous terrain. Desertions and rebellion spread among Afghan army units. For example, a unit at Bala Hissar fortress near Kabul rebelled on August 5, and the Rishkur barracks outside Kabul mutinied several weeks later. Both uprisings were suppressed.[28] In the midst of these difficulties for the Kabul regime in summer 1979, Hafizullah Amin, who had replaced Taraki as prime minister in March, also took over direct control of the Afghan armed forces and the security apparatus.[29]

Sometime in late August or early September, the Soviets evidently decided that they had to commit additional military resources to arrest a deteriorating military situation and to shore up the regime of their shaky Afghan Marxist clients. During the last part of August, another high-level Soviet mission arrived in Kabul, headed by General Ivan G. Pavlovskiy, commander-in-chief of Soviet ground forces. His arrival on the scene at a difficult juncture was reminiscent of the dispatch of General V.I. Petrov to Ethiopia in 1977; Petrov organized the joint Cuban-Soviet-Ethiopian offensive that bailed out the Mengistu regime.[30] Pavlovskiy, incidentally, had commanded the intervention forces in Czechoslovakia in 1968.

Pavlovskiy's arrival in Afghanistan roughly coincided with the taking over of Bagram air base about forty miles north of Kabul as the hub of Soviet transport and helicopter gunship operations, with 400 to 600 Soviet troops engaged in construction and guarding the base.[31] Some of the forty to fifty helicopter gunships were MI-24s, the most advanced in the Soviet inventory.[32] The Soviets also were reported to be expanding the military-base facilities at two other locations in western Afghanistan—near Farah, a town about sixty miles from the Iranian border, and at Shindand air base about seventy-five miles from Iran.[33] The buildup of Soviet advisory personnel in Afghanistan also continued, and by the end of October the number had risen to an estimated 3,500 to 4,000 Soviet military personnel and 2,000 to 3,000 civilian advisers.

Meanwhile, in September 1979, seeking an alternative political avenue to ease the insurgency situation in Afghanistan, the USSR may also have sought to encourage Taraki (who still retained the post of president of the country) to oust Amin and set up a new government prepared to make some concessions in the hope of defusing the opposition of the Moslem rebels. Though no solid evidence confirms it, there is a strong supposition that when Taraki stopped over in Moscow on September 10-11 on his return from the nonaligned conference in Havana, one of the reasons for the personal stamp of approval given him publicly by Brezhnev[34] was that he had been encouraged to move against Amin.[35]

Amin, however, acted first—tipped off, according to some accounts, by one of Taraki's bodyguards.[36] In a shoot-out on September 16, details of which still remain obscure, Taraki was killed,[37] and his remaining posts as president of the country, head of its ruling party, and chairman of the Revolutionary Council were taken over by Amin.[38]

At some point during the next three months, the USSR made the decisions that resulted in the December invasion of Afghanistan, Amin's demise, and his replacement by the Soviet-installed government of Babrak Karmal. What brought about these decisions is by no means fully known, but some reasonable surmises can be made.

Factors Contributing to the Invasion Decision

By December 1979, the initial Soviet involvement in Afghanistan had proved a manifest failure. Moscow by then had made an enormous political, military, and prestige investment in Afghanistan but saw continuation of the incumbent Amin regime as increasingly disastrous for Soviet interests.

Amin's repressive rule and fierce pursuit of radical change had antagonized all classes of Afghan society, but he stubbornly resisted Soviet suggestions to switch to so-called united-front tactics to mollify some sources of opposition.[39] Moreover, in addition to refusing to submit to Soviet control in this and other matters, Amin was increasingly unable to command the loyalty of much of the Afghan military establishment, which was eroding at an accelerated pace because of desertions, mutinies, and continued purges.

While Amin's power position appeared to be weakening, he nevertheless retained sufficient control over key military units in the Kabul area and over the internal-security apparatus to make it doubtful that he could be unseated by rival Afghan communist elements in a repeat performance along the lines of the recent unsuccessful anti-Amin coup attempt of September 16. There was thus the likelihood of continued deterioration of the unstable political-military situation in Afghanistan that might well result in the collapse of the revolutionary Marxist regime and its replacement by a government of uncertain orientation, possibly one hostile to Soviet interests.

Moreover, Amin's recalcitrant behavior toward the USSR, including his demand that Moscow replace its ambassador in Kabul for having sheltered some of Taraki's cohorts after the September shoot-out,[40] reportedly was accompanied in November by urgent overtures to Mohammed Zia ul-Haq of Pakistan.[41] While it is by no means clear that Amin was seeking to marshal outside support against Soviet interference in Afghanistan's internal affairs, as suggested by some observers, the Soviets might well have suspected that this was the case.[42]

On either count—possible collapse of the Kabul regime because of Amin's inflexibility and failure to quell the countrywide insurgency or his refusal to submit to Soviet control—Moscow evidently concluded that Amin must be replaced at the earliest opportunity by a more-compliant client regime and that the only feasible way to accomplish this and to bring the insurgency under control would be the large-scale introduction of Soviet forces, seasoned by a bit of guile.

Other considerations doubtless also lay behind the Soviet invasion decision, which some analysts believe the Politburo reached only after considerable internal debate.[43] The following were probably among these considerations:[44]

Moscow's long-standing geostrategic interest in military domination of Afghanistan as a wedge in the southward expansion toward the Indian Ocean, plus its more-recent interest in securing a foothold in proximity to the Persian Gulf oil route to the West and Japan;

A Politburo decision-making group sensitized to the dangers of a collapse of the Afghanistan communist regime by the turbulence in neighboring Iran and the beginning of a U.S. military buildup in littoral areas in response to the events in Iran;

Soviet concern about the potential spillover effects of Islamic fundamentalism on the USSR's Moslem community of 50 million in Central Asia, should the communist regime in Kabul succumb to the Moslem rebellion;

Soviet desire not only to forestall the penetration of Chinese influence into Afghanistan through aid to the tribal insurgency but also to forge another pro-Soviet link in a ring of containment around China instead.

Given the U.S. preoccupation with the Iranian crisis and U.S. vacilla-tion toward other Soviet interventions during the 1970s, the Soviets prob-ably reasoned that a stepped-up Soviet military intervention in Afghanistan would elicit little more than a rhetorical U.S. response. They probably reasoned further that relations with Washington had already deteriorated to the point that a SALT treaty ratification and other détente dividends were unlikely and, hence, no longer to be considered real constraints on forceful Soviet action in Afghanistan.

The Invasion and Occupation of Afghanistan

Contingency planning for the large-scale introduction of Soviet combat forces into Afghanistan doubtless began at least several months before the actual invasion, and by mid-December 1979 final preparations were well under way. These included new deployments and the bringing up to strength of Soviet ground and air units in areas along the Afghan and Iranian borders,[45] as well as a buildup of the Soviet military presence inside Afghan-istan, bringing the number of troops and advisers, according to U.S. offi-cials, to about 5,000, "including well over 1,000 in Soviet combat units."[46] Some reports from non-U.S. sources put the Soviet military influx by mid-December at a considerably higher figure.[47]

Even though a series of warnings and protests by Washington had called attention to Soviet preparations for the use of combat forces in Afghan-istan,[48] when the unprecedented invasion of a Third World client state and the accompanying coup took place in the midst of the Christmas season, these events came as a rude shock to many.[49]

The Use of Force and Deception

The USSR successfully employed both massive force and guile in the inva-sion of Afghanistan, carried out during the closing days of 1979. The initial elements of the Soviet invasion force, about 1,500 airborne troops, landed in Kabul on December 24.[50] Apparently, they came with the acquiescence of Amin, who reportedly continued for the next two days to believe Soviet assurances that the incoming combat forces were intended to bolster his regime rather than to facilitate its overthrow.[51]

By December 27, however—the day on which Amin met his demise—an airlift of 150 to 200 flights by AN-12, AN-22, and IL-76 transports had delivered from 5,000 to 6,000 additional troops and equipment to Kabul international airport and the Soviet air base at Bagram, and these troops now moved to seize control of communications and government centers in Kabul.[52]

At the same time, the first motorized rifle units of a five-division force of more than 50,000 men, which had been assembled along the Soviet-Afghan border, crossed into Afghanistan from Kushka and Termez and then fanned out toward Herat, Kabul, and the Pakistan border. The advance of motorized forces to Kabul was aided by the seizure of Salang Pass by airborne elements previously landed in the capital.[53]

Soviet forces encountered some local resistance from Afghan rebel groups and a few Afghan government troops, but it was neither strong nor coherent enough to impede the invasion operation, which also benefited from deception tactics. Armored units of the Amin regime guarding key installations around Kabul reportedly had been persuaded by Soviet advisers a few days before the invasion to turn in their tank batteries for winterizing and to undertake other housekeeping chores that left them virtually immobilized.[54]

The Removal of Amin

Details of the coup by which Amin was eliminated on December 27 remain somewhat obscure. The Soviets obviously meant to depose him since they had Babrak Karmal waiting in the wings with a prerecorded takeover message.[55] However, the Soviets may have sought up to the last minute to persuade or coerce Amin, as head of the incumbent government, to sign a document inviting them in, so as to have a demonstrable legal basis for the claim that their armed intervention had been sought to protect Afghanistan against counterrevolutionary forces supported from outside the country by the United States, China, Pakistan, Iran, and others.[56]

It may have been the mission of Lieutenant General Victor S. Paputin, a high Ministry of Internal Affairs (MVD) official who had been in Kabul since early December, to bring such a document back to Moscow.[57] If so, he evidently failed. A cryptic obituary in *Pravda* on January 3, 1980, disclosed that he had died December 28, 1979—the day after the Afghan coup.[58]

A coup scenario combining some available evidence with speculation might go something like this: With Soviet forces in the process of investing Kabul, Paputin goes to Duralaman palace, where Amin has taken up residence for security reasons—at Soviet suggestion, probably from Paputin himself—a few days before. There Paputin tells Amin that, under the circumstances, Amin had best step aside in favor of Babrak Karmal and that, as his last official service, Amin should sign the papers requesting Moscow to send troops.

Amin refuses to cooperate on both counts. A physical assault on the palace by Soviet troops (possibly a special MVD contingent under Paputin's command) follows, during which Amin is either deliberately or inadvertently

killed. Paputin either gets caught in the crossfire or possibly commits sui-
cide the next day for having botched his assignment to obtain Amin's cooperation in the intervention.

Whatever the merits of this scenario, Moscow obviously had trouble
finding a convincing justification for military intervention and the installation of a puppet government in Kabul. Its original undocumented and thus
flimsy claim that it had been invited to intervene by Amin was replaced by
the more-credible assertion that it had received the same invitation from
Babrak Karmal on December 28.[59] This post facto invitation, however, left
unsettled the awkward question of Amin's prior forcible removal from office and his death during the early stages of the Soviet intervention.

To deal with this question, the Soviets, in January 1980, first made what
Marshall Shulman has called an "astonishing allegation" that Amin was a
CIA agent who intended to betray the revolution.[60] Presumably, this was
meant to establish that Amin had merely met a well-deserved fate. Subsequently, Moscow advanced the equally implausible argument that there was
no connection between Amin's fate and the intervention. Rather, Karmal
was alleged to have returned to Afghanistan clandestinely in October 1979
and to have staged a coup that resulted in Amin's conviction by a revolutionary court for "crimes against the people."[61] As explained in one Soviet
account of events in Afghanistan:

> The fact that the removal of Amin took place concurrently with the be-
> ginning of the introduction of the Soviet contingent is a pure *coincidence in
> time* [emphasis in original], and there is no causal relationship between the
> two events. The Soviet units had nothing to do with the removal of Amin
> and his accomplices. That was done by the Afghans themselves.[62]

Whatever the Soviet pretenses concerning Amin's removal, the new
Karmal government was clearly even more dependent on Soviet administrative and security support than its predecessors.[63] It also appeared more
amenable to following a conciliatory line toward broad sectors of the population and toward the Islamic religion.[64]

Despite the new government's supposedly less-repressive policy line,
however, it could not surmount the stigma of being a Soviet puppet and its
other weaknesses. It soon became apparent not only that the Babrak regime
was failing to mollify the Islamic nationalism at the root of the insurgency
but also that it was unable to curb the internal strife between its Khalq and
Parcham factions and to halt the steady erosion of the Afghan armed
forces.[65] The USSR gives every indication, however, of intending to suppress the ongoing insurgency and to maintain the regime of its choice in
Kabul, despite the negative reaction of varied intensity in many quarters, including the UN and much of the Moslem world.[66]

The Lengthening Occupation

Rather than reducing the Afghan insurgency, the Christmas invasion produced a dramatic increase in resistance to the Kabul regime and to Soviet authority. As early as February 1980, it became apparent that one of the effects of the invasion was to accelerate the erosion of the Afghan armed forces, on which the Soviets initially had counted to share the counterinsurgency burden.[67]

By February, desertions and defections had reduced the Afghan forces to half their original strength of 100,000; by June the number had dropped to about a third.[68] Moreover, the defection of Afghan troops frequently was accompanied by wholesale transfers of arms, ammunition, and sometimes personnel to the rebels, leading the Soviets to disarm and disband some Afghan units in an effort to deny the insurgency this logistic conduit.[69] The internal source of arms supply was particularly important for the insurgents, since "only a trickle of arms" was reaching them from outside the country, despite Soviet allegations to the contrary.[70] The trickle apparently included some light weapons covertly supplied through Pakistan by the United States and other sympathetic countries.[71]

Efforts of the Karmal regime during 1980 and 1981 to find reliable new recruits to rebuild the shrinking Afghan military and security forces reportedly met with little success and aroused additional popular resentment. A new draft law promulgated in January 1981, which attempted to compensate for replacement shortfalls by lowering the draft age and extending the length of military service by six months to two and one-half years, provoked "police riots in Kabul and isolated instances of rebellion by troops." The regime's mobilization of reservists up to age thirty-five in September 1981 also set off antigovernment demonstrations and seemed equally unlikely to produce any significant increase in the Afghan army's strength, which remained at only about 30,000 at the beginning of 1982.[72]

With the combat effectiveness of the armed forces still eroding, it was apparent that any reorganization and rebuilding of an effective force would constitute an uphill and lengthy process. A factor complicating the situation was the high proportion of Khalq officers who still remained in what was left of the military establishment and who had little rapport with Babrak Karmal, a Parcham. However, should Karmal attempt a new purge of Khalq officers, he would risk further reducing the army's effectiveness.

A notable upsurge of popular sympathy and identification with the insurgents among Afghan youth and the urban citizenry was another effect of the December invasion that offered little prospect that the Soviet-installed Karmal regime would gain much support from the Afghan people. Attesting to the regime's uneasy position was the placing of Kabul under martial law when a week-long strike and series of anti-Soviet demonstrations broke out in February 1980, during which hundreds of civilians reportedly were killed by Soviet and Afghan riot-suppression troops.[73]

In April, students demonstrated for five days against the Soviet occupation;[74] in May, despite a curfew and armed patrols, leaflets extolling defiance of Soviet forces and the puppet regime were distributed nightly in Kabul by schoolchildren and their elders.[75] Five months later, it became necessary to enforce an even stricter curfew.[76]

Given factors such as the continuing deterioration of the Afghan army, growing public hostility toward the Soviet occupiers, the Kabul regime's inability to govern the country, and above all, the stubborn resistance of the Moslem rebels—who had come to be hailed as true patriots by most of the population—it was not surprising that the USSR failed to trim its post-invasion military presence in Afghanistan. On the contrary, despite a much-publicized pullout of about 5,000 troops and some equipment in June,[77] the Soviet occupation force increased in size and also changed in composition subsequent to the Christmas invasion.

From the initial combat force of at least 30,000 to 40,000 that invaded Afghanistan in December, Soviet troops increased to 80,000 by late January and leveled off soon afterward at about 85,000.[78] In June 1980, 5,000 troops that were unsuited to the Afghan terrain and guerrilla-style warfare were withdrawn and immediately replaced by "new and more useful units." During most of 1981, the Soviet occupation force in Afghanistan remained at about 85,000, with another 30,000 troops in neighboring Soviet territory committed to their direct support.[79]

Many of the troops in the original invasion force were reservists called up to fill out less than full-strength units, and a considerable number of them were Central Asians of Uzbek, Tadzhik, and Turkmen origin, closely akin to some of the peoples of Afghanistan's northern provinces.[80] It is not known whether their presence in the ranks of the invaders was merely a coincidence or a stratagem calculated to convince their Afghan brethren that they came as liberators. If the latter, however, the experiment apparently failed, for it was reported that many of the Soviet Central Asian troops developed morale problems after exposure to their fellow Moslems across the border.[81] By February the Central Asian soldiers were being replaced systematically by Slavic troops.[82] For these, in spring 1980, the tour of duty in Afghanistan was set at two years.[83]

Besides the personnel composition of the Soviet force in Afghanistan, its structure and the character of its field operations also underwent change as the counterinsurgency campaign against some 75,000 to 100,000 lightly armed and poorly coordinated Moslem guerrilla forces made slow progress.[84] The slow pace of the counterinsurgency campaign was probably all the more annoying to Soviet authorities in view of the fact that the Afghan mountain tribesmen often carried on old feuds among themselves in between ambushes or other clashes with the occupation troops.

Adaptation of Soviet equipment to the Afghan combat environment included the introduction of lighter tanks and armored personnel carriers for maneuverability in mountainous terrain, as well as the addition of more rocket-firing helicopter gunships (which had turned out to be one of the more-effective means of attacking rebels in their mountain strongholds) and fighter-bombers.[85] Other weapons brought into use against guerrilla forces were a light rifle that fired hollow-point bullets, flechette-loaded shells, and cluster bombs. Napalm also was used extensively, and by the end of 1981 there was mounting evidence of Soviet use of lethal chemical agents against Afghan insurgent bases.[86] In a sense, the Afghan conflict became a kind of proving ground for the Soviet military, offering a rich opportunity for test and evaluation of materiel and tactics in a non-European combat environment.[87]

Among changes in the structure of the occupation forces, the command of which fell to Marshal Sergey L. Sokolov, a first deputy minister of defense, one of the more interesting was the addition in midsummer 1980 of specially trained antiguerrilla units.[88] Another organizational change a month or so later was the establishment of seven regional command centers to oversee Soviet bases and operations in various sectors of the country.[89]

The expansion of existing military installations and construction of new ones at different regional locations began early in the occupation, and included the upgrading of key airfields, the building of permanent communications facilities, and the provision of permanent quarters for Soviet military personnel and dependents.[90]

These support programs not only testified to Soviet preparations for a long-term pacification of the country but also provided infrastructure for larger Soviet military deployments in Afghanistan should geostrategic considerations in southwest Asia and the Middle East require them. In fact, as one observer noted, the major buildup of facilities and troops around Shindand air base near Afghanistan's western border with Iran appeared to exceed the requirements of the counterinsurgency campaign itself.[91]

Operationally, Soviet forces, in the early months of the occupation, confined themselves mostly to establishing control in the Kabul area and a few provincial cities and to securing main roads and communications. The pattern began to change in midsummer.[92] Punitive attacks by air and motorized infantry began against villages in rebel-held territory. At harvest time, the Soviets burned crops and rounded up livestock in mountain valleys to deny food and shelter to the rebels. The Soviet forces also sought to flush out guerrilla groups in the mountainous border provinces by occasional sweeps and to seal off border-area infiltration routes from Pakistan by mining and cluster bombing.[93] To supplement these military operations in the counterinsurgency campaign, the Soviets tried to win over selected tribal leaders by bribes, appeals from pro-Soviet Moslems, and like tactics.

Despite these Soviet counterinsurgency efforts, the situation in Afghanistan showed no improvement in 1981 and, according to one State Department analyst, actually worsened. The reliability and morale of the Kabul regime's military forces continued to erode, while Moslem rebel attacks against government targets in both rural and urban areas increased and insurgent control of the countryside expanded. Moreover, the periodic Soviet offensive operations to reduce important rebel strongholds and to penetrate guerrilla base areas frequently proved unsuccessful. Among the more-notable Soviet setbacks were the failure to capture a key guerrilla redoubt in the eastern province of Nangarhar in June 1981; the abortive attempt by a combined Soviet-Afghan force one month later to drive Moslem guerrillas out of the Paghman Mountains, twelve miles northwest of Kabul; and Soviet failure over a long period to penetrate the Panjshir Valley, a major resistance base area that provided access to the main north-south supply route in the strategic Salang Pass area. Most of the central uplands of Afghanistan (Hazarajat) also reportedly remained "inaccessible to Soviet troops." The Soviet occupation army's manifest inability to suppress ambushes along all major roads and other guerrilla attacks was attributed, at least in part, to an excessive Soviet "concern with bureaucratic procedures" and to the "lack of zeal" of Soviet forces. Concern about the progress of the war apparently prompted the Soviets to introduce more troops into Afghanistan in late 1981 and early 1982, raising their total occupation force to around 100,000 when at full strength, a move that could presage additional, and perhaps more-substantial, reinforcements in the future.[94]

The price paid in terms of Soviet casualties to pursue the pacification of Afghanistan is a matter of some dispute. Claims by Moslem rebel sources that Soviet losses in the first nine months amounted to around 20,000 seem very much inflated.[95] U.K. sources estimated that casualties up to July 1980 came to about 5,000 wounded and 1,000 dead.[96] Others placed Soviet casualties up to September 1980 at 10,000 to 15,000, but these figures included large losses due to illnesses such as malaria and hepatitis.[97] A statement by a State Department intelligence specialist in May 1981 placed the number of Soviet dead and wounded up to that time at "about 5,000 or something like that."[98] At the close of 1981, U.S. Defense Department sources estimated the two-year toll of Soviet casualties in Afghanistan at about 5,000 killed and 5,000 wounded.[99]

How long the pacification effort may go on, and what its ultimate outcome may be remain unanswered questions at this writing. The Moslem guerrillas eventually may be ground down by a combination of military pressure and deprivation of logistic support as the exodus of refugees from their mountain villages—estimated in December 1981 at close to 3.5 million[100]— swells further. However, by the second anniversary of the 1979 invasion, it appeared that unless the Soviet counterinsurgency effort were to be at least doubled or perhaps trebled, the Moslem rebels could continue to hold out indefinitely,[101] sustained, as one writer put it earlier, by their Islamic zeal and traditional talent for guerrilla warfare.[102]

However, the Soviets are probably quite capable of carrying on a long and grueling campaign in Afghanistan, keeping the insurgency more or less stalemated, if not extinguishing it, while at the same time engaging in political maneuvers to neutralize reaction in Europe and the Moslem world. Thus, the notion that impatience in the Kremlin might prompt an early withdrawal from Afghanistan because Soviet forces had become bogged down there would appear at least questionable.[103]

Part II
Soviet Involvement in Third World Conflicts and Future U.S. Response Options

Part I has described the evolution of Soviet policy toward the Third World since 1946 broadly, canvassing political, diplomatic, and economic relations, as well as military activities. Part II, narrower and more analytical, concentrates on the patterns of Soviet military involvements in the Third World and what these patterns may portend.

To provide a contextual framework for assessing Soviet behavior, Part II begins with a brief overview of what the authors infer to be the major Soviet objectives in the Third World. A review of past Soviet involvements and distillation of our findings concerning the principal attributes and patterns of past Soviet Third World conflict behavior follow. In summarizing the patterns of past Soviet activity, we abstain initially from discussing Afghanistan but treat it later, in a comparative sense. We then discuss some of the trends that tend to increase Soviet Third World activism and prospects and some potential constraints on future Soviet policy. We conclude with speculations on the possible patterns of future Soviet behavior and suggest some implications for U.S. policy.

10 Soviet Policy Objectives in the Third World

Soviet objectives in the Third World have been a matter of some disagreement among Western observers, particularly with respect to whether Soviet policy is motivated more by Soviet national interests or by ideology. Adherents of the former view tend to see Soviet activities in the Third World as deriving primarily from the USSR's quest for great power status and promotion of traditional state interests, while those who emphasize the ideological bent see the spread of communism as more of a driving force. Elements of both are no doubt present in Soviet policy motivations and, whatever the genesis, can give rise to behavior equally threatening to U.S. interests.

Soviet objectives in the Third World are interrelated, mutually supporting, and long standing—even though some objectives have received shifting geographic and policy emphasis over time. Because the motivation of specific Soviet tactical shifts toward the Third World is covered in Part I, we limit our discussion here to what we infer to be the fundamental and more-enduring aims of Soviet Third World policies.

Our listing of Soviet objectives begins with the USSR's overriding aim to assure its own security, an aim that, among other things, has impelled the USSR to incorporate or dominate its neighbors.[1] Considerations of state security have also led Moscow to regulate its Third World activities so as to avoid situations that pose high risk of a direct Soviet-U.S. military conflict and that might escalate to involve the Soviet homeland.

A set of related, long-standing objectives has been evident in Soviet Third World policy since the mid-1950s. The first has been to weaken Western control and influence in the formerly colonial areas of Africa, the Middle East, and Asia. Latin America emerged somewhat later as a significant target of Soviet Third World political interest. A parallel objective has been to shape the sociopolitical and economic development of the newly independent countries and to bring the so-called nonaligned movement of the Third World into accord with Soviet goals and interests. Where feasible, the Soviets have sought also to foster the establishment of pro-Soviet Marxist governments and to sustain them in power against internal and external threats. This last goal seems to have moved up somewhat on the scale of Soviet Third World priorities, especially since the mid-1970s, as Angola, Ethiopia, South Yemen, and Afghanistan will attest.

Corollary to extending Soviet influence in the Third World, the USSR has tried to counter competition from and to isolate communist China—an aim that became increasingly evident as the Sino-Soviet rift began to widen in the early 1960s. Competition with China—manifest as early as 1960, when the Soviets undertook to provide military support to the Pathet Lao forces fighting in Laos—was an important factor motivating the Soviet intervention in Angola in 1975-1976. The Soviet aim of establishing an Asian collective-security system, first broached in 1969, also has lent itself to the objective of containing China, as has Moscow's support to New Delhi and Hanoi and its military lodgement in Afghanistan.

From the mid-1960s on—and especially with the failure of initial Soviet hopes for rapid transition of newly independent countries to Soviet-style socialism—we have seen accumulating evidence of the Soviet motivation to improve the USSR's global power position and military reach by securing access and basing arrangements in Third World areas. In addition to increasing the USSR's political influence and force-projection capabilities in the Third World, these basing arrangements also support the peacetime deployment and surveillance activities of Soviet naval and air forces (such as forward-deployed antisubmarine aircraft) and broaden Moscow's offensive options in the event of war. This objective has been accompanied by parallel Soviet efforts to erode existing U.S. overseas base structures and transit arrangements.

Finally, the USSR has sought over a long period to improve Soviet-bloc access to primary resources in the Third World[2] and, according to many observers, ultimately to control or deny the West access to such resources.[3] The time and manner in which this latter objective will receive definitive operational expression, however, is as yet unclear.

11

The Spectrum of Past Soviet Involvements in Third World Conflicts

As the chronological record presented in Part I amply demonstrates, Soviet involvement in Third World conflicts has been a fact of international life for some three decades now and has embraced at various times the following major categories of recurrent activity: direct combat involvement; cooperative intervention; materiel, logistic, training, and advisory support of combatants; and economic, diplomatic, and political-military support of clients.

Direct Combat Involvements

During the thirty years prior to the December 1979 invasion of Afghanistan, direct Soviet combat involvements had, for the most part, been circumspect, of limited magnitude and duration, confined mainly to air defense or small-scale tactical air support, and usually motivated by the need to fill some temporary void in a hard-pressed client's defenses.

Direct Soviet combat involvements in external conflicts had been confined largely to providing clients with air-defense support. During the Korean war, Soviet "volunteers" flew daylight air-defense missions in MIG alley over communist-controlled northwestern Korea (a fact only later admitted by the USSR)[1] and manned at least two night-fighter squadrons actively engaged in combat as well. Soviet advisers also are believed to have assisted in running the air-operations control room at the communist allied joint headquarters in Antung, Manchuria.[2]

The Soviet combat involvement in Vietnam was smaller and more circumspect than that in Korea. Although no Soviet fighter pilots are known to have operated in Vietnam, there is evidence that Soviet air-defense personnel exercised operational control over Hanoi's SAM system for at least some periods during 1965 and 1966.[3] After their arrival in the mid-1960s, Soviet technicians also helped man some of the North Vietnamese SAM sites until adequate North Vietnamese crews could be trained.[4] The number of Soviet military advisers and technicians in North Vietnam probably peaked at somewhat fewer than 3,000, the vast majority of whom performed training and support missions, principally in the use of SAM, aircraft, and other air-defense equipment.[5]

The most extensive Soviet combat involvement in an external conflict occurred in 1970, during the so-called Canal war or war of attrition in the Middle East. Between March and June 1970, the USSR deployed some 10,000 military personnel, including missile crews and pilots, to Egypt, along with a variety of advanced fighter aircraft and SAM systems, to help defend that country against Israeli "deep penetration" and other air raids.[6] Again, this deployment was intended as a temporary measure (Nasser told the Soviets that he wanted their crews to be there "for a limited time" only), while Egyptian air-defense personnel were undergoing training in the USSR.[7]

Prior to Afghanistan, Soviet combat involvement in internal Third World conflicts had been extremely limited and circumspect. Indeed, hard evidence of the extent of a direct Soviet combat role even in those few cases where it was strongly suspected is difficult to come by, in part because of the remoteness of the locales involved and the limited nature of the Soviet combat role. It is known that a few Soviet pilots temporarily provided close air support in late 1967 to beleaguered republican forces defending Sana, the capital of Yemen, during that country's civil war. The Soviets rushed pilots and aircraft to Sana to cope with the military emergency created by the sudden withdrawal of Egyptian forces from the republican side in that conflict.[8]

Numerous allegations of a direct Soviet combat involvement in the Sudanese civil war were made between late 1969 and mid-1971. While hard evidence is lacking, the southern Anya-Nya rebels fighting Sudanese government forces persistently reported bombing, rocket, and strafing attacks on their positions by Soviet-piloted helicopters and MIGs.[9]

Finally, Soviet pilots in MIG-23s also are believed to have conducted some limited bombing and strafing raids on Kurdish positions in support of the Iraq government's suppression campaign against Kurdish dissidents in 1974 and early 1975. Again the actual extent of the Soviet combat involvement is obscure, but the commitment seems to have been limited. The Soviet military involvement, while small scale, did produce important political effects in that it was a crucial factor in inducing the Iranian government to cease its support to the Kurdish revolt in March 1975.[10]

Cooperative Intervention

The USSR has on several occasions used the tactic of cooperative intervention, in which Moscow actively encourages and underwrites another state's participation in an ongoing conflict (see chapters 1 and 8). Cooperative intervention was first used during the Korean war, when the Soviets, in addition to sharing the aid-defense burden, also provided substantial materiel and logistic support to the Chinese air and ground forces that had intervened in that conflict.

An innovative use of cooperative intervention occurred in 1975, when the Soviets supplied weapons, munitions, and logistic support to the nearly

20,000 Cuban troops that had intervened in Angola late that year and in early 1976. This new type of cooperative intervention was repeated in Ethiopia during its war with Somalia over the Ogaden in 1977-1978, when the USSR not only supplied arms and munitions but also ships and aircraft that assisted in transporting an estimated 17,000 Cubans to Ethiopia.

In part because Moscow viewed intervention in Ethiopia as even less likely than the operation in Angola to provoke a U.S. response, the Soviet involvement in the Ethiopian conflict was more direct and extensive. In the case of Angola, the Cuban intervention forces were transported only on Cuban ships and initially only on Cuban aircraft, whereas in the case of Ethiopia the Soviets participated in the airlift of Cuban personnel from the very beginning and also provided Soviet passenger vessels to transport Cuban troops.[11] The Ethiopian intervention also marked a significant expansion in the numbers and functions of Soviet personnel. The Soviet in-country role in the Angolan conflict was modest, numbering at the highest no more than several hundred military advisers and technicians, whereas some 1,000 to 1,500 Soviet personnel were involved in Ethiopia. Again in contrast in Angola, Soviet personnel performed significant planning and command functions in Ethiopia, where senior Soviet officers were reported to have maintained close control over combat operations in both the Ogaden and Eritrea.[12]

Materiel, Logistic, Training, and Advisory Support of Combatants

By far the most dominant Soviet role has been the provision of materiel, logistic, training, intelligence, and advisory support to Third World clients engaged in internal as well as external conflicts. There have been numerous cases of Soviet arms tranfers to combatants prior to, during, and immediately following conflicts. The USSR provided much of the war materiel (including all the more-sophisticated aircraft and air-defense systems) used by communist forces fighting in Korea in the early 1950s. It was the principal arms supplier to Hanoi during the course of the Vietnam conflict, providing the North Vietnamese almost $3.3 billion of military assistance between 1965 and 1974. Other major Soviet arms-support efforts included several billion dollars' worth of equipment and munitions to Arab states in conjunction with various Middle East conflicts and extensive war materiel to MPLA (the communist-supported revolutionary movement) and Cuban troops in Angola and to the Mengistu forces and the Cubans operating in Ethiopia.

Several Third World conflicts have involved extensive air- and sealifts from the USSR. The largest military airlift occurred during the 1973 Yom

Kippur war and its immediate aftermath, when about 950 to 1,000 transport flights were made to Egypt, Syria, and Iraq. Seventy flights from the USSR were made during the Angola conflict, and about 100 flights were made to Ethiopia during the period of critical fighting in that country. The Soviets also carried out airlifts of varying size during the Laos and Congo conflicts in the early 1960s, the Yemen civil war in 1967-1968, the Canal war in 1970, the India-Pakistan war in 1971, and the China-Vietnam conflict in 1979.[13]

Although the USSR has airlifted high-priority equipment and some personnel, the vast bulk of Soviet arms and munitions has been delivered by sea. At the time of the Yom Kippur war, the tonnage of Soviet arms delivered by sea was more than five times that brought to the Arab combatants by air. Similarly, the great preponderance of the Soviet arms and munitions sent to Angola and Ethiopia went by sea.

Another long-standing and important element of Soviet logistic assistance to clients engaged in both external and internal conflicts has been the provision of intratheater shuttle airlift support. Such support was provided to Patrice Lumumba in the Congo on a limited scale in 1960 and to Kong Le and Pathet Lao forces in Laos on an extensive scale in 1960-1961, when Soviet aircraft flew more than 1,000 transport sorties from Hanoi to Vientiane and later to the Plain of Jars to sustain those forces logistically.[14] Soviet transport aircraft and helicopters are also reported to have provided extensive logistic assistance to Sudanese government forces during that country's civil war. Soviet AN-12 transports apparently provided similar shuttle support to indigenous and Cuban forces during the Angolan and Ethiopian conflicts.[15] In some cases, this shuttle support has been of critical importance in sustaining the indigenous clients' military operations. For example, the dozen Soviet-piloted AN-12 transport planes presently in Hanoi's service fly extensively between Ho Chi Minh City and western Cambodia, carrying supplies essential to Vietnam's military activities in Cambodia. A senior U.S. State Department official said in 1980 that "without such Soviet support the Vietnamese would be unable to maintain their effort in Cambodia at anything like its current level."[16]

The Soviets have also provided significant advisory, training, and technical support to Third World clients engaged in ongoing conflicts. This support has ranged from the more than 5,000 Soviet military advisers and technicians assigned to the Egyptian armed forces in the early 1970s[17] to the small military-training teams that Moscow occasionally dispatched to sympathetic neighboring African states during the 1960s and 1970s to work with various African liberation movements. For the most part, such Soviet advisory and training personnel seem to have been instructed to avoid active ground-combat zones and to keep to rear areas during Third World conflicts since few are proved to have been captured.[18]

Economic, Diplomatic, and Political-Military
Support of Clients

Over the years, Moscow has also rendered its Third World clients and allies a wide spectrum of other types of support in conflict situations. While Moscow typically has been less forthcoming with economic assistance than with military support, it has on occasion supplied important economic aid as well. For example, the USSR probably supplied more than $3 billion in economic assistance to North Vietnam between 1955 and 1974.[19] Moscow has also provided diplomatic support ranging from active efforts to terminate conflicts that were going badly for its clients (as in the case of the various Arab-Israeli wars) to the use of vetoes in the Security Council to fend off condemnation and early termination of a conflict going well for a Soviet-backed combatant (for example, India in 1971). The USSR has also sought to mobilize and pressure other Third World states to support Soviet clients politically in various conflict situations.[20]

In the political-and-diplomatic-support category, mention should be made of the friendship treaties that the Soviets signed with India in 1971, shortly before New Delhi's invasion of East Pakistan, and with Vietnam in 1978, prior to Hanoi's conquest of Cambodia. In both instances, the treaties (which contained similar security clauses) were in part designed to deter Chinese counterintervention in those conflicts.[21] There have also been a number of cases where the Soviets have rendered political-military support by mounting naval or other military shows of force or by issuing warnings in attempts to contain or discourage external attacks on their clients. For example, the Soviets conducted well-publicized maneuvers on USSR territory adjacent to Turkey so as to deter Turkish intervention in Syria in 1957 and in Iraq in 1958. Even more-important examples were Moscow's threats to intervene on behalf of beleaguered clients during the various Middle East conflicts, threats that constituted a type of political-military support that only a superpower could effectively render.

12 Attributes and Patterns of Soviet Military Involvements Prior to Afghanistan

The Soviets have intervened cautiously in the Third World, taking full advantage of the opportunities open to them but supporting military interventions mainly in conflicts to which they had reason to assume that the United States would not respond militarily. This tactical caution has been reflected also in Moscow's proclivity to move tentatively and incrementally, to minimize the visibility of its own involvement, and to keep Third World conflicts limited and localized. Where possible, the USSR has allowed other communist or indigenous troops to do the fighting and has seemed prepared to commit its own forces only in situations of dire necessity. Moscow's military support of its Third World clients usually has proved effective and responsive to battlefield requirements and has been accomplished at a relatively low economic and political cost to the USSR.

Largely Reactive but Assertively Opportunistic

In contrast to observers who argue that Soviet military involvements in the Third World derive directly from an overall master plan carefully manipulated from Moscow, we believe that such interventions have come largely in response to indigenous developments not of Moscow's making or to the action or inaction of other outside powers. In the case of Ethiopia, to cite but one example, the USSR's intervention evolved from a local development that it had not engineered—namely, the revolution that dethroned Haile Selassie and set Ethiopia on its leftward course in 1974.

Many initial arms-transfer agreements between the USSR and Third World states came about not so much because Moscow had long sought such agreements as because the United States or other Western powers refused to satisfy arms requests from those governments—as was the case with Egypt, Indonesia, Afghanistan, Somalia, and India. Most other Soviet military involvements have been in response to requests from local governments or some arguably legitimate political entity. Soviet support of movements waging so-called national-liberation wars may appear to be an exception, but most such Soviet-backed movements have been deemed legitimate and supported politically by numerous Third World states.

The assertively opportunistic character of Soviet behavior has been manifest in Moscow's propensity to exploit virtually every significant open-

135

ing presented to it in the Third World and to expand initially small opportunities into major positions of influence and presence. In Angola, a prime example of this ruthless opportunism, progressive increments of Soviet arms aid and, later, Cuban combat support succeeded in exploiting the political-military vacuum created by the Portuguese withdrawal and, in little more than a year, propelled a minority and initially militarily weaker liberation faction, the MPLA, to power and international legitimacy.

Moscow's recent willingness simultaneously to back several Third World clients engaged in ongoing conflicts in widely separate areas of the globe further reflects Soviet assertiveness. Already existing requirements to support the Angolan government against the UNITA insurgents and the Ethiopian regime against its Eritrean and Somali opponents did not deter the Soviets from accepting new and potentially more-far-reaching military obligations in former Indochina and in Afghanistan.

By stressing the largely reactive but opportunistic character of Soviet involvements, we are not suggesting that the Soviets are not assiduously pursuing their long-term objectives in the Third World or working to position themselves so as to be able to exploit opportunities that would serve their interests. Indeed, there are numerous examples of active and long-standing Soviet efforts to secure positions of influence through subversive activity, support for national-liberation movements, and attempts to proselytize Third World civilian and military leaders. Thus, the assertion that most Soviet involvements in the Third World are not the consequence of an overall master plan is not intended to downgrade the scope and depth of Soviet ambitions in these areas but to point up what should be an unremarkable finding: that the Soviet ability to foresee, create, and control events within the Third World is limited.

Low Risk in Terms of Possible Military Confrontation with the United States

Soviet-supported military interventions have occurred mainly in conflict situations where Moscow had reason to believe that a U.S. military response would be unlikely, either because of a lack of vital U.S. interests or commitments, existing political constraints, or an absence of viable response options. Moscow's backing of the North Korean invasion of South Korea might appear to have been an exception to this generalization, but the weight of evidence and scholarly opinion is that the Soviets considered any direct U.S. counteraction to the 1950 attack to be both unlikely and militarily difficult.[1]

The USSR had reason to view the external communist intervention in both Angola and Ethiopia as low-risk propositions. While cautious not to provoke an unwanted U.S. response in Angola, the Soviets and Cubans probably saw no great danger that their intervention would lead to a direct military confrontation with the United States, a perception partly conditioned by Washington's acquiescence to the collapse of South Vietnam in early 1975, the Watergate scandal, and the approaching U.S. presidential election.[2] Beyond these U.S. domestic considerations, however, communist calculations that Angola constituted a low-risk venture were probably also importantly shaped by Washington's passive reaction, at least initially, to developments in that African country and by the restrained behavior of the United States once it became involved.

During late 1974 and the first half of 1975, when the Soviets were assiduously arming the MPLA, the United States denied arms to the FNLA, providing instead limited, covert financial support, which it restricted to political uses.[3] Even when Washington later decided to supply arms, training, and other support to the FNLA and UNITA in late July 1975, the level and quality of this still covert aid were but a fraction of the Soviet and Cuban effort. In providing this assistance, U.S. objectives remained limited: to deny the Soviets an easy victory in Angola and to strengthen the bargaining position of the FNLA and UNITA in the event of a still hoped-for political settlement.[4] The United States also wanted to signal its concern to the Soviets and to allow them to scale down their intervention without an open confrontation.

The United States raised the issue of Soviet intervention with Moscow, privately, only in late October 1975,[5] and not until November 24, when the communist airlifts had already been under way for three weeks, did Washington begin to issue public warnings. These warnings, however, suggested political consequences only—that is, that continued Soviet intervention would inevitably threaten other Soviet-U.S. relationships and that Washington's emerging policy of reconciliation with Cuba could not survive that country's continued involvement.[6] Any residual communist concerns about a possible U.S. military counterintervention in Angola were dissolved in December 1975 by the U.S. Senate vote prohibiting further U.S. aid to UNITA and FNLA and by Ford administration statements explicitly ruling out the use of U.S. military force in that conflict.[7]

The Soviets and Cubans probably calculated the risk of any direct U.S. counteraction to their Ethiopian intervention to be even lower than was the case in Angola. Washington publicly had opposed the Somali invasion of the Ogaden and made it clear several months before Cuban combat forces arrived in Ethiopia that the United States would not become involved in the conflict.

Although Washington had agreed in principle in July 1977 to consider favorably Somali requests for defensive arms, the Somali invasion of the Ogaden quickly reversed this policy. On September 1, 1977, the State

138 Soviet Policy toward Third World Conflicts

Department announced that in view of the Ogaden fighting, the United States would not provide military equipment to Somalia. In late October, Washington announced that it would follow a policy of restraint toward the Somali-Ethiopia conflict, one that would emphasize support for diplomatic solutions, permit economic and humanitarian assistance to both sides but prohibit the supply of U.S. arms to either belligerent. Furthermore, the United States would continue to adhere to a policy of not "dramatizing the East-West factor" in Africa, despite its concerns about the Soviet and Cuban involvement there.[8]

The policy of muting the East-West factor had to be modified as the Soviet and Cuban involvement in Ethiopia escalated in late 1977 and early 1978. The United States conveyed its serious concern to Havana and Moscow both publicly and privately and, as in the case of Angola, warned the Soviets of "the dangers which their activities in Africa" posed for overall U.S.-Soviet relations.[9] However, the Carter administration eschewed the use of military signals—including, as Zbigniew Brzezinski had reportedly suggested, sending a "carrier task force to the area to intimidate the Soviets"—to reinforce these diplomatic warnings.[10] The United States became sufficiently aroused to warn of possible counteractions, like arms sales to the Somali government, only when it appeared that Ethiopian or Cuban forces might follow up a victory in the Ogaden by invading Somalia.[11] The Soviets and Ethiopians quickly provided assurances that no such invasion was contemplated.[12]

A similar point can be made about the USSR's encouragement and backing of Vietnam's invasion of Cambodia in 1978. Given the well-publicized U.S. abhorrence of the Pol Pot regime and the absence of any further U.S. commitment to preserving the status quo in former Indochina, Moscow had no reason to be concerned that Vietnam's move into Cambodia would provoke a military response from the United States. The USSR's 1978 treaty with Hanoi—which prepared the way for the invasion—was clearly designed to forestall possible military counteractions from China rather than the United States.

As South Vietnam (1975), Angola (1975-1976), Ethiopia (1977-1978), and Cambodia (1978) will attest, recent Soviet-supported battlefield successes in the Third World have come where the USSR and its communist allies have neither expected nor encountered direct military opposition from the United States. Inattention to this factor has sometimes made Soviet policy appear more adventurous than it really has been.

Hedged Commitments and Tailored Involvements
Where the Risks Are Uncertain

In Third World confrontations where U.S. forces or vital interests have been engaged directly, or where Moscow has been uncertain about a possible

U.S. military response or desirous not to provoke an unwanted U.S. reaction, the USSR has sought to hedge or tailor its commitments and involvements so as to hold the level of risk well below the threshold of a military conflict with the United States.

Although the Soviets on occasion have demonstrated a willingness to engage in courses of action that might involve potential high risks at some point downstream in a conflict scenario, they strive to keep the initial risks low, calculable, and controllable. In this way, as Alexander George and Richard Smoke have pointed out, "the potentially dangerous later stages of a conflict [are] sufficiently removed in time and by intervening events to allow crisis-control measures to be taken."[13] Such tactical caution in Third World conflict or crisis situations has been manifest in a variety of behavior patterns.

Tentative and Incremental Movements

When they are uncertain about a U.S. response or when anxious not to provoke one, the Soviets have demonstrated a propensity (particularly in the early stages of their involvements) to move tentatively and incrementally. The Soviet SAM systems deployed to Egypt in 1970, for example, were first emplaced deep within that country and pushed forward to the canal only in stages as Moscow discerned that the United States, which reacted with notable passivity to the Soviet combat presence, would not strongly back Israel in contesting this progressive encroachment.[14]

Although the Soviets had reason to view Angola as a low-risk involvement, they cautiously avoided unnecessary provocation to the United States and adopted an incremental approach that allowed them to monitor the risks of their actions at various stages of that conflict. It is noteworthy that the potentially most provocative Soviet moves, such as assisting with the airlift of Cuban forces from Cuba and the movement of major Soviet naval combatants to the Angolan theater, occurred only after the point of any possible confrontation with the United States had passed as a result of the Senate vote of December 19, 1975, that prohibited further U.S. aid to the anti-MPLA liberation movements in Angola.[15]

It should be emphasized here that this tentative and incremental pattern of behavior holds only as long as the risks remain uncertain. Once the Soviets have tested the waters and are convinced the risks of a given situation are low, they move forcefully and resolutely.

Low Visibility and Exposure

The USSR has also sought to control risks in such conflict situations by minimizing the magnitude and exposure of their own direct involvement.

For example, Khrushchev disclosed in his memoirs that Stalin had taken the precautionary step of withdrawing all Soviet advisers from their North Korean military units prior to the 1950 invasion of South Korea.[16] During the Jordanian crisis of 1970, Moscow cautiously did not allow Soviet advisers to accompany the Syrian armored units that temporarily invaded Jordanian territory.[17] In mid-1975, the USSR flatly turned down the MPLA's request that Soviet combat troops be deployed to Angola, apparently believing that such a step might provoke the United States. Moscow encouraged the MPLA to try the Cubans instead.[18]

To reduce their potential exposure as the principal arms supplier to Hanoi during the Vietnamese war, the Soviets insisted that their military supplies be transported to North Vietnam across China. Moscow anticipated from the beginning the possibility of a U.S. blockade or mining of North Vietnamese harbors and sought to finesse a possible military confrontation with the United States by maintaining the arms-supply route across China. The Soviets continued to follow the overland route despite harassment by Red Guards during the Cultural Revolution and despite public taunts from the Chinese government that sea routes were available for Soviet arms shipments to Vietnam. Deprecating the Soviet claim "that as the Soviet Union did not border on the Democratic Republic of Vietnam, its aid for the Vietnamese brothers could only reach them through Chinese territory," a Chinese foreign ministry spokesman stated in May 1966:

> Besides ground and air communications, there are sea routes to link various countries in the world. It is utterly groundless to say that aid cannot be rendered in the absence of a common boundary. The Soviet Union has no common boundary with Cuba which lies far away, yet it could ship rocket-nuclear weapons to and back from Cuba. It is not even that far from Vietnam; why can't it ship even conventional weapons there? Again, the Soviet Union has no common boundary with India, yet it could ship large quantities of military materials there by sea to help the Indian reactionaries attack China. Why then can't it ship aid materials by sea to help the Vietnamese people fight the United States?[19]

Notwithstanding this Chinese criticism, the Soviet decision to maintain the China route was vindicated when the United States mined the North Vietnamese harbors in spring 1972. Soviet and other communist arms shipments to Hanoi, rather than being reduced, actually were accelerated. Total Soviet, Chinese, and Eastern European arms shipments to Hanoi in 1972 were estimated at $750 million, more than double the $315 million worth delivered in 1971 and more than triple the $205 million provided in 1970.[20]

Judicious Use of Warnings

The Soviets have also been judicious in the timing and content of their declaratory statements in conflict or crisis situations when U.S. interests have been involved. We have seen the frequent tactic of the USSR firing off a warning after the point of crisis has passed, threatening retaliation in the event of straw-man contingencies that Moscow had high confidence were most unlikely actually to occur, or couching warnings in such general or carefully hedged terms as to provide ample leeway for backing off from any concrete action. Henry Kissinger comments in his memoirs on how non-specific and cautious the Soviet warnings to the United States were regarding any further U.S. escalation in Vietnam ("at no time did the Soviets even approach the hint of a threat"), but he discloses also that Washington took them "seriously at the time."[21]

Keeping Conflicts Localized and Limited

Notwithstanding the recurring U.S. fears during the Korean and Vietnam wars that the Soviets would move to counter the U.S. combat interventions by massive interventions of their own or by mounting military threats against other areas, say with probes in Europe, the Soviets have not threatened such escalation. Shortly after the Korean conflict broke out, diplomatic signals from Moscow clearly suggested that the USSR would not send its own ground forces into that confict,[22] and, as mentioned earlier, the eventual Soviet air-defense combat involvement was limited and circumspect. Aside from an occasional vague and carefully hedged statement about allowing some "volunteers" to assist North Vietnam if Hanoi should request them, the Soviets were careful to avoid any suggestion that they would assume a direct combat role in Vietnam. In neither conflict did Moscow threaten retaliatory military moves or increase its pressure in other geographic arenas.

Even during the Cuban missile crisis, when President Kennedy was absolutely convinced that the Soviets would close Berlin in response to the U.S. quarantine, they did not do so, nor did they mobilize their forces during the course of that crisis.[23] Indeed, Moscow's ambassador to the UN specifically ruled out any Soviet action against Berlin.[24]

Similarly, the Soviets have been cautious not to expand the geographic scope of their naval confrontations with U.S. forces during crisis situations. While they have frequently reinforced naval units in the immediate area of trouble, they have refrained from increasing "the deployment or readiness levels of combatants outside the crisis theater."[25] This practice, along with the various other "risk-controlling measures" consistently followed by the USSR in naval confrontation with the United States, appears designed both to reduce the likelihood of unintended hostilities and to control the level of the threat to U.S. naval forces.[26]

The United States, it is appropriate to note, has reciprocated fully the Soviet caution in avoiding actions that might provoke military conflict between the great powers. During the Cuban missile crisis, and most particularly during the Korean and Vietnam wars, the United States carefully avoided actions that Washington decisionmakers feared might trigger a direct Soviet combat response or reaction elsewhere. These concerns, as well as fears about a possible Chinese intervention in Vietnam, importantly shaped and constrained the manner in which the United States fought both the Korean and Vietnam wars.

**Intervention with Combat Forces
in Situations of Dire Necessity**

The Soviets seem prepared overtly to engage their own combat forces, or have implicitly threatened to do so with some credibility, only in situations where they have perceived the very existence of their clients to be at risk and/or the basic Soviet relationship with the client to be at stake. However, even in such instances, the risks of a direct military conflict with the United States have been low.

The Soviets threatened to intervene during the last days of the 1967 and 1973 Middle East wars only when Moscow had reason to believe that Syria, in 1967, and Egypt, in the case of the Yom Kippur war, were on the verge of catastrophic defeat. The 1967 threat was occasioned by the Israeli rout of the Syrian army on the Golan Heights and by the Soviet (and Syrian) fears that Israeli forces would thereafter move to capture Damascus. While this was not the Israeli intention, such an objective appeared credible to the Soviets and seemed entirely within Israeli capabilities, given the disintegration of the Syrian army and the fact that the Israelis, having seized the high ground less than forty miles from Damascus, would have confronted no additional natural obstacles en route to that capital.[27] These considerations, reinforced by the receipt in Moscow of a report that the Syrian government was about to flee from Damascus to Aleppo, motivated Kosygin to send a hot-line message to Washington on June 10, warning "that unless Israel unconditionally halted operations within the next few hours, the Soviet Union would take necessary actions, including military."[28]

Nasser's papers provide an interesting insight into the state of mind of the Soviet leadership that prompted this warning. According to Nasser, in July 1967 Brezhnev revealed in a conversation with two Arab presidents, Aref of Iraq and Boumédienne of Algeria, that Moscow had received word that the Syrian government planned to evacuate Damascus. Brezhnev is reported to have said:

> We have hardly slept for a whole month. How do we stop the Israeli army's march to Cairo or to Damascus? We received a cable to the effect that the Syrian government will move to Aleppo and this is why they asked for a

cease-fire. On our part, we have exerted pressure on the United States and the socialist countries have severed their relations with Israel. All these are serious steps and we have not taken anything like them in the past 10 years.[29]

The Soviet intervention threat at the close of the 1973 Yom Kippur war occurred at a point of extreme military peril for Egypt, with Israeli forces threatening the Egyptian Second Army's links to Cairo and, more important, in position to threaten the complete destruction of the surrounded Egyptian Third Army. Despite the agreement to observe a U.S.-Soviet-negotiated ceasefire on October 22, Israeli forces had taken advantage of subsequent Egyptian ceasefire violations to tighten their stranglehold on the Egyptian Third Army.[30] Following a public appeal from the now-desperate Sadat that the USSR and the United States jointly send forces to the Middle East to guarantee the ceasefire, Brezhnev sent a message to Nixon proposing common action "to compel observance of the cease-fire without delay" and warning that if Nixon should "find it impossible to act with us in this matter, we should be faced with the necessity urgently to consider the question of taking appropriate steps unilaterally."[31]

The Soviet warning was preceded on October 23 by a further upgrading in the alert status of seven Soviet airborne divisions that initially had been placed on an increased alert status on October 11, when Moscow perceived that the "Syrian front was in danger of collapsing." Fearing an Israeli thrust to Damascus, Moscow began to issue veiled threats toward Israel and, according to Chaim Herzog, informed Kissinger through Ambassador Dobrynin that "Soviet airborne forces were now on the alert to move to the defense of Damascus."[32]

While the United States rejected the Soviet threats in both 1967 and 1973 and responded by immediate shows of force of its own (including the DefCon 3 alert in 1973), the Soviet warnings occurred under conditions where Moscow probably perceived little risk of any resultant confrontation developing into a direct U.S.-Soviet conflict. In both cases, the Soviet threats came only after their Arab clients had agreed to ceasefires in place and when Moscow's demands clearly paralleled U.S. diplomatic objectives—namely, the observance of ceasefires and the halting of further Israeli advances. By addressing its warnings to Washington, Moscow obviously intended to motivate the United States to press further the Israelis to terminate their military operations—an objective immediately realized in both instances.

In connection with the U.S. response to Soviet warnings, Abba Eban states that "the United States was thrown into a global alarm" by the Soviet threats of 1967 and that President Johnson was urgently pressing the Israelis to "cease fire immediately." Eban recalls that "American representatives were openly hinting to us that Soviet intervention no longer seemed inconceivable.'' Pressures from Washington also intensified greatly follow-ing the Soviet intervention threat of 1973 and reportedly included a U.S. warning to Israel ''that if the Soviet Union dropped supplies to the Egyptian 3d Army, the United States could not oppose its action.''[33]

The Soviets decided to deploy air-defense systems to Egypt in 1970 also in response to a situation of dire necessity. Nasser realized that Egyptian air defenses were manifestly unable to cope with Israeli deep-penetration raids and other air attacks and believed that the Israeli objective was not only to force Cairo to terminate its war of attrition but also to break Egypt's morale and bring about the collapse of his regime.[34] He made a secret trip to Moscow on January 22, 1970, to seek Soviet assistance. When the Soviet leaders hesitated to accede to his request that the USSR provide Egypt with missile crews and Soviet-piloted aircraft (an act Brezhnev characterized as potentially leading to a crisis between the USSR and the United States), Nasser made it clear to them that their refusal to aid Egypt at that point would fundamentally alter the Soviet-Egyptian relationship, and he threat-ened to resign in favor of a ''pro-American president'' if help were not forthcoming.[35] Whereas Moscow had previously declined Cairo's requests for personnel to help man Egypt's air defenses, in this instance it agreed.[36]

A similar point can be made about the near-crisis battlefield situations that prompted the Soviets to support the deployment of major Cuban units to Angola in late 1975 and early 1976 and to Ethiopia in late 1977 and early 1978. In both cases, Moscow had reason to believe that their clients faced a serious prospect of catastrophic defeat and that an external rescue effort was mandatory (see pp. 147-149).

Preferred Pattern Allows Local Forces to Do the Fighting

Short of such catastrophic contingencies, the preferred Soviet pattern has been to provide arms, advisory, and logistic support but to allow other com-munist or indigenous forces to do the fighting, even when they had absorbed considerable punishment from external attacks and when a treaty relation-ship with the USSR existed. It should be noted, for example, that although both Angola and Mozambique have friendship treaties with the USSR, these treaty relationships have not been invoked in response to the cross-border air and ground attacks mounted against guerrilla sanctuaries and other targets in these countries by South African and former Rhodesian government forces. These attacks against Angola and Mozambique have at times resulted in extensive casualties and damage to indigenous targets of some economic importance and in the death of Soviet advisers, but they have not threatened the existence of the Marxist regimes in Luanda and Maputo.[37]

The most notable example of this restraint was the USSR's nonintervention during China's punitive attack on Vietnam in early 1979. Despite its treaty relationship with Hanoi, Moscow's behavior during the period of the Chinese buildup prior to the attack and during the hostilities was consistently restrained and cautious. The Soviets did not, for example, accelerate their prescheduled maneuvers on the Sino-Soviet border in response to the Chinese incursion but held these as previously planned—after China had withdrawn its forces from Vietnam.[38] During the period of mounting Sino-Vietnamese border tensions prior to the February 17 attack, Soviet media adopted a cautious posture, playing down the possibility of a conflict and "eschewing expressions of support for Hanoi or direct warnings to Beijing against launching an attack." Following the Chinese attack, Moscow warned China to "stop before it is too late" and pledged to honor the provisions of the Sino-Vietnamese treaty but remained cautiously noncommittal about how such a pledge would be carried out.[39]

Aside from the fact that Moscow probably perceived its military options against a nuclear-armed China to be unattractive, we would assume that the Soviets' restraint was influenced importantly by their understanding of the limited Chinese objectives in Vietnam, as the PRC had made it clear in statement and deed that its punitive operation was to be limited in both duration and territory. Had the Chinese advanced deep into Vietnam and threatened Hanoi, the chances of some Soviet military reaction obviously would have been much greater.

Military Effectiveness and Responsiveness

While the Soviets have by no means always backed the winning side in Third World conflicts, their military involvements and support operations have, in the main, been both effective and responsive to changing battlefield requirements. On a number of occasions, of course, Soviet clients (for example, the Arab states in the 1967 and 1973 Middle East wars) have suffered decisive military defeats, but it is not apparent that these resulted from inadequate Soviet materiel support.

Where Moscow has had a strong interest in sustaining a client in combat, it has proved an assiduous and responsive arms supplier, and where direct, external communist intervention has occurred, it has proved successful in securing immediate battlefield objectives. This capacity to get the job done is reflected in the military outcomes of several significant past cases.

Soviet Arms Aid to North Vietnam

There can be little question, for example, about the resolve Moscow displayed in providing military aid to Hanoi during the course of the Vietnam war or that this Soviet assistance was vital to Hanoi's continued and eventual successful prosecution of that war. Averaging some $325 million a year between 1965 and 1974, Soviet military aid accounted for about 70 percent of the DRV's external arms support.[40] This assistance, which was augmented by a significant but smaller amount of support from communist China,[41] furnished North Vietnam with an extensive air-defense system where none had existed before,[42] permitted the complete reequipment of both Viet Cong and North Vietnamese Army (NVA) forces with standardized communist weaponry well suited to the Indochina combat environment,[43] and provided Hanoi with the mobile, heavier weapons (armor, artillery, and mobile air-defense systems) and ammunition stocks necessary to mount the conventional general offensive launched at Easter in 1972 and the final, decisive attack in early 1975.[44]

Throughout the course of the Vietnam war, Moscow adamantly refused to cut back its arms support in return for Washington's proffered improvements in U.S.-Soviet relations. For example, when Kissinger told Soviet Ambassador Dobrynin in April 1969 that "a settlement in Vietnam was the key to everything" as far as progress in U.S.-Soviet relations was concerned, Dobrynin responded that the United States "had to understand the limitations of Soviet influence on Hanoi" and asserted "that the Soviet Union would never threaten to cut off supplies to their allies in North Vietnam."[45] As previously noted, the USSR significantly increased its military assistance to the DRV in 1972 despite the supposed flowering of détente in that year that resulted from the Nixon visit to Moscow.

Deployment of Air-Defense Systems to Egypt in 1970

Evaluated solely in terms of its immediate military objectives of defending against and deterring Israeli air attacks, the 1970 Soviet combat intervention in Egypt must be judged a success. Prior to Moscow's combat involvement, the Israeli air force had enjoyed near absolute air supremacy over Egypt, attacking military targets at will and "almost without loss" and conducting deep-penetration raids as close as five miles from the center of Cairo.[46] During the first four months of 1970, the Israelis mounted some 3,300 sorties and dropped an estimated 8,000 tons of ordnance on Egyptian territory.[47]

This bombing campaign was soon to be progressively closed down by the introduction of Soviet air-defensive systems and personnel that began in early 1970. The Israelis discontinued deep-penetration raids in mid-April, immediately after Jerusalem discerned that Soviet-piloted fighter aircraft were flying operational missions over Egypt.[48] In the following months, as the Soviet buildup continued and additional systems became operational, the Israelis, despite repeated air attacks, were unable to prevent the progressive forward movement of the Soviet-Egyptian air-defense coverage toward the Suez canal itself.[49] According to Yitzhak Rabin, then Israeli ambassador to Washington, Israeli "planes were helpless against the missile system that had crept forward to the canal."[50]

Growing aircraft losses and pressures from Washington, "which was increasingly anxious about the dangers of escalation," induced Israel to accept the U.S.-sponsored ceasefire, which previously had been accepted by Egypt and which became effective on August 7.[51] Although Israel had secured its primary military objective of ending the war of attrition, the outcome entailed significant costs for Israel in that the Soviet intervention had altered the existing Egyptian-Israeli military balance and helped to "pave the way to the Yom Kippur war."[52]

Cooperative Interventions with Cuba:
Angola and Ethiopia

In Angola and Ethiopia, the external communist interventions clearly proved the decisive factor in rescuing Soviet clients from rapidly deteriorating military situations and subsequently have contributed importantly to sustaining Marxist control in both countries. The contribution was even more significant in the case of Angola in that the external intervention, consisting of large amounts of Soviet weapons, a few hundred noncombatant Soviet advisers, and nearly 20,000 Cuban troops, actually propelled the MPLA to power in little more than a year (from fall 1974 to mid-February 1976), despite the opposition and counterintervention of the United States, People's Republic of China, South Africa, and Zaire.

This external support proved the critical determinant at several different stages of the Angolan conflict. Soviet arms deliveries during late 1974 and spring 1975 were a key factor in raising the MPLA from a position of comparative military weakness to the dominant indigenous military power in Angola by mid-summer 1975, permitting the MPLA progressiely to assume the offensive and gain control of the country's most important political and economic real estate: Luanda, the capital of Angola, and the oil-rich enclave of Cabinda. The subsequent introduction of heavier Soviet weapons, such as 122-mm truck-mounted multiple-rocket launchers, and the arrival of several thousand Cuban combat forces in September and October were decisive factors in the successful defense of MPLA positions in Cabinda and Luanda in early November 1975, when the MPLA appeared on the verge of defeat.[53] Finally, the rapid buildup of Cuban forces (which from November on did the bulk of the fighting) and the increased Soviet arms deliveries in late 1975 assured the eventual expulsion of anti-MPLA units from northern Angola and helped to persuade the South Africans to withdraw their intervention forces from the south in early 1976. It is clear that at each of these stages of the Angolan conflict, the quality, levels, and timing of the external communist support proved responsive to the battle-field requirements of the moment and sufficed to bring ultimate victory.

Although Soviet and Cuban intervention did not directly raise the Mengistu regime to power in Ethiopia, it effectively rescued that Marxist government from the situation of extreme peril that it faced at the end of 1977. For at that time, it "seemed more than likely" that Ethiopia "would fall apart under the pressure of the Somali invasion in the south, Eritrean guerrilla success in the north, and a variety of internal strains and revolts."[54] The Ethiopian army, which was proving to be of questionable reliability (some units had mutinied[55]) and was having difficulty in absorb-ing the large influx of new recruits and Soviet weapons, faced dangerous threats on two fronts. In Eritrea, guerrilla forces of the three Eritrean seces-sionist movements controlled more than 90 percent of the province and were exerting increasing pressure on the Ethiopian garrisons holed up in the few remaining government strongholds in the province.[56] In the Ogaden, regular Somali forces and guerrillas of the Western Somali Liberation Front had swept Ethiopian forces from most of that province and were in the pro-cess of attacking Harar, one of the last two remaining significant positions in the Ogaden still in Ethiopian hands.[57] It was believed that the loss of Harar, the provincial capital and site of the Ethiopian military academy, might threaten the future survival of the Mengistu regime.[58]

The Soviet and Cuban assistance rushed to Ethiopia in late 1977 and early 1978 brought about a dramatic easement of this military situation. A massive influx of Soviet munitions and heavy weapons, the introduction of some 17,000 Cuban troops (many of whom, as in Angola, were brought in by air), and the command, logistic, and technical support provided by the some 1,000 to 1,500 Soviet personnel managed to turn the tide decisively within a period of less than six months.

By January 1978, Cuban-piloted aircraft and the stiffening provided by some initial Cuban ground units, along with new Soviet heavy weapons (in-cluding T-54 and T-55 tanks and BM-21 truck-mounted rocket launchers) had assisted Ethiopian forces in relieving the Somali threat to Harar.[59] In the following month, Cuban mechanized brigades played a decisive role in a Soviet-planned and commanded counteroffensive that flanked the Somali invaders' major positions in the Ogaden and forced their withdrawal in early March.[60]

Once the Ogaden front was secure, additional Ethiopian forces, with the help of Soviet air and sea transport, were redeployed to Eritrea, where a series of successful offensives were launched in June and July, returning most of that province to government control.[61] While the Cubans apparently did not play a significant front-line ground role in these Eritrean offensives, Cuban officers reportedly took part in some operations (for example, by directing artillery fire), and the Soviets and Cubans provided vital planning and the logistic support for the operations.[62]

Communist Military Operations in the Third World

In the execution of their Third World support operations, the Soviets have demonstrated an impressive capability to accumulate and deliver substantial tonnages of weapons and munitions to distant conflict arenas on comparatively short notice. This capability is a function of both the massive inventories of readily accessible weapons stockpiled in the USSR (a condition that does not exist in the United States[63]) and the availability of large and proficient Soviet air- and sealift assets.

The Use of Air- and Sealifts

The Yom Kippur war and the fighting in Angola and Ethiopia, among other cases, have demonstrated the now well-developed Soviet capabilities for mounting substantial and responsive sea- and airlifts to Third World conflict arenas. Recent Soviet airlifts appear to have been conducted for the most part with a high degree of professionalism and without major operational problems. During the Yom Kippur war, for example, Soviet military-transport-aviation (VTA) resupply flights to Egypt demonstrated sufficiently short turnaround times to sustain a rate of two to three arrivals an hour over a one-week period.[64] The Soviet airlift to Ethiopia, though on a much smaller scale than the 1973 effort, reportedly suffered "few layovers or delays because of breakdowns."[65]

The USSR also has shown marked success in rapidly arranging overflight rights and refueling stops for its airlifts to Third World conflict arenas. In several instances (for example, the airlifts to Angola and Ethiopia), such arrangements apparently were secured in exchange for additional Soviet arms pledges to the countries granting the transit rights.[66] During the early stages of the Ethiopian airlift, however, the Soviets experienced unusual difficulties in obtaining and maintaining overflight clearances and were forced to change routes as Pakistan, Iran, and Egypt, in turn, objected to the transit of their territory. Iraq and Syria, despite their ties to Moslem Somalia and their support to Eritrean liberation movements, eventually provided transit facilities to the USSR.[67]

While the airlifts have been important in terms of the rapid deployment of high-priority equipment and munitions, and in some instances personnel, the great bulk of the arms and munitions was sent by sea. The tonnages delivered in several of these conflicts are striking. For example, in an eighteen-day period during the Yom Kippur war, Soviet ships carried some 63,000 tons of arms and munitions to various Middle East ports. In the first half of 1978, a period of intense fighting in the Ogaden and Eritrea, Moscow delivered more than 60,000 tons of military cargo to Ethiopia.[68] A number of these deliveries were made by Soviet roll-on/roll-off ships, which in the words of the U.S. Defense Department, "are ideal for transporting and rapidly loading and unloading wheeled and tracked vehicles, even in less developed harbors."[69]

When one considers that from 1973 on the Soviets have sequentially and, in some instances, simultaneously accommodated the burdens of providing logistic and weapons support to combatants in the Middle East, Angola, Ethiopia, Indochina,[70] and Afghanistan, while still managing to increase their arms transfers to other clients (including a significant upgrading of Cuba's weapon inventories as a compensation for its services in Angola and Ethiopia), one cannot but be impressed with the USSR's capabilities in this regard.

Cooperative Intervention: Efficacy against Inferior Forces

A second noteworthy attribute of the communist military operations in the Third World is the overall efficacy of the instrument of cooperative intervention. In both Angola and Ethiopia, Cuban military personnel demonstrated a considerable capacity to interact successfully with indigenous forces and to operate effectively with weapons delivered directly from the USSR, a demonstration of the advantages inherent in standardized communist weaponry and training. The Soviet-Cuban military cooperation and battlefield interaction in Ethiopia, which was much more extensive than in Angola where the Soviet advisory presence was far more limited, revealed the flexibility and competence of the two communist partners to work out a suitable division of labor. In addition to managing the logistic requirements of the Ethiopian campaign, Soviet personnel assumed primary responsibility for the planning and overall direction of operations, whereas Cuban officers focused in the main on tactical execution.[71] Ethiopia, in this among several other respects (like the transport of Cuban troops on Soviet vessels, which did not occur in Angola), denoted a further development of the interactive aspects of cooperative intervention.

While recognizing the overall efficacy of the Soviet and Cuban operations in Angola and Ethiopia, one should keep in mind that neither operation severely tested Soviet or Cuban capabilities (for example, the Soviet air- and sealifts were unopposed) and that both proved to be situations where even modest amounts of external aid and intervention were able to produce enormous leverage on the battlefield. In both Angola and Ethiopia, the Cubans faced for the most part significantly inferior military opposition.

For example, although the Somali forces in the Ogaden proved tenacious fighters, they were outnumbered and outgunned by their Ethiopian and Cuban opponents, lacked adequate air support, and operated from extended lines of communication that were both difficult to keep supplied once Soviet support had been cut off and vulnerable to Cuban mechanized envelopments. Except for the South Africans, who possessed better tactical leadership and were more skilled at mobile warfare than the Cubans, Havana's forces were clearly superior to the otherwise marginal military opposition they faced in Angola. Cuban-manned T-34 tanks and 122-mm truck-mounted multiple-rocket launchers had a devastating effect on the undisciplined and poorly led FNLA and Zairian forces, which frequently fled the battlefield at the first use of these weapons. UNITA's forces, while comparatively well led at the top and effective in guerrilla operations, were not adequately armed or trained to oppose the Cubans in conventional combat. The Cubans in both Angola and Ethiopia also possessed a marked advantage in firepower (which reflected the Soviet penchant for introducing and relying on a profusion of heavy weapons to dominate even Third World battlefields) and entered those conflicts with substantial foreknowledge of the military weaknesses of their opponents.

Avoidance of Entering Conflict Situations Unprepared

The last point mentioned deserves some further elaboration in that it demonstrates an additional attribute of Soviet-Cuban behavior—namely, that Moscow and Havana have not intervened to date in Third World conflict situations cold (that is, without the benefit of adequate on-the-spot assessments of the local balance of forces and battlefield situations) or without a reasonable prospect that their immediate military objectives could be achieved.

We must assume, for example, that Castro was well briefed by his senior advisers in Luanda about the limited military competence of the MPLA's opposition in Angola before he decided to commit troops to that conflict.[72] In the case of Ethiopia, the Soviets, after years of work with Somali military forces, were intimately familiar with Somali capabilities and could well estimate how their cutoff of spare parts and other logistic support to Mogadishu would affect Somali fighting effectiveness. Following a pattern now typical of Soviet interventions, Moscow also dispatched a senior military team to Addis Ababa to conduct an on-the-spot survey of the military situation before initiating its airlift to Ethiopia in late November 1977.[73] A similar point can be made about the 1970 Soviet decision to deploy air-defense systems to Egypt, in that with several thousand military advisers already in that country, the Soviet leaders had an ample basis for assessing the feasibility of and requirements for their intervention.

Poorer Results against Popular Insurgencies

It should be noted that external communist support and intervention have proved most effective in the more-conventional or set-piece stages of Third World conflicts. The Soviets and Cubans have been far less successful in combating and organizing their clients to cope with the popular-based insurgencies that still plague their Angolan and Ethiopian allies.

Despite the continued presence of 19,000 Cuban troops and military advisers in Angola, UNITA guerrillas still control much of the southern countryside in that country and have managed to keep the vital Benguela railroad closed. Even though it lacks the weapons and trained-force structure necessary to seize and hold the urban centers now protected by government and Cuban forces, UNITA is well organized for protracted guerrilla warfare, possesses wide popular support in its main areas of operation, and seems capable of sustaining its resistance over many years to come.[74] This insurgent threat, combined with the chronic political and economic problem still plaguing Angola, make it questionable whether the Marxist government in Luanda could long survive without Cuban troops to prop it up.[75]

Similarly, while Ethiopian forces (assisted by Cuban troops) retain control of nearly all towns in the Ogaden and Eritrea, they still have not stamped out the insurgencies in those areas. Ethiopian government units have suffered periodic setbacks in Eritrea, like the July 1979 series of unsuccessful assaults against Eritrean units holding the town of Nakfa, which reportedly cost the Ethiopians some 6,000 men.[76] In the Ogaden, WSLF guerrillas, at times supported by some regular Somali army units, continue to harass Ethiopian government outposts and frequently ambush resupply convoys in that region.[77] Much of the countryside remains under WSLF control, despite the draconian measures adopted by Ethiopian forces to purge the Ogaden of all populations sympathetic to the WSLF cause—a strategy that has resulted in a massive flight of refugees to Somali territory.

Low-Cost Approach

Until the recent invasion of Afghanistan, Soviet military involvements in the Third World had been conducted, in the main, with a low profile and at a low cost. The number of Soviet military personnel deployed had been relatively small, the largest contingent dispatched to any one country being the 20,000 or so sent to Cuba in 1962 and the some 15,000 combatants and advisers stationed in Egypt in 1970. Soviet casualties in Third World conflicts had been minimal, with a smattering of killed and wounded over the years in various conflicts in Asia, Africa, and the Middle East.

Because the USSR does not disclose casualties, estimates of Soviet Third World losses must be conjectured. It is known, for example, that some Soviet pilots were shot down during the Korean conflict and that four MIG-21s were downed by Israeli fighters during the 1970 war of attrition. It is also probable that the Soviets suffered some personnel losses as a result of U.S. air strikes on North Vietnamese SAM sites and from Israeli attacks on Egyptian air-defense systems in 1970. Limited Soviet casualties were reported also in the Yemeni and Sudanese civil wars, the Iraqi-Kurdish conflict, and the 1973 Yom Kippur war. Soviet losses in Afghanistan prior to the December 1979 invasion may have numbered over 100 as a result of Afghan army mutinies and Moslem guerrilla attacks.[78]

Except for an occasional merchant ship sunk or damaged and some aircraft losses (substantial only in the case of the Korean war), the USSR has suffered no appreciable destruction to its own property. The Israelis sank a Soviet merchant vessel at the Syrian port of Tartus during the Yom Kippur war, and four Soviet merchant ships accidentally were damaged "with loss of life" as a result of U.S. air attacks on Haiphong in 1972. Commenting on Moscow's strong diplomatic reaction to this latter event, Henry Kissinger wrote: "Like the Chinese, the Soviet protests about the bombing of North Vietnam took on a grave tone only when Soviet lives or property were in jeopardy."[79]

Soviet military and economic assistance to Third World combatants, while impressive in the aggregate, has not unduly strained Soviet resources.[80] As previously noted, Soviet production lines and accumulated weapon inventories permitted Moscow to supply its Third World clients while still building up Warsaw Pact forces. With a few major exceptions—such as the grant economic and military aid provided Hanoi during the Vietnam war and the subsidies and other assistance Moscow continued to render Cuba and Vietnam—Soviet aid has not produced a significant net drain on Soviet resources in that aid agreements provided for eventual repayment in one form or another, including hard currency in the case of some Arab clients.[81]

The political costs to the USSR prior to Afghanistan have also been low. Soviet military involvement has produced little if any sustained criticism from most Third World states. The Soviet and Cuban intervention in Angola has had the strong support of a number of key African countries, and such criticism as existed was muted by the more-vociferous condemnation of South Africa's involvement in that conflict. Ethiopia was another case where external communist intervention provoked little adverse response from Moscow's Third World constituency: Somalia's irredentist claims on the Ogaden have had only minimal support in Africa, and nearly all African countries opposed the Somali invasion of the Ethiopian province.

Similarly, Soviet adventures in the Third World have not seriously undermined Moscow's strategy of fostering detente in the overall East-West relationship, nor has detente seriously constrained Soviet behavior. Indeed, the Soviets have been largely successful in decoupling their involvements in Vietnam, Angola, and Ethiopia from other bilateral issues affecting U.S.-Soviet relations. President Johnson, to cite but one example, asserted that the United States concluded "more significant agreements with Moscow in the years 1963-1969 [which, it should be noted, included some of the bitterest U.S. fighting in Vietnam] than in the thirty years after we established diplomatic relations with the Soviet regime."[82] This is not to say, however, that there had not been a discernible negative cumulative effect of Soviet Third World adventures on the overall U.S.-Soviet relationship. Events in Indochina, Angola, and Ethiopia clearly fueled public criticism of détente within the United States and calls for an increased arms buildup.[83]

13 The Soviet Involvement in Afghanistan: Comparisons and Implications

The juxtaposition of Soviet involvement in Afghanistan with previous Soviet behavior reveals striking deviations from past patterns as well as significant continuities. Among other implications, the Afghanistan intervention may portend bolder future Soviet behavior in the Third World, particularly if Moscow ultimately judges the benefits of the invasion to outweigh the costs.

Differences

Even before the December 1979 invasion, Moscow's relationship with and military role in Afghanistan had acquired a character and degree of commitment that set Afghanistan apart from other Soviet Third World involvements. Soviet economic and military penetration of that border state had been growing since the mid-1950s, and while Afghanistan traditionally had sought to maintain a nonaligned position among the world powers, its location and inherent political and economic weakness made it especially vulnerable to Soviet influence.

As Afghanistan's largest source of economic aid and principal trading partner, the USSR had acquired a dominant role in Afghanistan's economic development. Soviet influence was equally pervasive in the military sphere, where the USSR had almost entirely equipped and trained the Afghan armed forces. No doubt with future contingencies in mind, the Soviets had also helped to construct Afghanistan's major airfields and two-thirds of Afghanistan's roads (which linked that country to the USSR's transportation system).[1] This Soviet-funded infrastructure greatly facilitated the 1979 invasion. As the U.K. prime minister, Mrs. Thatcher, put it, "Soviet tanks crossed Afghanistan on roads built with Soviet money, and their aircraft landed on airfields similarly financed."[2]

This special status and commitment Moscow accorded its interests in Afghanistan were also manifest in the December 1978 friendship treaty between the two countries, a treaty that clearly denoted a more-unequal relationship than had any previous Soviet treaty with a Third World country and that permitted the Soviets considerable leeway. Various clauses suggested a patron-client relationship, particularly Article 4 that, in a significant departure from other such treaties, stipulated that the two sides would take "appropriate measures to ensure the security, independence, and territorial integrity of the two countries."[3] The USSR interpreted this clause broadly; indeed, it subsequently was cited as providing a "firm legal foundation" for sending troops into Afghanistan.[4]

The USSR's unprecedented combat-command role in Afghanistan further set that country apart, even before the December all-out military occupation. While Moscow's initial response to the 1978 coup had followed a more-or-less expected pattern (a modest influx of military advisers, doubling the 350 Soviets already in the country, and a larger influx of civilian advisers and increased arms shipments), the unreliability and decimation of the frequently purged Afghan officer corps caused the Soviets progressively to expand both the numbers and functions of their military advisers as the insurgency widened. By early December 1979, an estimated 3,500 to 4,000 Soviet military personnel were positioned in the Afghan army at every level of command.[5] Soviet officers were providing day-to-day operational leadership to Afghan ground forces down to company level. Soviet control of the Afghan air force was equally pervasive. Soviet pilots were flying numerous combat missions, and the main air force base at Bagram was a virtual Soviet enclave, protected by Soviet troops.[6] In sum, prior to December the Soviets were already running the war in Afghanistan and had probably absorbed more ground-combat casualties than they had in any previous Third World venture.

The most striking deviation from previous patterns of Soviet Third World military involvements occurred with the December invasion. The direct use of Soviet forces to overthrow an existing government and the massive military occupation were without precedent outside Eastern Europe. Whereas previous Soviet military interventions had been requested by the local government or, at least in Third World eyes, some legitimate political entity, in the case of Afghanistan, the Soviets not only moved without Kabul's invitation (though there was a transparent attempt by Moscow to manufacture one after the fact) but also they used their own troops to eliminate the Amin government, an act that destroyed any semblance of legitimacy to their intervention.

Moscow's willingness to abandon its traditional low profile and to defy Third World sensitivities clearly signified a departure from previous behavior. In contrast to the limited and mostly temporary and defensive combat involvements of the past, the USSR for the first time assumed an open-ended commitment to pacify a Third World state with Soviet forces, an act that in turn provoked unprecedented condemnation and punitive responses from the world community and that has already resulted in far more Soviet dead and wounded than accumulated during the course of all other post-World War II Soviet military involvements.

Parallels

The USSR's actions toward Afghanistan also reflected certain continuities in Soviet behavior. First, the invasion of December 1979 seemed clearly to have been in response to a situation of dire necessity, one where the USSR had reason to perceive the continued existence of a client to be at risk had it failed to intervene. Amin's defiant refusal to submit to Soviet control, his increasingly bloody rule that was alienating all sectors of Afghan society, and the accelerating unreliability and erosion of the Afghan military establishment portended only a further deterioration of the political-military situation. Had it not invaded Afghanistan at the end of 1979, Moscow had every reason to expect the catastrophic collapse of the Marxist revolution in a country bordering on the USSR—a country in which Moscow had already invested enormous political and military capital—and the consequent loss of its own prestige.

Second, Moscow had earlier demonstrated its willingness to act resolutely to prevent a Marxist client state from being overthrown from within (as in Hungary in 1956) or to defend such a regime against outside threats. The major Soviet and Cuban interventions in Ethiopia and Angola were impelled by the desire to preserve positions of influence by rescuing pro-Soviet regimes threatened with defeat. The 27,000 or more Cubans still in Angola provide a striking parallel in the use of external communist forces and cadres to maintain a minority Marxist government in power against a popular-based insurgency. In this respect, the invasion of Afghanistan was the culmination of a policy trend increasingly evident in Soviet behavior during the latter part of the 1970s—namely, the willingness to sanction and actively support the use of external communist force to secure and defend additional footholds in the Third World. The successful intervention in Angola and Ethiopia had been followed immediately by Moscow's encouragement and backing of the Vietnamese invasion of Cambodia in 1978, an act that in itself signaled a more-cavalier attitude on the part of the Soviet leadership toward local Third World sensitivities.

Third, the Soviet actions in Afghanistan clearly again carried no risk of a direct military confrontation with the United States. To quote one recent U.S. ambassador to Afghanistan, U.S. support for Afghan independence had been "largely moral." The United States had manifested an unwillingness to extend its responsibilities into Afghanistan as early as the mid-1950s, when it declined to provide military assistance, in part because it was concerned about provoking a possible attack on Afghanistan from the USSR.[7] Washington had long tacitly accepted a preponderant Soviet influence in Afghanistan and had not reacted strongly to the April 1978 coup. Furthermore, since the early 1960s, the United States had exhibited little interest in competing militarily with the USSR in southern Asia and was clearly not positioned to do so in 1979.[8] While U.S. officials "repeatedly impressed on the Soviet government the dangers of more direct involvement in the fighting in Afghanistan," such public warnings contained no hint of a military response.[9] Expressions of "deep U.S. concern" about the growing involvement in Afghanistan apparently had little deterrent value, perhaps because Washington had voiced similar concerns without subsequent adverse consequences to the USSR about the Soviet and Cuban interventions in Angola and Ethiopia.

Fourth, as in past Moscow-orchestrated interventions, the USSR obviously did not project its forces into Afghanistan cold; various high-level Soviet fact-finding missions, as well as continuous field reporting from that country during 1979, surely provided Moscow with detailed firsthand information concerning the deteriorating situation in Afghanistan and the military requirements for intervention. Contingency planning for the large-scale introduction of Soviet troops probably had been under way for several months before the actual invasion, and the December military operations were carefully staged. While the logistic requirements of the invasion were not particularly demanding because of Afghanistan's proximity to bases in the USSR, the Soviets seem to have made good use of surprise and subterfuge to neutralize possible military opposition from Afghan forces. The ruses utilized to immobilize some Afghan armored elements (for example, the collection of ammunition stocks for inventory and of tank batteries for winterization) and the cover stories explaining Soviet troop movements remind of Moscow's tactical deceptions to thwart organized defense against its 1968 occupation of Czechoslovakia.[10] The Soviet battle plan for the invasion of Afghanistan, including the vertical envelopment tactics used to secure key logistic points, also closely paralleled the Soviet operations in Czechoslovakia in 1968.[11]

The intervention in Afghanistan also revealed once again the difficulties that external communist states face in attempting to organize Third World clients to cope with popular-based insurgencies. Despite the presence of some 7,000 Soviet advisers throughout the Afghan military and civilian structures, Moscow was manifestly unable to arrest the political and military deterioration that followed the April 1978 coup. The fundamental weaknesses that plagued the Marxist government from its inception (for example, lack of legitimacy and popular following, marginal support within the Afghan military, and bitter factional rivalries) intensified during 1978-1979. These weaknesses have been exacerbated further by the Soviet occupation, which itself has now become the dominant political issue sustaining continued Afghan resistance.

It remains to be seen whether the Soviets will succeed in recruiting reliable Afghan forces to do the fighting for them or whether the current

100,000-man occupation force will be sufficient to expand government control much beyond the urban centers now held.[12] Soviet counterinsurgency operations have not been impressive to date, even against a still poorly armed and largely uncoordinated tribal opposition. The Soviet approach to pacification in Afghanistan—like the Vietnamese approach in Cambodia and the Ethiopian in the Ogaden—is to erode resistance through the brutal application of firepower and repressive population-control measures and thus to generate a massive outflow of refugees to burden a neighboring country.[13]

Implications

A strong case may be made that the unprecedented use of Soviet forces to invade a Third World client state and install a regime of Moscow's choice was motivated initially by essentially defensive considerations, such as to prevent the collapse of a communist government and its replacement by a fundamentalist Islamic regime, perhaps aligned with Iran and Pakistan on the USSR's sensitive Central Asian borders.

Granted, however, that the Soviets acted in the first instance to avert a disastrous political setback and to defend gains that they had made in Afghanistan since the 1978 coup, it does not necessarily follow either that the events in Afghanistan are therefore of limited significance in terms of strategic and political gains or that they are likely to have little influence on Soviet conduct elsewhere in the Third World.

On the contrary, as Helmut Sonnenfeldt and others have pointed out with regard to the first point, the Afghanistan venture has had major strategic and political implications, whether or not they were contemplated by Moscow at the time the invasion was launched.[14] For example, the invasion has extended the USSR's military dominance beyond its previous Central Asian perimeter into territory that historically served as a buffer between the USSR and the Indian Ocean rimlands. This new projection of Soviet power, in turn, has multiplied the military options available to the USSR in a region of vital importance to the West for its oil resources and the crucial sea lanes.

Further, the USSR now finds itself in a position to bring new pressure on Pakistan and Iran, to include encouraging separatist-minded Baluchi tribesmen to carve out a pro-Soviet state at the expense of both—a move that would provide a corridor for southward Soviet access to the Arabian Sea and Strait of Hormuz. Finally, the invasion and occupation contribute to the Soviet aim of erecting a wall of containment around China, serving at the same time the broader strategic purpose of countering the emergence of a de facto Sino-U.S.-Japanese-West European alliance that Moscow has found patently objectionable.

The extent to which the USSR may seek to exploit the strategic options opened up by its military presence in Afghanistan obviously will depend on many factors: for example, Soviet progress in containing the insurgency in Afghanistan, the internal stability of neighboring countries in the so-called arc of crisis through southern Asia and the Middle East, and Moscow's perception of Western opposition to any new Soviet moves and its estimate of their chances of success.

Another salient question pertinent to Soviet moves to exploit the opportunities opened up by the invasion is how long the USSR may in fact maintain a large military presence in Afghanistan. As reiterated in a Soviet-Afghan statement at the close of Babrak Karmal's brief visit to Moscow in October 1980, the USSR will not withdraw its military forces until the rebellion threatening the legitimate Karmal government is put down—an eventuality that may be a long way off.[15] Even if the insurgency is contained, the military infrastructure the Soviets are building in Afghanistan suggests, as previously noted, that they are there for a long stay.

An indefinite Soviet occupation of Afghanistan, "legitimized" by treaty arrangements with whatever puppet government the USSR may choose to keep in power, does not necessarily mean that open Soviet military action will be taken against other countries in the region. However, even though the USSR may assiduously avoid direct military operations from Afghan bases against Pakistan or Iran—military operations such as hot pursuit, elimination of Afghan rebel sanctuaries, or even more-ambitious interventions—the political-military leverage afforded Moscow by the investment of Afghanistan appears by no means trivial. That is, the threat of intervention, fortified by the Afghan example, may prove sufficiently intimidating to bend shaky governments in the volatile arc of crisis toward policies that serve Soviet interests, as appears to have been the case when Pakistan initially declined a closer military association with the United States in the aftermath of the invasion.

With regard to Afghanistan's implications for Soviet conduct elsewhere in the Third World, one of the more obvious would appear to be what Marshall Shulman has termed the whetting of the Soviet appetite for similar armed intervention elsewhere if the Afghan venture turns out in the end to have yielded relatively risk-free political and geostrategic benefits.[16]

Looked at in cost/benefit terms from the Soviet viewpoint, the net balance of the Afghanistan intervention, at least up to the time of writing, probably appears relatively positive. The USSR succeeded in salvaging a weak communist regime and acquiring the various political-military advantages mentioned earlier at a price that, although not inconsequential, was nevertheless affordable. The material costs such as personnel casualties and the budgetary load of military campaigning to date are probably well within tolerable limits. Furthermore, the military commitments made to Afghanistan have absorbed only a very small portion of the USSR's total army and tactical air forces and have not significantly degraded Soviet capabilities for mounting simultaneous military operations elsewhere.[17]

Some of the political costs, such as the adverse (but transitory) reaction to the invasion in Western Europe and the boycott of the Olympic games held in Moscow, also may appear marginal to the Soviets. Others probably may weigh more heavily, such as the antagonism aroused in much of the Moslem world; the likelihood of closer Sino-U.S. collaboration; the negative effects on many Third World states, including some Soviet clients, located where they cannot be invaded readily by the USSR; and the resultant stimulus to U.S. arms spending and related military preparations.

Whatever the net judgment in Moscow, the negative factors may have the effect of increasing the value in Soviet eyes of conducting military interventions through proxy forces and thus prompting the USSR to rely on this instrument whenever possible in future interventions. Another effect may be to counsel more-effective setting up of the political prerequisites for intervention so as to preserve the appearance of responding to a properly legitimate invitation rather than to a transparently phony one as in the Afghanistan case.

As Harry Gelman pointed out, however, if the Soviets ultimately judge the benefits of the Afghanistan experience to have been worth the long-term costs, the fact that they invaded without a genuine invitation may embolden them to intervene elsewhere in the Third World.[18] Gelman reasons as follows: Until Afghanistan, appeals for intervention and support from a varied list of Third World clients, including Le Duan, Nasser, Sadat, Assad, Neto, and Mengistu, had been genuine, and it had not been necessary to stage thinly disguised coups with little local support so as to elicit such invitations. In effect, although the Soviets might attempt to nudge history a bit, they did not necessarily blatantly disregard the classical Marxist-Leninist precept that forcible action be keyed to the ripening of a revolutionary situation.

Thus, one implication of a successful Afghanistan invasion and coup may be that the Soviet leaders will find themselves less disposed than before to stand by until coups materialize objectively and rather more tempted to stimulate them artificially in Third World settings within geographic range of effective Soviet power-projection capabilities. Third World countries within this range and experiencing internal instability may, in other words, be considered open to the danger of intervention.

Such a trend of Soviet behavior might further be said to be reinforced by a perception on the part of the Soviet leaders that what they call the correlation of forces during the past decade has turned in their favor and that boldness in action can bring notable rewards. If this is the case, Afghanistan may prove to be the watershed separating an era of relatively cautious Soviet approach to Third World conflict situations from one marked by a distinctly bolder approach.

14 Future Soviet Involvement in the Third World

Having surveyed the patterns of past Soviet behavior, we now turn to the future and begin by reviewing some of the trends and other factors that may work for as well as against an increased Soviet activism and influence in the Third World.

Trends Suggesting Increased Soviet Activism

Changes in the Correlation of Forces

Improvements in Soviet force-projection capabilities, together with changes in the strategic and theater military balances and the other factors affecting what the Soviets call the worldwide correlation of forces, represent trends that may alter Soviet risk perceptions and lead to more-assertive behavior in the Third World. The Soviets hold that the correlation of forces is changing in their favor, and a major imponderable is whether they will continue to believe and, more important, increasingly act on this assumption. Moscow's behavior has in certain past Third World crises been constrained by its perceptions of the prevailing U.S.-Soviet military balance and by the concern that bolder actions on the USSR's part might lead to unwanted war with the United States.[1] However, one cannot be certain that Soviet restraint and caution will prevail in the future, particularly if the USSR were to come to believe that changes in the strategic and theater military balances to the Soviet advantage would serve to constrain U.S. response options and provide the Soviets an umbrella for more-assertive actions in the Third World.

Increased Force-Projection Capabilities

During the past two decades, the Soviets have made significant improvements in their capabilities to project military power to Third World areas, and these improvements have broadened the USSR's global military-political options. Among other capabilities, this enhancement program has produced highly ready airborne divisions with expanded mobile combat power and an improved ability to conduct independent operations; a military airlift capability that has undergone a fifty percent improvement in range and

163

payload since 1965; a major growth in Soviet out-of-area blue-water naval operations and an enlarged amphibious fleet (improved in capacity, range, sustainability, and time on station); a merchant marine that has been modernized and expanded to provide a major capability for rapid, long-distance movement of military assistance or military forces for speedy debarkation at unimproved port facilities; and fighter aircraft with improved ranges and payloads, able to operate with a minimum of ground-support equipment and to be ferried by air or delivered by carrier or container ship to many potential target areas.

Experience and Infrastructure

Through military- and economic-aid programs, the Soviets have accumulated a body of experience and infrastructure to facilitate not only the further penetration of Soviet influence in the Third World but also to extend the overseas reach and flexibility of the Soviet armed forces. While Third World states normally have been reluctant to provide the Soviets formal base rights, a number of recipients of Soviet military assistance grant Soviet forces use of their facilities when the need arises. The Soviet and Cuban intervention in Angola, for example, was made possible because the Congo was available as a secure rear base for those operations. Similarly, the communist intervention in Ethiopia was importantly facilitated by the availability of staging areas in South Yemen and Angola. Moreover, the potential availability of forward-positioned weapon stockpiles, such as the very large armored vehicle and aircraft inventories now stored in Libya, provides the Soviets with additional options should a beleaguered client require rapid logistic support in a nearby Third World conflict.[2] Military equipment acquired by some Third World states from the USSR has already been transferred to other clients that Moscow deemed in need of immediate reinforcement. Both Libya and South Yemen, for example, transferred Soviet-made weapons to Ethiopia in 1977.[3]

Cooperative Intervention

The innovative trend of the latter 1970s toward cooperative intervention with the Cubans—combining Soviet logistic, lift, and communications contributions with Cuban combat forces—places at Soviet disposal an instrument with further potential for intervening in selected situations before effective outside opposition can be mobilized and brought to bear. In this connection, it is pertinent that Cuban forces experienced in battle and in operating with indigenous Third World troops are positioned in numbers in the Horn and southern Africa where they could be moved into other conflict arenas on short notice. Recall the reported airlift of Cuban forces from Ethiopia to Aden in response to Saudi Arabia's military alert and partial mobilization during the 1979 conflict between South Yemen and North Yemen.[4]

Rising Radicalism and Persistent Third World Instabilities

The radicalism increasingly evident in many parts of the Third World, although not created by the Soviets, constitutes a political trend the USSR can comfortably encourage and exploit to the West's disadvantage.[5] The persistence of endemic political instabilities, ethnic and social conflicts, and grievous economic and population pressures in Third World states also serve to breed continued opportunities for Soviet exploitation and expansion.

The Validation of Soviet Great-Power Credentials

Finally, the Soviet policies and interventions that, in several important instances, have helped to shape the outcome of Third World conflicts to the advantage of Soviet clients have served to validate the USSR's credentials as a superpower patron to which other states or ambitious coup-minded military officers can turn for future help in resolving local or regional struggles for power. Furthermore, the USSR's growing military power and demonstrated willingness to employ force has increased Moscow's capacity to intimidate militarily vulnerable states and has fostered a greater reluctance on the part of some Third World nations to defy Soviet interests actively.

Potential Constraints on Greater Soviet Activism

U.S. Policies and Actions to Check the Soviets

Moscow's interest in avoiding military confrontation with the United States, preserving some form of East-West détente, discouraging Western rearmament, and warding off economic and political reprisals may in varying degrees serve to restrain future Soviet behavior in the Third World. The effectiveness of such constraints, however, will depend on the extent to which the United States may be perceived by the Soviets as resolved to commit and capable of committing its power and other resources to check their freedom of action.

Domestic Instability and Capriciousness of
Soviet Clients

The vulnerability of Third World governments to leadership coups and the propensity of such regimes to sudden policy shifts create important uncertainties for Moscow about the permanence of Soviet influence in many Third World states. Because of this inherent volatility, the Soviets have experienced considerable frustration in their attempts to forge a lasting network of reliable client states in the Third World. Egypt, Indonesia, Ghana, Guinea, Nigeria, Somalia, and Iraq are among examples of assiduously courted Third World countries that have proved intractable or unreliable in various measure. Cuba, Angola, Ethiopia, South Yemen, Afghanistan, and Vietnam, however, may prove more reliable over the longer run because of their heavy military and/or economic dependence on the USSR and because of the strong political and ideological orientation of their present regimes toward Moscow. However, the longer-term constancy of even some of these states may be uncertain. The Soviets seem uneasy, for example, about the future reliability of Ethiopia and consequently have pressed the Ethiopian government to institutionalize Marxist rule in that country through the creation of a mass party.[6]

Divergent Interests

The recognition by Third World states that their fundamental national interests diverge in important respects from those of the USSR may further constrain future Soviet involvements in the Third World. Indeed, much of the Third World manifests a healthy suspicion of Soviet motives, a suspicion that has been exacerbated by the recent Soviet actions in Afghanistan. Although economic ties between the Third World and the Soviet bloc have increased, the Soviets by no means have managed to preempt the economies of most Third World states. These states, by and large, continue to rely on the West for trade, investments, and technological assistance, areas in which Moscow cannot compete effectively or advantageously with the West. Over the years, a number of Third World states have become disenchanted with Soviet subversion and meddling, the arrogance and heavy-handedness of Soviet advisory personnel, and Moscow's propensity to engage in inequitable economic practices, a habit particularly manifest in the Soviet rapacious exploitation of local Third World fishery resources.[7] Many states also have been disappointed with the quality and magnitude of Soviet economic assistance and, in some cases, with Moscow's military assistance as well.[8]

Having to Take Sides in Local Conflicts

Regional and local conflicts in the Third World, which may place the USSR in the cross fire of ethnic, religious, and nationalist quarrels, inhibit Soviet policy, limit the Soviets' room for maneuver, and sometimes force Moscow to choose one set of interests over another. Support for one party in such disputes often means the alienation of another—as was the case in the Ethiopia-Somalia conflict.

National Sensitivities and Regional
Organization Ground Rules

The reluctance of some Third World recipients of Soviet aid to become overly dependent on Moscow and their fear of being drawn into East-West conflicts or of losing their nonaligned image by granting bases to the USSR also serve to constrain Soviet activities to some degree, as do the ground rules of regional organizations like the OAU, which emphasizes the sanctity of established borders and seeks to discourage great-power involvement in African affairs.

Constraints on the Use of Surrogates

Limits on the use of surrogate combat forces because of difficulties of geographic access, differences in the character of the opposition, and other factors impose potential constraints on Soviet intervention decisions. For example, while superior Soviet weaponry and Cuban troops have demonstrated a capability to dominate the battlefield against second- and third-rate opposition, there remains a serious question about how well the Cubans would do against more-competent opponents. Another constraining factor is Havana's capacity to absorb the political costs of significant military casualties in foreign interventions. As long as the potential targets of intervention are soft—that is, have small and poorly trained armed forces that easily can be overcome—the latter problem probably would not become a major constraint.

Potential Economic Considerations

Economic costs of Soviet Third World aid, while not a compelling constraint in the past, may be unpopular enough internally to mar consensual agreement among the Soviet leadership elite for support of large, new Third World undertakings, especially where marginal political, military, and economic returns may be in prospect.

Possible Patterns of Future Soviet Behavior

Any discussion of future Soviet behavior must, of course, be speculative in that Moscow's actions will be conditioned importantly by calculations of the possible benefits and risks of differing situations and by the nature of the opportunities it will confront. One possibility, and one to which we are inclined to adhere, is that the basic behavior patterns of the past will continue, much along the already established lines. In this event, Soviet behavior may be expected to exhibit the same elements of assertive opportunism combined with caution as before and to remain low cost and low profile where possible.

A continuation of past patterns would also suggest that future Soviet involvement and support of other external communist intervention in Third World conflict situations would be more likely to occur in circumstances when the USSR:

> Intervenes in response to a request from a local government or some arguably legitimate (in Third World eyes) political entity;

> Perceives the risk of direct military confrontation with the United States to be low because of a lack of vital U.S. interests or commitments, existing political constraints, or an absence of viable U.S. response options;

> Calculates that it can hedge or tailor its commitment and involvement so as to keep the initial risks low and controllable in situations where U.S. interests are engaged and the U.S. response is uncertain;

> Has had the opportunity to conduct on-the-spot assessments of the local balance of forces and prevailing battlefield situation and has determined that outside intervention has a good prospect of achieving immediate military objectives;

> Can keep its own direct combat role limited, circumspect, and/or temporary and thus reduce the risks of adverse reactions from Western and Third World states and avoid creating a justification for possible U.S. counteraction;

> Has access to the necessary base and transit infrastructure to support the outside intervention logistically, preferably including a proximate rear base in a neighboring country from which to stage resupply operations.

Continuation of Already Established Activities

Should established patterns persist, we may expect to see the following activities.

Arms Transfers. The USSR did not reciprocate the Carter administration's policy of exercising restraint in arms sales to Third World countries. Because the Soviets view military assistance as a major vehicle for establishing and maintaining their influence with Third World states, as well as an increasingly important source of hard-currency earnings, they may be expected to push for additional arms-transfer arrangements (including of more-sophisticated and -expensive weapons) with existing clients and usually will prove willing to fill any vacuum presented by U.S. or other Western refusals to satisfy arms requests from Third World countries. Given the overriding importance of arms transfers to Soviet Third World policy, it seems unlikely that the USSR will accept any meaningful restraints (for example, in future conventional arms-transfer negotiations) on its freedom to continue to exploit this instrument in the years ahead.[9]

Acquisition of Additional Basing and Overflight Arrangements. In keeping with their objective of expanding the geographic reach of their armed forces, the Soviets may be expected to continue to press for additional Third World basing and overflight arrangements and for the relaxation of host-government operational constraints (like the requirement for prior notification of use) covering some of their existing agreements. The Soviets' interest in acquiring the use of additional facilities derives from the need to support the growing peacetime deployments and surveillance activities of Soviet naval and air forces, the desire to broaden their military options for meeting differing contingencies, and their uncertainty about the long-term reliability of some of their existing arrangements.

As a hedge against future requirements along these lines, Moscow will continue to invest modestly in upgrading potentially useful facilities (such as the extension and improvement of airfields) in friendly Third World states and will attempt to use the leverage of its military assistance to secure naval and air privileges in other strategically located states.

Support of Selected National Liberation Movements. We may expect to see continued Soviet arms-supply and training support for guerrilla movements conducting so-called wars of national liberation, especially in Africa (for example, SWAPO against Namibia and the African National Congress against South Africa). Such support may be rendered increasingly through a division of labor with Warsaw Pact countries, Cuba, and a few other Soviet-oriented Third World states such as South Yemen and Ethiopia. Cuba will continue to provide training and arms support to various revolutionary movements in Central and South America such as El Salvador, Guatemala, and Colombia and covert support to leftist groups in the economically and politically vulnerable states of the Caribbean area. In the event that any of these movements were to succeed to the point where its takeover of power appeared imminent, external communist support could be expected to escalate (as was the case with the Cubans in Nicaragua) to assure total victory.

Support of New, "Progressive" Regimes Produced by Internal Coups and Uprisings. The Soviets may be expected to move promptly when requested by a legitimate entity to support favorable changes of regimes (with arms, advisers, and diplomacy)—for example, if a pro-Western or neutral Third World government were to be overthrown by an internal coup or uprising. Indeed, the Soviets may become more disposed than has been the case in the past to stimulate such coups with covert organizational assistance and assurances of immediate backing once power has been seized. Soviet action might include cooperative intervention using Cubans or perhaps other combat surrogates to help sustain such new governments in power. As long as surrogate troops were available and such interventions were to go essentially unopposed by competent outside forces, the Soviet leadership would have no reason to feel compelled to risk confrontation with the United States by introducing its own combat forces.

Low-Risk Probes. Soviet sanctioning of occasional low-risk and limited probes by Third World clients against neighboring states—for example, South Yemen's brief incursion into North Yemen in early 1979—can be expected to continue, particularly when Moscow can plausibly deny its own involvement. The Soviets will be less likely, however, to underwrite more-ambitious military adventures by their clients, like South Yemen's full-scale invasion of North Yemen, because of the risks of escalation and possible U.S. involvement.

Actions to Forestall the Reorientation of Regimes Closely Tied to Moscow. The Soviets appear anxious to hold on to the positions they have so far secured in the Third World and to prevent further setbacks such as those in Somalia and Egypt. Thus, in countries where external communist forces are already present, these forces may be expected to intervene when necessary and feasible to protect a favored government from overthrow by internal rivals or to assist in the unseating of a regime attempting to move out of the Soviet orbit.

The coup that unseated President Salim Rubai Ali of South Yemen in June 1978 seems at least in part to have been a reflection of this defensive policy. Prior to his overthrow, Rubai Ali was attempting to move South Yemen toward a closer accommodation with Saudi Arabia and North Yemen and away from excessive dependence on the USSR. That Moscow had reason to replace the increasingly unreliable Rubai Ali regime with a more staunchly pro-Soviet leadership and that Rubai Ali's ouster was largely engineered by South Yemen's Cuban-trained militia and air force strongly indicated a measure of Soviet and Cuban foreknowledge and involvement in the coup.[10]

Protection of Clients Threatened with Catastrophic Defeat. Moscow will be most inclined to threaten or actually to render direct combat assistance to important Third World clients in conflict situations of dire necessity—namely, when the client faces the loss of its capital city or the destruction of its military forces or, if the client is a Marxist regime, when it faces the loss of political control within the country. Thus, one may expect vigorous Soviet responses (including military) in the event Israeli forces were to move on Damascus in the course of another Middle East conflict or if a renewed Sino-Vietnamese conflict were to threaten a Chinese drive on Hanoi.

These various activities should not be construed as benign from the standpoint of U.S. interests since they would encompass actions similar to what has already been seen in Afghanistan, Angola, Ethiopia, South Yemen, and Vietnam. Indeed, several of these activities might involve the use of Cuban or other surrogate forces. However, to minimize risks of confrontation with the United States and to refurbish their political standing with the Third World and preserve elements of the East-West relationship, the Soviets will seek in the conduct of these activities to maintain a low profile in terms of their own direct military role and will be more inclined to act when they can count on political support from at least portions of their Third World constituency.

New Activities and More-Assertive Behavior

Significant modifications of Soviet risk perceptions might, however, lead to more-aggressive Soviet behavior. If, as noted before, the Soviets perceived increasingly favorable changes in the worldwide correlation of forces and if, for example, they perceived U.S. response options to be militarily or otherwise constrained, they might be encouraged to act more assertively in the Third World.[11] Certainly the Soviet invasion of Afghanistan has raised questions in the minds of many observers as to whether this may presage a new, more-adventurist phase of Soviet activity. Specific Soviet moves in the Third World cannot, of course, be predicted, but some examples of the types of contingencies where Soviet clients, or the Soviets themselves, might exhibit less restraint can be suggested.

Actions Involving Sanctuaries. We may see, for example, bolder communist actions to deal with one or more of the external sanctuaries that support continued resistance to Soviet clients in Africa and Asia. Such actions might include hot pursuit or even more-threatening cross-border air and ground operations by the Vietnamese against Thailand, by the Ethiopians against Somalia, or by the Soviets against Pakistan. Limited attacks have already taken place across the borders of each of these sanctuary states[12]; if the insurgents they now harbor should prove increasingly troublesome or receive substantially greater local-government support, more-serious counteractions might follow. These might involve a communist occupation of a portion of the host country's territory to seal off and eliminate guerrilla bases or an invasion thrust aimed at intimidating the sanctuary government into ceasing all further succor to the insurgents.[13]

The Soviets or Cubans could also be drawn into a greater involvement through the need to defend the sanctuary status of one of their own clients whose territory is being used as a base for insurgent operations against a neighboring state. One such case might arise if efforts to achieve a political settlement in Namibia were to break down and the South Africans were to intensify greatly or broaden their punitive and spoiling attacks against SWAPO's Angolan base areas.

Direct Action to Effect Political Change in Third World States. The Soviets may also find some opportunities too tempting to resist. One must admit, for example, the uncertainty of whether the Soviets will, over the long run, eschew the temptation to bring about political change by direct military intervention in a border state as turbulent, militarily vulnerable, and oil rich as Iran. The potential geostrategic benefits accruing to the USSR from a Soviet-dominated Iran—particularly with respect to the leverage that domination might provide for controlling Western and Japanese access to Persian Gulf oil—must be evident to Moscow.

At the same time, the USSR must realize that the very importance of the Gulf to the West increases the risks of a U.S. countermilitary action to any direct Soviet intervention in Iran. A Soviet invasion under existing circumstances would have other major drawbacks as well. Moscow would again face the specter of continuing, widespread guerrilla resistance, impeding reliable Soviet access to Iranian oil supplies, and the USSR would be forced to garrison and administer a country where its indigenous base of support would probably be even smaller than it is now in Afghanistan.

Because of the risks of provoking direct military confrontation with the United States and because Moscow would want to avoid premature actions that might harm its longer-term prospects in Iran, the Soviets may well be content to sit back and await the outcome of the political fermentation now in process, hoping that events will eventually bring to power a regime that would invite their support and be drawn increasingly into Moscow's orbit. The Soviet-backed Tudeh party and the other extreme Marxist factions in Iran are still comparatively weak, however, and their rise to eventual political control is, at best, uncertain.[14] This consideration, along with the opportunities that may unfold if the turbulence in Iran intensifies (say, in connection with the demand for autonomy by various ethnic groups, some of which are reportedly receiving clandestine assistance from the USSR[15]), might impel the Soviets to adopt a more-active role and conceivably even move forces into that country under the pretext of some local invitation or the need to defend the security of the Soviet state.[16]

Efforts to Deter or Counter U.S. Intervention. It is also uncertain how the Soviets might react to a U.S. military intervention in a Third World conflict, particularly in an area of strategic sensitivity to the USSR. Soviet doctrine has given increasing emphasis to the important role of the Soviet military in "resisting imperalist aggression" in the Third World, and favorable assessments of the evolving balance of forces could lead Moscow to assert itself to deter or counter such U.S. intervention. Iran might constitute one such strategically sensitive area, particularly because the 1921 Soviet-Iranian treaty (which Moscow repeatedly has refused to amend or see abrogated) gives the Soviets the right to intervene should a third country pursue a "policy of transgression" in Iran or use that country's territory as a base for possible military attacks against the USSR.[17]

15 Influencing Soviet Risk Perceptions and Other U.S. Responses

Given the spectrum of possible future challenges in the Third World, the United States will require an inventory of military and political response options that can be tailored to meet the requirements and particular context of differing situations.[1] Although we have not attempted to address such options in any comprehensive manner, say with regard to U.S. force postures or deployments, which lie beyond the scope of this study, our examination of past communist behavior and patterns of U.S.-Soviet interaction suggest several implications for future U.S. policy and practice.

Demonstrate U.S. Interests Early and Convincingly

The Soviet risk calculus in any future Third World conflict will be conditioned importantly by Moscow's perceptions of the degree of U.S. interest and commitment, comparative military capabilities, and the credibility of possible U.S. response options. Normally, the Soviets have been inclined to move where they have perceived U.S. interests to be low, commitments to be absent, or response options to be politically or militarily constrained. However, there have been important cases of Soviet miscalculations in this regard. In sanctioning the 1950 North Korean invasion of South Korea, for example, Moscow erroneously calculated that the attack would be a low-risk venture, believing that "Washington had neither the intention nor the capability for opposing a strong North Korean attack."[2]

One can conceive of some future challenge in a Third World country in which the United States may not have a strong intrinsic interest. This apparent lack of U.S. interest might lead the USSR leadership to assess possible Soviet intervention there as low risk. However, once that country becomes a likely target of Soviet intervention, the United States may be said to acquire a derivative interest in it—if only to forestall the cumulative accretion of Soviet influence in one Third World area after another. Such a derivative interest was acquired in Angola, where the United States became covertly engaged only after a significant Soviet involvement was discerned.[3]

To reduce the risk of a future Soviet miscalculation, the United States must define and articulate its interest in situations of potential intervention at the earliest point possible—and convince Moscow of its interest—before the Soviets acquire an investment and commitment that is difficult to reverse.

The credibility of any such U.S. diplomatic signals to the USSR would, of course, depend importantly on Moscow's perceptions of existing U.S. military capabilities and political resolve. Such signals would be enhanced if accompanied by appropriate U.S. preparatory military moves; efforts by administration officials to mobilize public support for possible U.S. counteractions, should the need for counteraction arise; and active support from the Congress to underline U.S. determination to resist any Soviet intervention.

Maintain Credibility of Possible U.S. Escalation

A second point regarding risk calculations concerns Soviet perceptions of U.S. willingness to escalate. Experience has shown that the Soviets have tended to move incrementally and cautiously in situations that might produce a direct military confrontation with the United States, in large part because they fear that such a confrontation may escalate to the use of nuclear weapons.[4] The United States should not relieve the Soviets of their anxieties in this regard; indeed, it must in some situations reinforce Soviet fears concerning the possible dangers of escalation, particularly where the United States may see it in its vital interests to deploy limited combat or trip-wire forces to areas where the Soviets or their clients possess a significant comparative advantage in conventional intervention capabilities. In situations where the United States is conventionally weaker, the most important deterrent to Soviet counteraction may be Moscow's perception of Washington's resolve to escalate in order to protect U.S. forces and vital interests.

Recognize Limitations of Linkage

While the threat of possible Western political and economic reprisals may constrain future Soviet behavior to some degree, it is doubtful that the instrument of linkage,[5] given the record to date, will itself deter the Soviets from attempting to exploit many Third World opportunities in the future. Even the clear-cut case of Afghanistan has pointed up the difficulties of organizing other governments to join with the United States in punitive responses when such governments have important foreign-policy interests or influential domestic constituencies with major investments in continued relations with Moscow. Punitive responses are even more difficult to organize in more-ambiguous situations (such as was the case in Ethiopia or Angola) where world opinion may be divided as to the significance and justification of the external communist intervention.

Moreover, when it comes to fundamental issues to the Soviets such as sustaining Marxist regimes in power or supporting certain wars of national liberation, the USSR and other communist states have over the years demonstrated a willingness to subordinate goodwill and prospects for improved relations with the West to these more-important (to them) immediate objectives, in part because they have been conditioned to believe that adverse political and economic repercussions will be of limited duration and/or magnitude. Thus the Soviets adamantaly refused to consider cutting back their arms support to North Vietnam in return for proffered improvements in U.S.-Soviet relations, and Havana has been quite willing to sacrifice progress toward the normalization of relations with the United States for its self-styled revolutionary obligation to assist insurgencies in Central America and Marxist regimes in Angola and Ethiopia.[6] Similarly, Hanoi has demonstrated its willingness to undercut its developing economic and political relations with Japan and the Association of Southeast Asian Nations (ASEAN) states, as well as normalization with the United States, to pursue the more-fundamental goal of controlling all of former Indochina by invading and overthrowing the Pol Pot regime in Cambodia.

Emphasize Crisis Management and Anticipatory Involvement

Third World contingencies that have proved particularly difficult to deal with after the fact are those in which an indigenous coup or revolution (in some cases without direct Soviet or Cuban assistance) brings to power a Marxist regime that, for reasons of ideological affinity or sustaining itself in power, invites in the Soviets or some other external communist force. The presence of a Cuban garrison, or a Soviet occupation force in the case of Afghanistan, and the imposition of ruthless internal-security measures (of late a special responsibility of East German advisory missions to Third World countries) foreclose the opportunity for future political change in the country.

Once in power, a Soviet-backed Marxist regime is difficult to dislodge—at least that has been the experience to date. Moreover, to the extent that such a regime must depend on outside communist support against internal and external enemies to remain in power, it is equally difficult to wean away from the USSR. Given the trend toward radicalism in the Third World and the evident vulnerability of some countries to internal political upheaval, separatist centrifugal forces, and the like, there will remain a persistent threat that additional Third World states may in time move into the Soviet orbit by this path.

One implication of the continued volatility of the Third World is that the U.S. policy and intelligence community must be better prepared than it has been in the past to manage the unique challenges presented by Third World countries already in the throes of internal conflict and upheaval. In such situations, there are sometimes opportunity windows, though perhaps of only brief duration, when the United States may have the chance to influence the course and direction of revolutionary change (for example, by actively backing outcomes that prevent radical extremists from seizing power) or otherwise moderate the impact of the internal political transformation. Critics of U.S. policies during the Nicaraguan and Iranian revolutions contend that Washington missed important opportunities to influence the course of events in those countries through a failure to assess correctly the dynamics of the local situations and through the application of ill-timed or counterproductive policies.[7]

Accurate and timely intelligence is vital to the design of effective diplomatic or military responses to such situations. For example, Washington policymakers seemed to have operated at a disadvantage during much of the Angolan conflict because of shortcomings in U.S. intelligence judgments concerning the USSR, Cuba, South Africa, and Angola.[8] These deficiencies contributed to misestimates of the levels and objectives of the external communist involvement in Angola and the likely efficacy of possible U.S. courses of action. The Ford administration's passive diplomatic reaction to the Soviet arms buildup and fighting in Angola during the first half of 1975 was attributable in large part to a failure to assess correctly Soviet and MPLA intentions in that country.[9] Misperceptions of the degree of Soviet commitment to an MPLA victory in Angola also seem to have encouraged Washington's erroneous hope in July 1975 that limited U.S. covert support of the FNLA and UNITA might persuade the Soviets to scale down their intervention without an open confrontation.

However, beyond better crisis-management capabilities lies a more-fundamental requirement for the United States and its allies in the years ahead: to design and sustain over the long term coherent policies and programs that will help to strengthen the political, economic, and military institutions of Third World states so as to reduce their vulnerability to such adverse internal political change. This type of anticipatory involvement is admittedly a complex and difficult task,[10] one at which the United States has not always proved adept and in which its influence is often limited, but it is an essential component of countering Soviet expansionism in the Third World.

Such anticipatory involvement will require, among other things, consistent focus on how U.S. military assistance and advisory programs can be best tailored to strengthen the capability, competence, and reliability of Third World military establishments, which more often than not are the final arbiters of their countries' domestic- and foreign-policy orientations.

The United States must adopt arms-transfer policies that are sufficiently flexible to meet the legitimate external-defense and internal-security requirements of Third World states seeking U.S. assistance. Along with providing military hardware and technical training, the United States and its allies must also use their influence and military aid to encourage the reform of patently vulnerable Third World military establishments by supporting programs that upgrade the quality of leadership and discipline in such forces, strengthen the popular base of the military within the country, and improve the living conditions of the rank-and-file, where necessary. Among the key events that triggered the revolution that brought Haile Selassie down and a Marxist government to power in Ethiopia were a series of military mutinies by enlisted men, noncommissioned officers, and junior officers who were protesting the gross inadequacies in their pay, food, water supplies, and other living conditions.[11] Similarly, the principal factor behind the European and African interventions in Zaire in 1977 and 1978 to contain Katangan incursions was the poor discipline and morale of Zairian army troops in the Shaba area, troops whose motivation and discipline had been undermined because they were apparently not paid regularly, fed properly, housed adequately, or led well.[12]

To the extent that Soviet policy in the Third World remains opportunistic, the United States will continue to be challenged to find ways to foreclose Soviet opportunities.

Appendix A
Chronology of Soviet
Third World Policy,
1917-1945

December 1917

Immediately after the Bolsheviks came to power, the Soviet government called on Persians, Turks, Arabs, Hindus, and other peoples of the East to overthrow their imperialist rulers. The policy they adopted—embodied in Lenin's and Stalin's famous appeal of December 5, 1919, "To All the Toiling Muslims of Russia and the East"—was aimed at supporting ultra-left-wing radical movements in the colonies.

July 1920

The Second Congress of the Comintern—Africa, incidentally, was not represented—took up the colonial question. Lenin argued that "all communist parties must give active support to revolutionary movements of liberation," while M.N. Roy of India argued against communist cooperation with nationalists. This issue was to recur in Soviet Third World policy deliberations for the next sixty years.

Lenin departed from Marxian doctrine on several points. First, he said that a proletarian revolution could not triumph without the help of peasant revolutionary movements in colonial states. Second, he said that a backward nation could skip the entire capitalist stage of economic development and proceed immediately to socialism through the use of state power, thus freeing the communist movement from the Marxist laws of economic development.

Lenin's underlying rationale is illustrated by the much-quoted line from his last article, "Luchshe menshe, da luchshe": "In the last analysis, the outcome [of revolutionary struggle] will be determined by the fact that Russia, India, China, and so forth, account for the overwhelming majority of the globe."

The chronology draws on the following accounts, among others: Alvin Z. Rubinstein, *The Foreign Policy of the Soviet Union* (New York: Random House, 1960); Roger E. Kanet, ed., *The Soviet Union and the Developing Nations* (Baltimore: Johns Hopkins University Press, 1974); Franz Borkenau, *World Communism* (Ann Arbor: University of Michigan Press, 1962); Jane Degras, ed., *The Communist International, 1919-1943: Documents* (London: Oxford University Press, 1956); Adam Ulam, *Expansion and Coexistence: The History of Soviet Foreign Policy, 1917-67* (New York: Frederick A. Praeger, 1968); and Lt. Colonel N. Larichev, "Fulfilling Internationalist Duty," *Soviet Military Review*, March 1980, pp. 46-48.

September 1920

The Congress of Peoples of the East, attended by some 1,891 delegates, took place in Baku. The Soviets (Zinoviev) urged toilers "living in Asia and Africa" to follow the European proletariat, saying: "We must conquer or perish together." The Baku conference created a "League for Liberation of the East," but it accomplished little.

1921-1926

This period was characterized by the NEP at home (1921-1923) and united front abroad, while the USSR sought a modus vivendi or, at least, temporary coexistence with the capitalist world. The Soviets began to moderate their support of more-radical revolutionary movements abroad, a policy that had been followed from 1917 to 1920, and Comintern interest in the colonial question in Asia decreased. At the Comintern congresses of 1922 and 1924, Asian delegates criticized the lack of attention to colonial states.

Soviet policy now called for a united front with social democrats in Europe and more-limited activity in colonial areas. The Comintern told Asian communists to cooperate with all types of nationalist movements.

1927-1928

The Comintern abruptly shifted to a militant line in this period. Abandoning the strategy of a united front from above—that is, communist collaboration with bourgeois-nationalist groups—the Comintern called for the development of communist parties in colonial areas, holding that only communists could lead national-liberation movements. Sanctioned by the Sixth Comintern Congress in 1928, this new program was the clearest statement of communist aims between the 1848 Manifesto and Zhdanov's 1947 Cominform speech. The 1928 Comintern ultrarevolutionary line, called "united front from below," reflected internal Soviet politics; it was used by Stalin against Bukharin, who was identified with the previous more-moderate line. This leftist, anticapitalist strategy remained in effect until 1935, when the Comintern adopted the popular-front tactic.

After 1928, and especially during the 1935-1945 period, Stalin pursued a moderate policy in underdeveloped areas, showing more interest in manipulating foreign communist parties to consolidate his own political position in the USSR and to maximize the long-term Soviet power position in international affairs than in spreading social revolution worldwide.

1930

The International Trade Union Committee of Negro Workers was set up in Hamburg under George Padmore to promote and coordinate revolutionary activity in Africa and the West Indies. However, with the coming of the popular front in 1935 and the shift from revolutionary agitation to collaboration, the USSR lost interest in the so-called Negro international.

1935

The establishment of the popular front in 1935 marked a return to cooperation with bourgeois-nationalist parties in underdeveloped countries and collaboration with the colonial powers themselves—as the threat of fascism grew. Soviet protests against Mussolini's invasion of Ethiopia in 1935 helped the USSR's anti-imperialist image, although at the same time the USSR tried to cement collective-security arrangements with the United Kingdom and France and did not cut off its substantial oil deliveries to Italy.

1936

During the Spanish Civil War (1936-1939), the USSR aided the left-wing Loyalist government against the Franco rebels backed by Germany and Italy.

1939-1945

During World War II, the Soviets showed little interest in support of liberation movements in underdeveloped countries. Interesting example: In 1943, the USSR urged the immediate solution of labor problems in Rhodesia in order to expedite maximum production of copper to support the war effort against the Axis powers. There was no reference to the rights and working conditions of Africans.

1945

Despite the crumbling of colonial empires and the widespread rise of nationalism in the postwar Third World, Stalin was slow to exploit the political opportunities presented by the postwar situation.

Appendix B
Chronology of Soviet
Military Aid and
Intervention, 1919-1945

1919

During the postrevolution civil war in Russia, Red Army units in the Ukraine were ordered to Hungary in March 1919 to aid the Bela Kun revolution. However, before the orders could be carried out, the situation in Russia worsened, and this first Soviet intervention abroad was abandoned.

1920

The Bolsheviks launched an unsuccessful invasion of Poland, after which Lenin reportedly told Trotsky that Red Army troops should never again be used directly to aid a revolution abroad.

In Iran, the Red Army supported a provincial rebellion that set up the Soviet Republic of Gilan and provided it with arms and military advisers. However, local communist dissension led the Red Army to withdraw in 1921, per a treaty concluded with Iran, and the Gilan Republic came to an end.

1921

The Red Army helped to establish communist rule in Georgia.

In Outer Mongolia, the Red Army set up the Mongolian People's Government, after a shadow government that requested Soviet military assistance had been established on Soviet soil. Outer Mongolia thus became the USSR's first satellite communist regime.

Also in 1921, by a similar arrangement, the Red Army helped set up the People's Republic of Tannu Tuva. In both cases, this meant restoring Russian protectorates of 1912-1917, now under Soviet auspices.

This chronology draws on the following sources, among others: Raymond L. Garthoff, "Military Influences and Instruments," in *Russian Foreign Policy: Essays in Historical Perspective*, ed. Ivo J. Lederer (New Haven: Yale University Press, 1962); Louis Fischer, *The Soviets in World Affairs*, vols. 1 and 2 (Princeton, N.J.: Princeton University Press, 1951); Roger E. Kanet, ed., *The Soviet Union and the Developing Nations* (Baltimore: Johns Hopkins University Press, 1974); Ivar Spector, *The Soviet Union and the Muslim World, 1917-1953* (Seattle: University of Washington Press, 1959); Walter Krivitsky, *In Stalin's Secret Service* (New York: Harper, 1939); and Lt. Colonel N. Larichev, "Fulfilling Internationalist Duty," *Soviet Military Review*, March 1980, pp. 46-48.

Military aid (arms, money, advisers) was furnished to Turkish rebels under Kemal, at the latter's request.

1923

The USSR provided military advisers and money to the Kuomintang after Sun Yat-sen sent Chiang Kai-shek to Moscow in 1923. Borodin and Galen, the top Soviet military advisers, and their staffs were withdrawn after Chiang's coups d'etat against communists in the Kuomintang in 1926-1927. Parallel Soviet military aid (mainly advisers) also was given to the northern warlords, Generals Fang Yu-hsiang and Kuo Sun-lin, in 1923-1925.

1931

The USSR signed a secret agreement to give military assistance to Chin Shu-jen, provincial governor of Sinkiang.

1933

The USSR reaffirmed the 1931 agreement with General Sheng Shih-ts'ai, Sinkiang's ruler from 1933-1943.

1934

At Sheng's request, the Soviets provided two brigades of troops of the People's Commissariat of Internal Affairs (NKVD) and combat air support to fight against other Chinese warlords. Soviet military aid to Sheng continued until 1942, when Sheng shifted allegiance to the Chungking government. During the late 1930s, the Soviets built an aircraft assembly plant at Urumchi and an aviation school at Kuldzha. Aircraft built at Kuldzha and Soviet flyers trained there helped the Chinese nationalists in 1937-1941.

The Soviets ordered two divisions to Afghanistan to aid pro-Soviet Emir Amanullah, but Amanullah was defeated before Soviet troops got to Afghanistan.

1936

Soviet aid to Loyalists in Spain involved clandestine Soviet support of the International Brigade (Western, but not Soviet, communists were allowed to join). The Soviet mission, headed by General Berzin, included 2,000 Red Army advisers and specialists, as well as weapons (including tanks and aircraft), which were tested in the Spanish conflict against German materiel.

1937-1941

Soviet military aid (including 885 aircraft and 200 "volunteer" pilots) was furnished to Chinese nationalists against the Japanese.

1938-1939

Soviet forces were employed against the Japanese in disputed territory along Soviet-Korean border (1938) and in Outer Mongolia (1939), where large-scale fighting developed.

1939-1940

The Soviet winter war against Finland occurred.

1940

The Red Army moved unopposed into the Baltic states and Bessarabia.

1941-1945

Soviet military activity in World War II concentrated mainly on containing the Nazi invasion and waging a successful counteroffensive against Germany. In Eastern and Central Europe (with the notable exception of Austria) and in North Korea—areas reached by Soviet military forces at the close of the war—communist regimes subsequently took power.

1945

The brief postwar presence of Soviet troops in Manchuria enabled the Chinese communists to establish a foothold against the Chinese nationalists. A similar situation prevailed in Inner Mongolia, where a combination of Soviet and Outer Mongolian troops aided the local communist forces.

In Soviet-occupied northern Iran, Soviet troops helped to establish allegedly autonomous Azerbaijan and Kurdish republics, but under strong Western pressure, Soviet forces were withdrawn in March 1946, and these puppet regimes fell, as had the Republic of Gilan in 1920.

Soviet demands were made on Turkey for the revision of the Montreux Convention, for a base on the Dardanelles, and for the return of Anatolian territories of Kars and Ardahan. These demands were refused, without the Soviets taking military action to enforce them. Similar Soviet demands to pick up the last fruits of World War II in areas not occupied by Soviet troops included efforts to obtain a trusteeship over one or more Italian colonies in the Mediterranean and Africa.

Some indirect Soviet support was rendered to communist-dominated guerrillas in Greece.

Endnotes

Chapter 1
Soviet Third World Policy
under Stalin, 1946-1953

1. Fritz Ermarth, "The Soviet Union in the Third World: Purpose in Search of Power," *Annals of the American Academy of Political and Social Sciences*, November 1969, p. 32.

2. Alvin Z. Rubinstein, *The Foreign Policy of the Soviet Union* (New York: Random House, 1960), pp. 376-378.

3. James F. Byrnes, *Speaking Frankly* (New York: Harper & Brothers, 1947), pp. 94-95, 300-301. See also Raymond L. Garthoff, "Military Influences and Instruments," in *Russian Foreign Policy: Essays in Historical Perspective*, ed. Ivo J. Lederer (New Haven: Yale University Press, 1962), p. 267; and Ivar Spector, *The Soviet Union and the Muslim World, 1917-1958* (Seattle: University of Washington Press, 1959), p. 204.

4. Garthoff (1962), p. 267; Roger E. Kanet, "The Soviet Union and the Colonial Question," in *The Soviet Union and the Developing Nations*, ed. Kanet (Baltimore: Johns Hopkins University Press, 1974), p. 26.

5. The Soviet Republic of Gilan had been set up briefly in northern Iran in 1920. See appendix B, "1920."

6. Andrey Zhdanov, "The International Situation," *For a Lasting Peace, For a People's Democracy*, November 10, 1947, p. 2.

7. Allan W. Cameron, "The Soviet Union and Vietnam: The Origins of Involvement," in *Soviet Policy in Developing Countries*, ed. W. Raymond Duncan (Waltham, Mass.: Ginn-Blaisdell, 1970), p. 175. See also Melvin Gurtov, *The First Vietnam Crisis* (New York: Columbia University Press, 1967), pp. 6-15; and George K. Tanham, *Communist Revolutionary Warfare: The Vietminh in Indochina* (New York: Frederick A. Praeger, 1961), pp. 68-69.

8. Rubinstein (1960), pp. 376-377.

9. Soviet policy had, of course, shifted between united-front collaboration with bourgeois -nationalist groups and an ultrarevolutionary communist line before World War II also. See appendix A, "1920-1936." In the immediate postwar period, a leading spokesman for the view that conditions in the colonial countries were favorable for evolutionary progress toward independence and an anti-imperialist alignment without the need for a violent revolutionary transition was the Soviet economist Evgeniy Varga. His theories came under attack in 1947, at about the time Zhdanov's two-camp line was laid down, from E.M. Zhukov, V.Ya. Vasileva, and others, on the grounds that economic and other prerequisites for peaceful transition in the

colonies were lacking. For further details, see Frederick C. Barghoorn, "The Varga Discussion and Its Significance," *American Slavic and East European Review*, no. 7 (1948), pp. 227-236; and Kanet (1974), pp. 16-20.

10. I.I. Potekhin, "Stalinist Theory of Colonial Revolution and the National-Liberation Movement in Tropical and Southern Africa," *Sovetskaya etnografiya*, no. 1 (1950), p. 24, cited by Kanet (1974), p. 21.

11. E.M. Zhukov, "Problems of the National-Liberation Struggle after the Second World War," *Voprosy ekonomiki*, no. 9 (1949), pp. 57-58.

12. Report of V.M. Khvostov, in *Vsesoyuznoye soveshchaniye o merakh uluchsheniya podgotovki nauchnopedagogicheskikh kadrov po istoricheskim naukam* [All-Union Conference on Measures to Improve the Preparation of Scholarly Pedagogical Cadres of the Historical Sciences] (Moscow: Izdatel'stvo Nauka, 1964), pp. 395-396.

13. Raymond L. Garthoff, "The Soviet Intervention in Manchuria, 1945-46," in *Sino-Soviet Military Relations*, ed. Garthoff (New York: Frederick A. Praeger, 1966), pp. 71-73; and David Dallin, *Soviet Russia and the Far East* (London: Hollis & Carter, Ltd., 1949), pp. 244-252.

14. O. Edmund Clubb, "Armed Conflict in the Chinese Borderlands, 1917-50," in Garthoff (1966), pp. 41-42.

15. Milovan Djilas, *Conversations with Stalin* (New York: Harcourt, Brace & World, 1962), p. 114. See also Thomas W. Wolfe, *Soviet Power and Europe: 1945-1970* (Baltimore: Johns Hopkins University Press, 1970), pp. 16-17.

16. *Khrushchev Remembers*, trans. and ed. Strobe Talbott (Boston: Little, Brown and Company, 1970), pp. 367-368. For other discussion of the origins of the Korean war, see Allen S. Whiting, *China Crosses the Yalu: The Decision to Enter the Korean War* (Stanford, Calif.: Stanford University Press, 1960), pp. 35-111; and Robert R. Simmons, *The Strained Alliance: Peking, Pyongyang, Moscow and the Politics of the Korean Civil War* (Glencoe, Ill.: Free Press, 1975), pp. 20-110.

17. Raymond L. Garthoff, "Sino-Soviet Military Relations, 1949-66," in Garthoff (1966), p. 85; and Kenneth R. Whiting, *The Chinese Communist Armed Forces*, AU-11 (Montgomery, Ala.: Air University Documentary Research Study, 1974), pp. 58, 78.

18. See p. 129 and notes 1 and 2, chapter 11. In addition to air force personnel, some accounts, citing U.S. intelligence estimates, have asserted that there were also as many as 25,000 Soviet troops in Korea, including ground, artillery, and engineer personnel. However, the Department of the Army's military histories of the Korean conflict neither mention the presence of substantial Soviet ground forces in Korea nor report Soviet ground troops to have been engaged in combat. See William Zimmerman, "The Korean and Vietnam Wars," in *Diplomacy of Power, Soviet Armed Forces*

as a Political Instrument, ed. Stephen S. Kaplan (Washington, D.C.: The Brookings Institution, 1981), pp. 333, 352. See also Robert F. Futrell, *The United States Air Force in Korea, 1950-1953* (New York: Duell, Sloan and Pearce, 1961), pp. 92, 477, 567; *Khrushchev Remembers* (1970), p. 369; and Mikhail S. Kapitsa, *KNR: Dva desyatiletiya—Dve politiki* [PRC: Two Decades—Two Policies] (Moscow: Politizdat, 1969), p. 36.

Chapter 2
Revived Soviet Interest in
the Third World, 1954-1957

1. Morton Schwartz, "The USSR and Leftist Regimes in Less Developed Countries," *Survey* (Spring 1973), pp. 211-212. See also Arthur Jay Klinghoffer, "The Soviet Union and Africa," in *The Soviet Union and the Developing Nations*, ed. Roger E. Kanet (Baltimore: Johns Hopkins University Press, 1974), p. 53.

2. Fritz Ermarth, "The Soviet Union in the Third World: Purpose in Search of Power," *Annals of the American Academy of Political and Social Sciences* (November 1969), p. 32. See also *Khrushchev Remembers: The Last Testament*, trans. and ed. Strobe Talbott (Boston: Little, Brown and Company, 1974), pp. 298-300, 330.

3. Uri Ra'anan, *The USSR Arms the Third World* (Cambridge, Mass.: MIT Press, 1969), pp. 125-126. See also Philip E. Mosely, "The Kremlin and the Third World," in *Soviet Policy in Developing Countries*, ed. W. Raymond Duncan (Waltham, Mass.: Ginn-Blaisdell, 1970), pp. 287-288.

4. "Report of the Central Committee to the 20th Party Congress," in *Current Soviet Policies II: The Documentary Record of the 20th Communist Party Congress and Its Aftermath*, ed. Leo Gruliow (New York: Frederick A. Praeger, 1957), p. 33.

5. At the Twentieth Congress, Khrushchev also emphasized the non-inevitability of war between the capitalist and communist systems and the possibility of parliamentary transition to communist regimes.

6. E. Zhukov, "Collapse of the Colonial System of Imperialism," *Partiynaya zhizn'*, no. 16 (1956), pp. 41-43; and E. Varga, *Osnovnyye voprosy ekonomiki i politiki imperializma posle Vtoroy mirovoy voyny* [Fundamental Economic and Political Problems of Imperialism after the Second World War], 2d ed. (Moscow: Gospolitizdat, 1957), pp. 339-340, cited by Kanet (1974), pp. 28-29.

7. The Baghdad Pact, which came into being in February 1955, was renamed the Central Treaty Organization (CENTO) in August 1959.

8. Mohamed Heikal, *The Sphinx and the Commissar: The Rise and Fall of Soviet Influence in the Middle East* (New York: Harper & Row, 1978), pp. 56-63. For other accounts, see Ra'anan (1969), pp. 2-85; Wynfred Joshua and Stephen P. Gibert, *Arms for the Third World: Soviet Military Aid Diplomacy*, (Baltimore: Johns Hopkins University Press, 1969), pp. 2-12; and Stockholm International Peace Research Institute, *The Arms Trade with the Third World* (New York: Humanities Press, 1971), p. 520.

9. Heikal (1978), p. 59.

10. Joshua and Gibert (1969), p. 65. See also Stockholm International Peace Research Institute (1971), p. 208.

11. Joshua and Gibert (1969), p. 12.

12. Ibid., pp. 57-58.

13. Elizabeth Kridl Valkenier, "Soviet Economic Relations with the Developing Nations," in Kanet (1974), p. 225.

14. Thomas W. Wolfe, *Soviet Power and Europe: 1945-1970* (Baltimore: Johns Hopkins University Pres, 1970), p. 81. For more-complete details of the 1956 Suez crisis, see Oles Smolansky, *The Soviet Union and the Arab East under Khrushchev* (Cranbury, N.J.: Associated University Presses, 1974), pp. 30-48; and Hugh Thomas, *Suez* (New York: Harper & Row, 1967), especially pp. 65-145.

15. Khrushchev wrote that the joint-intervention proposal had been made, in full knowledge that it would be rejected by Eisenhower, in order to "expose the hypocrisy of his public statement condemning the attack against Egypt." *Khrushchev Remembers*, trans. and ed. Strobe Talbott (Boston: Little, Brown and Company, 1970), p. 434.

16. J.M. Mackintosh, *Strategy and Tactics of Soviet Foreign Policy* (London: Oxford University Press, 1962), p. 188.

17. Ibid., p. 186. According to Mackintosh, TASS did not announce until November 10 that the USSR was ready to send volunteers. See also Hannes Adomeit, "Soviet Risk-Taking and Crisis Behaviour: From Confrontation to Coexistence?," Adelphi Paper 101 (London: International Institute for Strategic Studies, 1973), p. 9. Khrushchev wrote that the USSR was "recruiting volunteers to serve with the Egyptian army as tank operators, pilots, artillery specialists, and so on." He also said that the Israelis had been told in "very unambiguous terms" to pull back their troops or "they might find themselves faced with our volunteers." *Khrushchev Remembers* (1970), p. 436.

18. Anwar el-Sadat, *In Search of Identity* (New York: Harper & Row, 1977), p. 146.

19. Mackintosh (1962), p. 186. Interview by one of the authors with Nicholas G. Shadrin, former Soviet naval officer, July 11, 1972.

20. Mackintosh (1962), pp. 227-229.

Chapter 3
Khrushchev's Forward Strategy,
1958-1960

1. Thomas W. Wolfe, *Soviet Power and Europe: 1945-1970* (Baltimore: Johns Hopkins University Press, 1970), pp. 84-89.

2. Fritz Ermarth, "The Soviet Union in the Third World: Purpose in Search of Power," *Annals of the American Academy of Political and Social Sciences*, November 1969, p. 32.

3. As pointed out by some analysts, Khrushchev's embrace of this doctrine, which had grown partly out of theoretical work by a circle of academician-journalists and young political economists from the USSR's Near Eastern and African Institutes, apparently met internal resistance from more-orthodox elements of the party apparatus. See Uri Ra'anan, "Moscow and the 'Third World'," *Problems of Communism*, January-February 1965, pp. 24-26. See also Roger E. Kanet (ed.), *The Soviet Union and the Developing Nations* (Baltimore: Johns Hopkins University Press, 1974), pp. 32-35.

4. N.S. Khrushchev, "For New Victories of the World Communist Movement," *Kommunist*, no. 1 (January 1961), pp. 3-37.

5. Ermarth (1969), p. 35; Wolfe (1970), pp. 137-138.

6. Philip E. Mosely, "The Kremlin and the Third World," in *Soviet Policy in Developing Countries*, ed. W. Raymond Duncan (Waltham, Mass.: Ginn-Blaisdell, 1970), pp. 289-290.

7. Ibid., p. 290; Herbert S. Dinerstein, *Soviet Doctrine on Developing Countries: Some Divergent Views*, P-2725 (Santa Monica, Calif.: The Rand Corporation, March 1963), pp. 23-24.

8. Wynfred Joshua and Stephen P. Gibert, *Arms for the Third World: Soviet Military Aid Diplomacy* (Baltimore: Johns Hopkins University Press, 1969), pp. 58-59.

9. Stockholm International Peace Research Institute, *The Arms Trade with the Third World* (New York: Humanities Press, 1971), p. 481.

10. Joshua and Gibert (1969), pp. 33-35.

11. Ibid., p. 15.

12. See Roger E. Kanet, "Soviet Policy toward the Developing World: The Role of Economic Assistance and Trade," in *The Soviet Union in the Third World: Successes and Failures*, ed. Robert H. Donaldson (Boulder, Colo.: Westview Press, 1981), p. 344. It should be noted that Western estimates of the value of Soviet military aid to LDCs during various periods tend to differ considerably, owing not only to frequent lack of reliable data but also to the particular methodologies used to evaluate arms transfers. For a useful discussion of some of the data and methodological problems

involved, see Edward I. Laurance and Ronald G. Sherwin, "Understanding Arms Transfers through Data Analysis," in *Arms Transfers to the Third World: The Military Buildup in Less Industrialized Countries*, eds. Uri Ra'anan et al. (Boulder, Colo.: Westview Press, 1978), pp. 87-106.

13. North Korea, which had received major arms aid from the USSR during the 1950-1953 Korean war, continued to receive a reduced level of arms supplies in the 1955-1960 period. In addition to military assistance from China, North Vietnam in the latter 1950s received a small amount of military aid from the USSR, including small arms, transport aircraft, and a few surplus tanks. The first Soviet military shipments to Cuba began in 1960. See below, page 20. See also Joshua and Gibert (1969), p. 60; and Stockholm International Peace Research Institute (1971), pp. 192-194, 425-427.

14. The reader is owed an explanation for the ambiguity inherent in statistical compilations of Soviet military and economic aid to the Third World. Up to 1976, the principal unclassified government source of authoritative research on Soviet arms exports to the Third World was the serial publication by the Department of State's Bureau of Intelligence and Research, entitled *Communist States and Developing Countries: Aid and Trade* [pertinent year]. Publication of this annual report under a slightly differing title (*Communist Aid to Less Developed Countries of the Free World*, subsequently revised) was then taken over by a branch in CIA's Office of Economic Research.

In both cases, the guidelines used have excluded statistics on Soviet arms and economic aid to certain less-developed or Third World countries classifiable as belonging to the communist bloc—particularly North Korea, North Vietnam, and Cuba. However, a considerable gray area has emerged in the case of a number of LDCs that have slid into the Soviet orbit and come under the control of self-professed Marxist-Leninist regimes, such as Angola, Ethiopia, South Yemen, Afghanistan, and Kampuchea. These LDCs have remained part of the statistical data sets for recipients of Soviet and Eastern European aid to noncommunist, nonaligned Third World countries, even though they may no longer belong in this category.

A third basic source of unclassified government data on Soviet arms transfers has been a serial publication by the U.S. Arms Control and Disarmament Agency (ACDA), *World Military Expenditures and Arms Transfers*, first published in 1973. This publication includes all LDCs—whether noncommunist, communist, or gray area—in its data sets. However, lack of annual statistics on a donor-recipient basis, and the aggregating of the data in overlapping rather than sequential periods, limits the usefulness of this publication for keeping score of Soviet military aid over time.

15. Roger F. Pajak, "The Effectiveness of Soviet Arms Aid Diplomacy in the Third World," in *The Soviet Union in the Third World: Successes and Failures*, ed. Robert H. Donaldson (Boulder, Colo.: Westview Press, 1981), pp. 387-388; and Joshua and Gibert (1969), pp. 152-153.

16. Figures compiled from Marshall I. Goldman, *Soviet Foreign Aid* (New York: Frederick A. Praeger, Inc., 1967), pp. 73-185; and Joshua and Gibert (1969), pp. 102-103, indicate that Soviet-bloc economic-aid commitments came to about $2.4 billion, of which East European countries accounted for some $300 million.

17. Kanet (1981), p. 337.

18. Goldman (1967), pp. 60-74, 85-93.

19. Ibid., p. 108; Joshua and Gibert (1969), p. 117.

20. J.M. Mackintosh, *Strategy and Tactics of Soviet Foreign Policy* (London: Oxford University Press, 1962), p. 234.

21. Hannes Adomeit, "Soviet Risk-Taking and Crisis Behaviour: From Confrontation to Coexistence?" Adelphi Paper 101 (London: International Institute for Strategic Studies, 1973), p. 10.

22. Anwar el-Sadat, *In Search of Identity* (New York: Harper & Row, 1977), p. 153.

23. Mohamed Heikal, *The Cairo Documents* (New York: Doubleday & Company, 1973), p. 134. Heikal had accompanied Nasser on a secret trip to Moscow immediately after the coup in Iraq to find out specifically where the Soviets stood on the postcoup crisis. See also comments on the Soviet reaction to the U.S. Lebanon intervention in note 1, chapter 14.

24. "Statement by Spokesman of the Chinese Government: A Comment on Soviet Government Statement of August 21," *Peking Review*, no. 36 (September 6, 1963), p. 13.

25. Joshua and Gibert (1969), pp. 36-38.

26. Arthur J. Dommen, *Conflict in Laos: The Politics of Neutralization* (New York: Praeger Publishers, 1971), pp. 164-181.

27. Moscow probably assumed that Cuba was "one of the Latin American countries where the United States would be least likely to permit, and most able to prevent, significant internal or external communist influence" and that the United States would therefore take forceful measures to unseat the Castro regime. See Joshua and Gibert (1969), p. 84.

28. Ibid., pp. 84, 85.

29. By April 1961, Soviet weapon deliveries had reportedly included some 30 tanks, 19 assault guns, 78 76-mm field guns, and more than 100 heavy machine guns. Soviet and Czechoslovak military advisers in Cuba are estimated to have numbered about 100 at the time of the Bay of Pigs invasion. See ibid., p. 85.

30. See Peter Wyden, *Bay of Pigs: The Untold Story* (New York: Simon & Schuster, 1979), p. 103.

31. *Pravda*, July 9, 1960. Two years later, the Soviet government made a similar public pledge to protect Cuba by means of ICBMs based in the USSR (*Pravda*, September 11, 1962) at the same time MRBM and IRBM launchers were being deployed covertly in Cuba.

32. See William Hyland and Richard Wallace Shryock, *The Fall of Khrushchev* (New York: Funk & Wagnalls, 1968), p. 27.

Chapter 4
Peaking of Khrushchev's Third
World Expectations, 1961-1964

1. "Statement of Conference of Representatives of Communist and Workers' Parties," *Pravda*, December 6, 1960.

2. Morton Schwartz, "The USSR and Leftist Regimes in Less Developed Countries," *Survey* 19 (Spring 1973):212; and Roger E. Kanet, *The Soviet Union and the Developing Nations* (Baltimore: Johns Hopkins University Press, 1974), p. 39.

3. A. Sobolev, "National Democracy: The Way to Social Progress," *World Marxist Review*, no. 2 (February 1963), pp. 41-42. See also series of conference presentations under the title of "Socialism, Capitalism and the Less Developed Countries" by Soviet scholars such as G. Mirskiy, R. Avakov, R. Ulyanovskiy, V. Tyagunenko, and Yu. Ostrovityanov, *Mirovaya ekonomika i mezhdunarodnyye otnosheniya*, nos. 4 and 6 (1964).

4. Arthur Jay Klinghoffer, "The Soviet Union and Africa," in *The Soviet Union and the Developing Nations*, ed. Roger E. Kanet (Baltimore: Johns Hopkins University Press, 1974), pp. 62-81.

5. Ibid., pp. 57-58; and Robert Legvold, *Soviet Policy in West Africa* (Cambridge, Mass.: Harvard University Press, 1970), pp. 100-101, 129-146.

6. Uri Ra'anan, "Moscow and the 'Third World'," *Problems of Communism*, January-February 1965, pp. 26, 30.

7. See p. 19.

8. Schwartz (1973), p. 218; Legvold (1970), pp. 124-128.

9. It is worth noting that the phrase *national-liberation struggle* has had two different applications in Soviet usage: first, as a struggle for liberation from colonial rule; second, as the carrying out of socialist revolution within already independent Third World countries to liberate them from capitalist exploitation. Situations involving armed conflict have occurred in both types of national-liberation struggles.

10. Thomas W. Wolfe, *Soviet Power and Europe: 1945-1970* (Baltimore: Johns Hopkins University Press, 1970), p. 138.

11. Roger E. Kanet, "Soviet Policy toward the Developing World: The Role of Economic Assistance and Trade," in *The Soviet Union in the Third World: Successes and Failures*, ed. Robert H. Donaldson (Boulder, Colo.: Westview Press, 1981), p. 345; and Department of State, *Communist States and Developing Countries: Aid and Trade in 1972*, RECS-10 (Washington, D.C., June 15, 1973), appendix table 8.

12. Wynfred Joshua and Stephen P. Gibert, *Arms for the Third World: Soviet Military Aid Diplomacy* (Baltimore: Johns Hopkins University Press, 1969), p. 15.

13. Ibid., p. 59.

14. Ibid., p. 22.

15. The Soviet share came to about 65 percent of the $2.5 billion. For relevant data on economic aid during the period, see Marshall I. Goldman, *Soviet Foreign Aid* (New York: Frederick A. Praeger, Inc., 1967), pp. 61-206; George S. Carnett and Morris H. Crawford, "The Scope and Distribution of Soviet Economic Aid," in U.S. Congress, Joint Economic Committee, *Dimensions of Soviet Economic Power*, 87th Cong., 2d. sess., December 10 and 11, 1962, pp. 462-475; and Leo Tansky, "Soviet Foreign Aid: Scope, Direction and Trends," in U.S. Congress, Joint Economic Committee, *Soviet Economic Prospects for the Seventies*, Compendium of Papers, June 27, 1973, p. 768.

16. "Economic Aid to the Less Developed Countries," in U.S. Congress, Joint Economic Committee, *Soviet Economic Performance: 1966-67*, May 1968, p. 128, table 3.

17. Goldman (1967), p. 181.

18. U.S. Congress (1973), p. 767.

19. Ibid., p. 769.

20. Goldman (1967), p. 147.

21. Kanet (1981), pp. 337, 341.

22. *Pravda*, December 13, 1962.

23. *Khrushchev Remembers*, trans. and ed. Strobe Talbott (Boston: Little, Brown and Company, 1970), p. 493.

24. See Roberta Wohlstetter, *Cuba and Pearl Harbor: Hindsight and Foresight*, RM-4328-ISA (Santa Monica, Calif.: The Rand Corporation, April 1965), p. 8.

25. Graham T. Allison, *Essence of Decision: Explaining the Cuban Missile Crisis* (Boston: Little, Brown and Company, 1971), pp. 49, 105; and Secretary of Defense Robert S. McNamara and John Hughes, *Special Cuban Briefing*, State Department Auditorium, February 6, 1963, pp. 32, 35. For Castro's statement that Soviet military personnel in Cuba at the time of the 1962 missile crisis numbered "more than 40,000" see Lee Lescaze, "Castro Lists Soviet Strength in Cuba During 1962 Crisis," *Washington Post*, October 1, 1979.

26. Wohlstetter (1965), p. 10.

27. Wolfe (1970), p. 449; and *Khrushchev Remembers: The Last Testament*, trans. and ed. Strobe Talbott (Boston: Little, Brown and Company, 1974), pp. 326-327.

28. William J. Durch, "The Cuban Military in Africa and the Middle East: From Algeria to Angola," *Studies in Comparative Communism*, Spring/Summer 1978, p. 43.

29. Ibid., pp. 44-45.

30. Edgar O'Ballance, *The War in the Yemen* (Hamden, Conn.: Archon Books, 1971), pp. 9-42.

31. See also below, pp. 36-37 and 130. A detailed account of the Egyptian and Soviet involvement in the eight-year Yemen civil war may be found in Bruce D. Porter, "The USSR in Local Conflicts: Soviet Military Intervention in the Third World, 1917-1980," in manuscript, 1980, pp. 118-148.

32. Donald S. Zagoria, *Vietnam Triangle: Moscow, Peking, Hanoi* (New York: Pegasus, 1967), p. 42; and Richard Rosser, "The Soviets and Vietnam: A Tragic Miscalculation?" *South Atlantic Quarterly*, Summer 1973, pp. 392-394.

33. For figures on the level of Soviet arms support for the DRV, see pp. 145-146 and notes 40 and 42-44, chapter 12.

Chapter 5
Setbacks and Reappraisal of
Third World Policy, 1965-1969

1. Robert Legvold, *Soviet Policy in West Africa* (Cambridge, Mass.: Harvard University Press, 1970), p. 262; and John Hughes, *Indonesian Upheaval* (New York: David McKay Company, 1967).

2. Legvold (1970), pp. 262-268, 299-302; and Morton Schwartz, "The USSR and Leftist Regimes in Less Developed Countries," *Survey* 19 (Spring 1973):218. In the case of Ghana, according to Khrushchev, the Soviets had warned Nkrumah that he "ought to do something" to curb his officer corps because the situation "could lead to significant difficulties." *Khrushchev Remembers: The Last Testament*, trans. and ed. Strobe Talbott (Boston: Little, Brown and Company, 1974), pp. 334-335.

3. David E. Albright, "The USSR and Africa: Soviet Policy," *Problems of Communism*, January-February 1978, pp. 24-25; Elizabeth K. Valkenier, "Recent Trends in Soviet Research on the Developing Countries," *World Politics*, July 1968, pp. 644-659; and Carol R. Saivetz, "The Soviet Perception of Military Intervention in Third World Countries," in *Soviet Policy in the Third World*, ed. W. Raymond Duncan (New York: Pergamon Press, 1980), p. 137.

4. For a discussion of Moscow's changing views of the political rewards that could be expected from economic aid, see Department of State, Bureau of Intelligence and Research, *Communist States and Developing Countries: Aid and Trade in 1969*, RECS-5 (Washington, D.C., July 9, 1970), pp. iv, 7.

5. K.N. Brutents, "African Revolution: Gains and Problems," *International Affairs* (Moscow), January 1967, p. 21; and V.L. Tyagunenko, commentary on "The Theory and Practice of the Non-Capitalist Way of Development," *International Affairs* (Moscow), November 1970, p. 14.

6. Tyagunenko (1970), p. 14.

7. David Morison, "USSR and Third World," *Mizan* 12 (October 1970):7-8; and Elizabeth K. Valkenier, "Sino-Soviet Rivalry in the Third World," *Current History*, October 1969, p. 202. See also Schwartz (1973), pp. 218-222.

8. G. Kim and A. Kaufman, "On Sources of Socialist Conceptions in Developing Countries," *World Marxist Review*, December 1971, p. 128; and Prof. R. Ulyanovskiy, "The 'Third World'—Problems of Socialist Orientation,' *Mezhdunarodnaya zhizn'*, no. 8 (August 1977), pp. 38-42. Ulyanovskiy, an economist, is also a high-ranking official of the Central Committee department dealing with formulation of Soviet policy toward Third World states of Asia and Africa.

9. R. Ulyanovskiy, "Some Features of the Present Stage of the National Liberation Movement," *Pravda*, January 3, 1968.

10. See pp. 64-66.

11. N.A. Simoniya, "On the Character of the National Liberation Revolutions," *Narody Azii i Afriki*, no. 6 (1966), p. 14. See also Simoniya, "Afro-Asian Concepts of Socialism," *World Marxist Review*, December 1971, p. 34.

12. See Albright (1978), p. 25; and Arthur Jay Klinghoffer, "The Soviet Union and Africa," in *The Soviet Union and the Developing Nations*, ed. Roger E. Kanet (Baltimore: Johns Hopkins University Press, 1974), pp. 60-63.

13. G.I. Mirskiy, *"Armiya i politika v stranakh Azii i Afriki* [The Army and Politics in the Countries of Asia and Africa] (Moscow: Izdatel'stvo Nauka, 1970), p. 4. Among other points of interest in this book are the following:

Only recently had social categories, such as the army, which play an important role in the developing countries, become an object of serious Soviet study (p. 4).

The sense of cohesiveness and nationality bred in the army in many formerly colonial countries puts the military in a more-favorable position than other institutions (pp. 9-12).

Nobody feels the backwardness of a state so keenly (and thus becomes a proponent of modernizing change) as the officer who, in the course of his military education abroad, has become familiar with the military, economic, scientific, and cultural achievements of more-developed countries (p. 10).

The initiators of military coups in developing countries always underscore their striving to combat the corruption, ineffectiveness, and demagoguery of the ruling circles (p. 15).

Younger officers usually have more-radical views and are more disposed to overthrow the existing system than officers of the older generation oriented toward the Western powers and ideals (p. 302).

The overthrow of military dictatorships usually is possible only when the middle- and junior-officer strata join the opposition and bring the mass of troops along with them (p. 11).

Even in countries with revolutionary-democratic regimes, however, a considerable part of the officer corps is inclined to oppose creation of a vanguard revolutionary political party (pp. 17, 302).

The West has been searching for a substitute for the bourgeoisie in the Third World to serve as the instrument of capitalist development, and it calculates that the military ought to provide such a surrogate (p. 333).

With evident approval, Mirskiy also quoted from a book by C.L. Sulzberger: "That foreign power which furnishes arms and spare parts, exerts in a given situation decisive influence."

14. Schwartz (1973), p. 224. See also Morison (1970), pp. 12-13; and V. Solodovnikov, "Some Aspects of Non-Capitalist Development," *International Affairs*, no. 6 (1973), p. 47.

15. Yu.G. Sumbatyan, "The Army in the Political System of National Democracy," *Narody Azii i Afriki*, no. 4 (1969), pp. 34-39; A. Iskenderov, "The Army, Politics, and the People," *Izvestiya*, January 17, 1967; Mirskiy (1970), pp. 9-12; and R.E. Sevortyan, *Armiya v politicheskom rezhime stran sovremennogo vostoka* [The Army in the Political Regime of Countries of the Contemporary East] (Moscow: Izdatel'stvo Nauka, 1973), pp. 80-86.

16. A.S. Kaufman, "Socialist Doctrines in the Developing Countries," *Narody Azii i Afriki*, no. 4 (1968), pp. 54-55.

17. Iskenderov (1967).

18. Ibid. See also Maj. Gen. V. Mozolev, "In Foreign Armies: The Role of the Army in the Developing Countries," *Voyenno-istoricheskiy zhurnal*, no. 4 (April 1980), p. 67.

19. G.B. Starushenko, "The Struggle against Right and Left Opportunism in Africa," in *Leninizm i bor'ba protiv burzhuaznoy ideologii i anti-Kommunizma na sovremennom etape* [Leninism and the Struggle against Bourgeois Ideology and Anti-Communism at the Present Stage], ed. M.B. Mitin

(Moscow: 1970), pp. 180-197. See also *The Soviet Union and the Developing Nations,* ed. Roger E. Kanet (Baltimore: Johns Hopkins University Press, 1974), p. 40. The term *vanguard* was a euphemism to avoid classifying the variety of single-party organizations in the Third World as communist. A kind of prototype communist party was what these writers evidently had in mind.

20. Mirskiy (1970), p. 336. See also Mirskiy's later book, *"Tretiy mir":* *Obshchestvo, Vlast', Armiya* [The "Third World": Society, Power, Army] (Moscow: Izdatel'stvo Nauka, 1976), pp. 385, 389-391. A similar argument that even progressive military elements could not be expected to serve as a substitute for a vanguard party was advanced by V. Tikhmenev, "Leninism and the Revolutionary Process in Latin America," *Kommunist,* no. 3 (February 1971), p. 118.

21. D. Zarine, "Classes and Class Struggle in Developing Countries," *International Affairs,* no. 4 (April 1968), pp. 51-52.

22. Robert O. Freedman, *Soviet Policy toward the Middle East since 1970* (rev.) (New York: Praeger Publishers, 1978), pp. 21-22. After the Cultural Revolution ended in 1969, China resumed its Third World competition with the USSR, particularly in Africa, where strong Chinese backing was given to a number of African liberation movements. See Albright (1978), p. 33.

23. For data on Soviet support of Vietnam, see below, pp. 35-36 and 129.

24. Because of factors such as those mentioned in note 12, chapter 3, published estimates of the value of Soviet military aid for the years 1965-1969 vary from about $1.7 billion to around $2.4 billion. A figure of approximately $2 billion for the USSR, plus perhaps $300 million for Eastern Europe, would seem reasonable. See Roger E. Kanet, "Soviet Policy toward the Developing World: The Role of Economic Assistance and Trade," in *The Soviet Union in the Third World: Successes and Failures,* ed. Robert H. Donaldson (Boulder, Colo.: Westview Press, 1981), p. 345; Central Intelligence Agency, *Communist Aid to Less Developed Countries of the Free World, 1975,* ER 76-10372U (Washington, D.C., July 1976), p. 1; and Central Intelligence Agency, *Communist Aid to Less Developed Countries of the Free World, 1977,* ER 78-10478U (Washington, D.C., November 1978), p. 1.

25. Wynfred Joshua and Stephen P. Gibert, *Arms for the Third World: Soviet Military Aid Diplomacy* (Baltimore: Johns Hopkins University Press, 1969), pp. 26-27; Bradford Dismukes and James McConnell, eds., *Soviet Naval Diplomacy* (New York: Pergamon Press, 1979), p. 337.

26. Anwar el-Sadat, *In Search of Identity* (New York: Harper & Row, 1977), pp. 175-176.

27. Stockholm International Peace Research Institute, *The Arms Trade with the Third World* (New York: Humanities Press, 1971), pp. 627-630.

28. John de St. Jorre, *The Brothers' War: Biafra and Nigeria* (Boston: Houghton Mifflin Co., 1972), pp. 181-184; Joshua and Gibert (1969), pp. 44-45; and Klinghoffer (1974), p. 64.

29. Bruce D. Porter, "The USSR in Local Conflicts: Soviet Military Intervention in the Third World, 1917-1980" (Manuscript, 1980), p. 169.

30. Ibid., pp. 152-153; Legvold (1970), pp. 311-330.

31. Mohamed Heikal, *The Sphinx and the Commissar: The Rise and Fall of Soviet Influence in the Middle East* (New York: Harper & Row, 1978), p. 208.

32. See below, pp. 130 and 132.

33. U.S. Department of State, Bureau of Intelligence and Research, *Communist States and Developing Countries: Aid and Trade in 1970*, RECS-15 (Washington, D.C., September 22, 1971), pp. 16-18; and Central Intelligence Agency (1978), p. 1.

34. Department of State (1970), pp. 2-3; and Central Intelligence Agency (1978), p. 1.

35. U.S. Congress, Joint Economic Committee, *Soviet Economic Performance: 1966-67*, May 1968, p. 125.

36. U.S. Congress, Joint Economic Committee, *Soviet Economic Prospects for the Seventies*, Compendium of Papers, June 27, 1973, p. 769; and Marshall I. Goldman, *Soviet Foreign Aid* (New York: Frederick A. Praeger, Inc., 1967), p. 153. The first Soviet aid agreement with Turkey in 1964 was for $168 million, increased later in the period to about $390 million; the agreement included a dam, steel mill, and oil refinery.

37. U.S. Congress (1968), p. 125.

38. Lagging deliveries of economic aid stemmed not only from long lead times inherent in heavy industrial-project assistance but also from administrative problems in both the USSR and the LDCs and from lack of adequate infrastructure and skilled personnel in the LDCs to absorb project-type aid. See U.S. Congress (1973), p. 770; and Orah Cooper, "Soviet Economic Aid to the Third World," in U.S. Congress, Joint Economic Committee, *Soviet Economy in a New Perspective*, Compendium of Papers, October 14, 1976, p. 190.

39. Klinghoffer (1974), pp. 59-60; and Elizabeth Kridl Valkenier, "Soviet Economic Relations with the Developing Nations," in *The Soviet Union and the Developing Nations*, ed. Roger E. Kanet (Baltimore: Johns Hopkins University Press, 1974), pp. 226-230.

40. Vladimir Lee, "The National Liberation Movement Today," *International Affairs* (Moscow), December 1969, p. 42; and N.A. Simoniya (1966), pp. 3-21.

41. Points are from Kaznacheev's lecture, "Soviet Tactics in Underdeveloped Areas" (Presented at the Institute for Sino-Soviet Studies,

George Washington University, Washington, D.C., December 9, 1969). Kaznacheev is the author of *Inside a Soviet Embassy*.

42. Valkenier (1974), pp. 218-234; U.S. Congress (1973), p. 769; and Kanet (1981), p. 352.

43. Major planning decisions for the Eighth Five-Year Plan, 1966-1970, customarily would have been made in 1965.

44. This thesis is advanced in James M. McConnell and Bradford Dismukes, "Soviet Diplomacy of Force in the Third World," *Problems of Communism*, January-February 1979, pp. 19-22. A fuller treatment of the subject, to which the same authors contributed, may be found in Dismukes and McConnell (1979), especially pp. 21-29, 281-300. Another analysis advancing essentially the same thesis, and backed up by a thorough survey of Soviet military doctrine and related materials, has been made by William F. Scott and Harriet Fast Scott, *A Review and Assessment of Soviet Policy and Concepts on the Projections of Military Presence and Power*, vol. 2 of *Soviet Projection of Military Presence and Power* (McLean, Va.: General Research Corporation, January 1979).

45. Compare V.D. Sokolovskiy (ed.), *Voyennaya Strategiya*, 2d ed. (Moscow: Voyenizdat, 1963), pp. 228-229; 3d ed., 1968, p. 222.

46. Lt. Col. N. Zagorodnikov, "The Military Might of the Socialist System and the World Revolutionary Process," *Kommunist vooruzhennykh sil*, no. 16 (August 1966), pp. 43-44; and N.P. Pankratov, "V.I. Lenin on the International Character of the Armed Forces of a Socialist State," in *V.I. Lenin i voyennaya istoriya* [V.I. Lenin and Military History] ed. M.V. Zakharov (Moscow: Voyenizdat, 1970), p. 223. For a later Soviet statement on the same theme, see Lt. Col. N. Larichev, "Fulfilling Internationalist Duty," *Soviet Military Review*, March 1980, pp. 46-48.

47. *Pravda*, March 30, 1966.

48. A.M. Dudin and Yu.N. Listvinov, "Problems of the New Stage in the Arms Race," in *Voyennaya sila i mezhdunarodnyye otnosheniya* [Military Power and International Relations] ed. V.M. Kulish et al. (Moscow: Izdatel'stvo Mezhdunarodnyye otnosheniya, 1972), pp. 134-136.

49. See Thomas W. Wolfe, *The Soviet Quest for More Globally Mobile Military Power*, RM-5554-PR (Santa Monica, Calif.: The Rand Corporation, December 1967); Dismukes and McConnell (1979), pp. 21-29 and appendixes A and B. For discussion of how Soviet economic-aid programs often contributed to creation of a network of airports, harbors, and communications facilities accessible to the USSR in the Third World, see Valkenier (1974), pp. 231-236.

50. Hannes Adomeit, "Soviet Risk-Taking and Crisis Behaviour: From Confrontation to Coexistence?" Adelphi Paper 101 (London: International Institute for Strategic Studies, 1973), p. 12. In the view of some observers,

the USSR had been in the process of reducing its involvement in Vietnam in 1964 but was manipulated by the North Vietnamese through devices like the Pleiku provocation of February 1965 to furnish increasing support to demonstrate that it was a "strong and reliable" friend of a small, fraternal socialist state. See William Zimmerman, "The Korean and Vietnam Wars," in *Diplomacy of Power. Soviet Armed Forces as a Political Instrument*, ed. Stephen S. Kaplan (Washington, D.C.: The Brookings Institution, 1981), pp. 341-345, 353.

51. Heikal (1978), p. 162.

52. See p. 129 and notes 3-5, chapter 11.

53. Soviet military aid to North Vietnam is estimated to have been around $1.485 billion for the period 1965-1969 and around $3.245 billion for 1965-1974. See International Institute for Strategic Studies, *Strategic Survey 1972* (London, 1973), p. 50; and U.S. Arms Control and Disarmament Agency, *World Military Expenditures and Arms Transfers 1965-1974* (Washington, D.C., 1976a), p. 74. See also Porter (1980), p. 27; Zimmerman (1981), p. 347; pp. 145-146; note 100, chapter 7; and notes 40, 42-44, chapter 12.

54. Lyndon Baines Johnson, *The Vantage Point: Perspectives of the Presidency, 1963-1969* (New York: Holt, Rinehart and Winston, 1971), p. 302.

55. Ibid., pp. 302-303.

56. Wolfe (1970), p. 444. The Soviet Fifth *Eskadra* in the Mediterranean more closely resembles a numbered U.S. fleet in size than a squadron. For a description of the growth of the Soviet naval presence in the Mediterranean, see Robert G. Weinland, "Soviet Transits of the Turkish Straits: 1945-1970," in *Soviet Naval Developments: Capability and Context*, ed. Michael MccGwire (New York: Praeger Publishers, 1973), pp. 325-343.

57. Sadat (1977), pp. 162-163, 214.

58. Thomas W. Wolfe, "Soviet Naval Interaction with the United States and Its Influence on Soviet Naval Developments," in *Soviet Naval Developments: Capability and Context*, ed. Michael MccGwire (New York: Praeger Publishers, 1973), p. 261.

59. See Dismukes and McConnell (1979), p. 262.

60. McConnell and Dismukes (1979), p. 18.

61. Dismukes and McConnell (1979), pp. 123-124. For an informative case study of the trawler episode, see David K. Hall, "Naval Diplomacy in West African Waters," in *Diplomacy of Power. Soviet Armed Forces as a Political Instrument*, ed. Stephen S. Kaplan (Washington, D.C.: The Brookings Institution, 1981), p. 519-538.

62. Heikal (1978), p. 210. See also Galia Golan, *The Soviet Union and the PLO* (Jerusalem: Soviet and East European Research Center, Hebrew University, 1976), pp. 1-3.

Chapter 6
Furthering of Soviet Strategic
Interests in the Third World,
1970-1974

1. David E. Albright, "The USSR and Africa: Soviet Policy," *Problems of Communism* (January-February 1978), pp. 26-28.

2. Anwar el-Sadat, *In Search of Identity* (New York: Harper & Row, 1977), p. 230; Mohamed Heikal, *The Sphinx and the Commissar: The Rise and Fall of Soviet Influence in the Middle East* (New York: Harper & Row, 1978), p. 244.

3. Department of State, *Communist States and Developing Countries: Aid and Trade in 1972*, RECS-10 (Washington, D.C.: June 15, 1973), p. 13; Central Intelligence Agency, *Communist Aid to Less Developed Countries of the Free World, 1977*, ER 78-10478U (Washington, D.C.: November 1978), p. 29.

4. Robert F. Pajak, "Soviet Arms and Egypt," *Survival*, July/August 1975, p. 169.

5. See Sadat (1977), p. 230; Heikal (1978), p. 244; Heikal, *The Road to Ramadan* (New York: Quadrangle/New York Times Book Co., 1975), pp. 164-175; and Dismukes and McConnell, *Soviet Naval Diplomacy*, Pergamon Policy Studies 37, ed. Bradford Dismukes and James McConnell (New York: Pergamon Press, 1979), pp. 372-374. For a discussion of the effects of the withdrawal of Egyptian facilities upon the Soviet naval position in the Mediterranean, see Robert G. Weinland, "Land Support for Naval Forces: Egypt and the Soviet Escadra 1962-1976," *Survival*, March/April 1978, pp. 73-79.

6. Sadat (1977), pp. 230-231.

7. Heikal (1975), pp. 174-175.

8. Ibid., p. 175.

9. Galia Golan, *Yom Kippur and After: The Soviet Union and the Middle East Crisis* (New York: Cambridge University Press, 1977), pp. 24-25; Robert O. Freedman, *Soviet Policy toward the Middle East since 1970*, rev. (New York: Praeger Publishers, 1978), p. 88; and Pajak (1975), p. 169.

10. O. Orestov, "Independent Africa in the Making," *International Affairs* (Moscow), November 1975, p. 75.

11. V. Solodovnikov and N. Gavrilov, "Africa: Tendencies of Non-Capitalist Development," *Mezhdunarodnaya zhizn'*, no. 2 (February 1976), p. 34.

12. Ibid., p. 35. See also G. Mirskiy, *"Tretiy mir": Obshchestvo, Vlast', Armiya* [The "Third World": Society, Power, Army] (Moscow: Izdatel'stvo

Nauka, 1976), p. 385. In addition to calling for vanguard parties, mainly in African states, the USSR in 1972-1973 had sought in the Middle East to get Iraq and Syria to bring their indigenous communist parties into national fronts. This was a reversal of the earlier Soviet advice to Egypt's communist party to dissolve itself. See R.A. Ulyanovskiy, "On the Unity of the Anti-Imperialist Front of Progressive Forces in the Newly Independent States," *Mirovaya ekonomika i mezhdunarodnyye otnosheniya*, no. 9 (September 1972), pp. 76-86.

13. Solodovnikov and Gavrilov (1976), p. 34.

14. Dismukes and McConnell (1979), pp. 303-304; and Albright (1978), pp. 35-37.

15. See David Lynn Price, "Moscow and the Persian Gulf," *Problems of Communism*, March-April 1979, p. 9; and William E. Griffith, *Soviet Power and Policies in the Third World: The Case of Africa*, Adelphi Paper 152 (London: International Institute for Strategic Studies, 1979), pp. 39-45.

16. Albright (1978), p. 34; and Freedman (1978), pp. 88-89.

17. Dismukes and McConnell (1979), pp. 127-133.

18. See, for example, B. Ponomarev, "Topical Problems of the Theory of the Revolutionary Process," *Kommunist*, no. 15 (October 1971), p. 62; and V. Bushuyev, "Latin America: Year One of New Decade," *International Affairs* (Moscow), no. 3 (March 1972), pp. 43-44. For an analysis in depth of the shift in Soviet attitude toward the new military regimes, which Moscow initially had sized up in an entirely negative fashion, see Leon Gouré and Morris Rothenberg, *Soviet Penetration of Latin America* (Miami, Fla.: Center for Advanced International Studies, University of Miami, 1975), pp. 81-95.

19. Ponomarev (1971), p. 15.

20. Jorge Texier, "General and Distinct Features of the Liberation Process," *World Marxist Review*, April 1972, p. 106.

21. See Gouré and Rothenberg (1975), pp. 105-113.

22. For a discussion of this latter point, see William H. Luers, "The U.S.S.R. and the Third World," in *The U.S.S.R. and the Sources of Soviet Policy*, Occasional Paper no. 34 (Seminar sponsored by the Council on Foreign Relations and the Kennan Institute for Advanced Russian Studies, The Wilson Center, Washington, D.C., April-May 1978), p. 15.

23. Central Intelligence Agency, *Communist Aid Activities in Non-Communist Less Developed Countries, 1979 and 1954-79*, ER 80-10318U (Washington, D.C., October 1980a), p. 13.

24. Sadat (1977), pp. 197-198, 220-229; and Heikal (1975), p. 167.

25. William B. Quandt, *Soviet Policy in the October 1973 War*, R-1864-ISA (Santa Monica, Calif.: The Rand Corporation, May 1976), pp. 4-6.

26. This complaint, among others about the unsatisfactory status of the Soviet-Egyptian relationship, was contained in a message from Sadat to Brezhnev on August 30, 1972. See Sadat (1977), p. 318.

27. Although denying TU-22s to Egypt, the Soviets, following a treaty with Iraq in April 1972, sent a small number of these aircraft to Iraq in summer 1973, an act that for Sadat no doubt added insult to injury. The next year Libya also received some TU-22s from Moscow. See Jon Glassman, *Arms for the Arabs: The Soviet Union and War in the Middle East* (Baltimore: Johns Hopkins University Press, 1975), pp. 96, 112, 116; Central Intelligence Agency, *Communist Aid to Less Developed Countries of the Free World, 1975*, ER 76-10372U (Washington, D.C.: July 1976), p. 12.

28. Somewhere between 15 and 30 SCUD (SS-1) launchers reportedly were delivered to Egypt by August 1973 or earlier. Two of these were fired during the Yom Kippur war in October 1973, probably with the assistance of Soviet personnel, although apparently the missiles were placed under Egyptian operational control. See Glassman (1975), pp. 105, 113. See also p. 51, below.

29. According to Heikal (1975, p. 162), the Soviets backed out of this promise to provide MIG-23s, even though the Egyptians had "undertaken to pay hard currency for them." Moscow "offered a modified version of the MIG-21 instead."

30. Ibid., pp. 168 and 171.

31. Sadat (1977), pp. 196, 221, and 258.

32. Glassman (1975), pp. 105-109; Stockholm International Peace Institute, *The Arms Trade with the Third World* (New York: Humanities Press, 1971), p. 839.

33. Glassman (1975), pp. 105-109.

34. Heikal (1975), p. 181.

35. Heikal (1978), pp. 253-254; and Freedman (1978), pp. 122-124.

36. Golan (1977), p. 40.

37. International Institute for Strategic Studies, *Strategic Survey 1976* (London: 1977), p. 60; and Colin Legum, "The USSR and Africa: The African Environment," *Problems of Communism*, January-February 1978, p. 14. See also Tom J. Farer, *War Clouds on the Horn of Africa: A Crisis for Detente* (Washington, D.C.: Carnegie Endowment for International Peace, 1976), p. 111.

38. International Institute for Strategic Studies, *Strategic Survey 1973* (London: 1974), p. 82. See also Roger Hamburg, "The Soviet Union and Latin America," in *The Soviet Union and the Developing Nations*, ed. Roger E. Kanet (Baltimore: Johns Hopkins University Press, 1974), pp. 191-202; and Gouré and Rothenberg (1975), pp. 168-169.

39. See International Institute for Strategic Studies, *Strategic Survey 1975* (London: 1976), p. 31.

40. Central Intelligence Agency (1976), p. 12.

41. Department of State, Bureau of Intelligence and Research, *Communist States and Developing Countries: Aid and Trade in 1974*, Report No. 298 (January 27, 1976), p. ii.

42. Central Intelligence Agency, *Communist Aid Activities in Non-Communist Less Developed Countries, 1979 and 1954-79*, ER 80-10318U (Washington, D.C.: October 1980a), p. 17.

43. U.S. Congress, Joint Economic Committee, *Soviet Economy in a New Perspective*, Compendium of Papers (October 14, 1976b), p. 194; U.S. Congress, Joint Economic Committee, *Soviet Economic Prospects for the Seventies*, Compendium of Papers (June 27, 1973), p. 775.

44. U.S. Congress (1976b), p. 193.

45. See below, pp. 146-147.

46. Sadat (1977), p. 197. See also pp. 43-44, above. Sadat indicates that the Soviets promised to furnish some TU-16s by April 1970 to augment the dozen or so previously furnished to Egypt. The Egyptians received a few additional TU-16s during ensuing months but no TU-22s. See Glassman (1975), p. 105.

47. Sadat, as Nasser's personal emissary, and Egyptian War Minister Fawzi had worked out a deal with the Soviet leaders in December 1969 for new air-defense hardware, including SA-3 missiles, delivery of which was scheduled to begin in June 1970. See Sadat (1977), p. 197; and Glassman (1975), p. 73.

48. Nasser's January 1970 request included training of Egyptian replacement crews for the SA-3 missiles, but according to Sadat (1977, p. 197), this was expected to take at least until August 1970. Heikal (1975, p. 86) put the number of Egyptian trainees at 1,800. The numbers of Soviet personnel to man some 75 to 85 SAM sites and about 150 interceptors in the air defense of Egypt have been estimated to be between 7,500 and 15,000. A figure toward the lower end of the spread is probably closer to the mark. See Glassman (1975), p. 75; *Strategic Survey 1970*, p. 47; Stockholm International Peace Research Institute (1971), p. 527; and Central Intelligence Agency (1980a), p. 5.

49. Heikal (1975), pp. 87-88.

50. Ibid.

51. See Glassman (1975), p. 75.

52. See Henry Kissinger, *White House Years* (Boston: Little, Brown and Company, 1979), pp. 560-561.

53. See Dismukes and McConnell (1979), p. 340.

54. According to some accounts, four Soviet-piloted MIG-21s were shot down on July 30, 1970, in an aerial ambush laid by the Israelis, after earlier Soviet attacks on Israeli fighter-bombers. See Glassman (1975), p. 79.

55. International Institute for Strategic Studies, *Strategic Survey 1972* (London: 1973), p. 27; Heikal (1975), p. 162; and Avi Shlaim and Raymond Tanter, "Decision Process, Choice and Consequences: Israel's Deep-Penetration Bombing in Egypt, 1970," *World Politics* (July 1978):494-506.

56. Marvin Kalb and Bernard Kalb, *Kissinger* (Boston: Little, Brown and Company, 1974), p. 192; and Kissinger (1979), p. 569.

57. Kalb and Kalb (1974), p. 198. The reminiscences of both Sadat and Heikal skip over the question of ceasefire violations and the Soviet role therein. See also note 51, chapter 12.

58. See Freedman (1978), p. 38; and Neville Brown, "Jordanian Civil War," *Military Review*, September 1971, pp. 38-48.

59. Kalb and Kalb (1974), pp. 201, 207.

60. Reportedly, Soviet diplomats had rushed to Damascus on September 21 to "turn off the invasion." Ibid., p. 207.

61. Ibid., pp. 202-207; and Dismukes and McConnell (1979), pp. 168-177.

62. See William B. Quandt, *Decade of Decisions* (Berkeley: University of California Press, 1977), pp. 118-119.

63. Kalb and Kalb (1974), p. 212. See also George H. Quester, "Missiles in Cuba, 1970," *Foreign Affairs*, April 1971, pp. 493-497; and Barry M. Blechman and Stephanie E. Levinson, "Soviet Submarine Visits to Cuba," *U.S. Naval Institute Proceedings*, September 1975, pp. 30-39.

64. Besides a diesel- and a nuclear-powered attack submarine, the visiting Soviet flotilla combinations included a nuclear-powered cruise-missile submarine. However no nuclear-powered ballistic-missile submarines were used. See Kissinger (1979), pp. 650-652.

65. John M. Goshko, "Soviet Construction of Pier at Cuban Base Is Reported," *Washington Post*, October 31, 1979.

66. For one account of these airlifts, see Dismukes and McConnell (1979), pp. 344-345.

67. Ibid., pp. 130-133.

68. See David K. Hall, "Naval Diplomacy in West African Waters," in *Diplomacy of Power: Soviet Armed Forces as a Political Instrument*, ed. Stephen S. Kaplan (Washington, D.C.: The Brookings Institution, 1981), pp. 539-569. See also James M. McConnell, "The Soviet Navy in the Indian Ocean," in *Soviet Naval Developments: Capability and Context*, ed. Michael MccGwire (New York: Praeger Publishers, 1973), p. 398.

69. See Hall (1981), pp. 565-566.

70. Ibid. (1981), p. 563; and Dismukes and McConnell (1979), p. 57.

71. See "Intelligence Role of Journalists," *The Times* (London), May 23, 1980; and "Strategy in Africa," *The Times* (London), May 27, 1980.

72. Freedman (1978), pp. 58-61; Heikal (1975), pp. 141-143; and Cecil Eprile, *War and Peace in the Sudan, 1955-1972* (London: David & Charles, Ltd., 1974), pp. 120-123.

73. Freedman (1978), pp. 4, 116.

74. Dismukes and McConnell (1979), pp. 117, 137.

75. Congressional Research Service (Senior Specialists Division), Library of Congress, *The Soviet Union and the Third World: A Watershed in Great Power Policy?* (Report to Committee on International Relations, U.S. House of Representatives, May 8, 1977), pp. 79-80.

76. Dismukes and McConnell (1979), pp. 134-136; and Golan (1977), p. 57.

77. Sadat (1977), pp. 246, 249, 264. A discussion of the extent of Soviet complicity in the starting of the Yom Kippur war may be found in Bruce D. Porter, "The USSR in Local Conflicts: Soviet Military Intervention in the Third World, 1917-1980," manuscript (1980), pp. 191-199.

78. Heikal (1978), pp. 253-254. See also Quandt (1976), pp. 4-8; Dismukes and McConnell (1979), pp. 192-193; and Golan (1977), pp. 36-41, 74.

79. Quandt (1976), pp. 13-15; and Golan (1977), pp. 75-80. See also Lawrence L. Whetten, "June 1967 to June 1971: Four Years of Canal War Reconsidered," *New Middle East*, June 1971, p. 21.

80. Sadat (1977), p. 253; and Heikal (1975), p. 245.

81. Kalb and Kalb (1974), pp. 465-472.

82. According to the Yugoslavs, overflight rights granted the Soviets were at the behest of the Arabs rather than the USSR. See *Strategic Survey 1973*, pp. 14, 27; and Golan (1977), p. 87.

83. Bonner Day, "Soviet Airlift to Ethiopia," *Air Force Magazine*, September 1978, p. 33; and Dismukes and McConnell (1979), p. 338.

84. See Quandt (1976), pp. 18-26; Dismukes and McConnell (1979), pp. 198-203, 336-347; and Robert Legvold, "The Soviet Union's Strategic Stake in Africa," in *Africa and the United States: Vital Interests*, ed. Jennifer Seymour Whitaker (New York: New York University Press, 1978), p. 158.

85. Glassman (1975), pp. 136-138; and Porter (1980), pp. 204-208.

86. The intensified Soviet diplomacy included a trip to Cairo by Kosygin, October 16-19, to try to wring agreement to a ceasefire from Sadat, followed by Brezhnev's invitation to Kissinger to fly to Moscow on October 20 for "urgent consultations on the Middle East." See Sadat (1977), pp. 258-259; and Kalb and Kalb (1974), p. 481.

87. Kalb and Kalb (1974), p. 490.

88. Among the other indicators reinforcing Washington's conviction that some sort of Soviet military move was imminent was the discovery on the evening of October 24 that elements of the East German armed forces were to be put on alert and that eight Soviet AN-22 transports were slated to fly to Egypt within the next few hours. See Henry Kissinger, *Years of Upheaval* (Boston: Little, Brown and Company, 1982), p. 589. Also see Dismukes and McConnell (1979), pp. 193-207; Kalb and Kalb (1974), p. 488;

Elmo R. Zumwalt, Jr., *On Watch* (New York: Quadrangle/The New York Times Book Co., 1976), pp. 437-447; and Golan (1977), p. 123.

89. Kalb and Kalb (1974), pp. 491-492; *Strategic Survey 1973*, pp. 29-30; and Kissinger (1982), pp. 589-599.

Chapter 7
Increased Soviet Third
World Involvement, 1975-1980

1. For useful discussion of the upcoming change of leadership genera-tions in the USSR, see Jerry F. Hough, "The Generation Gap and the Brezhnev Succession," *Problems of Communism*, July-August 1979, pp. 1-16; R. Judson Mitchell, "The Soviet Succession: Who, and What, Will Follow Brezhnev?" *Orbis*, Spring 1979, pp. 9-34; and Thane Gustafson, "The Soviet Leadership Succession and the Political Agenda for the 1980s," (Unpublished paper given at U.S.-China Conference on the Soviet Union, Washington, D.C., November 8-11, 1979), 12 pages.

2. Angola has been termed by some analysts as Moscow's "first major Third World breakthrough," while Ethiopia is said to have demonstrated in the Third World that alignment with the USSR was "superior to alignment with the United States." See William E. Griffith, "The Implications of Afghanistan," *Survival*, July-August 1980, p. 148; and Steven David, "Realignment in the Horn: The Soviet Advantage," *International Security*, Fall 1979, p. 70.

3. G. Kim, "Successes of the National-Liberation Movement and Their Influence on World Affairs," *Mezhdunarodnaya zhizn'*, no. 1 (1979), p. 95. See also E. Tarabrin, "Africa at a New Turn of the Liberation Strug-gle," *Mirovaya ekonomika i mezhdunarodnyye otnosheniya*, no. 2 (Feb-ruary 1979), p. 45.

4. In the case of Rhodesia, where the USSR had been backing guerrilla leader Joshua Nkomo, the peace settlement and elections, which brought rival guerrilla groups and whites together in a Zimbabwe coalition govern-ment under Robert Mugabe in March 1980, represented at least a temporary dimming of prospects for a radical, Soviet-oriented regime in that country. However, Zimbabwe's long-term stability was probably questionable enough to keep alive the prospect of a fresh round of guerrilla warfare such as that reportedly directed previously from Zambia by the USSR ambassador, Vasiliy Solodovnikov, who also is a leading Soviet expert on Africa. See John F. Burns, "Friction Grows in Zimbabwe Coalition," *The New York Times*, July 28, 1980.

5. See John F. Burns, "Cease-Fire for Rhodesia; War Plans for South Africa," *The New York Times*, December 23, 1979; and Caryle Murphy, "S. African Guerrillas Gain New Vigor," *Washington Post*, August 19, 1980.

6. The pro-Soviet group headed by Abdul Fattah Ismail and Ali Nasir Muhammad al-Hasani took over power in South Yemen after executing President Selim Rubai Ali on June 26, 1978, two days after North Yemen's President Ahmad Hussein Ghashmi was assassinated by a bomb carried to his office in Sana by a South Yemeni envoy. The Rubai Ali regime, which had been installed in 1969, two years after South Yemen's independence, was of Marxist complexion, but Ali was apparently trying to broaden his contacts with conservative Arab states and the West. International Institute for Strategic Studies, *Strategic Survey 1978* (London: 1979), pp. 58, 133. Also see below, pp. 170-171.

7. "South Yemen Replaces President," *The New York Times*, April 22, 1980.

8. For various explanations of this complicated issue, see Edward Cody, "President Quits in Aden Citing Health, but Analysts Suspect Power Struggle," *Washington Post*, April 22, 1980; Amos Perlmutter, "The Yemen Strategy," *The New Republic*, July 5-12, 1980, p. 16; Christopher Wren, "Big Power Rivalry Echoed in Latest Yemen Shake-Up," *The New York Times*, April 27, 1981; and Pranay B. Gupte, "South Yemen Seeks to Widen Arab Ties," *The New York Times*, June 15, 1980.

9. See pp. 88-90. Because local communist parties in the Third World often exhibit ideological impurities like overt nationalism that prevent their establishing true communist regimes when they take power, the Soviets usually refer to such new governments as socialist oriented or on the path to socialism rather than as socialist or communist. See Sylvia W. Edgington, " 'The State of Socialist Orientation' as Soviet Developmental Politics" (Paper delivered at the 1980 Annual Meeting of the American Political Science Association, Washington, D.C., August 28-31, 1980).

10. Robert O. Freedman, *Soviet Policy toward the Middle East since 1970*, rev. (New York: Praeger Publishers, 1978), pp. 25, 110, 205, 218.

11. "Soviet Asked to Explain Turkish Border Buildup," *Baltimore Sun*, August 27, 1980; and Alfred Friendly, "Soviet Aid Bolsters Militants in Turkey," *Washington Post*, July 6, 1980.

12. The first public Soviet indictment of the Iranian revolution, attacking both Khomeini's rule and Islamic fundamentalism, was made in early September 1979 in an article by Aleksandr Bovin, "With Koran and Saber!" *Nedelya*, no. 36 (September 4, 1979). See also Kevin Klose, "Khomeini Denounced by Soviets," *Washington Post*, September 9, 1979.

13. During the early weeks after seizure of the U.S. embassy, the amount of inflammatory, anti-U.S. material in clandestine Soviet broadcasts to Iran varied considerably, suggesting some debate in Moscow over the response to be given U.S. protests about the Soviet attitude. By early December 1979, however, when a *Pravda* article first came out openly on Iran's side, a uniform line had been adopted. See A. Petrov, "Display Prudence and

Restraint," *Pravda*, December 5, 1979. See also Craig R. Whitney, "Moscow Backs Iran on Hostages While Conceding Breach of Rules," *The New York Times*, December 6, 1979; Whitney, "U.S. Aides in Soviet Angered over Iran," *The New York Times*, December 7, 1979; Whitney, "Moscow Again Warns Washington over Use of Force in Iran Crisis," *The New York Times*, December 10, 1979; and Foreign Broadcast Information Service, *National Voice of Iran: November 1978-November 1979*, Special Report, December 10, 1979, pp. 286-290.

14. Jonathan C. Randal, "Iranian Leftists Emerge from Isolation," *Washington Post*, December 3, 1979; and Editorial, "Moscow Tilts toward Qum," *The New York Times*, December 9, 1979.

15. Jay Ross, "High-Level Soviet Diplomat Expelled from Iran on Charges of Espionage," *Washington Post*, July 1, 1980; and "Teheran Threat to Recall Envoy from Moscow," *The Times* (London), August 9, 1980.

16. For commentary on how regional aggression by Third World clients of the USSR has tended in several cases to follow the signing of friendship and cooperation treaties, see letter to the editor by Donald S. Zagoria, "Moscow's Friendship: Catalyst for Third World Aggression," *The New York Times*, January 19, 1979.

17. Soviet warships visited Cam Ranh Bay for the first time in March 1979, under provisions of the November 1978 treaty. Four months later Soviet destroyers were said by U.S. Admiral Harry D. Train to be using the port of Danang while Soviet technicians were installing radio facilities at Cam Ranh Bay. According to the Chinese, the Soviets also had been given access to naval facilities in Haiphong and to air-base facilities near Ho Chi Minh City. By early 1980, Soviet submarine and air patrols reportedly were being carried out by naval forces deployed to Vietnamese facilities. See Richard Burt, "Soviet Ships Arrive at Cam Ranh Bay," *The New York Times*, March 29, 1979; Drew Middleton, "U.S. Seeks a Strategy to Employ Its Conventional Forces," *The New York Times*, July 9, 1979; and James Foley, "Soviet Subs Stationed in S. China Sea," *Philadelphia Inquirer*, May 2, 1980.

18. See Myles R.R. Frechette, director of the office of Cuban Affairs, statement submitted to the Subcommittee on Inter-American Affairs of the House Foreign Affairs Committee on April 17, 1980, *Department of State Bulletin*, July 1980, p. 78.

19. For an account of the coup in Grenada, see the interview with Grenadian labor leader Curtis Stuart, *AFL-CIO Free Trade Union News* 35 (April 1980):4-5.

20. Ibid.

21. See Frechette (1980), p. 78.

22. See Richard Burt, "U.S. Asserts Cubans Are Supplying and Training Rebels in Nicaragua," *The New York Times*, June 23, 1979, pp. 1, 3; and

Department of State, Bureau of Public Affairs, *Cuba's Renewed Support for Violence in Latin America*, Special Report no. 90 (Washington, D.C., December 14, 1981), p. 6.

23. See Frechette (1980), p. 78; Don Oberdorfer, "U.S. Details 'Covert Activities' by Cubans in Latin America," *Washington Post*, December 2, 1981, pp. 1 and 20; Richard Halloran, "Nicaragua Arms Called Peril to Area," *The New York Times*, December 3, 1981, p. 12; Oberdorfer, "Haig Asks Joint Action on Cuba," *Washington Post*, December 5, 1981, p. 20; and Oberdorfer, "U.S., in Secret Dialogue, Sought Rapprochement with Nicaragua," *Washington Post*, December 10, 1981, pp. 1 and 12.

24. R. Tuchnin, "On International Themes: An Irreversible Process," *Izvestiya*, August 5, 1979.

25. Graham Hovey, "U.S. Fears Unrest in Central America," *The New York Times*, July 22, 1979.

26. O. Ignat'yev, "The Victory of the People of Nicaragua," *Kommunist*, no. 13 (September 1979), p. 95.

27. See Department of State, Bureau of Public Affairs, *Communist Interference in El Salvador*, Special Report no. 80 (Washington, D.C., February 23, 1981); and Department of State, *Communist Interference in El Salvador*, Documents Demonstrating Communist Support of the Salvadoran Insurgency (Washington, D.C., February 23, 1981). After the State Department published the report and documents, serious questions were raised about the apparent mistranslations, omissions, ambiguities, errors, and extrapolations. However, while acknowledging certain shortcomings in the report, the State Department strongly defended the report's main conclusions, stating that the "unification of guerrilla groups by the Cubans, the gathering of arms and military supplies from the Vietnamese, the Ethiopians, and East Europeans, and the transshipment of these arms to Cuba and Nicaragua are fully confirmed." See Juan de Onis, "State Dept. Defends Report on Salvador," *The New York Times*, June 9, 1981, p. A3; de Onis, "U.S. Officials Concede Flaws in Salvador White Paper but Defend Its Conclusions," *The New York Times*, June 10, 1981, p. A6; Jonathan Kwitny, "Tarnished Report? Apparent Error, Cloud U.S. 'White Paper' on Reds in El Salvador," *Wall Street Journal*, June 8, 1981, pp. 1, 10; Robert G. Kaiser, "White Paper on El Salvador Is Faulty," *Washington Post*, June 9, 1981, pp. A1, A14; and Department of State, "Response to Stories Published in the *Wall Street Journal* and the *Washington Post* about Special Report no. 80," June 17, 1981. For earlier charges about Cuban interference in El Salvador, see "U.S. Cites Cuba's Role in El Salvador," *Washington Post*, March 26, 1980, p. 1.

28. See Department of State, Bureau of Public Affairs, *Cuba's Renewed Support for Violence in Latin America*, Special Report no. 90 (Washington, D.C., December 14, 1981), pp. 7-9.

29. Some sixteen guerrillas were reported killed and seventy-five captured, including several key leaders. Among those captured were Carlos Toledo Plata, founder of the guerrilla group, and several M-19 guerrillas who had participated in the 1980 seizure of the Dominican Embassy in Bogota and who subsequently had been given safe passage to Cuba. Colombia suspended relations with Cuba on March 23, 1981, charging that Cuba is widening "the geographical orbit" of its "offensive" beyond the Caribbean and Central America by its training of Colombian guerrillas. See James Nelson Goodsell, "Castro Cast Adrift in Caribbean by Worried Latin Neighbors," *Christian Science Monitor*, March 25, 1981, p. 3; *Washington Post*, March 19, 1981, p. A27; and Department of State, Special Report no. 90 (1981), p. 11.

30. Karen DeYoung, "Nonaligned Summit Closes after Final Wrangle," *Washington Post*, September 10, 1979; and Flora Lewis, "Beyond the Havana Talks: Castro Sows Trouble for U.S.," *The New York Times,* September 12, 1979. See also note 5, chapter 14.

31. Mohamed Heikal, *The Sphinx and the Commissar: The Rise and Fall of Soviet Influence in the Middle East* (New York: Harper & Row, 1978), pp. 269-270. In addition to abrogation of the Soviet-Egyptian treaty, other actions taken by Sadat at Soviet expense included cancellation in April 1976 of the Soviet navy's rights to use facilities at Alexandria, Port Said, and Mersa Matruh; stopping of Egyptian cotton exports to the USSR; and a unilateral ten-year suspension of debt repayments for Soviet military aid.

32. See Freedman (1978), pp. 303-310.

33. In addition to Ethiopia and Somalia, the proposed federation was to include South Yemen, Djibouti, and Eritrea. See "Soviet Said to Propose African Confederation," *The New York Times*, May 16, 1977. See also Marina and David Ottaway, *Ethiopia: Empire in Revolution* (New York: Africana Publishing Co., 1978), p. 169; and Dimitri K. Simes, "Imperial Globalism in the Making: Soviet Involvement in the Horn of Africa," *Washington Review of Strategic and International Studies*, Special Supplement, May 1978, p. 33.

34. International Institute for Strategic Studies, *Strategic Survey 1977* (London: 1978), p. 25.

35. See Marina and David Ottaway (1978), pp. 169-170; Freedman (1978), p. 310; and William G. Hyland, "U.S. Policy Options," *Washington Review of Strategic and International Studies*, Special Supplement, May 1978, p. 26.

36. John Darnton, "Somalia Is Ordering Soviet Advisers Out, Halts Use of Bases," *The New York Times*, November 14, 1977.

37. *Strategic Survey 1978*, p. 99; John Darnton, "Envoys Wonder if Somalia Is Returning to Soviet Orbit," *The New York Times*, January 11, 1979; and David (1979), pp. 69, 81.

38. Somalia previously had sought to interest the United States in using the military facilities from which it had expelled the Soviets, presumably to court U.S. support in the event of a Soviet-backed invasion from Ethiopia. Not until the impact of Iran and Afghanistan had produced an about-face in U.S. policy, however, was a deal worked out for U.S. use of facilities in Somalia, following completion of similar arrangements for U.S. access to bases in Oman and Kenya. See "Naval Base in Somalia—Exit Russia, Enter U.S.," *U.S. News & World Report*, March 3, 1980, p. 24; Robert B. Cullen, "Somalia Agrees to Let U.S. Use Ports, Airstrips," *Washington Post*, August 21, 1980; and Henry S. Bradsher, "U.S. Concludes Deal to Use Somali Base," *Washington Star*, August 22, 1980.

39. Freedman (1978), p. 252; Colin Legum, "The USSR and Africa: The African Environment," *Problems of Communism* (January-February 1978), p. 13; and *Strategic Survey 1977*, p. 25. The Soviet military experts expelled by Nimeiry were replaced by Egyptians, Yugoslavs, and Chinese.

40. David Lamb, "Soviets Lose Base in Equatorial Guinea," *Los Angeles Times*, January 28, 1980.

41. "Press Conference of M. al-Shaer," *Pravda*, July 15, 1979; and P. Demchenko, "What Is Going on in Lebanon," *Pravda*, July 16, 1976. For detailed discussion of Soviet reaction to Syria's intervention in Lebanon, see Freedman (1978), pp. 229-240.

42. Reuters dispatch, "Syrian Arms Minister in Soviet: Rift on Weapons May Be Subject," *The New York Times*, January 5, 1979.

43. Freedman (1978), p. 257.

44. *Strategic Survey 1977*, p. 41.

45. Ibid.

46. Christopher Wren, "Modern Soviet Arms on Way to Damascus," *The New York Times*, November 4, 1979; and Reuters dispatch, "Soviet Said to Cancel Syrian Debt," *The New York Times*, November 4, 1979.

47. David B. Ottaway, "Syrian Leader Assad Gambling in Attempt to Bolster Position," *Washington Post*, October 22, 1980. Incidentally, during the 1981 Syrian-Israeli crisis, the Soviets pointed out that the treaty applied only to Syria proper and not to Syrian troops in Lebanon; see the *Washington Post*, May 17, 1981, p. A19.

48. David Lynn Price, "Moscow and the Persian Gulf," *Problems of Communism* (March-April 1979), p. 7.

49. Flora Lewis, "Reports from Iraq Indicate Crisis in Its Leadership," *The New York Times*, July 28, 1979; Marvine Howe, "Iraq's New Chief Purging Leaders in an Effort to Bolster His Position," *The New York Times*, July 30, 1979; and "Iraq Reported to Hold 36 in High-Level 'Plot' to Take Over Regime," *The New York Times*, August 1, 1979.

50. Bonner Day, "Soviet Airlift to Ethiopia," *Air Force Magazine* (September 1978), p. 33.

51. Marvine Howe, "Surrounded by Turmoil, Iraq Is Shifting Its Posture," *The New York Times*, January 7, 1979; and "Iraq Now Has Powerful Claim to Leadership of Arab World," *The New York Times*, July 22, 1979.

52. See Francis Fukuyama, *New Directions for Soviet Middle East Policy in the 1980's: Implications for the Atlantic Alliance*, P-6443 (Santa Monica, Calif.: The Rand Corporation, February 1980), pp. 5-9.

53. Bernard Gwertzman, "Moscow's Gulf Opportunities," *The New York Times*, October 11, 1980; and David B. Ottaway, "Soviets Move to Bolster Influence in Iraq," *Washington Post*, May 5, 1981.

54. Donald S. Zagoria, "Into the Breach: New Soviet Alliances in the Third World," *Foreign Affairs*, Spring 1979, p. 738.

55. Hannah Negaran (pseudonym), "The Afghan Coup of April 1978: Revolution and International Security," *Orbis*, Spring 1979, pp. 93-94. See also Richard Pipes, "Soviet Global Strategy," *Commentary*, April 1980, p. 37; and Harry Gelman, *The Politburo's Management of Its America Problem*, R-2707-NA (Santa Monica, Calif.: The Rand Corporation, April 1981), pp. 23, 60.

56. Francis Fukuyama, "A New Soviet Strategy," *Commentary*, October 1979, pp. 52-58; and Fukuyama (1980a), pp. 10-12.

57. A.I. Levkovskiy, "Practical Class Problems of the Developing Countries," *Rabochiy klass i sovremennyy mir*, no. 2 (March-April 1975), pp. 141-151; "Specific Character and Limits of Capitalism in a Transitional Society of the 'Third World'," *Mirovaya ekonomika i mezhdunarodnyye otnosheniya*, no. 1 (1974), p. 114; and *Tretiy mir v sovremennom mire* [The Third World in the Contemporary World] (Moscow: Izdatel'stvo Nauka, 1970), pp. 8, 110-115. See also, L.I. Reisner, *Razvivayushchiyesya strany: Ocherk teorii ekonomicheskogo rosta* [The Developing Countries: An Outline Theory of Economic Growth] (Moscow: Izdatel'stvo Nauka, 1976), pp. 51-65, 67-72, 320. Also "Debate on N. Simoniya's book *Countries of the East: Paths of Development*," *Narody Azii i Afriki*, no. 3 (May-June 1977), pp. 54-64.

58. V. Chirkin, "The Government of a Modern Transitional Society," *Aziya i Afrika segodnya*, no. 9 (September 1978), pp. 28-31; and A.V. Roslavlev, "Once More about the 'Theory' of Multiple Elements in Countries of the 'Third World'," *Rabochiy klass i sovremennyy mir*, no. 1 (January-February 1977), pp. 136-145.

59. The countries named as having acquired a vanguard party were Congo, Benin, Mozambique, Angola, and Ethiopia. See Tarabrin (1979), p. 39.

60. K.N. Brutents, "The Soviet Union and the Emerging Countries," *Mezhdunarodnaya zhizn'*, no. 3 (1979), pp. 12-13.

61. R. Ulyanovskiy, "Concerning the Countries of Socialist Orientation," *Kommunist*, no. 11 (July 1979), p. 118.

62. See Foreign Broadcast Information Service, *Soviet Guidelines for Third World Regimes: Political Control, Economic Pluralism*, March 12, 1981, p. 5.

63. B. Ponomarev, "Joint Struggle of the Worker and National-Liberation Movement against Imperialism and for Social Progress," *Kommunist*, no. 16 (November 1980), especially p. 42.

64. Foreign Broadcast Information Service (1981), p. 7.

65. Col. Ye. Dolgopolov, "National-Democratic Revolution and the Army," *Soviet Military Review* (Moscow), no. 4 (April 1980), pp. 49-50.

66. Central Intelligence Agency, *Communist Aid Activities in Non-Communist Less Developed Countries, 1979 and 1954-79*, ER 80-10318U (Washington, D.C., October 1980a), table A-1, p. 13.

67. Ibid., pp. 1, 13. At the end of the 1970s, estimates of the dollar value of Soviet arms transfers began to reflect an upward revision due in part to higher ruble prices for given items of Soviet equipment, the rising dollar value of the ruble, and the increased sophistication, and hence cost, of some of the arms furnished.

68. Central Intelligence Agency, *Communist Aid to the Less Developed Countries of the Free World, 1976*, ER 77-10296U, August 1977, pp. 2-3; Central Intelligence Agency, *Communist Aid Activities in Non-Communist Less Developed Countries, 1978*, ER 79-10412U (Washington, D.C., September 1979), pp. 19, 20, 32; Central Intelligence Agency (1980a), pp. 29-30.

69. See p. 63.

70. Central Intelligence Agency (1977), p. 3.

71. Central Intelligence Agency (1980a), pp. 13, 14.

72. U.S. Arms Control and Disarmament Agency, *World Military Expenditures and Arms Transfers 1969-1978* (Washington, D.C., December 1980), p. 161.

73. Ibid.

74. Central Intelligence Agency (1979), p. 3; U.S. Congress, Joint Economic Committee, *Soviet Economy in a New Perspective*, Compendium of Papers (October 14, 1976b), pp. 192-193.

75. Central Intelligence Agency, *Communist Aid to Less Developed Countries of the Free World, 1977*, ER 78-10478U (Washington, D.C., November 1978), p. 1.

76. Bernard Gwertzman, "U.S. Fears Soviet Arms Deal Might Harm Ties to India," *The New York Times*, May 30, 1980.

77. See Francis Fukuyama, *The Soviet Union and Iraq since 1968*, N-1524-AF (Santa Monica, Calif.: The Rand Corporation, July 1980), pp. 46-76.

78. See pp. 63-64. See also Central Intelligence Agency (1979), pp. 32, 34; and Central Intelligence Agency (1980a), p. 1.

79. Central Intelligence Agency (1977), p. 4; Central Intelligence Agency (1978), p. 2; Central Intelligence Agency (1979), p. 29; and U.S. Arms Control and Disarmament Agency (1980), p. 162.

80. See pp. 58-60.

81. Central Intelligence Agency (1980a), p. 5.

82. The front-line states identified by Soviet sources as supporting the national-liberation struggle against Rhodesia and South Africa included—in addition to Mozambique, Zambia, and Tanzania—Angola and Botswana. See Kim (1979), p. 95.

83. Murphy (1980).

84. Price (1979), p. 9; and Legum (1978), p. 17. See also James M. Markham, "Alliances, Allegiances Switch Often in Western Sahara War," *The New York Times*, February 17, 1980.

85. This argument was made by Representative Stephen J. Solarz of New York after a trip to the Sahara in 1979, "Arms for Morocco?" *Foreign Affairs*, Winter 1979/80, especially pp. 286-292.

86. Central Intelligence Agency (1980a), p. 13.

87. The available published data for Soviet military aid to North Korea, North Vietnam, and Cuba are incomplete for some years, but on the basis of the figures available, a conservative estimate would place the total dollar value at about $7 billion at least, of which North Vietnam's share would come to around $3.7 billion. See Stockholm International Peace Research Institute, *The Arms Trade with the Third World* (New York: Humanities Press, 1971), pp. 192-194, 409, 425, 687; U.S. Arms Control and Disarmament Agency, *World Military Expenditures and Arms Transfers 1968-1977* (Washington, D.C., October 1979), p. 156; and U.S. Arms Control and Disarmament Agency (1980), p. 162.

88. Central Intelligence Agency (1980a), pp. 15-16.

89. For an interesting discussion of this point, see Jane Rosen, "How the Third World Runs the U.N.," *The New York Times Magazine*, December 16, 1979, pp. 36-84. See also Louis Halasz, "Soviet Losing Its Grip with Third World," *Baltimore Sun*, November 2, 1980.

90. Roger F. Pajak, "The Effectiveness of Soviet Arms Aid Diplomacy in the Third World," in *The Soviet Union in the Third World: Successes and Failures*, ed. Robert H. Donaldson (Boulder, Colo.: Westview Press, 1981), p. 395.

91. See p. 70. See also Central Intelligence Agency (1980a), p. 13; and Roger E. Kanet, "Soviet Policy toward the Developing World: The Role of Economic Assistance and Trade," in *The Soviet Union in the Third World: Successes and Failures*, ed. Robert H. Donaldson (Boulder, Colo.: Westview Press, 1981), pp. 347-348.

92. Central Intelligence Agency (1980a), p. 17.

93. Ibid.

94. U.S. Congress (1976b), p. 193.

95. Central Intellience Agency (1980a), pp. 7-8.

96. Ibid., pp. 6-9.

97. Ibid.; and Kanet (1981), p. 352.

98. This estimate of Soviet economic assistance is drawn from data presented in Central Intelligence Agency, *Handbook of Economic Statistics 1980*, ER 80-10452 (Washington, D.C., October 1980), table 78, p. 110; Goldman (1967), pp. 37-38; U.S. Congress (1973), table 4, p. 776; and Central Intelligence Agency and Defense Intelligence Agency, *Communist Military and Economic Aid to North Vietnam 1970-1974*, Memorandum, March 5, 1975, p. 4.

99. Nguyen Lam, chairman of the Vietnam State Planning Commission, told an interviewer that during his country's second five-year plan period (1976-1980), the USSR provided Vietnam $757.5 million (500 million rubles) in economic assistance each year. See Nayan Chanda, "Bickering Begins as Old Friends Fall Out," *Far Eastern Economic Review* (Hong Kong) 111 (February 27, 1981):32.

100. Soviet military and economic aid to Vietnam, estimated at about $3 million a day in 1979, reportedly doubled in 1980, amounting to about $1.9 billion to $2 billion for the year. About 45 percent of this aid was believed to have been economic and 55 percent military. See Richard C. Holbrooke, assistant secretary of state for East Asian and Pacific Affairs, Statement before the Subcommittee on Asian and Pacific Affairs of the Senate Foreign Relations Committee on March 24, 1980, *Department of State Bulletin* 80 (June 1980):28; and Douglas Pike, "Vietnam in 1980: The Gathering Storm?" *Asian Survey* 21 (January 1981):90.

101. Edward Gonzalez, "Cuban Policy toward Africa: Activities, Motivations, and Outcomes" (Draft paper, May 1980), table 2, to appear in David E. Albright and Jiri Valenta, *The Communist States in Africa* (Bloomington: Indiana University Press, forthcoming).

102. For an exposition of these arguments, see Herbert E. Meyer, "Why We Should Worry about the Soviet Energy Crunch," *Fortune*, February 25, 1980, pp. 82-88; and Meyer, "Russia's Sudden Search for Raw Materials," *Fortune*, July 28, 1980, pp. 43-44.

103. See James Arnold Miller, Daniel I. Fine, and R. Daniel McMichael (eds.), *The Resource War in 3-D: Dependency, Diplomacy, Defense* (Pittsburgh, Pa.: World Affairs Council of Pittsburgh, June 1980).

104. Elizabeth Kridl Valkenier, "The USSR, The Third World and the Global Economy," *Problems of Communism*, July-August 1979, pp. 17-33. Among indications of greater Soviet-LDC-Western economic interdependence cited by Valkenier were several joint Soviet-Western development ventures undertaken in the latter 1970s in the Third World, including in Afghanistan, Nigeria, and Argentina.

105. A departure from orthodox Marxist-Leninist thinking on Third World economic-development issues may be found in Ye. Bragina, *Razvivayushchiyesya strany: Gosudarstvennaya politika i promyshlennost'* [The Developing Countries: State Policy and Industry] (Moscow: Izdatel'stvo Mysl', 1977); and A. Yelyanov, *Razvivayushchiyesya strany: Problemy ekonomicheskogo razvitiya i rynok* [The Developing Countries: Problems of Economic Development and the Market] (Moscow: Izdatel'stvo Mysl', 1976). These authors share an outlook on Third World development problems similar to that of Levkovskiy, Reisner, and Simoniya, the writers cited in note 57. For an analysis of several current Soviet schools of thought on the subject, see Elizabeth Kridl Valkenier, "Development Issues in Recent Soviet Scholarship," *World Politics*, no. 4 (July 1980), pp. 485-508; and Foreign Broadcast Information Service, *Soviet Guidelines for Third World Regimes: Political Control, Economic Pluralism*, Analysis Report, March 12, 1981, pp. 1-4.

106. Maj. Gen. A. Zaytsev and Col. V. Kondrashov (Ret.), "The Downfall of Imperialism's Colonial System," *Kommunist vooruzhennykh sil*, no. 5 (March 1980), p. 79. For commentary on a Soviet book, *Strategiya i ekonomika* [Strategy and Economics], by Maj. Gen. A.N. Lagovskiy, in which arguments are made for exploiting the U.S. weak link in strategic materials, see Richard T. Ackley, "The Weak Link in U.S. National Strategy: USSR Is Self-Sufficient; U.S. Is Not," *Sea Power*, August 1974, pp. 24-27.

Chapter 8
The Introduction of
Cooperative Intervention

1. See Harry Gelman, *The Politburo's Management of Its America Problem*, R-2707-NA (Santa Monica, Calif.: The Rand Corporation, April 1981), pp. 20-21, 60-62. See also Congressional Research Service, Library of Congress, *Soviet Policy and United States Responses in the Third World*, March 1981, pp. 111-145.

2. See text of President Ford's state-of-the-world speech to a joint session of Congress, Department of State news release, April 10, 1975, p. 6.

3. See above, p. 45.

4. For various accounts of the Angola conflict and the role of external powers, see John Marcum, *The Angolan Revolution: Exile Politics and Guerrilla Warfare (1962-1976)*, vol. 2 (Cambridge, Mass.: MIT Press, 1978); Jiri Valenta, "The Soviet-Cuban Intervention in Angola," *Studies in Comparative Communism*, Spring/Summer 1978, pp. 1-33; William J. Durch, "The Cuban Military in Africa and the Middle East: From Algeria to Angola," *Studies in Comparative Communism* (Spring/Summer 1978),

pp. 61-74; John Stockwell, *In Search of Enemies* (New York: W.W. Norton and Company, 1978); Colin Legum, "Foreign Intervention in Angola," in *After Angola: The War over Southern Africa*, eds. Legum and Tony Hodges (New York: Africana Publishing Company, 1976); Tony Hodges, "How the MPLA Won in Angola," in *After Angola: The War over Southern Africa*, eds. Legum and Hodges (New York: Africana Publishing Company, 1976); Nathaniel Davis, "The Angolan Decision of 1975: A Personal Memoir," *Foreign Affairs*, Fall 1978, pp. 109-124; U.S. Congress, Senate, Committee on Foreign Relations, Subcommittee on African Affairs, *Angola*, 94th Cong., 2d. sess., January 29, February 3, 4, and 6, 1976; and *Soviet Naval Diplomacy*, Pergamon Policy Studies 37, ed. Bradford Dismukes and James McConnell (New York: Pergamon Press, 1979), pp. 144-153.

5. See William E. Griffith, in *Prospects of the Soviet Power in the Nineteen Eighties*, ed. Christoph Bertram (Hamden, Conn.: Shoe String Press, 1980), pp. 40-41.

6. See Durch (1978), pp. 64-67; Davis (1978), pp. 120-121; and Stockwell (1978), p. 206.

7. The request reportedly was made by Iko Carreira, the MPLA's minister of defense, during a visit to Moscow. Robert Moss gives an account of the MPLA's approach to the USSR for troop support and its subsequent request to Cuba in *The Sunday Telegraph* (London), January 30, 1977, pp. 8 and 9. Some analysts have suggested that Soviet troop intervention was opposed in Moscow by elements in the foreign and defense ministries on grounds of damage to détente and expense. See Peter Vanneman and Martin James, "The Soviet Intervention in Angola: Intentions and Implications," *Strategic Review*, Summer 1976, p. 97.

8. Some Cuban sources have indicated that an initial decision to send between 200 to 300 military advisers was made sometime in the May-June 1975 period. Around mid-August, Castro probably made another decision to commit an expeditionary force of up to 3,000 troops, but the buildup to around 20,000 Cubans probably was not decided until sometime in late October or early November. See Valenta (1978), p. 11; Durch (1978), pp. 65-67; William E. Schaufele, Jr., assistant secretary of state for African Affairs, *The African Dimension of the Angolan Conflict* (Washington, D.C.: Department of State, Bureau of Public Affairs, February 6, 1976), p. 3; and Gabriel Garcia Marquez, "Operation Carlota," *New Left Review*, February-April 1977, p. 124.

9. Valenta (1978), pp. 11, 26.

10. The initial Cuban expeditionary contingent reportedly was drawn from a special armored unit known as "the prime minister's reserve troops." Durch (1978), pp. 66-67.

11. See Jorge I. Dominguez, "The Cuban Operation in Angola: Costs and Benefits for the Armed Forces," *Cuban Studies* 8 (January 1978), pp. 11-12.

12. See Legum and Hodges (1976), p. 19; and Vanneman and James (1976), p. 94.

13. Durch (1978), p. 67; International Institute for Strategic Studies, *Strategic Survey 1975* (London, 1976), p. 34.

14. For accounts of the Cuban airlift, see Durch (1978), pp. 68-70; and Dismukes and McConnell (1979), pp. 144-145, 340-341.

15. Among the cargo reportedly carried in the airlift were crated MIG aircraft, light tanks, and tactical missiles. Prior to the Angolan independence day (November 11, 1975), the Soviet airlift terminated at Brazzaville; thereafter it flew directly to Luanda. The shorter-range AN-12s also apparently made refueling stops at Bamako, Mali. Soviet oilers and merchant tankers are believed to have supported the airlift by delivering fuel to Conakry, Guinea. See Dismukes and McConnell (1979), pp. 144-147, 340-341.

16. See Statement by Secretary of State Henry Kissinger in U.S. Congress, Senate, Committee on Foreign Relations, Subcommittee on African Affairs, *Angola*, 94th Cong., 2d. sess. (January 29, February 3, 4, and 6, 1976), p. 19.

17. See Dismukes and McConnell (1979), p. 145.

18. Valenta (1978), p. 28; Colin Legum, "Angola and the Horn of Africa," in *Diplomacy of Power: Soviet Armed Forces as a Political Instrument*, ed. Stephen S. Kaplan (Washington, D.C.: The Brookings Institution, 1981), p. 595; Durch (1978), p. 69; and International Institute for Strategic Studies, *Strategic Survey 1976* (London, 1977), pp. 44-46.

19. Speech by Fidel Castro to the National Assembly of People's Power, December 27, 1979, cited in Edward Gonzalez, "Cuban Policy toward Africa: Activities, Motivations, and Outcomes," draft paper (May 1980a), p. 35, to appear in *The Communist States in Africa*, ed. David Albright and Jiri Valenta (Indiana University Press, forthcoming).

20. See Dismukes and McConnell (1979), pp. 146-151.

21. Although the Alligator-class amphibious landing ship (LST) assumed a patrolling station off the Congo, Zaire, and northern Angola at the end of the first week of December, the first major Soviet naval combatant (a Kotlin-class guided-missile destroyer) did not reach its operating area off Angola until the first week of January, some two weeks after the December 19 Senate vote that ruled out U.S. intervention. The possibility of any U.S. military involvement in Angola also was disclaimed explicitly on December 20, when President Ford stated that the United States "had no intention whatsoever of ever sending any U.S. military personnel there." Despite the low probability of any direct U.S. intervention, the Soviets may have anti-

cipated a possible diversion of a U.S. naval task group to the Angolan theater to "show the flag" in January and seemed to have made a concerted effort to monitor and hopefully to discourage any such deployment. See Dismukes and McConnell (1979), pp. 146-151; and Gerald Ford, *Department of State Bulletin*, January 19, 1976, p. 78.

22. See Dismukes and McConnell (1979), pp. 146-147.

23. Ibid., p. 148.

24. During November and early December, the Cubans suffered several defeats from South African forces, which possessed better tactical leadership and proved more skilled in mobile warfare than the Cubans. The battle of bridge 14, which took place between December 9 and 12 in the Catofe area north of Santa Comba, proved a particularly severe defeat for the Cubans. According to the South African account of this engagement, a mixed South African-FNLA-UNITA force consisting of four companies and an armored-car squadron, along with artillery and other supporting units, decisively defeated a substantially larger Cuban-MPLA force of three battalions (one Cuban, one MPLA, and one mixed battalion with 122-mm rocket launchers, artillery, and mortar support). The South Africans claim that some 400 Cuban and MPLA troops were killed in this engagement, at a cost of only 4 South Africans dead.

Even before this mid-December defeat, the Cubans apparently viewed their military prospects with considerable alarm, even to the point of contemplating a possible withdrawal from Angola. According to Gabriel Garcia Marquez, the Cubans saw the war "at the point of being lost" during the first week of December and the situation "so desperate that consideration was being given to the possibility of establishing a stronghold in Cabinda and setting aside a beachhead around Luanda in order to begin the evacuation." Such a retreat proved unnecessary, as the South Africans decided to go on the defensive in mid-December, presumably to hold down casualties (they claim to have lost less than forty killed in combat during the course of the conflict) and to await the outcome of the debate in the U.S. Senate over continued U.S. military aid to Angola. For South Africa's version of its involvement in Angola, see "Nature and Extent of the SADF's Involvement in the Angolan Conflict," South African Defense Forces Headquarters, Pretoria, February 3, 1977. For an account reflecting Cuban views on the situation, see Gabriel Garcia Marquez, "Cuba and Its Intervention in Angola," *La Prensa* (Lima, in Spanish), January 10-16, 1977, translated in Joint Publications Research Service, *Translations on Latin America*, no. 1613 (February 25, 1977), p. 29.

25. On January 23, South Africa began to move its forces to a fifty-mile cordon on the Angola side of the border with Namibia; at the end of March, it completely withdrew these forces from Angola. The South African military commitment to FNLA-UNITA had amounted to about 2,000

troops at the front and perhaps twice that number in support along the Namibian border. Another reason for South African disengagement, besides African political pressure and the U.S. aid cutoff, was that the continuing buildup of Cuban troops would have required larger South African manpower commitments than Pretoria was prepared to make.

26. *Strategic Survey 1976*, p.44; Valenta (1978), p. 29.

27. While no reliable data exist on the total military casualties suffered by the MPLA, FNLA, and UNITA during the course of the Angolan struggle, they are believed to have been light and possibly fewer than the civilian casualties resulting from the stand-off-and-fire character of the warfare.

28. See, for example, Tony Hodges, "The Struggle for Angola," *The Round Table* (London), no. 262 (April 1976), p. 180; and *Strategic Survey 1975*, p. 31.

29. Inasmuch as Yugoslavia was a consistent, early, and active supporter of the MPLA, Washington picked a difficult target for its protests.

30. Central Intelligence Agency, *Communist Aid Activities in Non-Communist Less Developed Countries, 1978*, ER 79-10412U (Washington, D.C.: September 1979), pp. 4 and 14.

31. See Legum (1981), pp. 600-601; Edward Gonzalez, "Cuba, the Soviet Union, and Africa," in *Communism in Africa*, ed. David E. Albright (Bloomington: Indiana University Press, 1980), p. 156; and Gerald J. Bender, "Angola, the Cubans, and American Anxieties," *Foreign Policy*, Summer 1978, pp. 23-26.

32. For a more-detailed account of the incursions, see Peter Mangold, "Shaba I and Shaba II," *Survival* 21 (May/June 1979):107-112.

33. Ibid., pp. 108-109; and David Binder, "Castro Says He Told U.S. He Tried to Halt Invasion into Zaire," *The New York Times*, June 11, 1978, pp. 1 and 6. Some analysts, apparently finding the U.S. intelligence assertions about Cuban involvement less than persuasive, and believing that Havana had sound reasons for opposing the Katangan invasion, tend to accept Castro's protestations about Cuban noninvolvement as plausible. Also see Gonzalez (1980a), p. 28.

34. According to a CIA memorandum dated June 2, made public by the Carter administration, the March 1977 incursion was supported by Cuban personnel who were with the Katangan forces in Angola "before and at the time of the invasion." The memorandum also asserted that after the 1977 invasion, Cuban and East German instructors continued to provide military training to the Katangans, including 5,000 new recruits, at various bases in Angola. Prior to the 1978 invasion, the Cubans reportedly helped to transport "large quantities of weapons" to a Katangan camp near Zaire and organized and accompanied the movement of a large number of Katangan troops from northeast Angola toward the Zambian border area, where the incursion into Zaire was launched. However, the CIA memoran-

dum said that there was "no independent information" to confirm that any Cubans had accompanied the Katangans into Zaire. See Bernard Gwertzman, "White House Cites CIA Material on a Cuban Role in Zaire Invasion," *The New York Times*, June 16, 1978, p. A1; and John M. Goshko, "U.S. Releases Summary of Its Evidence," *Washington Post*, June 15, 1978, p. 1. For a follow-on press account of the U.S. intelligence findings that "Cuba was deeply involved in training and supplying the invaders," see Richard Burt, "Lesson of Shaba: Carter Risked Serious 'Credibility Gap'," *The New York Times*, July 11, 1978, p. A2.

35. See Central Intelligence Agency, *Communist Aid to Less Developed Countries of the Free World, 1977*, ER 78-10478U (Washington, D.C., November 1978), p. 39.

36. See Richard M. Moose (then assistant secretary for African Affairs), "The United States and Angola," *Department of State Bulletin*, December 1980, p. 30; and Captain William H.J. Manthorpe, Jr., U.S. Navy (Ret.), "The Soviet Navy in 1979: Part I," *U.S. Naval Institute Proceedings*, April 1980, pp. 116 and 119.

37. See Flora Lewis, "With Neto Gone, Angola Rebel Renews Plea for Talks to End Civil War," *The New York Times*, September 15, 1979.

38. David Lamb, "Angola Growing Uneasy with Soviets," *Washington Post*, June 5, 1980.

39. This and eight other reasons for expecting no further Cuban military ventures in Africa may be found in Abraham F. Lowenthal, "Cuba's African Adventure," *International Security*, Summer 1977, pp. 3-10. See also Gregory F. Treverton, "Cuba after Angola," *The World Today*, January 1977, p. 21.

40. Dimitri K. Simes, "Imperial Globalism in the Making: Soviet Involvement in the Horn of Africa," *Washington Review of Strategic and International Studies*, Special Supplement (May 1978), p. 37.

41. Legum (1981), pp. 613, 627; Bruce D. Porter, "The USSR in Local Conflicts: Soviet Military Intervention in the Third World, 1917-1980," manuscript (1980), p. 284.

42. Legum (1981), pp. 612-615; and *Strategic Survey 1976*, pp. 55-60.

43. The best account of Soviet-Ethiopian arms dickering is that of Porter (1980), pp. 283-294. See also Marina and David Ottaway, *Ethiopia: Empire in Revolution* (New York: Africana Publishing Co., 1978), p. 167.

44. Porter (1980), pp. 286-288.

45. Ibid., p. 287.

46. Simes (1978), p. 33; and Legum (1981), p. 615.

47. See p. 61.

48. Marina and David Ottaway (1978), p. 168.

49. S. Sergeyev, "The Formation of a New Ethiopia," *Mezhdunarodnaya zhizn'*, no 4 (1979), pp. 13-15; V. Sidenko, "USSR-Ethiopia: Shoulder to Shoulder," *New Times* (Moscow), no. 48 (November 1978), p. 6.

50. Legum (1981), p. 615; Marina and David Ottaway (1978), p. 168; Don Oberdorfer, "The Superpowers and Africa's Horn," *Washington Post*, March 5, 1978; and U.S. Arms Control and Disarmament Agency, *World Military Expenditures and Arms Transfers 1968-1977* (Washington, D.C., October 1979), pp. 127, 157.

51. Roger W. Fontaine, "Cuba on the Horn," *Washington Review of Strategic and International Studies*, Special Supplement, May 1978, p. 40.

52. Legum (1981), p. 620.

53. Marina and David Ottaway (1978), p. 168.

54. Ibid., Oberdorfer, *Washington Post*, March 5, 1978; International Institute for Strategic Studies, *Strategic Survey 1977* (London: 1978), p. 20.

55. See Legum (1981), pp. 618, 619. See also p. 138 and note 8, chapter 12.

56. *Strategic Survey 1977*, p. 21.

57. Legum (1981), pp. 616, 617.

58. See p. 62.

59. *Strategic Survey 1977*, p. 20.

60. Ibid.

61. Roger W. Fontaine, "Cuban Strategy in Africa: The Long Road of Ambition," *Strategic Review* 6 (Summer 1978): 23; Steven David, "Realignment in the Horn: The Soviet Advantage," *International Security* 4 (Fall 1979): 80; International Institute for Strategic Studies, *Strategic Survey* 1978 (London, 1979), p. 13; and Legum (1981), pp. 620-621.

62. *Strategic Survey 1978*, p. 13. One report, for example, erroneously cited estimates that in the first few weeks of the airlift, 225 transport aircraft, or about 12 percent of the Soviet military transport fleet, had flown to Ethiopia. See Drew Middleton, "Airlift to Ethiopia Seen as Soviet Test," *The New York Times*, January 8, 1978.

63. *Strategic Survey 1978*, p. 13.

64. Bernard Gwertzman, "U.S. Aides Frustrated over Soviet Gains in Ethiopia," *The New York Times*, December 29, 1977.

65. Legum (1981), p. 622.

66. *Strategic Survey 1978*, pp. 13-14; Peter Vanneman and Martin James, "Soviet Threat into the Horn of Africa: The Next Targets," *Strategic Review* (Spring 1978), p. 36; and Major David T. Twining, "Soviet Activities in the Third World: A New Pattern," *Military Review*, June 1980, p. 6.

67. See John Darnton, "Cuba Said to Expand Military Force in Ethiopia by over 1000 a Month," *The New York Times*, February 18, 1978, pp. 1 and 5; and Graham Hovey, "Brzezinski Asserts that Soviet General Leads Ethiopia Units," *The New York Times*, February 25, 1978, p. 1.

68. Drew Middleton, "Eritrean Situation Has NATO Worried," *The New York Times*, July 15, 1978, p. 5. According to *Strategic Survey 1978*, p. 98, Soviet arms deliveries in 1977-1978 included some 550 tanks, 80 MIG

aircraft, "more than 300 armored personnel carriers and large quantities of M-21 rocket launchers, 155 mm and 185 mm guns and light arms." While the USSR reportedly gave or lent some of these weapons, the question remained as to how Ethiopia, with its one-crop economy (coffee), would find the hard currency to pay for the remainder.

69. Some estimates placed the number of Cubans as high as 20,000 at the peak of the Ethiopian intervention, but the usually accepted figure from official U.S. sources was around 17,000. By August 1979, the Cuban military presence in Ethiopia reportedly was reduced by several thousand, including both advisers and combat troops. See Murrey Marder, "Cubans Expand Role in Ethiopia, U.S. Says," *Washington Post*, April 1, 1978; Legum (1981), pp. 623, 627; *Strategic Survey 1978*, p. 13; and Graham Hovey, "Limited Cuban Pullout in Ethiopia Is Reported by American Officials," *The New York Times*, August 4, 1979.

70. See note 19.

71. General Petrov was a first deputy commander-in-chief of Soviet ground forces, while Barisov had been the ranking Soviet officer in Somalia up to November 1977. Subsequent to his military stint in Ethiopia, General Petrov became commander of a new Far East theater organization set up by the USSR in early 1979 and in December 1980 was promoted to commander-in-chief of Soviet ground forces. Legum (1981), pp. 623-624; and Kim Williamson, "Red Stars over Africa," *Newsweek*, March 13, 1978, p. 39.

72. For discussion of a Soviet attempt to strike a deal with the ELF, one that would have offered a chance for a political solution in Eritrea, see Stephen Larrabee, *Somalia and Moscow's Problems on the Horn of Africa,* Radio Liberty Research Paper no. RL 158/77, July 5, 1977, p. 11. See also Legum (1981), pp. 630-631.

73. There is considerable variance in estimates of Cuban ground-force participation in the Eritrean fighting, with some sources crediting the Cubans with conducting "tank, antitank and air warfare" in Eritrea and others attributing to them chiefly air-support and garrison roles. The Soviets, in addition to field command, reportedly participated in air- and naval-support operations in Eritrea. See *Strategic Survey 1978*, p. 13; Legum (1981), pp. 625-627; "Soviet Navy Accused of Shelling Eritreans," *The New York Times*, June 18, 1978; and "Cubans Said to Halt Participation in Drive on Eritrea," *The New York Times*, June 22, 1978.

74. See "Ethiopia: The Other Side of the Hill," *Economist*, October 6-12, 1979, pp. 71-72.

75. Edward Girardet, "Ethiopia Enlists Soviet Arms to Crush Stubborn Eritreans," *Christian Science Monitor*, July 17, 1980; and "Russia Said to Send Copters to Ethiopia," *International Herald Tribune*, June 14-15, 1980.

76. Henry L. Trewhitt, "Somalia-Ethiopia Conflict Continues Its Devastation," *Baltimore Sun*, August 4, 1980; and Christopher Wren, "Forgotten War in Ethiopia: Ogaden Heats up Again," *The New York Times*, May 26, 1980.

77. See Richard Burt, "U.S. Aides Disclose Soviet Airmen Help in Defense of Cuba," *The New York Times*, February 14, 1978.

78. See statement of Lt. Col. John A. Fesmire, Defense Intelligence Agency analyst, in U.S. Congress, House, Committee on International Relations, Subcommittee on Inter-American Affairs, *Impact of Cuban-Soviet Ties in the Western Hemisphere*, 95th Cong., 2d. sess., March 14, 1978, p. 5.

79. "Moscow's Helping Hands," *Time*, February 20, 1978, p. 29; and Legum (1981), p. 626.

80. Richard F. Sherman, "Marxism on the Horn of Africa," *Problems of Communism*, September-October 1980, p. 64; and "Soviet Naval Presence Doubles in Indian Ocean, Lacks Support," *Aviation Week & Space Technology*, April 6, 1981, p. 10.

81. Daniel S. Papp, "The Soviet Union and Cuba in Ethiopia," *Current History*, March 1979, p. 129.

82. U.S. warnings during the Ethiopian intervention that Soviet and Cuban military involvement must be reduced were, for example, dismissed by the Soviets on the grounds that helping the Ethiopians to repel aggression was justification for their military presence. See Bernard Gwertzman, "Carter Warns Soviet Official on Ethiopia," *The New York Times*, January 26, 1978; Henry S. Bradsher, "1977 U.S. Arms Offer to Somalia Ill-Timed?" *Washington Star*, January 14, 1978; Richard Burt, "Soviet Reportedly Cool to Linking Cuban, Somali Pullout in Ethiopia," *The New York Times*, March 16, 1978; and Legum (1981), pp. 624-625.

83. See p. 133 and note 21, chapter 11.

84. Craig R. Whitney, "Moscow Says Drive into Cambodia Is by Vietnamese-Supported Rebels," *The New York Times*, January 5, 1979; and Richard Burt, "Soviet Places Ships off Vietnam Coast," *The New York Times*, February 8, 1979.

85. See David K. Shipler, "Soviet Terse in Invasion Report, Implying No Decision on Action," *The New York Times*, February 18, 1979.

86. Soviet ships reportedly transported Vietnamese troops and equipment from the ports of Ho Chi Minh City (formerly Saigon), and Kompong Som in Cambodia to Hanoi's port of Haiphong. Other troops were moved to Hanoi by Soviet transport aircraft. See Henry Kamm, "Soviets Reported to Be Transporting Vietnamese Forces and Equipment," *The New York Times*, March 16, 1979, p. 1.

87. According to Thai sources, there were seventy-nine Soviet overflights of Thailand in February and March 1979. These continued at a

lower rate in the next few months but jumped to forty-six in September, presumably in support of a Vietnamese dry-season offensive in Cambodia. While these flights ostensibly were made by Aeroflot aircraft, "the pilots did not speak in English over the radio, as airline pilots throughout the world usually do." John McBeth, "Bringing Down the High Fliers," *Far Eastern Economic Review* 107 (February 29, 1980):10.

88. Nayan Chanda, "Vietnam: An Alliance Based on Mutual Need," *Far Eastern Economic Review* 105 (August 24, 1979):22; and Richard C. Holbrooke, assistant secretary of state for East Asian and Pacific Affairs, Statement before the Subcommittee on Asian and Pacific Affairs of the Senate Foreign Relations Committee on March 24, 1980, *Department of State Bulletin* 80 (June 1980):28.

89. Ibid.

90. Douglas Pike puts Soviet military assistance to Vietnam during 1980 at between $1.045 billion and $1.1 billion. Douglas Pike, "Vietnam in 1980: The Gathering Storm?" *Asian Survey* 21 (January 1981):90.

91. David R. Griffiths, "Lull in Vietnamese Thai Invasion," *Aviation Week & Space Technology*, July 7, 1980, pp. 16-17.

92. Don Oberdorfer, "Asians Reject Soviet Ship Visits," *Washington Post*, September 19, 1979, p. A19.

93. See Chanda (1979), p. 22; and Holbrooke (1980), p. 28.

94. Holbrooke (1980), p. 28.

95. While Hanoi has apparently not granted the USSR formal base rights on its territory, Soviet aircraft and naval vessels have made increasing use of Vietnamese facilities. Up to March 1980, a total of ninety-one Soviet surface-combat ships (including the carrier *Minsk*), submarines, amphibious craft, and auxiliaries had called at Vietnamese ports. A small number of Soviet vessels also are now regularly forward deployed from Vietnamese ports. See Nayan Chanda, "Indochina: Too Close for Comfort," *Far Eastern Economic Review* 110 (November 14, 1980):27; George C. Wilson, "Soviet Use of Cam Ranh Bay as Sub Base Arouses U.S. Concern," *Washington Post*, May 10, 1979, pp. A1 and A21; and Holbrooke (1980), p. 28. See also pp. 56-57.

96. Oberdorfer, *Washington Post*, September 19, 1979, p. A19.

97. According to the former U.S. military attaché to North Yemen, the first weeks of February 1979 were marked by "an increasing frequency of clashes along the border of the two Yemens by insurgent forces from both countries operating against military targets in the region." See Lt. Col. John J. Ruszkiewicz, USA (Ret.), "How the US Lost Its Footing in the Shifting Sands of the Persian Gulf—A Case History in the Yemen Arab Republic," *Armed Forces Journal International*, September 1980, p. 66.

98. Marvine Howe, "Southern Yemen Blends Marxism with Islam and Arab Nationalism," *The New York Times*, May 25, 1979.

99. TASS broadcast, February 27, 1979, in Foreign Broadcast Information Service, Daily Report, *Soviet Union*, February 28, 1979, pp. F4, F5.

100. Michael Tingay, "Yemen War Stalemate as Iraq Neutralises Soviet Moves," *Financial Times* (London), March 29, 1979, p. 4.

101. Marvine Howe, "Yemen Seeks U.S. Aid on Border Force," *The New York Times*, June 12, 1979.

102. Central Intelligence Agency (1979), p. 4.

103. These troop movements were reported by the Kuwaiti newspaper *Al Siyasa*; see AP, "Soviet Said to Enter Yemen Conflict," *The New York Times*, March 9, 1979, p. A8.

104. See "A Mideast Buildup," *Newsweek*, March 19, 1979, p. 33.

105. The U.S. military attache to North Yemen found little evidence of any serious fighting in the border region; see Ruszkiewicz (1980), pp. 70 and 72.

106. Besides sending the carrier *Constellation* and three other ships to the Arabian Sea, the United States airlifted almost $400 million worth of fighter aircraft and armored equipment to the Arabian peninsula, destined for North Yemen. Richard Burt, "U.S. Sends Ships to Arabian Sea in Yemen Crisis," *The New York Times*, March 7, 1979; and "Intervention in Yemen War Signals Foreign Policy Shift," *The New York Times*, March 18, 1979.

107. Pranay B. Gupte, "Soviet Activity Found Growing in Aden Region," *The New York Times*, June 10, 1980.

108. UPI, "Soviet Naval Force Stages Show for Southern Yemenis," *The New York Times*, May 31, 1979.

109. Gupte, *The New York Times*, June 10, 1980, p. A13; and Manthorpe (1980), p. 119.

110. Central Intelligence Agency, *Communist Aid Activities in Non-Communist Less Developed Countries, 1979 and 1954-79*, ER 80-10318U (Washington, D.C., October 1980a), p. 15.

111. See Gupte, *The New York Times*, June 10, 1980, p. A13; Drew Middleton, "Oman Wary of Soviet Buildup in Southern Yemen," *The New York Times*, June 4, 1979, p. 3; and "Only There for the Port," *Economist*, November 3-9, 1979, p. 53.

112. Richard Burt, "Saudis Said to Delay Weapons for Yemen, " *The New York Times*, December 19, 1979.

113. The Soviet aid package reportedly included 36 MIG-21 fighters, 24 SU-22 ground-attack jets, approximately 500 tanks, and a number of armored personnel carriers and rocket launchers. See Christopher Wren,

"In Yemen, the East and West Do Meet," *The New York Times*, May 7, 1980; and Edward Cody, "U.S., Saudi Concern Increasing at Soviet Arms Aid to N. Yemen," *Washington Post*, June 5, 1980.

114. The early months of 1980 found both Soviet and U.S. military personnel instructing North Yemen's forces. The U.S. number had declined by midyear from about seventy to eight.

115. Moscow, either directly or through East European countries, had supplied arms intermittently to Sana between 1956 and 1975 and from 1967 to 1970 had intervened actively in Yemen's civil war. See pp. 25-26 and 130.

116. See p. 25.

117. Durch (1978), pp. 46-50.

118. Edward Gonzalez, "Complexities of Cuban Foreign Policy," *Problems of Communism*, November-December 1977, p. 3; and Durch (1978), pp. 53-54.

119. See p. 96.

120. Gonzalez (1977), p. 3.

121. See James D. Theberge, *Russia in the Caribbean*, Part Two (Washington, D.C.: Center for Strategic and International Studies, Georgetown University, 1973), pp. 53-60; and "Cuba Said To Keep Its Forces Overseas," *The New York Times*, October 21, 1979.

122. See p. 93.

123. For views on Cuban accommodation to Soviet direction, see George Volsky, "Cuba's Foreign Policies," *Current History*, February 1976, pp. 69-72; Lyn D. Bender, *The Politics of Hostility—Castro's Revolution and United States Policy* (San German, Puerto Rico: Inter-American University Press, 1975), pp. 55-56; Vanneman and James (1976), pp. 92-103; and Theberge (1973), p. 54.

124. Other expositions of the view that Cuba is a compliant surrogate of the USSR in the Third World may be found in David Rees, *Soviet Strategic Penetration of Africa*, Conflict Studies no. 77 (London: Institute for the Study of Conflict, November 1977), pp. 1-21; Irving Louis Horowitz, "Military Outcomes of the Cuban Revolution," in *Cuban Communism*, ed. Horowitz (New Brunswick, N.J.: Transaction Books, 1977), p. 94; and Hugh Thomas, "Cuba's 'Civilizing Mission': Lessons of the African Adventures," *Encounter*, February 1978, pp. 51-55.

125. For interpretations emphasizing the autonomous element in Cuban policy, see statement of Lourdes Casal in U.S. Congress, House, Committee on Foreign Relations, Subcommittee on Inter-American Affairs, *Impact of Cuban-Soviet Ties in the Western Hemisphere*, 95th Cong., 2d sess., April 12, 1978, pp. 80-85; Nelson P. Valdes, "Revolutionary Solidarity in Angola," in *Cuba in the World*, eds. Cole Blaiser and Carmelo Mesa-Lago (Pittsburgh, Pa.: University of Pittsburgh Press, 1978), pp. 110-113; Cole Blaiser, "The Soviet Union in the Cuban American Conflict," in *Cuba in*

the World, eds. Blaiser and Carmelo Mesa-Lago (Pittsburgh, Pa.: University of Pittsburgh Press, 1978), pp. 37-38; and W. Raymond Duncan, "Cuba: National Communism in the Global Setting," *International Journal*, Winter 1976, p. 71.

126. The mobilization thesis for Cuban involvement abroad, rather than subservience to Soviet dictates, has been advanced by A.M. Kapcia, "Cuba's African Involvement: A New Perspective," *Survey* 24 (Spring 1979):153-159.

127. Informative discussions of this and other interpretations of the Soviet-Cuban relationship may be found in Gonzalez (1980b), pp. 147-165; and in a review article by Cole Blaiser, "The Cuban-Soviet Link," *Problems of Communism*, November-December 1978, pp. 59-62. See also William J. Durch, "The Cuban Military in Africa and the Middle East: From Algeria to Angola," *Studies in Comparative Communism*, Spring/Summer 1978, pp. 34-36; Jorge I. Dominguez, "Cuban Foreign Policy," *Foreign Affairs*, Fall 1978, pp. 91-95, 98; and Michael A. Samuels et al., *Implications of Soviet and Cuban Activities in Africa for U.S. Policy* (Washington, D.C.: Center for Strategic and International Studies, Georgetown University, 1979), pp. 43-50.

128. Jorge I. Dominguez, "The Armed Forces and Foreign Relations," in *Cuba and the World*, ed. Cole Blaiser and Carmelo Mesa-Lago (Pittsburgh, Pa.: University of Pittsburgh Press, 1978), p. 73.

129. Durch (1978), p. 61.

130. See Brian Crozier, *The Surrogate Forces of the Soviet Union*, Conflict Studies no. 92 (London: Institute for the Study of Conflict, February 1978), pp. 4-7.

131. Melvin Croan, "A New Afrika Korps?" *Washington Quarterly*, Winter 1980, pp. 27-33; John F. Burns, "East German Afrika Korps: Force to Be Reckoned With," *The New York Times*, November 18, 1979; and Central Intelligence Agency (1980a), p. 39.

132. Crozier (1978), pp. 4-7; and Croan (1980), pp. 27-32. Some 9,000 to 10,000 East Germans reportedly are stationed in Africa. Although some of them are involved in advising local internal-security and intelligence organizations like those described earlier, the great majority of East Germans, like the other Eastern European communists in Africa, probably serves as economic technicians. The 23,500 Eastern Europeans and Soviets in Libya, for example, are engaged largely in public works and agriculture. See Central Intelligence Agency (1980a), p. 3. See also William F. Robinson, *Eastern Europe's Presence in Black Africa*, RAD Background Report/142, Radio Free Europe Research (Eastern Europe), June 21, 1979.

133. Dismukes and McConnell (1979), p. 145. In addition to logistics help, the East Germans also reportedly provided arms, medical supplies, and training to MPLA forces and allowed MPLA wounded to recuperate in

GDR hospitals. Similar East German assistance reportedly was rendered "on a larger scale" to Frelimo forces fighting the Portuguese in Mozambique. See Croan (1980), pp. 27-28.

134. See Department of State, Bureau of Public Affairs, *Communist Interference in El Salvador*, Special Report no. 80 (Washington, D.C.: February 23, 1981), and *Communist Interference in El Salvador*, Documents Demonstrating Communist Support of the Salvadoran Insurgency (Washington, D.C., February 23, 1981).

135. For a discerning analysis of the institutional constituencies within the Cuban leadership and the foreign-policy tendencies associated with them, see Edward Gonzalez, "Institutionalization, Political Elites, and Foreign Policies," in *Cuba in the World*, ed. Cole Blaiser and Carmelo Mesa-Lago (Pittsburgh, Pa.: University of Pittsburgh Press, 1978), pp. 3-36. See also Jorge I. Dominguez, "The Armed Forces and Foreign Relations," in ibid., pp. 60-61. Dominguez makes the point that an important change in Cuban military doctrine occurred with Angola, after which an overseas combat mission for the armed forces was explicitly justified and rewarded, which in turn boosted the standing of the military in the Cuban political system and gave the military an institutional stake in a vigorous Cuban interventionist policy abroad.

136. This and other points in our discussion of the Soviet-Cuban connection have been drawn from Rose E. Gottemoeller, "The Potential for Conflict between Soviet and Cuban Policies in the Third World," P-6668 (Santa Monica, Calif.: The Rand Corporation, August 1981), p. 23.

137. See below, pp. 150-151. During a visit to the United States in November 1979, Jonas Savimbi asserted that his UNITA guerrilla forces had beaten Cuban troops in their encounters in southern Angola, without immediate South African participation. Bernard D. Nossiter, "Angola Rebel Leader Says His Forces Are Beating Cubans," *The New York Times*, November 8, 1979.

138. In the years 1976-1979, Soviet economic aid to Cuba was estimated at more than $9.6 billion, while for the preceding fifteen years the total was slightly more than $7 billion. See Gonzalez (1980a), table 2.

139. John M. Goshko and Walter Pincus, "Sense of Duty behind Cuba's Global Role," *Washington Post*, September 21, 1979.

140. *Strategic Survey 1978*, p. 13.

141. Nossiter (1979).

142. See Avigdor Haselkorn, "Soviet Military Casualties in Third World Conflicts," *Conflict* 2 (1980):80.

143. Michael A. Samuels et al., *Implications of Soviet and Cuban Activities in Africa for U.S. Policy* (Washington, D.C.: Center for Strategic and International Studies, Georgetown University, 1979), p. 50.

144. The customary pattern of naval deployments was the visit twice annually of a group of four or five warships that spent several weeks in Cuba and usually included exercises in the Gulf of Mexico in their schedule. The air deployments involved flights by pairs of TU-95 (Bear D) aircraft from northern fleet bases up to eleven times a year. See U.S. Congress (1978a), March 14, pp. 7-9; and U.S. Congress (1979), April 25, pp. 8-9.

145. According to data released by the U.S. government, the brigade was commanded by a Soviet colonel and had three motorized infantry battalions and one tank battalion, and its equipment included forty tanks, sixty armored personnel carriers, and other hardware. Department of State, Bureau of Public Affairs, *Background on the Question of Soviet Troops in Cuba*, Current Policy no. 93 (Washington, D.C., October 1, 1979), p. 1.

146. For accounts covering the combat-brigade issue, see ibid., pp. 1-4; Department of State, Bureau of Public Affairs, Secretary of State Vance, Press Conference, *Soviet Troops in Cuba*, Current Policy no. 85 (Washington, D.C., September 5, 1979), pp. 1-7; Department of State, Bureau of Public Affairs, President Carter, Broadcast, *Soviet Troops in Cuba*, Current Policy no. 92 (Washington, D.C., October 1, 1979); David Binder, "Soviet Brigade: How the U.S. Traced It," *The New York Times*, September 13, 1979; and Don Oberdorfer, "The 'Brigade': An Unwelcome Sighting in Cuba," *Washington Post*, September 9, 1979.

147. See above, pp. 24-25.

148. "By Whom and for What Is This Needed," *Pravda*, September 11, 1979; Richard Burt, "Soviet Says Troops Are to Advise Cuba: Denies Combat Role," *The New York Times*, September 11, 1979; and Karen DeYoung, "Castro Denounces Carter, Calls Troop Charge False," *Washington Post*, September 29, 1979.

149. Richard Burt, "U.S. Said to Develop Policy Options on Issue of Soviet Force in Cuba," *The New York Times*, September 19, 1979; and Bernard Gwertzman, "Brzezinski Cautions Soviet on Cuba Unit," *The New York Times*, September 23, 1979.

150. See U.S. Congress (1979), April 25, pp. 5-10. See also Don Oberdorfer and Walter Pincus, "Soviet Troops Talks Continue Amid a Swirl of Controversy," *Washington Post*, September 12, 1979; and the testimony before a Senate Foreign Relations Subcommittee of Fred C. Iklé, undersecretary of defense for policy, reported by George C. Wilson, "'Contingency Plans' for Caribbean Being Drafted, Pentagon Tells Hill," *Washington Post*, December 16, 1981, p. A20; and Richard Halloran, "U.S. to Train 1,500 Salvadoran Soldiers," *The New York Times* (December 16, 1981), p. A5.

151. For an informative survey of trends in the Caribbean basin, see Richard Sim and James Anderson, *The Caribbean Strategic Vacuum*, Con-

flict Studies no. 121 (London: Institute for the Study of Conflict, August 1980), pp. 1-23. See also Richard Burt, "U.S. Asserts Cubans Are Supplying and Training Rebels in Nicaragua," *The New York Times*, 23 June 1979; Henry S. Bradsher, "Experts See New Cuba Role in Hemisphere Revolutions," *Washington Star*, February 18, 1980; and Karen Elliott House and Beth Nissen, "Southern Strategy: U.S. Tries to Influence the Unrest in Central American Lands but Finds the Task Tricky," *Wall Street Journal*, April 29, 1980.

Chapter 9
The Soviet Intervention in Afghanistan

1. See pp. 11-12.

2. See Arnold Fletcher, *Afghanistan: Highway of Conquest* (Ithaca, N.Y.: Cornell University Press, 1965); William E. Griffith, "The Implications of Afghanistan," *Survival* (London: July–August 1980b), pp. 146–147; Ronald R. Rader, "The Russian Military and Afghanistan: An Historical Perspective," in *Soviet Armed Forces Review Annual*, vol. 4, ed. David R. Jones (Gulf Breeze, Fla.: Academic International Press, 1980), pp. 308–318.

3. The Khalq-Parcham rivalry within the communist-oriented People's Democratic Party of Afghanistan (PDPA), which had been founded in 1965 by Nur Mohammed Taraki, began two years later, when Babrak Karmal led a Parcham splinter group out of the party. The Parcham faction has been considered closer to Moscow than the more independent-minded Khalq faction. For details, see Hannah Negaran, pseudonym, "The Afghan Coup of April 1978: Revolution and International Security," *Orbis* (Spring 1979) pp. 96–100; and Louis Dupree, "Afghanistan under the Khalq," *Problems of Communism*, July–August 1979, pp. 34–35.

4. See David Chaffetz, "Afghanistan in Turmoil," *International Affairs* (London), January 1980, pp. 17–18.

5. Reportedly, Daoud had discussed his intention to seek true nonalignment with Sadat not long before the 1978 coup. Negaran (1979), p. 99. For a discussion of the various steps Daoud had taken to lessen Afghan dependence on the USSR, including the expanding Afghan relationship with Iran, see Selig W. Harrison, "The Shah, Not Kremlin Touched off Afghan Coup," *Washington Post*, May 13, 1977, pp. C1 and C5.

6. Theodore L. Eliot, Jr., "Afghanistan after the 1978 Revolution," *Strategic Review*, Spring 1979, p. 58.

7. See especially David Rees, *Afghanistan's Role in Soviet Strategy*, Conflict Studies no. 118 (London: Institute for the Study of Conflict, May 1980), pp. 1–2.

8. Louis Dupree, *Red Flag Over the Hindu Kush, Part II: The Accidental Coup, or Taraki in Blunderland*, American Universities Field Staff Reports, no. 45 (Hanover, N.H.: 1979), pp. 4–6.

9. For accounts of the coup, see ibid.; Dupree, *The Democratic Republic of Afghanistan 1979*, American Universities Field Staff Reports, no. 32 (Hanover, N.H.: 1979), p. 2; and Nancy Peabody Newell and Richard S. Newell, *The Struggle for Afghanistan* (Ithaca, N.Y.: Cornell University Press, 1981), pp. 67–72.

10. Negaran (1979), p. 101.

11. Some observers believe that "there was little or no direct Soviet involvement in the coup or in its timing." They reason that the Soviets had closer ties with the Parcham faction than with the Khalq, and that the Khalq played the predominant role in the seizure of power, while the Parcham apparently "played a lesser, even a passive role in the coup." According to this view, the dominance of the Khalq faction in the takeover resulted in the installation of a Marxist regime in Afghanistan that "was ideologically derived from Moscow but whose leaders owed it nothing for the power they had grabbed." See Newell and Newell (1981), pp. 112–113.

12. Dupree (1979a), p. 47.

13. Soviet advisers and technicians in Afghanistan prior to the Taraki takeover reportedly were numbered somewhere between 1,000 and 3,000, including 300 to 400 military personnel. See Don Oberdorfer, *Washington Post*, May 29, 1978. The CIA estimated the number of Soviet and Eastern European advisers and technicians at 350 military and 1,350 economic in 1967 and 700 military and 2,075 economic in 1968. See Central Intelligence Agency, *Communist Aid to Less Developed Countries of the Free World, 1977*, ER 78-10478U (Washington, D.C.: November 1978), pp. 3 and 9; and Central Intelligence Agency, *Communist Aid Activities in Non-Communist Less Developed Countries, 1978*, ER 79-10412U (Washington, D.C.: September 1979), pp. 4 and 15.

14. Eliot (1979), p. 58.

15. See William Borders, "New Afghan Leader Denies Aim Is to Move Closer to Soviet Union," the *New York Times*, May 7, 1978; "New Regime Moving Afghanistan Deeper into Soviet Orbit," *The New York Times*, November 16, 1978; and Craig R. Whitney, "20-Year Treaty Brings Afghans Closer to Soviet," *The New York Times*, December 6, 1978.

16. See Eliza Van Hollen, *Soviet Dilemmas in Afghanistan*, Department of State, Special Report no. 72 (Washington, D.C., June 1980), p. 2. Karmal was first sent out of the country as ambassador to Czechoslovakia; later, when Amin summoned him to Kabul—perhaps to be purged physically—he went underground until the Soviets brought him back.

17. Ibid., p. 4. See also David Lynn Price, "Moscow and the Persian Gulf," *Problems of Communism* (March–April 1979), pp. 8–9; and Robert

Trumbull, "Foes of Afghan Rulers Are Hoping Skirmishes Will Bring on Rebellion," *The New York Times*, February 5, 1979.

18. For useful background on the ethnic and tribal factors in the spreading rebellion, see "Crisis Over Afghanistan," International Institute for Strategic Studies, *Strategy Survey 1979* (London: 1980), pp. 49-52.

19. In both a State Department press briefing on March 28, 1979, and a note to the Soviet government several days earlier, the United States had cautioned Moscow not to intervene in the Afghan civil struggle and had denied Soviet allegations that the United States was interfering in the internal affairs of the country. For its part, the USSR—besides accusing the United States, Iran, and Pakistan of interference in Afghanistan—also took the public position that the Afghans had enough manpower and equipment to deal with insurgency, which was blamed on the "reactionary clergy" assisted from outside. See David Binder, "U.S. Cautions Moscow to Avoid Any Military Role in Afghanistan," *The New York Times*, March 24, 1979; U. Verbin, "Defending the Gains of the Revolution," *Izvestiya*, March 20, 1979; and A. Petrov, "Rebuff to the Forces of Reaction and Imperialism," *Pravda*, March 21, 1979.

20. Aside from MI-24 Hind-type helicopter gunships, the best quality equipment the USSR had provided to Afghanistan at this point included MIG-21 fighter aircraft and T-62 tanks. See Jonathan C. Randal, "Afghanistan: Moscow's Vietnam?" *Washington Post*, May 10, 1979; see also "Afghans Said to Obtain Soviet Copter Gunships," *Washington Post*, May 4, 1979.

21. Stuart Auerbach, "Soviets Seen Boosting Aid to Afghans," *Washington Post*, March 28, 1979; and Richard Burt, "Russians Said to Die in Afghan Fighting," *The New York Times*, April 12, 1979.

22. At this time, about 2,000 to 3,000 Soviet civilian advisers were in position in Afghanistan. See "Afghans Said to Obtain Soviet Copter Gunships," *Washington Post*, May 4, 1979.

23. William Borders, "Afghan Insurgency Threatening Regime," *The New York Times*, April 13, 1979.

24. Randal (1979a); and David Binder, "U.S. Aides Say Afghanistan Army Is Crumbling under Rebel Pressure," *The New York Times*, July 13, 1979.

25. The term *left infantilism* derives from a 1920 work by Lenin entitled *Left-Wing Communism: An Infantile Disorder*, in which he castigated overenthusiastic and undisciplined communists who tried to set a more-extreme revolutionary pace than objective circumstances would allow.

26. See Lt. Gen. B. Balakirev, "Guarding the April Revolution," *Krasnaya zvezda*, April 25, 1979.

27. Michael T. Kaufman, "Soviet Role in Afghan Clash Shows Signs of Toughening," *The New York Times*, September 6, 1979.

28. Reuters dispatch, "Afghan Army Unit Reported to Rebel in 4-Hour Battle," *The New York Times*, August 6, 1979; and Michael T. Kaufman, "Afghan Guerrillas Boast of Success in Struggle against Soviet-Backed Regime," *The New York Times*, August 14, 1979.

29. Jiri Valenta, "The Soviet Invasion of Afghanistan: The Difficulty of Knowing Where to Stop," *Orbis*, Summer 1980, p. 205.

30. Robert C. Toth, "New Soviet Afghan Mission," *Washington Post*, September 5, 1979.

31. "Soviet Escalation in Afghanistan," *Soviet Report*, vol. 1 (Washington, D.C.: Center for Strategic and International Studies, Georgetown University, November 1979), p. 1.

32. According to U.S. intelligence sources, twelve MI-24 helicopter gunships had been supplied to Afghanistan by early May 1979. See "Afghans Said to Obtain Soviet Copter Gunships," *Washington Post*, May 4, 1979.

33. Drew Middleton, "In Afghanistan, 2 Soviet Trends Now Emerging," *The New York Times*, October 30, 1979. The location of the bases in western Afghanistan prompted some speculation that the Soviets might use such bases to apply military pressure on Iran.

34. "In the Center of Attention," *Pravda*, September 12, 1979.

35. *Strategic Survey 1979*, p. 49.

36. The bodyguard alleged to have betrayed Taraki was Major Sayed Daoud Tarun of the Afghan air force. See Zalmay Khalilzad, "Afghanistan and the Crisis in American Foreign Policy," *Survival*, July–August 1980, p. 155.

37. According to some Soviet accounts, Amin's bodyguards killed Taraki not with bullets but by smothering him with pillows.

38. "New Afghan Leader, Taking Over, Promises a 'Better Socialist Order'," *The New York Times*, September 18, 1979; "Afghans' New President Is Termed Survivor of Ambush on Weekend," *The New York Times*, September 20, 1979; and Michael T. Kaufman, "Taraki's Downfall Came Immediately after a Visit to Moscow," *The New York Times*, September 23, 1979.

39. *Soviet Report* (1979), p. 2.

40. Valenta (1980a), p. 206. On November 8, 1979, Moscow complied with Amin's demand, replacing Ambassador Aleksandr Pusanov with Fikryat Tabeev, a Tatar Muslim. Herman Nickel, "The U.S. Gropes for a Mideast Strategy," *Fortune*, February 25, 1980, p. 74.

41. Ibid. See also Selig S. Harrison, "Did Moscow Fear an Afghan Tito?" *The New York Times*, January 13, 1980; and "Amin Reportedly Appealed to Zia," *Washington Post*, February 14, 1980.

42. See Vladimir Petrov, "New Dimensions of Soviet Foreign Policy," in *Evolving Strategic Realities: Implications for U.S. Policymakers*, ed.

Franklin D. Margiotta (Washington, D.C.: National Security Affairs Institute 1979–1980 Seminar Series, 1980), p. 32.

43. Some observers believe that Moscow made the basic decision to occupy Afghanistan as early as October, whereas others place the date of this decision as late November. See Valenta (1980a), p. 211.

44. Ibid., p. 210; V. Petrov (1980), p. 33; Griffith (1980b), p. 149; Dimitri K. Simes, "Those Soviet Bombshells," *Washington Star*, January 6, 1980; Seweryn Bialer, "A Risk Carefully Taken," *Washington Post*, January 18, 1980; and Hedrick Smith, "Russia's Power Strategy," *The New York Times Magazine*, January 27, 1980, pp. 28–30.

45. Rees (1980), p. 3.

46. Henry S. Bradsher, "Soviet Combat Battalion Enters Afghanistan; U.S. Aides Concerned," *Washington Star*, December 13, 1979; and "U.S. Says Soviet Buildup Continues in Afghanistan," *Washington Post*, December 16, 1979.

47. According to the unconfirmed claims of a spokesman for the Afghan guerrillas, for example, the Soviet military presence in Afghanistan had jumped to 25,000 in early December 1979. Although at the time this figure was exaggerated, it was soon to be exceeded. Michael T. Kaufman, "Afghan Guerrilla Says Soviet Has Greatly Expanded Adviser Forces," *The New York Times*, December 11, 1979.

48. Richard Burt, "U.S. Voices Concern Repeatedly to Moscow over Afghan Buildup," *The New York Times*, December 23, 1979.

49. The shock effect of the invasion was perhaps best epitomized by President Carter's New Year's Eve statement: "This action of the Soviets has made a more dramatic change in my own opinion of what the Soviets' ultimate goals are than anything they've done in the previous time I've been in office." See Bernard Gwertzman, "Carter's Russian Lesson Is One in a Long Series," *The New York Times*, January 6, 1980.

50. *Strategic Survey 1979*, p. 53. Some of the initial elements of the invasion force may have been special KGB and MVD troops. See John J. Dziak, "Soviet Intelligence and Security Services in the Eighties: The Paramilitary Dimension," *Orbis*, Winter 1981, p. 782.

51. According to David Rees, Amin had told an Arab journalist on the morning of December 26 that the USSR had no designs against his regime. Assurances that the USSR had no intention to interfere in Afghanistan's internal affairs and charges that U.S. reports of Soviet "combat troops" in Afghanistan were "pure invention" were voiced in *Pravda* as late as December 23. See Rees (1980), p. 3; and Arkadiy Maslennikov, "Vain Attempts: Behind-the-Scenes Events," *Pravda*, December 23, 1979.

52. Drew Middleton, "Soviet Display of Flexibility," *The New York Times,* December 28, 1979; Donald E. Fink, "Afghan Invasion Likened to 1968 Action," *Aviation Week & Space Technology*, July 14, 1980, pp. 20–23; and *Strategic Survey 1979*, pp. 53–54.

53. Rees (1980), p. 3. Most of the forces for the invasion were evidently drawn from the Turkestan and Central Asia Military Districts of the USSR.

54. Ibid.; and Valenta (1980a), p. 214.

55. The initial announcements over Kabul radio of Karmal's takeover came from a transmitter in the USSR. Karmal himself was not seen in Kabul until January 1, but he may have been flown in from Moscow a few days before. See William Branigin, "Soviet Kabul Coup Carefully Staged," *Washington Post*, January 7, 1980; and Department of State, *Soviet Invasion of Afghanistan*, Special Report no. 70 (Washington, D.C., April 1980), p. 1.

56. Kevin Klose, "Moscow Justifies Actions in Kabul on Basis of Pact," *Washington Post*, December 29, 1979; and "Soviets Claim Troops to Repel 'Aggression'," *Washington Star*, December 31, 1979.

57. Paputin, first deputy minister of internal affairs, presumably had come to Kabul to look after Amin's security, a task that could have given him a central role in the coup planning. For several alternative hypotheses concerning Paputin's coup role, see David Binder, "U.S. Links Afghan Events and Soviet General's Death," *The New York Times*, February 3, 1980; and Dziak (1981), pp. 781-783.

58. See Marshall D. Shulman, *Tales of Afghanistan, Moscow Style*, Current Policy no. 143 (Washington, D.C.: Department of State, Bureau of Public Affairs, March 1980), p. 2.

59. The December 1978 Soviet-Afghan treaty of friendship and cooperation was cited as the basis for Babrak's request for military help. The request was first aired over Kabul radio on December 28.

60. Shulman (1980), p. 2.

61. Rees (1980), p. 3.

62. Victor Sidenko, "Two Years of the Afghan Revolution," *New Times* (Moscow), no. 17 (April 1980), p. 23.

63. About 4,000 additional Soviet administrators reportedly were flown to Kabul within days after the invasion to help run the government. Virtually all senior positions were filled by Soviet officials. Some East German personnel also were brought in. Rees (1980), p. 4; and Van Hollen (1980), p. 3.

64. Valenta (1980a), p. 215.

65. Stuart Auerbach, "Afghan Guerrillas Bar Conciliation with New Rulers," *Washington Post*, December 29, 1979.

66. See Text of UN's Afghanistan Resolution, *The New York Times*, January 15, 1980. For a rundown of international reaction to the invasion—including condemnatory steps taken by the U.S. government—see Department of State, Special Report no. 70 (1980), pp. 2-4.

67. *Strategic Survey 1979*, p. 54.

68. Van Hollen (1980), p. 4.

69. Rees (1980), p. 5; and AP, "Soviets Reportedly Take Afghan Allies' Heavy Arms," *Washington Post*, September 13, 1980.

70. See Marvine Howe, "United Front Still Eludes Afghan Guerrillas," *The New York Times*, May 28, 1980; and Edith M. Lederer, "Afghan Rebels Reportedly Stronger but Still Outgunned," *Washington Post*, July 11, 1980.

71. David Binder, "U.S. Supplying Afghan Insurgents with Arms in a Covert Operation," *The New York Times*, February 16, 1980.

72. See Van Hollen (1980), p. 4; Eliza Van Hollen, "Afghanistan: A Year of Occupation," *Department of State Bulletin*, March 1981a, pp. 20 and 21; and Van Hollen, *Afghanistan: 2 Years of Occupation*, Special Report no. 91 (Washington, D.C.: Department of State, Bureau of Public Affairs, December 1981c), p. 3.

73. James F. Sterba, "Gunfire Said to Continue in Kabul As Strike Keeps Businesses Closed," *The New York Times*, February 25, 1980; "Anti-Soviet Rioting Brings Martial Law to Afghan Capital," *The New York Times*, February 23, 1980; and "Soviet Commander Appears in Charge in Afghan Capital," *The New York Times*, February 26, 1980.

74. Michael T. Kaufman, "Travelers Tell of Afghan Students' Bloody Protests," *The New York Times*, May 11, 1980.

75. Michael T. Kaufman, "Afghan Leaflets Extolling Defiance Again Distributed Nightly in Kabul," *The New York Times*, May 16, 1980.

76. Stuart Auerbach, "Afghan Rebels Said to Press Urban Attacks," *Washington Post*, October 17, 1980.

77. The Soviet announcement on June 22 that the USSR was withdrawing "some army units whose stay in Afghanistan is not necessary at present" was timed to coincide with a summit conference of Western leaders in Venice. Politically, the move was taken to have purposes such as sharpening differences among the Western allies and putting a better face on the occupation in advance of the July Olympic games in Moscow. Militarily, it amounted to the removal of some heavy weapons and air-defense and surface-to-surface missiles that had proved of no use in counterinsurgency operations. The limited nature of the move also appeared consonant with statements by Brezhnev in February and the Afghan government in May that a phased withdrawal of Soviet forces would be contingent on guarantees against the arming and infiltration of insurgents from outside. See Craig R. Whitney, "Soviet Seen Attempting to Sow Discord in West," *The New York Times*, June 23, 1980; Whitney, "Afghans Offer Way for Soviet Pullout," *The New York Times*, May 15, 1980; and George C. Wilson, "Departing Soviets Unneeded in Afghanistan War," *Washington Post*, June 26, 1980.

78. Van Hollen (1981a), p. 19. Included in this 85,000-man force were "elements of three rifle divisions, two airborne divisions, and at least two other independent units." See David R. Griffiths, "Afghan Problems Stall

Soviets," *Aviation Week & Space Technology*, April 21, 1980, p. 18. For other estimates of Soviet troop strengths, see *Strategic Survey 1979*, p. 54; and Edith M. Lederer, "Soviet Said to Hold to Its Afghan Force," *The New York Times*, July 11, 1980.

79. Van Hollen (1981a), p. 19; and Eliza Van Hollen, "Afghanistan: 18 Months of Occupation," *Department of State Bulletin*, October 1981b, p. 64.

80. *Strategic Survey 1979*, p. 54; and Lederer, *The New York Times*, July 11, 1980. Observers in Kabul, according to Francis Fukuyama, also noted Central Asians in the Afghan capital wearing the uniform of Soviet MVD troops, which differs from that of the Soviet army. As previously mentioned, MVD troops may have helped to spearhead the seizure of Kabul, as they had done in Prague in 1968.

81. Alexandre Bennigsen, "Soviet Muslims and the World of Islam," *Problems of Communism*, March–April 1980, pp. 47–48; and Rader (1980), pp. 322–323. See also S. Enders Wimbush and Alex Alexiev, *Soviet Central Asian Soldiers in Afghanistan*, N–1634–NA (Santa Monica, Calif.: The Rand Corporation, January 1981), p. 16.

82. Bennigsen (1980), p. 47.

83. Van Hollen (1980), p. 3.

84. The number of effective fighting men in rebel ranks was probably unknown to the rebels themselves, who owed their allegiance to some 946 local chiefs, or shalliks, but the consensus among the better-informed observers put it at no more than 75,000 to 100,000.

85. During 1980, the number of Soviet helicopter gunships in Afghanistan quadrupled to about 240. Other combat aircraft included MIG-21s, MIG-23s, SU-17s, and some venerable IL-28 bombers. See Van Hollen (1981a), p. 19; Michael T. Kaufman, "Soviet Units in Afghanistan Dig in As If for a Long Stay," *The New York Times*, October 9, 1980; and R.D.M. Furlong and Theodor Winkler, "The Soviet Invasion of Afghanistan," *International Defense Review* (Cointrin-Geneva), no. 2 (1980), p. 169.

86. See Drew Middleton, "Soviet Troops Said to Test New Weapons in Afghanistan," *The New York Times*, July 10, 1980; Van Hollen (1981c), p. 3; and Department of State, Bureau of Public Affairs, *Chemical Warfare in Southeast Asia and Afghanistan*, Special Report no. 98, Report to the Congress from Secretary of State Alexander M. Haig, Jr., Washington, D.C., March 22, 1982, pp. 14–17.

87. Stuart Auerbach, "Soviets Test Weapons in Afghan War," *Washington Post*, October 9, 1979.

88. AP, "Moscow Is Said to Send New Units to Kabul," *The New York Times*, July 4, 1980.

89. Kaufman, *The New York Times*, October 9, 1980.

90. Van Hollen (1980), p. 3.

91. Rees (1980), p. 5.

92. Drew Middleton, "Afghans May Confront New Soviet Tactics," *The New York Times*, April 21, 1980; and Michael T. Kaufman, "Soviet, Changing Its Conduct of War, Presses Attacks on Afghan Villages," *The New York Times*, July 15, 1980.

93. Michael T. Kaufman, "India Hears of Growing Afghan Resistance," *The New York Times*, October 17, 1980; and Kaufman, "Soviet Units in Afghanistan Dig in As If for a Long Stay," *The New York Times*, October 9, 1980.

94. Since the actual Soviet presence in Afghanistan varies from day to day, the number of troops may be as much as 10 percent lower than this 100,000-man figure at any one time. See statement of Deputy Secretary of State Walter J. Stoessel, Jr., before the Senate Foreign Relations Committee on March 8, 1982, *Department of State Bulletin*, April 1982, p. 85; Van Hollen (1981b), pp. 64–65; and Van Hollen (1981c), pp. 1–3. For other accounts of the situation in Afghanistan as of late 1981, see Stuart Auerbach, "Standoff in Afghanistan Hurts Soviet Troops' Image," *Washington Post*, December 27, 1981, pp. A1, A24; and Richard Halloran, "Soviets Ready to Bolster Its Afghan Force," *The New York Times*, December 24, 1981, p. A3.

95. Michael T. Kaufman, "Afghan Guerrillas Tell of Soviet Drive," *The New York Times*, October 5, 1980.

96. Middleton, *The New York Times*, July 10, 1980.

97. William Beecher, "Soviets Trying to Hide Toll of Afghan War," *Washington Star*, September 18, 1980.

98. "Soviet Military Said to Have Morale, Drinking Problems," *Baltimore Sun*, May 7, 1981. This 1981 casualty estimation is somewhat lower than an earlier State Department estimate that placed Soviet casualties at 7,000 killed and wounded by the beginning of April 1980. See Department of State, Special Report no. 70 (1980), p. 2.

99. Auerbach, *Washington Post*, December 27, 1981.

100. As of December 1981, an estimated 2.5 million Afghan refugees were in Pakistan and about 1 million in Iran. See Van Hollen (1981c), p. 6; and "Russia in Afghanistan: the Tribesmen Who Took on a Titan," *Economist*, May 23-29, 1981, p. 35.

101. *Economist*, May 23-29, 1981, p. 34.

102. Nicholas Gage, "Islamic Zeal and Talent for War Help Afghan Rebels to Hold Out," *The New York Times*, July 20, 1980.

103. The authors are indebted to William G. Hyland for this observation on the bogging-down thesis.

Chapter 10
Soviet Policy Objectives in the Third World

1. As Henry Kissinger put it: "Absolute security for Russia has meant infinite insecurity for all its neighbors." Henry Kissinger, *White House Years* (Boston: Little Brown and Company, 1979), p. 118.

2. As noted on pp. 77-78, recent trends pointing to increased Soviet imports of strategic minerals (some of which were previously exported in large amounts by the USSR) and forecasts predicting an eventual downturn in Soviet oil production suggest that the USSR's interest in acquiring Third World resources will become substantially greater in the years ahead.

3. Richard Pipes, for example, contends that a principal aim of Soviet strategy toward the Third World "has been to cut off capitalist countries from sources of raw materials and cheap labor. . . . The single-minded persistence with which the USSR, its failures notwithstanding, has advanced its influence in the Middle East has had (and continues to have) as one of its prime motives the desire to establish control over the oil supplies of that region." See Richard Pipes (ed.), *Soviet Strategy in Europe* (New York: Crane, Russak & Company, 1976), pp. 26 and 37.

Chapter 11
The Spectrum of Past Soviet Involvements in
Third World Conflicts

1. Although at the time the Soviets took pains to mask their involvement in the Korean conflict, they have since claimed credit for their support. According to one Soviet history, "Soviet fliers shot down scores of U.S. aircraft and reliably safeguarded northeast China against air raids. Battle-steeled Soviet fighter pilots took part in these operations." See B. Ponomarev, A. Gromyko, V. Khvostov (eds.) *History of Soviet Foreign Policy, 1945-1970* (English edition) (Moscow: Progress Publishers, 1974), p. 195. A prominent Soviet specialist on the Far East, Mikhail S. Kapitsa, wrote that in 1950 the Soviet government transferred several Soviet air divisions to northeastern China. He maintained also that had the situation worsened, the USSR was prepared to send five divisions to help the North Koreans "repulse the American aggression." See Kapitsa, *KNR: Dva desyatiletiya—Dve politiki* [PRC: Two Decades—Two Policies] (Moscow: Politizdat, 1969), pp. 36-37. Similar claims are to be found in Ponomarev, Gromyko, and Khvostov (1974, p. 195) and in a history of the Soviet armed forces compiled by the Institute of Military History of the Ministry of Defense, USSR. See S.A. Tyushkevich (ed.), *Sovetskiye vooruzhennyye*

sily: Istoriya stroitel'stva [The Soviet Armed Forces: The History of Their Construction] (Moscow: Voyenizdat, 1978), p. 378.

2. See Robert F. Futrell, *The United States Air Force in Korea, 1950-1953* (New York: Duell, Sloan and Pearce, 1961), pp. 370 and 571. According to one authority, most of the fighter squadrons actively engaging USAF F-86s in Korea "were Soviet squadrons being rotated through the front at about six-week intervals." See General William W. Momyer, USAF (Ret.), *Air Power in Three Wars (WWII, Korea, Vietnam)* (Washington, D.C.: Department of the Air Force, 1978), p. 114. Soviet participation was not limited to the air war: Soviet intelligence officers were reported to be participating in the interrogation of U.S. prisoners of war, and thirty Russians were known to have assembled and supervised the laying of 3,000 mines in Wonsan harbor in October 1950, complicating and delaying the U.S. landing at Wonsan. Roy E. Appleman, *United States Army in the Korean War: South to the Naktong, North to the Yalu (June–November 1950)* (Washington, D.C.: Office of the Chief of Military History, Department of the Army, 1961), p. 635.

3. It was reported in August 1965 that "from radio interceptions, ground espionage, aerial reconnaissance and deduction from other known facts, most, if not all, the missiles are believed to be under Soviet management." Max Frankel, "U.S. Thinks Missile-Site Raids Have Hit Russians," *The New York Times*, August 22, 1965, p. 3. In October 1966, it was revealed that Russian voices had been heard on the radio network that tied North Vietnam's air-defense system together and that from these conversations, "it appeared that the Soviet advisers were helping to coordinate the system against American attacks." John W. Finney, "Soviet Operational Role Is Seen in North Vietnam's Air Defense," *The New York Times*, October 4, 1966, p. 10. See also William Zimmerman, "The Korean and Vietnam Wars," in *Diplomacy of Power: Soviet Armed Forces as a Political Instrument*, ed. Stephen S. Kaplan (Washington, D.C.: The Brookings Institution, 1981), pp. 346–347.

4. According to Momyer (1978, p. 123), the SAMs at all locations apparently were "operated almost entirely by the Russians and North Vietnamese with the Russians acting as technical advisors most of the time."

5. *Za rubezhom*, a Soviet weekly news magazine, disclosed on December 14, 1968, that since the beginning of 1965, about 3,000 Soviet experts had been sent to North Vietnam and that these experts were helping "in various fields of the national economy and the defense of North Vietnam." Given the USSR's heavy training and advisory involvement with North Vietnam's air-defense system during this period, it is probable that the bulk of these experts was military. See "Soviets Sent 3,000 Experts," *The New York Times*, December 15, 1968, p. 26.

It is possible that the USSR initially contemplated stationing a somewhat larger advisory mission in North Vietnam. According to Chinese accounts, Moscow proposed in March 1965 that China "permit transit of 4,000 Soviet army personnel to Vietnam, 'without first obtaining [Vietnam's] consent'." Hannes Adomeit, "Soviet Risk-Taking and Crisis Behaviour: From Confrontation to Coexistence?" Adelphi Paper 101 (London: International Institute for Strategic Studies, 1973), p. 12. This proposal was apparently but one of several Soviet requests for special arrangements with China to support the North Vietnamese war effort. The USSR also reportedly requested but was refused "an air corridor" over China to facilitate the airlift of Soviet military supplies and at least one Chinese airfield (Kunming) for "the special use of the Soviet Union" for the purpose of "aiding Vietnam with 12 MIG-21 aircraft." Hoang Van Hoan, "Distortions of Facts about Militant Friendship between Viet Nam and China Is Impermissible," *Beijing Review*, no. 49 (December 7, 1979), p. 18. Hoang, one-time vice-chairman, standing committee, North Vietnamese national assembly, had subsequently defected to China. While denying the USSR an air corridor and bases, the Chinese permitted the transport of Soviet and Eastern European military equipment and other aid supplies to Vietnam across China. The USSR and PRC apparently also cooperated in the training of North Vietnamese fighter pilots, who were given basic pilot training in the USSR and final combat training in China. See Momyer (1978), p. 137.

6. Henry Kissinger, *White House Years* (Boston: Little Brown and Company, 1979), p. 576. By the time Soviet forces were expelled from Egypt in mid-1972, the number of Soviet military personnel assigned to operational units in that country had been reduced to about 7,500. Department of State, *Communist States and Developing Countries: Aid and Trade in 1972*, RECS-10 (Washington, D.C.: June 15, 1973), p. 13.

7. Mohamed Heikal, *The Road to Ramadan* (New York: Quadrangle/New York Times Book Co., 1975), pp. 85–86, 88.

8. In November 1969, forty to fifty Soviet aviation personnel were flown to Sana with some twenty-four MIG-19s. Soon thereafter, a Soviet-piloted MIG was shot down, and Syrian pilots reportedly replaced the Soviets. See Wynfred Joshua and Stephen P. Gibert, *Arms for the Third World: Soviet Military Aid Diplomacy* (Baltimore: Johns Hopkins University Press, 1969), p. 27; and Edgar O'Ballance, *The War in the Yemen* (Hamden, Conn.: Archon Books, 1971), p. 193.

9. For a discussion of the evidence ("much of which would not stand up in a court of law") concerning possible Soviet combat involvements, see Cecil Eprile, *War and Peace in the Sudan, 1955–1972* (London: David & Charles, Newton Abbot, 1974), pp. 104–114. The Sudanese government consistently denied any direct Soviet combat involvement.

10. See Alvin Z. Rubinstein, "Air Support in the Arab East," in *Diplomacy of Power: Soviet Armed Forces as a Political Instrument*, ed. Stephen S. Kaplan (Washington, D.C.: The Brookings Institution, 1981), pp. 504, 507.

11. See John D. Harbon, "Cuba's Maritime Outreach," *U.S. Naval Institute Proceedings*, September 1978, p. 44; and Don Oberdorfer, "The Superpowers and Africa's Horn," *Washington Post* (March 5, 1978), p. 1.

12. For reports on the various Soviet planning and command roles in Ethiopia, see "War in the Horn," *Newsweek*, February 13, 1978, p. 46; "Red Stars Over Africa," *Newsweek*, March 13, 1978, p. 39; and Oliver LeBrun, "Ethiopians Put Pressure on Desert Rebels," *Manchester Guardian Weekly*, June 3, 1979, p. 7.

13. See pp. 51, 82-83, 92; see also *Soviet Naval Diplomacy,* Pergamon Policy Studies 37, ed. Bradford Dismukes and James McConnell (New York: Pergamon Press, 1979), pp. 337-343.

14. The Soviets flew over 1,000 sorties between December 1960 and March 23, 1961. A Soviet deputy foreign minister, G.M. Pushkin, told Averell Harriman that "apart from the Second World War, this was the highest priority Soviet supply operation since the Revolution." See Arthur M. Schlesinger, Jr., *A Thousand Days: John F. Kennedy in the White House* (Boston: Houghton Mifflin Company, 1965), pp. 331, 333.

15. Dismukes and McConnell (1979), p. 340; and Bonner Day, "Soviet Airlift to Ethiopia," *Air Force Magazine* (September 1978), p. 33.

16. See Richard C. Holbrooke, assistant secretary of state for East Asian and Pacific Affairs, statement before the Subcommittee on Asian and Pacific Affairs of the Senate Foreign Relations Committee on March 24, 1980, *Department of State Bulletin* 80 (June 1980), p. 28.

17. The Department of State (1973, p. 13) puts the number of Soviet military advisers and technicians in Egypt in early 1972 at 5,500. Most of these advisers, along with the estimated 7,500 Soviets who had been assigned to operational units, were withdrawn from Egypt in mid-1972.

18. One of the rare instances of the capture of Soviet personnel occurred in southwestern Angola on November 23, 1980, when two Soviet airmen piloting what was reported to be an AN-26 were shot down and taken prisoner by UNITA forces. UNITA displayed photographs of the two Soviet airmen as evidence of their capture. See Bernard D. Nossiter, "Angolan Rebels Report Capturing 2 Soviet Airmen," *The New York Times*, December 13, 1980, p. 3.

19. See p. 77 and note 98, chapter 7. As of February 1968, Soviet economic assistance to North Vietnam included "trucks, railroad equipment, barges, machinery, petroleum, fertilizer and food." See statement of Secretary of Defense Robert McNamara in *The Pentagon Papers* (Senator Gravel edition), vol. 4 (Boston: Beacon Press, undated), p. 231.

20. For example, the Soviets unsuccessfully pressed Idi Amin of Uganda (then chairman of the OAU and a recipient of considerable Soviet military aid) to recognize the MPLA government that assumed power in Angola in November 1975. Amin rejected this "arrogant" Soviet demand and briefly

broke diplomatic relations with the USSR. See Colin Legum, "Foreign Intervention in Angola," in *After Angola: The War over Southern Africa*, ed. Legum and Tony Hodges (New York: Africana Publishing Company, 1976), p. 17.

21. Departing from the customary exceedingly noncommittal security provisions of Soviet friendship and cooperation treaties with Third World states, the treaties with India and Vietnam become operative in the event of an "attack or threat of attack" and promise "effective measures" to ensure the peace and security of the two countries.

Article 9 of the Indo-Soviet Treaty of Peace, Friendship, and Cooperation, signed August 9, 1971, specifies that "in the event of either Party being subjected to an attack or a threat thereof, the High Contracting Parties shall immediately enter into mutual consultations in order to remove such a threat and to take appropriate effective measures to ensure peace and security of their countries."

Article 6 of the Treaty of Friendship and Cooperation between the Socialist Republic of Vietnam and the USSR, signed November 3, 1978, provides that "in case either party is attacked or threatened with attack, the two parties signatory to the treaty shall immediately consult each other with a view to eliminating that threat, and shall take appropriate and effective measures to safeguard peace and the security of the two countries."

With the exception of the December 1978 friendship treaty with Afghanistan, which contains unique provisions that could be construed to permit Soviet intervention under a number of circumstances (see pp. 155-156), Soviet Third World treaties call only for immediate consultation and coordination of positions in the event of a "threat to the peace" or "breach of the peace." For example, Article 7 of the Treaty of Friendship and Cooperation between the USSR and the People's Republic of Angola, signed October 8, 1976, states that "in the event of situations arising which create a threat to peace or a breach of the peace, the high contracting parties will immediately contact each other with a view to coordinating their positions in the interests of eliminating the threat that has arisen or restoring peace."

Similar formulations appear in the Soviet treaties with Egypt, May 1971 (abrogated in March 1976); Iraq, April 1972; Somalia, October 1974 (abrogated in November 1977); Mozambique, March 1977; Ethiopia, November 1978; South Yemen, October 1979; Syria, October 1980; and Congo, May 1981.

None of the treaties, including those with Afghanistan, India, and Vietnam, provides the binding military commitments found in the Soviet treaties with Mongolia (February 27, 1946), North Korea (July 6, 1961), and the Warsaw Pact countries, which pledge military assistance from the USSR in the event the signatories are the object of an armed attack. Compare, for example, Article 10 of the May 6, 1970, treaty of friendship, cooperation, and military aid with Czechoslovakia, which provides that "in the event that one of the High Contracting Parties is subjected to an armed attack by any state or group of states, the other Contracting Party, regarding this as an attack against itself, will immediately give the first party all possible assistance, including military aid, and will also give it support with all means at its disposal."

The texts of the Soviet treaties with Third World states may be found in the following issues of Foreign Broadcast Information Service, Daily Report, *Soviet Union*: Egypt (FBIS-SOV-71-104, May 28, 1971, pp. B1–B4); India (FBIS-SOV-71-153, August 9, 1971, pp. B3–B6); Iraq (FBIS-SOV-72-70, April 10, 1972, pp. B1–B3); Somalia (FBIS-SOV-74-212, November 1, 1974, pp. H1–H3); Angola (FBIS-SOV-76-198, October 12, 1976, pp. H1–H4); Mozambique (FBIS-SOV-77-64, April 4, 1977, pp. H2–H5); Vietnam (FBIS-SOV-78-214, November 3, 1978, pp. L6–L9); Ethiopia (FBIS-SOV-78-225, November 21, 1978, pp. H6–H8); Afghanistan (FBIS-SOV-78-235, December 6, 1978, pp. J10–J13); South Yemen (FBIS-SOV-79-210, October 29, 1979, pp. H2–H5); Syria (FBIS-SOV-80-198, October 9, 1980, pp. H6–H8); and Congo (FBIS-SOV-81-096, May 19, 1981, pp. J1–J3).

The text of the USSR's treaty with Mongolia appears in USSR, Ministry of Foreign Affairs, *Sbornik deystvuyushchikh dogovorov, soglasheniy i konventsiy, zaklyuchennykh SSSR s inostrannymi gosudarstvami* [Collection of Treaties, Agreements, and Conventions in Force, Concluded by the USSR with Foreign Governments], no. 12 (Moscow: Izdatel'stvo Politicheskoy literatury, 1956), pp. 11–13. The treaty with North Korea appears in *Current Digest of the Soviet Press* 13 (August 2, 1961): 23–24. The Soviet treaty with Czechoslovakia may be found in Robin Alison Remington, *The Warsaw Pact: Case Studies in Communist Conflict Resolution* (Cambridge, Mass.: MIT Press, 1971), pp. 231–234.

Chapter 12
Attributes and Patterns of
Soviet Military Involvements
Prior to Afghanistan

1. See, for example, Charles E. Bohlen, *Witness to History, 1929-1969* (New York: W.W. Norton & Company, 1973), pp. 293-295; and Alexander L. George and Richard Smoke, *Deterrence in American Foreign Policy: Theory and Practice* (New York: Columbia University Press, 1974), pp. 159-162.

2. Commenting on how the Cubans' perceptions of the prevailing political climate in the United States had weighed in their decision to commit troops to Angola, Gabriel Garcia Marquez, who apparently had access to official Cuban views, wrote: "The possibility that the United States might intervene overtly rather than through mercenaries or South Africa, as it had done thus far, was unquestionably one of the most disturbing enigmas. Nevertheless, a quick analysis warranted the expectation that it would consider this at least more than three times after it had just left the swamps of Vietnam and the Watergate scandal, with a President whom no one had elected, with the CIA harassed by Congress and discredited in the eyes of the public, with the need to be careful not to appear. as an ally of racist South Africa not only to the majority of the African countries, but also to the black population of the United States itself, and, in addition, at the height of the election campaign during the new bicentennial year." Gabriel Garcia Marquez, "Cuba and Its Intervention in Angola," *La Prensa* (Lima, in Spanish) (January 10-16, 1977), translated in Joint Publications Research Service, *Translations on Latin America*, no. 1613 (February 25, 1977a), pp. 23-24.

3. The declared policy of the United States toward Angola was also notably passive during the period. Official commentary stated that Washington was following developments in Angola with "great interest" and that it viewed the coming independence with "great satisfaction." The United States indicated a readiness to provide what assistance it could, but it did not attempt actively to promote the Alvor agreement. According to William E. Schaufele, Jr., assistant secretary of state for African Affairs, the United States "quietly told people that we supported" the Alvor arrangement but considered it to be "an African process." He said also that the Administration did not think it productive to get involved in an "active and pressurizing way." See U.S. Congress, Senate, Committee on Foreign Relations, Subcommittee on African Affairs, *Angola*, 94th Cong., 2d sess. (January 29, February 3, 4, and 6, 1976), pp. 191-192. See also the statement of Nathaniel Davis, assistant secretary of state for African Affairs, before the Subcommittee on Africa of the Senate Foreign Relations Committee, July 14, 1975, *Department of State Bulletin*, August 11, 1975, pp. 212-213.

4. Secretary Kissinger testified as follows on the limited U.S. aims: "We have never sought to 'overcome' the Cubans and Russians with our modest support but instead to achieve a balance on the ground that would lead to a negotiated settlement and the departure of all foreign forces." U.S. Congress, *Angola* (1976), p. 50.

5. Without naming the USSR, the United States first voiced a "cautionary word" about the "interference of extracontinental powers in

Angola" on September 23, but only in late October and November did it begin to raise the issue privately with the USSR by offering, in Kissinger's words, "to use our influence to bring about a cessation of foreign involvement in Angola and to encourage an African solution" if the Soviets would do the same. Kissinger said that the Soviet response to these overtures was "evasive but not totally negative." U.S. Congress, *Angola* (1976), pp. 10, 17-18, 52. U.S. officials revealed that they saw no purpose in raising the Angolan issue directly with the Soviets earlier, because "the Soviets do not respond to diplomatic pressure unless there is something behind it." Washington believed that it was necessary first to strengthen the FNLA and UNITA—"to help get something on the ground"—before initiating "some kind of dialogue with the Soviet Union on the subject." The administration's view was that the United States simply did not have the bargaining chips to talk with the USSR earlier. See ibid., pp. 193-194.

6. See Secretary Kissinger's November 24 speech before the Economic Club of Detroit, Department of State Press Release no. 578, November 24, 1975. However, the United States threatened neither to cancel the grain deal negotiated with the Soviets the previous summer nor to stop the ongoing SALT negotiations. In January 1976, Kissinger testified before the African Subcommittee of the Senate Committee on Foreign Relations on why these options were not pursued. See U.S. Congress, *Angola* (1976), p. 19. He earlier had summarized his view of the limitations of this type of leverage as follows: "We should not have the idea we can substitute in our bilateral relations with the Soviet Union for the situation on the ground." Department of State Press Release no. 627, December 23, 1975.

Moscow's public response to Washington's warnings that continued Soviet involvement in Angola might endanger détente was consistently negative. A December 2 *Izvestiya* article explicitly denied any such linkage between détente and Soviet support of wars of national liberation: "Some people would like us to believe that the process of easing tensions in the world and support for the national liberation struggle are incompatible. . . . The détente process does not mean—and never has meant—the freezing of the sociopolitical status quo in the world or the end of the people's anti-imperialist struggle for a better, just lot and against foreign interference and oppression." See Foreign Broadcast Information Service, *Trends in Communist Media,* December 17, 1975, p. 1.

7. According to Kissinger, there never had been "any intention of committing U.S. forces there to counteract the Soviets and Cubans." U.S. Congress, *Angola* (1976), p. 50.

8. The U.S. position on the Somali-Ethiopian conflict was spelled out by Anthony Lake, director of the State Department policy planning staff, on October 27, when he stated that the United States believed the "wisest course" was to pursue "a policy of restraint. . . . This means: a refusal to supply arms to either side; support for peaceful diplomatic initiatives by the

Africans themselves, including the Organization of African Unity; and a willingness to provide economic and humanitarian assistance to both sides, to relieve human suffering and to convey symbolically our desire for good relations with both." Lake also reiterated the U.S. policy of not "dramatizing the East-West factor" in Africa. After quoting an earlier statement by Secretary Vance to the effect that "a negative, reactive American policy that seeks only to oppose Soviet or Cuban involvements in Africa would be both dangerous and futile," Lake went on to say: "This does not mean we are unconcerned about the presence of Cuban troops in Africa or the flow of Soviet arms there—on the contrary. But I am convinced that we do more harm than good by dramatizing the East-West factor. Such dramatic exercises can make crises more dangerous; they can cut across that sense of African nationalism that is the surest barrier to external intervention; and they can inhibit the African diplomatic efforts that offer the best hope of resolving disputes before they become conflicts. When we look at African questions as East-West rather than African in their essential character, we are prone to act more on the basis of abstract geopolitical theorizing than with due regard for local realities." See Anthony Lake, "Africa in a Global Perspective," Christian A. Herter Lecture at the Johns Hopkins University School of Advanced International Studies, Washington, D.C., on October 27, 1977, *Department of State Bulletin* (December 12, 1977): 843, 845.

9. As in the case of Angola, the United States did not choose to link the Soviet intervention in Ethiopia to the ongoing SALT negotiations. As Secretary of State Cyrus Vance put it: "We do not believe that it is in our national interest to make a negotiating linkage between reaching a good SALT agreement, which is clearly in our basic security interests, and the inevitable competition with the Soviets which will continue to take place in Africa and elsewhere in the Third World." See U.S. Congress, Senate, Committee on Foreign Relations, Subcommittee on African Affairs, *U.S. Policy toward Africa,* 95th Cong., 2d. sess., May 12, 1978, p. 8.

10. See Leslie H. Gelb, "Muskie and Brzezinski: The Struggle over Foreign Policy," *The New York Times Magazine,* July 20, 1980, p. 39.

11. See Graham Hovey, "Brzezinski Asserts That Soviet General Leads Ethiopia Units," *The New York Times* (February 25, 1978), p. 5.

12. See Graham Hovey, "Soviet Assures U.S. Ethiopians Will Stop at Somalia's Border," *The New York Times,* February 11, 1978, p. 1; and "Ethiopia Sends U.S. Promise on Somalia," *The New York Times,* February 22, 1978, p. 1. See also Transcript of Questions and Answers at President Carter's News Conference, *The New York Times,* March 3, 1978, p. 10.

13. George and Smoke (1974), p. 465.

14. Kissinger described the pattern of forward missile deployments as one where there was "a seemingly marginal Soviet move, followed by a pause for consolidation and analysis of our reaction, succeeded by a rapid,

Notes to Pages 139-142

dramatic buildup." Henry Kissinger, *White House Years* (Boston: Little Brown and Company, 1979), p. 587.

15. See pp. 83-84.

16. When Khrushchev questioned Stalin about this, the Soviet leader reportedly "snapped back . . . 'It's too dangerous to keep our advisors there. They might be taken prisoner. We don't want there to be evidence for accusing us of taking part in this business. It's Kim Il-sung's affair.' " *Khrushchev Remembers,* trans. and ed. Strobe Talbott (Boston: Little, Brown and Company, 1970), p. 370.

17. Kissinger (1979, pp. 630-631) wrote that on September 25, 1970, "Dobrynin assured me that the Soviet Union had not known of the Syrian plan to invade Jordan. He weakened his case considerably by reassuring me that Soviet advisers had left their Syrian units before the latter crossed the frontier!"

18. See p. 81 and note 7, chapter 8.

19. "Malinovsky Is a Liar," *Peking Review* (May 3, 1966), quoted in Donald S. Zagoria, *Vietnam Triangle: Moscow, Peking, Hanoi* (New York: Pegasus, 1967), pp. 204-206.

20. See Central Intelligence Agency and Defense Intelligence Agency, *Communist Military and Economic Aid to North Vietnam, 1970-1974,* Memorandum, March 5, 1975, p. 4.

21. Kissinger (1979), p. 160.

22. After reviewing various Soviet communications on Korea, President Truman concluded on June 29, 1950, that "the Soviets are going to let the Chinese and the North Koreans do their fighting for them." Glenn D. Paige, *The Korean Decision* (New York: Free Press, 1968), p. 248.

23. David Detzer, *The Brink* (New York: Thomas Y. Crowell, Publishers, 1979), p. 258.

24. Ibid., p. 203.

25. *Soviet·Naval Diplomacy,* Pergamon Policy Studies 37, ed. Bradford Dismukes and James McConnell (New York: Pergamon Press, 1979), p. 212.

26. Other Soviet risk-controlling measures include the deployment usually of "only a portion of the naval forces available to them" in crisis situations involving the United States, the avoidance of overflying U.S. carriers with aircraft "capable of carrying cruise missiles," and the operation of their ships "with prudence in the presence of U.S. vessels." Ibid.

27. Moshe Dayan, *Moshe Dayan: Story of My Life* (New York: William Morrow and Company, 1976), p. 377.

28. Also on June 10, the Soviet ambassador to the UN informed the Israeli government that it was severing relations because Israel was "carrying out the conquest of Syrian territory and moving toward Damascus." See Abba Eban, *Abba Eban: An Autobiography* (New York: Random House, 1977), pp. 422-423.

29. " 'Abd-al-Nasir's Secret Papers," *Al-Dustur* (London, in Arabic), June 12-November 5, 1978, translated in Joint Publications Research Service, *Translations on Near East and North Africa,* JPRS 72223, no. 1865 (November 14, 1978):22.

30. See Chaim Herzog, *The War of Atonement* (Boston: Little, Brown, and Company, 1975), p. 250.

31. William B. Quandt, *Soviet Policy in the October 1973 War,* R-1864-ISA (Santa Monica, Calif.: The Rand Corporation, May 1976), p. 32.

32. See Herzog (1975), pp. 135-136; and William B. Quandt, *Decade of Decisions* (Berkeley: University of California Press, 1977), p. 197, note 70.

33. See Eban (1977), pp. 422, 536-537. Dayan (1976, pp. 543-544) reports that Washington was threatening Israel with "grave steps" if it did not observe the 1973 ceasefire and demanded, "more or less in the form of an ultimatum," that Egypt be allowed to resupply the encircled Third Army.

34. According to Heikal, Egypt's perceptions of Israeli motives in these attacks were (1) to forestall Egypt's building up a "missile wall which could cover an attack across the canal," (2) to break "the morale of the home front," and (3) to make Egypt "appear totally impotent, and so bring about the collapse of the regime and the disruption of the proposed union with Libya and the Sudan." Mohamed Heikal, *The Road to Ramadan* (New York: Quandrangle/New York Times Book Co., 1975), pp. 82, 84. In their analysis of Israel's deep-penetration bombing campaign, Shlaim and Tanter report that Israel's military objectives were (1) "to reduce further Egyptian military pressure," (2) to deter Egypt "from planning a full-scale war," and most important, (3) "to bring the war of attrition to an end and compel Egypt to observe the cease-fire." The authors say also that at least some Israeli decision makers apparently also hoped that the air attacks would "break the Egyptian morale, create a credibility gap between Nasser and the Egyptian people, and bring about the downfall of the Nasser regime." Avi Shlaim and Raymond Tanter, "Decision Process, Choice and Consequences: Israel's Deep-Penetration Bombing in Egypt, 1970," *World Politics* 30 (July 1978): 491-492.

35. See pp. 46-47 and Heikal (1975), pp. 86-88.

36. Sadat states: "We had repeatedly asked the Soviet Union to help us with our air defense, since the 1967 defeat, so much so, in fact, that Nasser even asked for a Soviet air commander to take over our defense." Anwar el-Sadat, *In Search of Identity* (New York: Harper & Row, 1977), p. 197. Yitzhak Rabin, then Israeli ambassador to Washington, is quoted as saying that the Soviets intervened "to avert an Egyptian military defeat." See Shlaim and Tanter (1978), p. 509.

37. According to President Machel, during the course of the Rhodesian conflict, Rhodesian forces attacked Mozambique "350 times, killing 1335 Mozambicans, injuring 1538, capturing 751, and costing Mozambique $550

million in revenue from transport and services, trade and tourism."
Gregory Jaynes, "Marxist Mozambique, Limping Along, Makes Slight
Gesture toward the West," *The New York Times,* October 13, 1980, p. A8.

38. While the planning for the Soviet war games held in late March
1979 "probably preceded Peking's assault into Vietnam," the scale of the
exercises evidently was beefed up as a show of force to China. The war
games, the largest ever staged on the Sino-Soviet border, involved nearly
250,000 Soviet troops. See William Beecher, "Soviets Staging War Games
near China," *Boston Globe,* March 28, 1979, p. 1.

39. See Foreign Broadcast Information Service, *Trends in Communist
Media,* FB TM 79-004, January 24, 1979, pp. 7-9; FB TM 79-007, February
14, 1979, pp. 4-5; FB TM 79-008, February 23, 1979, pp. 5-6; and FB TM
79-009, February 28, 1979, pp. 5-8.

40. Soviet military assistance over this ten-year period is estimated to
have been $3.25 billion. Total external communist assistance was $4.63
billion. See U.S. Arms Control and Disarmament Agency, *World Military
Expenditures and Arms Transfers 1965-1974* (Washington, D.C.: 1976), p.
74.

41. Between 1965 and 1974, North Vietnam received from the PRC
about 30 percent of its military assistance, amounting to some $1,355
billion. Ibid.

42. At the end of 1964, the very weak North Vietnamese air-defense
system consisted of no SAMs, about 700 AAA weapons, 20 early-warning
radars with limited tracking capability, and 34 MIG-15 and MIG-17 fighter
aircraft. By mid-1977, an extensive air-defense system had been built up, including about 200 SAM sites, 7,000 AAA weapons, numerous early-
warning and ground-control intercept radars, and some 75 to 80 MIG-15,
MIG-17, and MIG-21 fighters. While the PRC provided some fighter aircraft, the greater part of this new air-defense equipment came from the
USSR. See U.S. Air Force, *The Tale of Two Bridges* and *The Battle for the
Skies over North Vietnam,* USAF Southeast Asia Monograph Series
(Washington, D.C.: U.S. Government Printing Office, 1976), pp. 112 and
113; U.S. Grant Sharp, Adm., USN (Ret.), *Strategy for Defeat: Vietnam in
Retrospect* (Novato, Calif.: Presidio Press, 1979), p. 189; and *The Pentagon Papers* (Senator Gravel edition), vol. 4 (Boston: Beacon Press, un-
dated), p. 231.

43. These forces previously had been equipped with a hodgepodge of
French and other World War II-vintage weapons.

44. Communist ammunition deliveries to North Vietnam were closely
attuned to the requirements of these offensives, reaching their highest levels
during the 1972 offensive and in 1974, in preparation for the DRV's attack
in early 1975. See Central Intelligence Agency and Defense Intelligence
Agency (1975), pp. 2 and 4.

45. Richard Nixon, *The Memoirs of Richard Nixon* (New York: Grosset & Dunlap, 1978), p. 391.

46. See Shlaim and Tanter (1978), p. 494.

47. International Institute for Strategic Studies, *Strategic Survey 1970* (London: 1971), p. 46. Only a small portion of these sorties was in support of deep-penetration raids, which numbered but twenty between January 7 and April 13, 1970, including eight within thirty kilometers of Cairo. See Shlaim and Tanter (1978), p. 494, note 44.

48. Israeli aircraft encountered a formation of MIG-21s "carrying Egyptian markings but manned by Russian pilots" while raiding deep into Egypt on April 18. The Israeli aircraft broke off and returned to base. Shlaim and Tanter (1978), p. 495. Heikal (1975, p. 90) disclosed that the Soviet pilots did not attempt to maintain secrecy about their nationality since all intercom communications between them were in Russian. He ascribes this to "how the game was played between the superpowers: It was a signal to the Americans that the Russians had arrived in Egypt."

49. *Strategic Survey 1970,* p. 48. The Israeli air force vigorously contested and for a time effectively impeded this forward deployment process by persistently attacking new missile sites. On July 30, Israeli aircraft shot down four Soviet-piloted MIG-21s.

50. Yitzhak Rabin, *The Rabin Memoirs* (Boston: Little, Brown and Company, 1979), p. 178.

51. Shlaim and Tanter (1978), p. 506. Between June 30 and August 7, the Israelis suffered an unprecedented loss of seven aircraft. Flagrantly violating the ceasefire, the Soviets and Egyptians moved additional SAM units into the canal area after August 7, thus completing a forward missile-defense arc within reach of the canal between Ismailia and Suez.

52. Among other costs, the Soviet intervention and buildup of Egypt's missile defenses had eroded Israel's previous air superiority over Egypt and restricted future Israeli military options, particularly with respect to staging "reprisal attacks at will anywhere in Egypt" and the "ability to launch a massive preemptive strike, if necessary, to forestall an anticipated Egyptian crossing of the canal." Ibid., p. 508.

53. Soviet rockets and Cuban troops were instrumental in defeating the joint FNLA-Zairian task force that attempted to capture Luanda around November 11, 1975. Starting from ten miles north of the capital, a column of up to 1,500 FNLA and Zairian troops and Portuguese army veterans, supported by a dozen armored cars and a few artillery pieces, began to advance south across the Quifangondo valley toward Luanda's outer defensive positions, manned by an estimated 800 Cubans and MPLA units stiffened by Cuban cadres. The attack ended in total disaster for the FNLA-Zairian force, partly because of the incompetent tactics employed but also because of the devastating effect of Cuban firepower, particularly the

122-mm truck-mounted rockets, on the exposed attacking force. According to one account, "Observers estimated that two thousand rockets rained on the task force as it broke and fled in panic, scattering across the valley in aimless flight, abandoning weapons, vehicles and wounded comrades alike." John Stockwell, *In Search of Enemies* (New York: W.W. Norton and Company, 1978), pp. 213-214. See also Robert Moss, "Battle of Death Road," *The Sunday Telegraph,* February 13, 1977, p. 8.

54. International Institute for Strategic Studies, *Strategic Survey 1978* (London: 1979), p. 94.

55. After a week-long battle, Jijiga (a key Ethiopian town and tank base in the Ogaden) fell on September 14, 1977, when "some 1000 troops of Ethiopia's Third Army Division and 10th Mechanized Brigade mutinied and fled through the mountain passes behind it." International Institute for Strategic Studies, *Strategic Survey 1977* (London: 1978), p. 21.

56. The towns remaining in government hands were Asmara (the provincial capital), Barentu, Adi Caieh, and the ports of Massawa and Assab. All but Assab were tightly besieged by Eritrean guerrilla forces. Even though the Eritreans were outnumbered, they frequently prevailed on the battlefield because of their ability to pick the time and place of their attacks and because of the low morale of their Ethiopian opponents, who often chose to surrender rather than fight. See *Strategic Survey 1978,* p. 96; and "Nearing Victory, Eritrean Rebels Fear Division," *Baltimore Sun,* December 28, 1977, p. 2.

57. The town of Dire Dawa, sitting astride the supply route to Harar, was the only other significant position in the Ogaden still controlled by government forces. By this time, a large proportion (by some accounts, close to 90 percent) of Somalia's 30,000-man regular army had been committed to the Ogaden. Don Oberdorfer, "The Superpowers and Africa's Horn," *Washington Post,* March 5, 1978.

58. Steven David, "Realignment in the Horn: The Soviet Advantage," *International Security* (Fall 1979), p. 79.

59. *Strategic Survey 1978,* p. 95.

60. See "Red Stars over Africa," *Newsweek,* March 13, 1978, p. 39.

61. The maintenance of a large Cuban combat garrison in the Ogaden made it safe for the Ethiopians to redeploy additional forces from that front to Eritrea. *Strategic Survey 1978,* p. 96.

62. Ibid.

63. The United States, for example, found it difficult to rebuild rapidly some of the U.S. armor inventories drawn down to support Israel during the Yom Kippur war.

64. Dismukes and McConnell (1979), p. 344.

65. Bonner Day, "Soviet Airlift to Ethiopia," *Air Force Magazine* (September 1978), p. 33.

66. Algeria, Mali, and Guinea are reported to have received commitments for increased military assistance from the USSR in return for their provision of facilities to support Soviet logistic operations in Africa. See Central Intelligence Agency, *Communist Aid to Less Developed Countries of the Free World, 1977,* ER 78-10478U (Washington, D.C.: November 1978), pp. 13, 18, 21.

67. In return for these transit rights, Moscow reportedly agreed to provide Iraq additional military equipment and to forgive some of the accumulated military-arms debt that Syria owed the USSR. Syria, Iraq, and South Yemen also provided refueling stops for the airlift. Day (1978).

68. See above, p. 92.

69. See Department of Defense, *Annual Report, Fiscal Year 1981,* (Washington, D.C.: January 29, 1980), p. 106.

70. Following China's short-lived punitive operation against Vietnam, Soviet seaborne military deliveries to Vietnam increased significantly. Some 90,000 tons were reportedly delivered in the first six months of 1979 alone. See above, p. 95.

71. Some Cuban officers also apparently participated in the overall operational planning with Soviet and Ethiopian officers, most notably Arnaldo Ochoa, the commander of the Cuban expeditionary force, who shared a joint headquarters in Addis Ababa with his immediate superior, Soviet General Vasiliy I. Petrov. Three lesser Soviet generals are reported to have directed military operations in the Ogaden from a forward command post near Harar. See "War in the Horn," *Newsweek* (February 13, 1978), p. 48; and "Red Stars over Africa," *Newsweek* (March 13, 1978), p. 39.

72. The MPLA's initial request for Cuban combat troops reportedly was transmitted to Havana through "three senior Cuban advisers in Luanda." See Moss, *The Sunday Telegraph* (London), January 30, 1977, p. 9.

73. See Oberdorfer, *Washington Post,* March 5, 1978.

74. Interviewed at his headquarters in southeastern Angola in July 1981, UNITA leader Jonas Savimbi claimed that his movement had a fighting force of 15,000 guerrillas operating in groups of 30 to 150 men throughout south and central Angola. Savimbi said also that UNITA had equipped and trained ten conventional combat battalions and would field an additional five battalions by the end of 1981. Although its operations involve mainly guerrilla-type hit-and-run attacks and ambushes, UNITA apparently won a major set-piece battle in September 1980 when it routed a 2,000-man MPLA garrison guarding Mavinga in southeastern Angola. Subsequent MPLA counterattacks to retake the town—unaided by Cuban forces—had been repulsed, according to Savimbi, with heavy MPLA casualties. By Savimbi's account, the Cubans have virtually retired from offensive operations in Angola, restricting their activities to garrisoning the larger towns and providing static defense for strategic assets such as fac-

tories, bridges, diamond mines, and Gulf oil facilities. Indeed, Savimbi indicated that UNITA has had no significant engagements with Cuban forces during the past few years. Although Savimbi acknowledges that his forces cannot win a complete military victory while Cuban forces remain in Angola, he believes that UNITA "will succeed when the MPLA cracks" and "when it becomes obvious to all that they cannot govern." See Richard Harwood, "Angola: A Distant War," *Washington Post,* July 20, 1981, pp. 1, 8, and July 21, 1981, pp. 1 and 8. See also the assessment of UNITA by Jack Foisie, "Elusive Savimbi Pursues Quest," *Washington Post,* June 4, 1980, pp. 21-22.

75. David Lamb, "20,000 Cubans Prop Up Regime," *Washington Post,* June 4, 1980, pp. 21-22.

76. "The Hills with a View over Ethiopia's Dead," *Economist,* September 1-7, 1979, p. 43.

77. As of mid-1980, remnants of three Somali regular battalions reportedly were still operating in the Ogaden. See Gregory Jaynes, "The U.S. Finds High Prices on East Africa's Bargain Bases," *The New York Times,* September 14, 1980, Section 4, p. 6. See also Edward Cody, "Somali Guerrillas Intensify Fight for Ethiopian Region," *Washington Post,* May 20, 1980, pp. A1, A28, A29; and Christopher S. Wren, "Forgotten War in Ethiopia's Ogaden Heats up Again," *The New York Times,* May 26, 1980, p. 2.

78. For one account of Soviet Third World losses, which the author puts at possibly in the "hundreds," see Avigdor Haselkorn, "Soviet Military Casualties in Third World Conflict," *Conflict* 2 (1980): 80; also see above, p. 117.

79. Kissinger (1979), p. 1122.

80. According to the Central Intelligence Agency, "Economic aid has imposed a negligible drain on Soviet domestic resources, even considering that aid requirements must be wedged into an already overcommitted economy." *Communist Aid Activities in Non-Communist Less Developed Countries, 1979 and 1954-79,* ER 80-10318U (Washington, D.C.: October 1980a), p. 8.

81. Full repayment by some countries, however, will be long in coming, if indeed it ever materializes. The Soviets must doubt, for example, Ethiopia's capacity to repay its debt, because of its one-crop economy (coffee) and lack of hard-currency earnings. Egypt's debt reimbursement to the USSR will, at best, be a drawn-out process, given Cairo's decision in 1977 to halt all military-assistance repayments to the Soviets for ten years and to cut its annual economic-aid repayments to Moscow to only $20 million a year. See Central Intelligence Agency (1978), p. 29.

82. Lyndon Baines Johnson, *The Vantage Point: Perspectives of the Presidency, 1963-1969* (New York: Holt, Rinehart and Winston, 1971), p. 476.

83. The Soviet actions in Angola, for example, while not leading to a cancellation of the 1975 U.S.-Soviet grain-sale agreement or a suspension of the SALT II negotiations, caused President Ford to campaign in 1976 for "peace through strength" rather than "détente" and may have contributed to the failure to consummate SALT II. See Dimitri Simes, "The Death of Dente?" *International Security* (Summer 1980): 19-20.

Chapter 13
The Soviet Involvement in
Afghanistan: Comparisons
and Implications

1. See Central Intelligence Agency, *Communist Aid Activities in Non-Communist Less Developed Countries, 1979 and 1954-79,* ER-80-10318U (Washington, D.C.: October 1980a), p. 34; and Central Intelligence Agency, *Communist Aid to Less Developed Countries of the Free World, 1977,* ER-78-10478U (Washington, D.C.: November 1978), p. 36.

2. Quoted in David Rees, *Afghanistan's Role in Soviet Strategy*, Conflict Studies no. 118 (London: Institute for the Study of Conflict, May 1980), p. 1.

3. In contrast to the other Soviet treaties with Third World states, the Soviet-Afghan treaty does not specify the circumstances that would trigger such appropriate measures: "The high contracting parties, acting in the spirit of the traditions of friendship and good neighbourliness, as well as the U.N. Charter, shall consult each other and take by agreement of the two sides, appropriate measures to ensure the security, independence, and territorial integrity of the two countries" (Article 4, Treaty of Friendship, Good Neighbourliness, and Cooperation between the USSR and the Democratic Republic of Afghanistan, signed December 5, 1978). See Foreign Broadcast Information Service, Daily Report, *Soviet Union*, December 6, 1978, p. J11. All other Soviet Third-World treaties call for consultation only under specific circumstances—namely, when there is a "threat to peace" or "breach of the peace" or, in the cases of India and Vietnam, when there is an "attack" or "threat of attack."

4. This Soviet claim was, of course, quite specious in that Article 4 called for the taking of "appropriate measures" only after consultation and "by agreement of the two sides," and Amin clearly did not invite the Soviets into Afghanistan to overthrow his regime. A revealing insight into how the USSR interpreted Article 4 as guaranteeing Soviet security interests in Afghanistan was provided by a Soviet political commentator who wrote: "This article should be interpreted not only in the sense that the Soviet Union pledged itself to extend a helping hand to the Afghan people in the event of external aggression, but also in the sense that the Afghan side was

to contribute in every way to preserving peace and stability on the Soviet Union's southern borders and to prevent the emergence there of a seat of military danger threatening the Soviet Union." Victor Sidenko, "Two Years of the Afghan Revolution," *New Times* (Moscow), no. 17 (April 1980), p. 23.

5. As of December 10, 1979, U.S. government specialists were reporting about "3000 to 4000 Soviet military advisers and an equal number of civilian advisers in Afghanistan." See "U.S. Puts Advisers at 8,000," *The New York Times*, December 11, 1979, p. 4. These estimates closely parallel the CIA's projection of 4,000 Soviet and Eastern European military advisers and 3,700 Soviet and Eastern European economic technicians in Afghanistan at the end of 1979. See Central Intelligence Agency (1980a), pp. 15 and 21.

6. For reports on the pervasive Soviet role in the Afghan war by late 1979, see Stuart Auerbach, "Soviet Test Weapons in Afghan War," *Washington Post*, October 9, 1979, p. 1; "Brezhnev's Breath on Amin's Neck," *The Economist*, November 3-9, 1979, pp. 52-53; Henry S. Bradsher, "Soviet Advisers Increase Role in Afghan War," *Washington Star*, November 30, 1979, p. 3; and M. Aftab Khan, "Rebels Claim Killing 40 Afghan Aides," *Washington Star*, December 27, 1979, pp. 1 and 10.

7. U.S. arms assistance to Afghanistan also was inhibited by concerns about the effect that such aid might have on "U.S. relations with its CENTO partner, Pakistan." Theodore L. Eliot, "Afghanistan after the 1978 Revolution," *Strategic Review* 7, no. 2 (Spring 1979): 58 and 61.

8. In the words of one observer, South Asia had by 1965 "become an area of little interest to the United States. For all practical purposes, the United States chose against a competitive role in the region vis-à-vis the Soviet Union when Washington decided not to challenge Moscow's efforts to mediate the 1965 Indo-Pakistini war." Leo E. Rose, "The Superpowers in South Asia: A Geostrategic Analysis," *Orbis* (Summer 1978):398.

9. One such public warning was made on September 26, 1979, when a senior State Department official said: "Direct interference in Afghanistan by any country, including the Soviet Union, would threaten the integrity of that nation and peace in the area and would be a matter of deep concern to the United States." This warning was accompanied by a reiteration of the U.S. desire "for normal and friendly relations" with Afghanistan, despite Washington's important differences with the government in Kabul, and a reassurance that the U.S. government "seeks no special position in Afghanistan." See Harold H. Saunders, assistant secretary of state for Near Eastern and South Asian Affairs, statement before the Subcommittee on Asian and Pacific Affairs of the House Foreign Affairs Committee on September 26, 1979, *Department of State Bulletin* 79 (December 1979):53.

10. In the case of Czechoslovakia, the Soviets arranged an unexpected military exercise of Czechoslovak forces "to divert the attention of the

Czechoslovak generals from the forthcoming invasion" and succeeded in lowering fuel and ammunition stocks by transferring these to East Germany. Jiri Valenta, "From Prague to Kabul: The Soviet Style of Invasion," *International Security* (Fall 1980):134.

11. See Donald E. Fink, "Afghan Invasion Likened to 1968 Action," *Aviation Week & Space Technology* (July 14, 1980), p. 22.

12. As previously noted, some observers believe that it would take "at least three times" the present force level "to give the Russians a hope of subduing the country." "Russia in Afghanistan: The Tribesmen Who Took on a Titan," *Economist* (May 23-29, 1981), p. 34.

13. For one description of Soviet pacification operations, which includes the leveling of Afghan villages by air attacks and the systematic destruction of crops to deny the guerrillas winter food, see "Keeping Warm in Cities," *Economist* (November 22-28, 1980), pp. 38 and 41.

14. Helmut Sonnenfeldt, "Implications of the Soviet Invasion of Afghanistan for East-West Relations," *NATO Review*, no. 2 (April 1980), pp. 1-3; William E. Griffith, "The Implications of Afghanistan," *Survival* (London) (July-August 1980b), pp. 146-150; and Jiri Valenta, "The Soviet Invasion of Afghanistan: The Difficulty of Knowing Where to Stop," *Orbis* (Summer 1980a), pp. 215-217.

15. Anthony Austin, "Soviet Stands Firm on Keeping Troops in Afghanistan," *The New York Times*, October 20, 1980.

16. See Marshall D. Shulman, *Tales of Afghanistan, Moscow Style*, Current Policy no. 143 (Washington, D.C.: Department of State, Bureau of Public Affairs, March 1980), p. 2.

17. As of mid-1981, the USSR had some 85,000 men in Afghanistan and another 30,000 just across the Soviet border; these constituted only about 5 percent of the more than 2 million men then serving in the Soviet army and tactical air forces. For estimates of 1981 Soviet force strengths, see International Institute for Strategic Studies, *The Military Balance 1980-1981* (London, 1980), pp. 10 and 12.

18. Harry Gelman, *The Politburo's Management of Its America Problem*, R-2707-NA (Santa Monica, Calif.: The Rand Corporation, April 1981), pp. 63-67.

Chapter 14
Future Soviet Involvement
in the Third World

1. During the 1958 Middle East crisis, for example, when the United States intervened in Lebanon and Moscow's Arab clients were concerned that the United States and the United Kingdom would also move to overthrow the new revolutionary government that had recently seized power in

Iraq, Nasser flew to Moscow to seek Soviet support. Khrushchev, citing the "possibility of a nuclear war," counseled Nasser against any provocative actions and opined that the new leaders in Iraq should "reassure the West that its supplies of oil will not be interrupted." Khrushchev rejected Nasser's suggestion that the USSR state publicly that it was "prepared to intervene if the West invades or threatens invasion" because it "would raise the temperature" and "could produce unforeseeable consequences." The Soviet leader instead indicated that Moscow would limit its response to increasing the "scale of the Warsaw Pact manoeuvres due to take place near the Bulgarian-Turkish frontier" and emphasized that "of course it must be made plain that these were only manoeuvres." See Mohamed Heikal, *The Sphinx and the Commissar: The Rise and Fall of Soviet Influence in the Middle East* (New York: Harper & Row, 1978), pp. 79-99.

The cautious stance of the Soviet leadership in the 1958 crisis was anticipated by President Eisenhower and Secretary of State John Foster Dulles because of their confidence in the then prevailing U.S. military superiority. Eisenhower recalled in his memoirs that, in a discussion of the likely Soviet reaction to a U.S. intervention in Lebanon, he asked the secretary of state: " 'Foster, give us your analysis of an American intervention in Lebanon. What would the Russians do?' He [Dulles] replied, 'The Russians will probably make threatening gestures—toward Turkey and Iran especially—but will not act unless they believe the results of a general war would be favorable to them.' Foster did not believe the Soviets would put this to the test because of their respect for our power—especially overwhelming in bombers." See Dwight D. Eisenhower, *The White House Years: Waging Peace, 1956-1961* (New York: Doubleday & Company, 1965), pp. 270-271.

2. See Drew Middleton, "Soviet Said to Build Arms Caches in Libya, Syria, Persian Gulf Area," *The New York Times*, March 14, 1980, p. 11.

3. Central Intelligence Agency, *Communist Aid to Less Developed Countries of the Free World, 1977*, ER 78-10478U (Washington, D.C.: November 1978), pp. 14 and 34.

4. See p. 105.

5. Although Moscow has never succeeded in obtaining the solid support of the ninety-two countries of the nonaligned movement behind Soviet policies, at the sixth nonaligned conference in Havana in September 1979, thanks largely to Castro's intercession on Soviet behalf, a majority of these countries assumed increasingly pro-Soviet positions. The USSR's invasion of Afghanistan subsequently has tarnished Moscow's image, particularly among Third World Moslem nations, but the lasting effects of this action are yet to be determined. For an account of the Sixth Conference of Heads of State or Government of Non-Aligned Countries, Havana, September

3-9, 1979, see *Review of International Affairs* (Belgrade), September 20, 1979.

6. See "Cuba Gets the Bigger Thank-You," *Economist*, September 22-28, 1979, pp. 61-62.

7. The USSR's rapacious exploitation of local fishing resources and failure to live up to fishing agreements have created problems with a number of African states. Mozambique protested the low-quality fish it received in return for Soviet fishing rights. In Guinea-Bissau, the Soviets were blamed for fish shortages in Bissau markets. Sierra Leone charged the USSR with failing to live up to its 1976 fishing agreement and claimed some "$4 million of annual losses from Soviet fishing in its territorial waters." The USSR has come under fire for similar practices in Mauritius. See Central Intelligence Agency (1978), pp. 18, 21, and 23; and Central Intelligence Agency, *Communist Aid Activities in Non-Communist Less Developed Countries, 1978*, ER 79-10412U (Washington, D.C.: September 1979), p. 26.

8. The 1979 Nigerian decision to cut back from forty to five the Soviet training mission for the Nigerian air force reportedly stemmed from the "inefficient performance and 'condescending attitudes' of the Soviet advisors." The Nigerians were "displeased with the inability of the Soviets to service and maintain" their MIG-21 fighters and were alienated "by frequent displays of arrogance" from the Soviet technicians. Richard Burt, "Nigeria Orders Soviet to Reduce Advisors from 40 to 5," *The New York Times*, August 22, 1979, p. 3.

9. According to a Senate Foreign Relations Committee report, "The December 1978 Conventional Arms Transfer (CAT) negotiations with the Soviets in Mexico City ended with no real progress, and subsequent negotiations scheduled for Helsinki were postponed and have never been rescheduled. Neither the Soviet Union nor the major West European suppliers have agreed to restrain their transfers of arms and, in fact, statistics show that their transfers have increased significantly during the past three years." U.S. Congress, "Report to the Senate from the Committee on Foreign Relations on U.S. Conventional Arms Transfer Policy" (draft), June 3, 1980, p. 3.

10. See "A Tale of Two Yemens," *Newsweek*, July 10, 1978, p. 39; Richard L. Homan, "Pro-Soviet Coup in S. Yemen," *Washington Post*, June 27, 1978, p. 1; David Lynn Price, "Moscow and the Persian Gulf," *Problems of Communism* (March-April 1979), p. 13; and Amos Perlmutter, "The Yemen Strategy," *The New Republic* (July 5-12, 1980), p. 16.

11. Francis Fukuyama, among others, suggested in a private communication two possible factors that might encourage Soviet risk-taking propensities. First, the generational change in the Soviet leadership eventually will bring to power younger men whose outlook toward conflict and its

consequences has not been shaped intimately by the destruction and personnel losses suffered by the USSR during World War II. Second, the prospect
of the closing, by the late 1980s, of what some analysts now see as a window
of vulnerability in certain U.S. strategic- and conventional-force com-
ponents may induce the Soviets to act assertively while they still possess a
comparative military advantage.

12. In June 1980, Vietnamese forces attacked several Cambodian refugee
encampments on the Thai border, purportedly in response to Thailand's decision to repatriate to Cambodia refugees sympathetic to Pol Pot. Continued
Somali claims to the Ogaden and support to the Ogaden insurgents have provoked periodic Ethiopian air strikes and ground attacks on Somali border
towns. Even though the Pakistini government has attempted to avoid provoking Soviet attacks on its territory by eschewing active military support to
the Afghan insurgents, six helicopter gunships from Afghanistan strafed an
Afghan refugee camp ten miles inside Pakistan on October 25, 1980. See
"Lashing Out," *Economist*, June 28-July 4, 1980, p. 32; "Somalia Says
Ethiopia Attacked Two Towns," *The New York Times*, September 22, 1980,
p. A7; and *Baltimore Sun*, October 26, 1980, p. 2.

13. For a discussion of Pakistani concerns about such possible Soviet
attacks on Pakistan, as well as contingencies involving armed action from
India, see Francis Fukuyama, *The Security of Pakistan: A Trip Report*,
N-1584-RC (Santa Monica, Calif.: The Rand Corporation, September
1980), pp. 10-20.

14. While the Tudeh party apparently has made some progress in
recruiting members among students, oil workers, and ethnic minority
groups, it has yet to generate much mass appeal in Iran, in part because of
its long and close ties to the USSR. In contrast to other major leftist
movements, the Tudeh apparently possesses no military organization of its
own and therefore has concentrated on infiltrating and establishing cells in
the Iranian armed forces. Up to the present, the Tudeh, no doubt with
Moscow's encouragement, has followed an expedient policy of formal support for the Khomeini regime now in power. For analyses of the comparative strengths and future prospects of the Tudeh and the two other
major leftist groups in Iran—the Feda'iyin-e Khalq and the Mojahedin-e
Khalq—see Shahram Chubin, "Leftist Forces in Iran," *Problems of Communism*, July-August 1980, pp. 1-25; and John Kifner, "Iran Declares a
'Holy War' against Ideas from the Left," *The New York Times*, April 27,
1980, p. E3.

15. The Iranian government has, for example, charged the USSR with
supplying arms to the Kurdish insurgents seeking autonomy from Iran. See
Jim Gallagher, "Soviets Play Risky Game Encouraging Iran Terror,"
Chicago Tribune, November 19, 1979, p. 6.

16. Among other contingencies, the Soviets might occupy a portion of Iran (for example, Azerbaijan) or massively invade the entire country, capturing Tehran and the Khuzestan oilfields, which would constitute a far richer economic and political prize.

17. Under Article 5 of the treaty, " 'the Soviet government of Russia' and Persia each undertook to prevent the use of its territory by groups fighting the other. Each would also prevent 'the sojourn in its territory' of any third country's armed forces that 'may threaten the frontier, or the interests of, or the order in the country of the other.' " In Article 6 the two parties agreed that " 'in case any third countries intend to pursue a policy of transgression in Persian territory, or to make Persian territory a base for military attacks against Russia, and if thereby a danger threatens 'the frontier of Soviet Russia,' and Persia cannot remove the danger, 'the Soviet government shall have the right to send its army into Persia in order to take the necessary military steps in its own defense.' " The treaty was of unlimited duration and lacked any provision for amendment or renunciation. In 1941, the treaty was invoked as a "basis for a Soviet invasion of Iran in cooperation with a British move to oust Nazi German agents influencing Reza Shah, who was deposed in favor of his young son." Various Iranian governments have attempted unsuccessfully to eliminate or change Articles 5 and 6 through the years (for example, in 1935, 1958, 1959, and 1979, when Iran's revolutionary council unilaterally announced the cancellation of the two articles), but Moscow adamantly has rejected any changes, holding that "all articles of the 1921 treaty are unalterable." See Henry S. Bradsher, "Iran-Soviet Treaty Dates from Era of British Empire," *Washington Star*, November 21, 1979, p. A2.

Chapter 15
Influencing Soviet Risk
Perceptions and Other
U.S. Responses

1. For some thoughtful suggestions as to the various steps the United States and its allies might take to cope better with future Soviet challenges in the Third World, see Seyom Brown, "An End to Grand Strategy," *Foreign Policy*, no. 32 (Fall 1978), pp. 22-46; Donald S. Zagoria, "Into the Breach: New Soviet Alliances in the Third World," *Foreign Affairs* (Spring 1979), pp. 733-754; and Atlantic Council of the United States, *After Afghanistan—The Long Haul: Safeguarding Security and Independence in the Third World*, Policy Papers (Washington, D.C.: Atlantic Council's Working Group on Security Affairs, March 1980).

2. See Alexander L. George and Richard Smoke, *Deterrence in American Foreign Policy: Theory and Practice* (New York: Columbia University Press, 1974), pp. 160-162. Khrushchev disclosed that while Stalin "was worried that the Americans would jump in," he and other leaders "were inclined to think that if the war were fought swiftly—and Kim Il-sung was sure that it could be won swiftly—then intervention by the USA could be avoided." See *Khrushchev Remembers*, trans. and ed. Strobe Talbott (Boston: Little, Brown and Company, 1970), p. 368. The Soviets seem also to have miscalculated in the decision to deploy offensive missiles to Cuba. The Soviet leaders apparently believed that the "missiles could be made operational in Cuba before they were discovered" and that even if "they were discovered in the process, that the initial U.S. response would probably be a hesitant one, and would almost certainly be diplomatic and political rather than military in character." Khrushchev also viewed President Kennedy "as weak, inexperienced, and irresolute . . . ," and Soviet leaders "were genuinely surprised when Kennedy reacted as firmly as he did." See George and Smoke (1974), pp. 463-465.

3. The authors are indebted to Helmut Sonnenfeldt for the concept of derivative interest as applied to U.S. policy toward Angola.

4. McGeorge Bundy asserts that *"uncertainty*—the real and unpredictable risk of an escalation out of control" was of critical importance to the successful resolution of the Cuban missile crisis: "As a force for resolving the crisis I think it [uncertainty] ranks right with the visible and effective American superiority in the region around Cuba, and well above any imbalance in the strategic forces of the two countries." See McGeorge Bundy, "The Best of All Possible Nuclear Worlds," *International Security* 5 (Summer 1980):175.

5. A discussion of earlier attempts to use linkage to influence Soviet behavior is presented in Helmut Sonnenfeldt, "Linkage: A Strategy for Tempering Soviet Antagonism," *NATO Review*, no. 1 (February 1979), pp. 3-5, 20-23.

6. Shortly before Castro sent combat troops to Angola in 1975, the United States had cooperated in easing the inter-American boycott of Cuba and had been discussing further reconciliation with Havana. To this end, William D. Rogers, assistant secretary of state for Latin American affairs, had held private meetings with Cuban representatives. By July 1975, the two sides "were looking at a wide variety of ways to move toward resolving the issues" separating them. Rogers said on September 23 that the United States was prepared "to improve our relations with Cuba" and "to enter into a dialogue with Cuba." At the final meeting, in late November, the United States made clear its firm opposition to Cuba's military involvement in Angola but "did not slam the door on further talks." See David Binder, "U.S. and Cubans Discussed Links in Talks in 1975," *The New York Times* (March 29, 1977), pp. 1 and 8.

In May 1977, the United States had again expressed interest in working toward improved relations with Havana but made it clear that any major Cuban involvement in Ethiopia could jeopardize the resumption of discussions on normalizing relations. Immediately on the heels of its intervention in Ethiopia, Havana reportedly asked in March 1978 that a secret negotiating channel be set up with the Carter administration to work toward improved ties. The two sides held a series of top-level meetings over a period of more than a year, but the negotiations foundered over Cuba's refusal to cut its support of revolutionary activity in Latin America and Africa to U.S. satisfaction. See "Aide to Carter Says U.S., Cuba Talked Secretly," *Washington Star*, July 7, 1981, p. 5. See also Bernard Gwertzman, "50 Cuban Advisers Reported Training Troops in Ethiopia," *The New York Times*, May 26,1977, p. 1; and President Carter's May 30, 1977, statement on U.S.-Cuban relations, *Department of State Bulletin*, July 4, 1977.

7. In his postmortem of U.S. policy during the collapse of the Somoza regime in Nicaragua, William M. LeoGrande asserts that "there was nothing inevitable about the final outcome in Nicaragua" and that the United States failed to exploit available opportunities to assist moderate forces to power in that country. "As events unfolded in Nicaragua, the United States consistently tried to fit a square peg of policy into the round hole of reality. By failing to assess accurately the dynamics of Somoza's decline, the United States produced proposals which were invariably six months out of date. When the political initiative lay with the moderate opposition, the United States acted as if it still lay with Somoza. When the initiative shifted to the radicals, the United States acted as if it lay with the moderates. And when, at the last moment, the United States recognized that the radicals held the initiative, it seemed to think it could cajole them into returning it to the moderates." See William M. LeoGrande, "The Revolution in Nicaragua: Another Cuba?" *Foreign Affairs*, Fall 1979, p. 37.

In the case of the Iranian revolution, the former ambassador to Iran, William H. Sullivan, charged that the United States, through policy failure, missed a crucial opportunity to "broker an arrangement" that would have permitted "the armed forces to remain intact" in Iran and prevent the "disintegration of the armed forces and eventually the disintegration of Iran." See William H. Sullivan, "Dateline Iran: The Road Not Taken," *Foreign Policy*, Fall 1980, pp. 179-180, 184. For a comprehensive analysis of the various U.S. policy misperceptions and failures during the months prior to Khomeini's seizure of power in February 1980, see Michael Ledeen and William Lewis, *Debacle: The American Failure in Iran* (New York: Alfred A. Knopf, 1981).

8. Senior U.S. policy officials clearly did not anticipate the degree of foreign involvement in Angola. In an interview with a group of *Spiegel* editors, Kissinger said that the United States was surprised by both the Cuban involvement and the extent of Soviet involvement in Angola, as "we

did not expect either." See "Dr. Kissinger on World Affairs," *Encounter*, November 1978, p. 12. The United States seems also to have been surprised by South Africa's direct military intervention in the conflict. Members of Congress were assured in administration briefings at the end of July 1975 that South Africa was not going to become involved and thus would not prove an embarrassment to the United States. See U.S. Congress, Senate, Committee on Foreign Relations, Subcommittee on African Affairs, *Angola*, 94th Cong., 2d sess. (January 29, February 3, 4, and 6, 1976), p. 31. Washington also apparently lacked sufficient information about the comparative military capacities of the various liberation movements fighting for power in Angola. According to the former chief of the CIA Angola task force, even at the end of the war the United States had little "detailed knowledge of our allies" and "our knowledge of the MPLA was nil." John Stockwell, *In Search of Enemies* (New York: W.W. Norton and Company, 1978), pp. 180-181.

9. Washington initially perceived the Soviet arms buildup as simply an attempt to bring the MPLA up to parity with the stronger FNLA. As Secretary Kissinger testified on January 29, 1976, the "magnitude of the Soviet effort and the lengths to which the Soviet Union was prepared to go were not clear to us until later in October." When asked why the USSR was not "approached diplomatically when the Administration first discovered that it was providing substantial military assistance to the MPLA," Kissinger responded: "It appeared to us that the early shipments of Soviet arms to the MPLA were merely part of an effort to strengthen that group so it could compete militarily with the then much stronger FNLA. It wasn't until later that the Soviet arms deliveries to the MPLA seemed to do more than achieve parity with FNLA." U.S. Congress, *Angola* (1976), pp. 38 and 52.

10. As Seyom Brown, from whose article "anticipatory involvement" was drawn, points out, it is also "still difficult, so soon after Vietnam, to engender popular and congressional support for such a policy of involvement in the Third World." See Brown (1978), p. 40.

11. The first mutiny occurred on January 12, 1974, at Negelle in the southern Ethiopian province of Borana, when noncommissioned officers and soldiers of the Fourth Brigade detained their brigade commander and all their officers. The mutiny was generated by two immediate local grievances: the poor quality of the food and the absence of potable water. The broken pump of the enlisted men's well had gone unrepaired for several months, and while the officers could draw clean water from their own well, they refused to allow others to use it. When Haile Selassie uncharacteristically failed to act decisively against the Negelle mutineers, but chose to negotiate with them instead, "what soon came to be known as the 'Negelle flu' " rapidly spread to other military units throughout the country, where the soldiers had similar grievances about their living conditions

and pay and infected other segments of Ethiopian society as well, including workers, students, civil servants, the police, and professional classes. By early March, Ethiopian enlisted men, along with noncommissioned officers and some junior officers, had "virtually taken over the army, arrested their senior officers, got the Prime Minister and his cabinet to resign, and obtained from the Emperor the promise of a democratic constitutional monarchy." See Colin Legum (ed.), *Africa Contemporary Record: Annual Survey and Documents, 1974-1975*, vol. 7 (New York: Africana Publishing Company, 1975), pp. B160-B168.

12. These and other shortcomings in the Zairian military establishment reportedly were being corrected as of 1980 with the help of Belgian and French military advisers working with various Zairian military units in Shaba. See the statement of Ambassador Lannon Walker, deputy assistant secretary of state for African Affairs, before the Subcommittee on Africa of the House Foreign Affairs Committee on March 5, 1980, *Department of State Bulletin* (August 1980), pp. 47-48.

Bibliography

Ackley, Richard T. "The Weak Link in U.S. National Strategy: USSR Is Self-Sufficient; U.S. Is Not." *Sea Power,* August 1974.

Adomeit, Hannes. "Soviet Risk-Taking and Crisis Behaviour: From Confrontation to Coexistence?" Adelphi Paper 101. London: International Institute for Strategic Studies, 1973.

"Afghan Army Unit Reported to Rebel in 4-Hour Battle." *The New York Times,* August 6, 1979.

"Afghans Said to Obtain Soviet Copter Gunships." *Washington Post,* May 4, 1979.

"Afghans' New President Is Termed Survivor of Ambush on Weekend." *The New York Times,* September 20, 1979.

"Aide to Carter Says U.S., Cuba Talked Secretly." *Washington Star,* July 7, 1981.

Albright, David E. "The USSR and Africa: Soviet Policy." *Problems of Communism,* January-February 1978.

―――――, ed. *Communism in Africa.* Bloomington: Indiana University Press, 1980.

Allison, Graham T. *Essence of Decision: Explaining the Cuban Missile Crisis.* Boston: Little, Brown and Company, 1971.

"Amin Reportedly Appealed to Zia." *Washington Post,* February 14, 1980.

"Anti-Soviet Rioting Brings Martial Law to Afghan Capital." *The New York Times,* February 23, 1980.

Appleman, Roy E. *United States Army in the Korean War: South to the Naktong, North to the Yalu (June-November 1950).* Washington, D.C.: Department of the Army, Office of the Chief of Military History, 1961.

Atlantic Council of the United States. *After Afghanistan—The Long Haul: Safeguarding Security and Independence in the Third World.* Policy Papers of the Atlantic Council's Working Group on Security Affairs, Washington, D.C., March 1980.

Auerbach, Stuart. "Soviets Seen Boosting Aid to Afghans." *Washington Post,* March 28, 1979.

―――――. "Soviets Test Weapons in Afghan War." *Washington Post,* October 9, 1979.

―――――. "Afghan Guerrillas Bar Conciliation with New Rulers." *Washington Post,* December 29, 1979.

―――――. "Afghan Rebels Said to Press Urban Attacks." *Washington Post,* October 17, 1980.

―――――. "Standoff in Afghanistan Hurts Soviet Troops' Image." *Washington Post,* December 27, 1981.

Austin, Anthony. "Soviet Stands Firm on Keeping Troops in Afghanistan." *The New York Times,* October 20, 1980.

Balakirev, Lt. Gen. B. "Guarding the April Revolution," *Krasnaya zvezda,* April 25, 1979.

Barghoorn, Frederick C. "The Varga Discussion and Its Significance," *American Slavic and East European Review,* no. 7, 1948.

Beecher, William. "Soviet Staging War Games near China." *Boston Globe,* March 28, 1979.

_____ . "Soviets Trying to Hide Toll of Afghan War." *Washington Star,* September 18, 1980.

Bender, Gerald J. "Angola, the Cubans, and American Anxieties." *Foreign Policy,* Summer 1978.

Bender, Lyn D. *The Politics of Hostility—Castro's Revolution and United States Policy.* San German, Puerto Rico: Inter-American University Press, 1975.

Benningsen, Alexandre. "Soviet Muslims and the World of Islam." *Problems of Communism,* March-April 1980.

Bertram, Christoph, ed. *Prospects of the Soviet Power in the Nineteen Eighties.* Hamden, Conn.: Shoe String Press, 1980.

Bialer, Seweryn. "A Risk Carefully Taken." *Washington Post,* January 18, 1980.

Binder, David. "U.S. and Cubans Discussed Links in Talks in 1975." *The New York Times,* March 29, 1977.

_____ . "Castro Says He Told U.S. He Tried to Halt Invasion into Zaire." *The New York Times,* June 11, 1978.

_____ . "U.S. Cautions Moscow to Avoid Any Military Role in Afghanistan." *The New York Times,* March 24, 1979.

_____ . "U.S. Aides Say Afghanistan Army is Crumbling under Rebel Pressure." *The New York Times,* July 13, 1979.

_____ . "Soviet Brigade: How the U.S. Traced It." *The New York Times,* September 13, 1979.

_____ . "U.S. Links Afghan Events and Soviet General's Death." *The New York Times,* February 3, 1980.

_____ . "U.S. Supplying Afghan Insurgents with Arms in a Covert Operation." *The New York Times,* February 16, 1980.

Blaiser, Cole. "The Cuban-Soviet Link." *Problems of Communism,* November-December 1978.

_____ . "The Soviet Union in the Cuban-American Conflict." In *Cuba in the World,* edited by Blaiser and Carmelo Mesa-Lago. Pittsburgh, Pa.: University of Pittsburgh Press, 1978.

Blaiser, Cole, and Carmelo Mesa-Lago, eds. *Cuba in the World.* Pittsburgh, Pa.: University of Pittsburgh Press, 1978.

Blechman, Barry M., and Stephanie E. Levinson. "Soviet Submarine Visits to Cuba." *U.S. Naval Proceedings,* September 1975.

Bohlen, Charles E. *Witness to History, 1929-1969.* New York: W.W. Norton & Company, 1973.

Borders, William. "New Afghan Leader Denies Aim Is to Move Closer to Soviet Union." *The New York Times,* May 7, 1978.

————. "Afghan Insurgency Threatening Regime." *The New York Times,* April 13, 1979.

Borkenau, Franz. *World Communism.* Ann Arbor: University of Michigan Press, 1962.

Bovin, Aleksandr. "With Koran and Saber!" *Nedelya,* no. 36, September 4, 1979.

Bradsher, Henry S. "1977 U.S. Arms Offer to Somalia Ill-Timed?" *Washington Star,* January 14, 1978.

————. "Iran-Soviet Treaty Dates from Era of British Empire." *Washington Star,* November 21, 1979.

————. "Soviet Advisers Increase Role in Afghan War." *Washington Star,* November 30, 1979.

————. "Soviet Combat Battalion Enters Afghanistan; U.S. Aides Concerned." *Washington Star,* December 13, 1979.

————. "Experts See New Cuba Role in Hemisphere Revolutions." *Washington Star,* February 18, 1980.

————. "U.S. Concludes Deal to Use Somali Base." *Washington Star,* August 22, 1980.

Bragina, Ye. *Razvivayushchiyesya strany: Gosudarstvennaya politika i promyshlennost'* [The Developing Countries: State Policy and Industry]. Moscow: Izdatel'stvo Mysl', 1977.

Branigin, William. "Soviet Kabul Coup Carefully Staged." *Washington Post,* January 7, 1980.

Brown, Neville. "Jordanian Civil War." *Military Review,* September 1971.

Brown, Seyom. "An End to Grand Strategy." *Foreign Policy,* no. 32, Fall 1978.

Brutents, K.N. "African Revolution: Gains and Problems." *International Affairs* (Moscow), January 1967.

————. "The Soviet Union and Emerging Countries." *Mezhdunarodnaya zhizn',* no. 3, 1979.

Bundy, McGeorge. "The Best of All Possible Nuclear Worlds." *International Security* 5 (Summer 1980).

Burns, John F. "East German Afrika Korps: Force to Be Reckoned With." *The New York Times,* November 18, 1979.

————. "Cease-Fire for Rhodesia; War Plans for South Africa." *The New York Times,* December 23, 1979.

————. "Friction Grows in Zimbabwe Coalition." *The New York Times,* July 28, 1980.

Burt, Richard. "U.S. Aides Disclose Soviet Airmen Help in Defense of Cuba." *The New York Times,* February 14, 1978.

_____ . "Soviet Reportedly Cool to Linking Cuban, Somali Pullout in Ethiopia." *The New York Times,* March 16, 1978.

_____ . "Lesson of Shaba: Carter Risked Serious 'Credibility Gap'." *The New York Times,* July 11, 1978.

_____ . "Soviet Places Ships off Vietnam Coast." *The New York Times,* February 8, 1979.

_____ . "U.S. Sends Ships to Arabian Sea in Yemen Crisis." *The New York Times,* March 7, 1979.

_____ . "Soviet Ships Arrive at Cam Ranh Bay." *The New York Times,* March 29, 1979.

_____ . "Russians Said to Die in Afghan Fighting." *The New York Times,* April 12, 1979.

_____ . "U.S. Asserts Cubans Are Supplying and Training Rebels in Nicaragua." *The New York Times,* June 23, 1979.

_____ . "Nigeria Orders Soviet to Reduce Advisors from 40 to 5." *The New York Times,* August 22, 1979.

_____ . "Soviet Says Troops Are to Advise Cuba: Denies Combat Role." *The New York Times,* September 11, 1979.

_____ . "U.S. Said to Develop Policy Options on Issue of Soviet Force in Cuba." *The New York Times,* September 19, 1979.

_____ . "Saudis Said to Delay Weapons for Yemen." *The New York Times,* December 19, 1979.

_____ . "U.S. Voices Concern Repeatedly to Moscow over Afghan Buildup." *The New York Times,* December 23, 1979.

Bushuyev, V. "Latin America: Year One of New Decade." *International Affairs* (Moscow), no. 3, March 1972.

Byrnes, James F. *Speaking Frankly.* New York: Harper & Brothers, 1947.

"By Whom and for What Is This Needed." *Pravda,* July 15, 1979.

Cameron, Allan W. "The Soviet Union and Vietnam: The Origins of Involvement." In *Soviet Policy in Developing Countries,* edited by W. Raymond Duncan. Waltham, Mass.: Ginn-Blaisdell, 1970.

Carter, Jimmy. "Statement on U.S.-Cuban Relations." *Department of State Bulletin,* July 4, 1977.

_____ . Transcript of news conference. *The New York Times,* March 3, 1978.

_____ . *"Soviet Troops in Cuba"* (text of broadcast). Bureau of Public Affairs, Current Policy no. 921. Washington, D.C.: Department of State, October 1, 1979.

Central Intelligence Agency. *Communist Aid to Less Developed Countries of the Free World, 1975.* ER 76-10372U. Washington, D.C., July 1976.

_____ . *Communist Aid to the Less Developed Countries of the Free World, 1976.* ER 77-10296U. Washington, D.C., August 1977.

_____. *Communist Aid to Less Developed Countries of the Free World, 1977.* ER 78-10478U. Washington, D.C., November 1978.

_____. *Communist Aid Activities in Non-Communist Less Developed Countries, 1978.* ER 79-10412U. Washington, D.C., September 1979.

_____. *Communist Aid Activities in Non-Communist Less Developed Countries, 1979 and 1954-79.* ER 80-10318U. Washington, D.C., October 1980a.

_____. *Handbook of Economic Statistics 1980.* ER 80-10452. Washington, D.C., October 1980b.

Central Intelligence Agency and Defense Intelligence Agency. *Communist Military and Economic Aid to North Vietnam, 1970-1974.* Memorandum, Washington, D.C., March 5, 1975.

Chaffetz, David. "Afghanistan in Turmoil." *International Affairs* (London), January 1980.

Chanda, Nayan. "Vietnam: An Alliance Based on Mutual Need." *Far Eastern Economic Review* (Hong Kong) 105 (August 24, 1979).

_____. "Indochina: Too Close for Comfort." *Far Eastern Economic Review* (Hong Kong) 110 (November 14, 1980).

_____. "Bickering Begins as Old Friends Fall Out," *Far Eastern Economic Review* (Hong Kong) 111 (February 27, 1981).

Chirkin, V. "The Government of a Modern Transitional Society." *Aziya i Afrika Segodnya,* no. 9, September 1978.

Chubin, Shahram. "Leftist Forces in Iran." *Problems of Communism,* July-August 1980.

Clubb, O. Edmund. "Armed Conflict in the Chinese Borderlands, 1917-50." In *Sino-Soviet Military Relations,* edited by Raymond L. Garthoff. New York: Frederick A. Praeger, 1966.

Cody, Edward. "Somali Guerrillas Intensify Fight for Ethiopian Region." *Washington Post,* May 20, 1979.

_____. "President Quits in Aden Citing Health, but Analysts Suspect Power Struggle." *Washington Post,* April 22, 1980.

_____. "U.S., Saudi Concern Increasing at Soviet Arms Aid to N. Yemen." *Washington Post,* June 5, 1980.

Congressional Research Service. Library of Congress. *Soviet Policy and United States Responses in the Third World,* March 1981.

Congressional Research Service. Senior Specialists Division. Library of Congress. *The Soviet Union and the Third World: A Watershed in Great Power Policy?* Report to Committee on International Relations. U.S. House of Representatives, May 8, 1977.

Croan, Melvin. "A New Afrika Korps?" *Washington Quarterly,* Winter 1980.

Crozier, Brian. "The Surrogate Forces of the Soviet Union." Conflict Studies no. 92. London: Institute for the Study of Conflict, February 1978.

"Cuba Gets the Bigger Thank-You." *Economist,* September 22-28, 1979.

"Cuba Said to Keep Its Forces Overseas." *The New York Times,* October 21, 1979.

"Cubans Said to Halt Participation in Drive on Eritrea." *The New York Times,* June 22, 1978.

Cullen, Robert B. "Somalia Agrees to let U.S. Use Ports, Airstrips." *Washington Post,* August 21, 1980.

Current Digest of the Soviet Press 13 (August 2, 1961).

Dallin, David. *Soviet Russia and the Far East.* London: Hollis & Carter, Ltd., 1949.

Darnton, John. "Somalia Is Ordering Soviet Advisers Out, Halts Use of Bases." *The New York Times,* November 14, 1977.

_____ . "Cuba Said to Expand Military Force in Ethiopia by over 1000 a Month." *The New York Times,* February 18, 1978.

_____ . "Envoys Wonder If Somalia Is Returning to Soviet Orbit." *The New York Times,* January 11, 1979.

_____ . "Mozambique, with Cuban Help, Is Shoring up Its Internal Security." *The New York Times,* June 24, 1979.

David, Steven. "Realignment in the Horn: The Soviet Advantage." *International Security* 4 (Fall 1979).

Davis, Nathaniel. "Statement before the Subcommittee on Africa of the Senate Foreign Relations Committee, July 14, 1975." *Department of State Bulletin,* August 11, 1975.

_____ . "The Angolan Decision of 1975: A Personal Memoir." *Foreign Affairs,* Fall 1978.

Day, Bonner. "Soviet Airlift to Ethiopia." *Air Force Magazine,* September 1978.

Dayan, Moshe. *Moshe Dayan: Story of My Life.* New York: William Morrow and Company, 1976.

"Debate on N. Simoniya's Book *Countries of the East: Paths of Development.*" *Narody Afriki i Azii,* no. 3, May-June 1977.

Degras, Jane, ed. *The Communist International, 1919-1943: Documents.* London: Oxford University Press, 1956.

Demchenko, P. "What Is Going on in Lebanon." *Pravda,* July 16, 1976.

de Onis, Juan. "State Dept. Defends Report on Salvador." *The New York Times,* June 9, 1981.

de Onis, Juan. "U.S. Officials Concede Flaws in Salvador White Paper but Defend Its Conclusion." *The New York Times,* June 10, 1981.

Detzer, David. *The Brink.* New York: Thomas Y. Crowell, 1979.

DeYoung, Karen. "Nonaligned Summit Closes after Final Wrangle." *Washington Post,* September 10, 1979.

_____ . "Castro Denounces Carter, Calls Troop Charge False." *Washington Post,* September 29, 1979.

Dinerstein, Herbert S. *Soviet Doctrine on Developing Countries: Some Divergent Views.* P-2725. Santa Monica, Calif.: The Rand Corporation, March 1963.

Dismukes, Bradford, and James McConnell, eds. *Soviet Naval Diplomacy.* Pergamon Policy Studies, 37. New York: Pergamon Press, 1979.

Djilas, Milovan. *Conversations with Stalin.* New York: Harcourt, Brace & World, 1962.

Dolgopolov, Col. Ye. "National-Democratic Revolution and the Army." *Soviet Military Review* (Moscow), no. 4 (April 1980).

Dominguez, Jorge I. "The Cuban Operation in Angola: Costs and Benefits for the Armed Forces." *Cuban Studies* 8 (January 1978).

———. "Cuban Foreign Policy." *Foreign Affairs,* Fall 1978.

———. "The Armed Forces and Foreign Relations." In *Cuba in the World,* edited by Cole Blaiser and Carmelo Mesa-Lago. Pittsburgh, Pa.: University of Pittsburgh Press, 1978.

Dommen, Arthur J. *Conflict in Laos: The Politics of Neutralization.* New York: Praeger Publishers, 1971.

Donaldson, Robert H., ed. *The Soviet Union in the Third World: Successes and Failures.* Boulder, Colo.: Westview Press, 1981.

"Dr. Kissinger on World Affairs." Interview with *Spiegel* editors. *Encounter,* November 1978.

Dudin, A.M., and Yu.N. Listvinov. "Problems of the New Stage in the Arms Race." In *Voyennaya sila i mezhdunarodnyye otnosheniya* [Military Power and International Relations], edited by V.M. Kulish. Moscow: Izdatel'stvo Mezhdunarodnyye Otnosheniya, 1972.

Duncan, W. Raymond, ed. *Soviet Policy in Developing Countries.* Waltham, Mass.: Ginn-Blaisdell, 1970.

———. ed. *Soviet Policy in the Third World.* New York: Pergamon Press, 1980.

———. "Cuba: National Communism in the Global Setting." *International Journal* (Toronto), Winter 1976.

Dupree, Louis. "Afghanistan under the Khalq." *Problems of Communism,* July-August 1979a.

———. *The Democratic Republic of Afghanistan 1979.* American Universities Field Staff Reports, no. 32, 1979b.

———. *Red Flag over the Hindu Kush, Part II: The Accidental Coup, or Taraki in Blunderland.* American Universities Field Staff Reports, no. 45, 1979c.

Durch, William J. "The Cuban Military in Africa and the Middle East: From Algeria to Angola." *Studies in Comparative Communism,* Spring/Summer 1978.

Dziak, John J. "Soviet Intelligence and Security Services in the Eighties: The Paramilitary Dimension." *Orbis,* Winter 1981, p. 782.

Eban, Abba. *Abba Eban: An Autobiography.* New York: Random House, 1977.

Edgington, Sylvia W. "'The State of Socialist Orientation' as Soviet Developmental Politics." Paper delivered at the 1980 Annual Meeting of the American Political Science Association, Washington, D.C., August 28-31, 1980.

Eisenhower, Dwight D. *The White House Years: Waging Peace, 1956-1961.* New York: Doubleday & Company, 1965.

Eliot, Theodore L. "Afghanistan after the 1978 Revolution." *Strategic Review* (Spring 1979).

Eprile, Cecil. *War and Peace in the Sudan, 1955-1972.* London: David & Charles, Newton Abbot, 1974.

Ermarth, Fritz. "The Soviet Union in the Third World: Purpose in Search of Power." *Annals of the American Academy of Political and Social Sciences,* November 1969.

"Ethiopia: The Other Side of the Hill." *Economist,* October 6-12, 1979.

Farer, Tom J. *War Clouds on the Horn of Africa: A Crisis for Detente.* Washington, D.C.: Carnegie Endowment for International Peace, 1976.

Fink, Donald E. "Afghan Invasion Likened to 1968 Action." *Aviation Week & Space Technology,* July 14, 1980.

Finney, John W. "Soviet Operational Role Is Seen in North Vietnam's Air Defense." *The New York Times,* October 4, 1966.

Fletcher, Arnold. *Afghanistan: Highway of Conquest.* Ithaca, N.Y.: Cornell University Press, 1965.

Foisie, Jack. "Elusive Savimbi Pursues Quest." *Washington Post,* June 4, 1980.

Foley, James. "Soviet Subs Stationed in S. China Sea." *Philadelphia Inquirer,* May 2, 1980.

Fontaine, Roger W. "Cuba on the Horn." *Washington Review of Strategic and International Studies,* Special Supplement, May 1978.

_____ . "Cuban Strategy in Africa: The Long Road of Ambition." *Strategic Review* 6 (Summer 1978).

Ford, Gerald. State-of-the-world speech to joint session of Congress, Department of State news release, April 10, 1975.

_____ . "Statement of December 20, 1975." *Department of State Bulletin,* January 19, 1976.

Foreign Broadcast Information Service. Analysis Report. *Soviet Guidelines for Third World Regimes: Political Control, Economic Pluralism,* March 12, 1981.

_____ . Daily Report. *Soviet Union,* May 28, 1971.

_____ . Daily Report. *Soviet Union,* August 8, 1971.

_____ . Daily Report. *Soviet Union,* April 10, 1972.

_____ . Daily Report. *Soviet Union,* November 1, 1974.

_____ . Daily Report, *Soviet Union,* October 12, 1976.

_____ . Daily Report. *Soviet Union,* April 4, 1977.

_____ . Daily Report. *Soviet Union,* November 3, 1978.

_____ . Daily Report. *Soviet Union,* November 21, 1978.

_____ . Daily Report. *Soviet Union,* December 6, 1978.

_____ . Daily Report. *Soviet Union,* February 28, 1979.

_____ . Daily Report. *Soviet Union,* October 29, 1979.

_____ . Daily Report. *Soviet Union,* October 9, 1980.

_____ . Daily Report. *Soviet Union,* May 19, 1981.

_____ . Special Report. *National Voice of Iran: November 1978-November 1979,* December 10, 1979.

_____ . *Trends in Communist Media,* December 17, 1975.

_____ . *Trends in Communist Media,* January 24, 1979.

_____ . *Trends in Communist Media,* February 14, 1979.

_____ . *Trends in Communist Media,* February 23, 1979.

_____ . *Trends in Communist Media,* February 28, 1979.

Frankel, Max. "U.S. Thinks Missile-Site Raids Have Hit Russians." *The New York Times,* August 22, 1965.

Frechette, Myles R.R. Statement submitted to the Subcommittee on Inter-American Affairs of the House Foreign Affairs Committee on April 17, 1980. *Department of State Bulletin,* July 1980.

Freedman, Robert O. *Soviet Policy toward the Middle East since 1970,* rev. ed. New York: Praeger Publishers, 1978.

Friendly, Alfred. "Soviet Aid Bolsters Militants in Turkey." *Washington Post,* July 6, 1980.

Fukuyama, Francis. "A New Soviet Strategy." *Commentary,* October 1979.

_____ . *New Directions for Soviet Middle East Policy in the 1980's: Implications for the Atlantic Alliance.* P-6443. Santa Monica, Calif.: The Rand Corporation, February 1980a.

_____ . *The Soviet Union and Iraq since 1968.* N-1524-AF. Santa Monica, Calif.: The Rand Corporation, July 1980b.

_____ . *The Security of Pakistan: A Trip Report.* N-1584-RC. Santa Monica, Calif.: The Rand Corporation, September 1980c.

Furlong, R.D.M., and Theodor Winkler. "The Soviet Invasion of Afghanistan." *International Defense Review* (Cointrin-Geneva), no. 2 (1980).

Futrell, Robert F. *The United States Air Force in Korea, 1950-1953.* New York: Duell, Sloan and Pearce, 1961.

Gage, Nicholas. "Islamic Zeal and Talent for War Help Afghan Rebels to Hold Out." *The New York Times,* July 20, 1980.

Gallagher, Jim. "Soviets Play Risky Game Encouraging Iran Terror." *Chicago Tribune,* November 19, 1979.

Garthoff, Raymond L. "Military Influences and Instruments." In *Russian Foreign Policy: Essays in Historical Perspective,* edited by Ivo J.

Lederer. New Haven, Conn.: Yale University Press, 1962.

———. ed. *Sino-Soviet Military Relations*. New York: Frederick A. Praeger, Inc., 1966.

———. "The Soviet Intervention in Manchuria, 1945-46." In *Sino-Soviet Military Relations,* edited by Garthoff. New York: Frederick A. Praeger, Inc., 1966.

———. "Sino-Soviet Military Relations, 1949-66." In *Sino-Soviet Military Relations*, edited by Garthoff. New York: Frederick A. Praeger, Inc., 1966.

Gelb, Leslie. "Muskie and Brzezinski: The Struggle over Foreign Policy." *The New York Times Magazine*, July 20, 1980.

Gelman, Harry. *The Politburo's Management of Its America Problem*. R-2707-NA. Santa Monica, Calif.: The Rand Corporation, April 1981.

George, Alexander L., and Richard Smoke. *Deterrence in American Foreign Policy: Theory and Practice*. New York: Columbia University Press, 1974.

Girardet, Edward. "Ethiopia Enlists Soviet Arms to Crush Stubborn Eritreans." *Christian Science Monitor*, July 17, 1980.

Glassman, Jon. *Arms for the Arabs: The Soviet Union and War in the Middle East*. Baltimore: Johns Hopkins University Press, 1975.

Golan, Galia. *The Soviet Union and the PLO*. Jerusalem: Soviet and East European Research Center, Hebrew University, 1976.

———. *Yom Kippur and After: The Soviet Union and the Middle East Crisis*. New York: Cambridge University Press, 1977.

Goldman, Marshall I. *Soviet Foreign Aid*. New York: Frederick A. Praeger, Inc., 1967.

Gonzalez, Edward. "Complexities of Cuban Foreign Policy." *Problems of Communism*, November-December 1977.

———. "Institutionalization, Political Elites, and Foreign Policies." In *Cuba in the World*, edited by Cole Blaiser and Carmelo Mesa-Lago. Pittsburgh, Pa.: University of Pittsburgh Press, 1978.

———. "Cuban Policy toward Africa: Activities, Motivations, and Outcomes." Draft paper, May 1980a, to appear in *The Communist States in Africa*, edited by David Albright and Jiri Valenta. Bloomington: Indiana University Press, forthcoming.

———. "Cuba, the Soviet Union, and Africa." In *Communism in Africa*, edited by David Albright. Bloomington: Indiana University Press, 1980b.

Goodsell, James Nelson. "Castro Cast Adrift in Caribbean by Worried Latin Neighbors." *Christian Science Monitor*, March 25, 1981.

Goshko, John M. "U.S. Releases Summary of Its Evidence." *Washington Post*, June 15, 1978.

———. "Soviet Construction of Pier at Cuban Base Is Reported." *Washington Post*, October 31, 1979.

Goshko, John M., and Walter Pincus. "Sense of Duty behind Cuba's Global Role." *Washington Post*, September 21, 1979.

Gottemoeller, Rose E. "The Potential for Conflict between Soviet and Cuban Policies in the Third World." P-6668. Santa Monica, Calif.: The Rand Corporation, August 1981.

Gouré, Leon, and Morris Rothenberg. *Soviet Penetration of Latin America*. Miami: Center for Advanced International Studies, University of Miami, 1975.

Griffith, William E. "Soviet Power and Policies in the Third World: The Case of Africa." Adelphi Paper 152. London: International Institute for Strategic Studies, 1979.

————. "Soviet Power and Policies in the Third World: The Case of Africa." In *Prospects of the Soviet Power in the Nineteen Eighties*, edited by Christoph Bertram. Hamden, Conn.: Shoe String Press, 1980a.

————. "The Implications of Afghanistan." *Survival* (London), July-August 1980b.

Griffiths, David R. "Afghan Problems Stall Soviets." *Aviation Week & Space Technology*, April 21, 1980.

————. "Lull in Vietnamese Thai Invasion." *Aviation Week & Space Technology*, July 7, 1980.

Gupte, Pranay B. "Soviet Activity Found Growing in Aden Region." *The New York Times*, June 10, 1980.

————. "South Yemen Seeks to Widen Ties." *The New York Times*, June 15, 1980.

Gurtov, Melvin. *The First Vietnam Crisis*. New York: Columbia University Press, 1967.

Gustafson, Thane. "The Soviet Leadership Succession and the Political Agenda for the 1980s." Unpublished paper given at U.S.-China Conference on the Soviet Union, Washington, D.C., November 8-11, 1979.

Gwertzman, Bernard. "50 Cuban Advisers Reported Training Troops in Ethiopia." *The New York Times,* May 26, 1977.

————. "U.S. Aides Frustrated over Soviet Gains in Ethiopia." *The New York Times*, December 29, 1977.

————. "Carter Warns Soviet Official on Ethiopia," *The New York Times,* January 26, 1978.

————. "White House Cites CIA Material on a Cuban Role in Zaire Invasion." *The New York Times*, June 16, 1978.

————. "Brzezinski Cautions Soviet on Cuba Unit." *The New York Times,* September 23, 1979.

————. "Carter's Russian Lesson Is One in a Long Series." *The New York Times*, January 6, 1980.

————. "U.S. Fears Soviet Arms Deal Might Harm Ties to India." *The New York Times*, May 30, 1980.

_____ . "Moscow's Gulf Opportunities." *The New York Times*, October 11, 1980.

Haig, Alexander M., Jr., "Chemical Warfare in Southeast Asia and Afghanistan." Report to the Congress. Special Rept no. 98. Washington, D.C.: Department of State, Bureau of Public Affairs, March 22, 1982.

Halasz, Louis. "Soviet Losing Its Grip with Third World." *Baltimore Sun,* November 2, 1980.

Hall, David K. "Naval Diplomacy in West African Waters." In *Diplomacy of Power. Soviet Armed Forces as a Political Instrument*, edited by Stephen S. Kaplan. Washington, D.C.: The Brookings Institution, 1981.

Halloran, Richard. "Nicaragua Arms Called Peril to Area." *The New York Times*, December 3, 1981.

_____ . "U.S. to Train 1,500 Salvadoran Soldiers." *The New York Times,* December 16, 1981.

_____ . "Soviets Ready to Bolster Its Afghan Force." *The New York Times*, December 24, 1981.

Hamburg, Roger. "The Soviet Union and Latin America." In *The Soviet Union and the Developing Nations*, edited by Roger E. Kanet. Baltimore: Johns Hopkins University Press, 1974.

Harbon, John D. "Cuba's Maritime Outreach." *U.S. Naval Institute Proceedings*, September 1978.

Harrison, Selig W. "The Shah, Not Kremlin Touched off Afghan Coup." *Washington Post*, May 13, 1977.

_____ . "Did Moscow Fear an Afghan Tito?" *The New York Times*, January 13, 1980.

Harwood, Richard. "Angola: A Distant War." *Washington Post*, July 20 and 21, 1981.

Haselkorn, Avigdor. "Soviet Military Casualties in Third World Conflicts." *Conflict* no. 1 (1980).

Heikal, Mohamed. *The Cairo Documents*. New York: Doubleday & Company, 1973.

_____ . *The Road to Ramadan*. New York: Quadrangle/New York Times Book Co., 1975.

_____ . *The Sphinx and the Commissar: The Rise and Fall of Soviet Influence in the Middle East*. New York: Harper & Row, 1978.

Herzog, Chaim. *The War of Atonement*. Boston: Little, Brown and Company, 1975.

"The Hills with a View over Ethiopia's Dead." *Economist*, September 1-7, 1979.

Hoang Van Hoan. "Distortions of Facts about Militant Friendships between Viet Nam and China Is Impermissible." *Beijing Review*, no. 49 (December 7, 1979).

Hodges, Tony. "The Struggle for Angola." *The Round Table* (London), no. 262 (April 1976).

Holbrooke, Richard C. "Statement before the Subcommittee on Asian and Pacific Affairs of the Senate Foreign Relations Committee on March 24, 1980." *Department of State Bulletin* 80 (June 1980).

Homan, Richard L. "Pro-Soviet Coup in S. Yemen." *Washington Post*, June 27, 1978.

Horowitz, Irving Louis. "Military Outcomes of the Cuban Revolution." In *Cuban Communism*, edited by I.L. Horowitz. New Brunswick, N.J.: Transaction Books, 1977.

Hough, Jerry F. "The Generation Gap and the Brezhnev Succession." *Problems of Communism*, July-August 1979.

House, Karen Elliott, and Beth Nissen. "Southern Strategy: U.S. Tries to Influence the Unrest in Central American Lands but Finds the Task Tricky." *Wall Street Journal*, April 29, 1980.

Hovey, Graham. "Soviet Assures U.S. Ethiopians Will Stop at Somalia's Border." *The New York Times*, February 11, 1978.

_____ . "Ethiopia Sends U.S. Promise on Somalia." *The New York Times,* February 22, 1978.

_____ . "Brzezinski Asserts That Soviet General Leads Ethiopia Units." *The New York Times*, February 25, 1978.

_____ . "U.S. Fears Unrest in Central America." *The New York Times*, July 22, 1979.

_____ . "Limited Cuban Pullout in Ethiopia Is Reported by American Officials." *The New York Times*, August 4, 1979.

Howe, Marvine. "Surrounded by Turmoil, Iraq Is Shifting Its Posture." *The New York Times*, January 7, 1979.

_____ . "Southern Yemen Blends Marxism with Islam and Arab Nationalism." *The New York Times*, May 25, 1979.

_____ . "Yemen Seeks U.S. Aid on Border Force." *The New York Times*, June 12, 1979.

_____ . "Iraq Now Has Powerful Claim to Leadership of Arab World." *The New York Times*, July 22, 1979.

_____ . "Iraq's New Chief Purging Leaders in an Effort to Bolster His Position." *The New York Times*, July 30, 1979.

_____ . "United Front Still Eludes Afghan Guerrillas." *The New York Times*, May 28, 1980.

Hughes, John. *Indonesian Upheaval*. New York: David McKay Company, 1967.

Hyland, William G. "U.S. Policy Options." *Washington Review of Strategic and International Studies*. Special Supplement, May 1978.

Hyland, William G., and Richard Wallace Shryok. *The Fall of Khrushchev*. New York: Funk & Wagnalls, 1968.

Ignat'yev, O. "The Victory of the People of Nicaragua." *Kommunist*, no. 13 (September 1979).

"Intelligence Role of Journalists." *The Times* (London), May 23, 1980.

International Institute for Strategic Studies (IISS). *Strategic Survey 1970*. London, 1971.

———. *Strategic Survey 1972*. London, 1973.

———. *Strategic Survey 1973*. London, 1974.

———. *Strategic Survey 1975*. London, 1976.

———. *Strategic Survey 1976*. London, 1977.

———. *Strategic Survey 1977*. London, 1978.

———. *Strategic Survey 1978*. London, 1979.

———. *Strategic Survey 1979*. "Crisis Over Afghanistan." London, Spring 1980.

———. *The Military Balance 1980-1981*. London, 1980.

"Intervention in Yemen War Signals Foreign Policy Shift." *The New York Times*, March 18, 1979.

Interview with Grenadian labor leader Curtis Stuart. *AFL-CIO Free Trade Union News*, 35 (April 1980), p. 4-5.

"In the Center of Attention." *Pravda*, September 12, 1979.

"Iraq Reported to Hold 36 in High-Level 'Plot' to Take Over Regime." *The New York Times*, August 1, 1979.

Iskenderov, A. "The Army, Politics, and the People." *Izvestiya*, January 17, 1967.

Jaynes, Gregory. "The U.S. Finds High Prices on East Africa's Bargain Bases." *The New York Times*, September 14, 1980.

———. "Marxist Mozambique, Limping Along, Makes Slight Gesture toward the West." *The New York Times*, October 13, 1980.

Johnson, Lyndon Baines. *The Vantage Point: Perspectives of the Presidency, 1963-1969*. New York: Holt, Rinehart & Winston, 1971.

Joint Publications Research Service. "'Abd-al-Nasir's Secret Papers." *Al-Dustur* (London, in Arabic), June 12-November 5, 1978. Translated in JPRS 72223, *Translations on Near East and North Africa*, no. 1865 (November 14, 1978).

Joshua, Wynfred, and Stephen P. Gibert. *Arms for the Third World: Soviet Military Aid Diplomacy*. Baltimore: Johns Hopkins University Press, 1969.

Kaiser, Robert G. "White Paper on El Salvador Is Faulty." *Washington Post*, June 9, 1981.

Kalb, Marvin, and Bernard Kalb. *Kissinger*. Boston: Little, Brown and Company, 1974.

Kamm, Henry. "Soviets Reported to Be Transporting Vietnamese Forces and Equipment." *The New York Times*, March 16, 1979.

Kanet, Roger E., ed. *The Soviet Union and the Developing Nations*. Baltimore: Johns Hopkins University Press, 1974.

———. "The Soviet Union and the Colonial Question." In *The Soviet Union and the Developing Nations*, edited by Kanet. Baltimore: Johns Hopkins University Press, 1974.

——— . "Soviet Policy toward the Developing World: The Role of Economic Assistance and Trade." In *The Soviet Union in the Third World: Successes and Failures*, edited by Robert H. Donaldson. Boulder, Colo.: Westview Press, 1981.

Kapcia, A.M. "Cuba's African Involvement: A New Perspective." *Survey* (London) 24 (Spring 1979).

Kapitsa, Mikhail S. *KNR: Dva Desyatiletiya—Dve Politiki* [PRC: Two Decades—Two Policies]. Moscow: Politizdat, 1969.

Kaplan, Stephen S. ed. *Diplomacy of Power. Soviet Armed Forces as a Political Instrument*. Washington, D.C.: The Brookings Institution, 1981.

Kaufman, A.S. "Socialist Doctrines in the Developing Countries." *Narody Azii i Afriki*, no. 4 (1968).

Kaufman, Michael T. "Afghan Guerrillas Boast of Success in Struggle against Soviet-Backed Regime." *The New York Times*, August 14, 1979.

——— . "Soviet Role in Afghan Clash Shows Signs of Toughening." *The New York Times*, September 6, 1979.

——— . "Taraki's Downfall Came Immediately after a Visit to Moscow." *The New York Times*, September 23, 1979.

——— . "Afghan Guerrilla Says Soviet Has Greatly Expanded Adviser Forces." *The New York Times*, December 11, 1979.

——— . "Travelers Tell of Afghan Students' Bloody Protests." *The New York Times*, May 11, 1980.

——— . "Afghan Leaflets Extolling Defiance Again Distributed Nightly in Kabul." *The New York Times*, May 16, 1980.

——— . "Soviet, Changing Its Conduct of War, Presses Attacks on Afghan Villages." *The New York Times*, July 15, 1980.

——— . "Afghan Guerrillas Tell of Soviet Drive." *The New York Times*, October 5, 1980.

——— . "Soviet Units in Afghanistan Dig in As If for a Long Stay." *The New York Times*, October 9, 1980.

——— . "India Hears of Growing Afghan Resistance." *The New York Times*, October 17, 1980.

Kaylor, Robert. "Cuba's Africa Role Said Growing." *Washington Post*, January 21, 1979.

"Keeping Warm in Cities," *Economist*, November 22-28, 1980.

Kennan, George. "The Source of Soviet Conduct." *Foreign Affairs*, July 1947.

Khalilzad, Zalmay. "Afghanistan and the Crisis in American Foreign Policy." *Survival* (London), July-August 1980.

Khan, M. Aftab. "Rebels Claim Killing 40 Afghan Aides." *Washington Star*, December 27, 1979.

Khrushchev, N.S. "For New Victories of the World Communist Movement." *Kommunist*, no. 1 (January 1961).

Khrushchev Remembers. Trans. and ed. by Strobe Talbott. Boston: Little, Brown and Company, 1970.

Khrushchev Remembers: The Last Testament. Trans. and ed. by Strobe Talbott. Boston: Little, Brown and Company, 1974.

Khvostov, V.M. In *Vsesoyuznoye soveshchaniye o merakh uluchsheniya podgotovki nauchnopedagogicheskikh kadrov po istoricheskim naukam* [All-Union Conference on Measures to Improve the Preparation of Scholarly Pedagogical Cadres of the Historical Sciences]. Moscow: Izdatel'stvo Nauka, 1964.

Kifner, John. "Iran Declares a 'Holy War' against Ideas from the Left." *The New York Times,* April 27, 1980.

Kim, G. "Successes of the National-Liberation Movement and Their Influence on World Affairs." *Mezhdunarodnaya zhizn',* no. 1 (1979).

Kim, G., and A. Kaufman. "On Sources of Socialist Conceptions in Developing Countries." *World Marxist Review* (Toronto), December 1971.

Kissinger, Henry. Speech before Economic Club of Detroit. Department of State Press Release no. 578, November 24, 1975.

_____ . Press conference. Department of State Press Release no. 627, December 23, 1975.

_____ . Testimony. In U.S. Congress. Senate. Committee on Foreign Relations. Subcommittee on African Affairs. *Angola.* 94th Cong., 2d. sess., January 29, 1976.

_____ . "Dr. Kissinger on World Affairs." Interview with *Spiegel* editors. *Encounter,* November 1978.

_____ . *White House Years.* Boston: Little, Brown and Company, 1979.

_____ . *Years of Upheaval.* Boston: Little, Brown and Company, 1982.

Klinghoffer, Arthur Jay. "The Soviet Union and Africa." In *The Soviet Union and the Developing Nations,* edited by Roger E. Kanet. Baltimore: Johns Hopkins University Press, 1974.

Klose, Kevin. "Khomeini Denounced by Soviets." *Washington Post,* September 9, 1979.

_____ . "Moscow Justifies Actions in Kabul on Basis of Pact." *Washington Post,* December 29, 1979.

Kwitny, Jonathan. "Tarnished Report? Apparent Errors Cloud U.S. 'White Paper' on Reds in El Salvador." *Wall Street Journal,* June 8, 1981.

Lake, Anthony. "Africa in a Global Perspective." Christian A. Herter Lecture at the Johns Hopkins University School of Advanced International Studies, Washington, D.C., October 27, 1977. *Department of State Bulletin* 77 (December 12, 1977).

Lamb, David. "Soviets Lose Base in Equatorial Guinea." *Los Angeles Times,* January 28, 1980.

_____ . "20,000 Cubans Prop up Regime." *Washington Post,* June 4, 1980.

_____ . "Angola Growing Uneasy with Soviets." *Washington Post,* June 5, 1980.

Larichev, Lt. Col. N. "Fulfilling Internationalist Duty." *Soviet Military Review* (Moscow), March 1980.

Larrabee, Stephen. "Somalia and Moscow's Problems on the Horn of Africa." Radio Liberty Research Paper RL 158/77, July 5, 1977.

"Lashing Out." *Economist,* June 28-July 4, 1980.

Laurance, Edward I., and Ronald G. Sherwin. "Understanding Arms Transfers through Data Analysis." In *Arms Transfers to the Third World: The Military Buildup in Less Industrialized Countries,* edited by Uri Ra'anan, Robert L. Pfaltzgraff, Jr., and Geoffrey Kemp. Boulder, Colo.: Westview Press, 1978.

LeBrun, Oliver. "Ethiopians Put Pressure on Desert Rebels." *Manchester Guardian Weekly,* June 3, 1979.

Ledeen, Michael, and William Lewis. *Debacle: The American Failure in Iran.* New York: Alfred A. Knopf, 1981.

Lederer, Edith M. "Soviet Said to Hold to Its Afghan Force." *The New York Times,* July 11, 1980.

_____ . "Afghan Rebels Reportedly Stronger but Still Outgunned." *Washington Post,* July 11, 1980.

Lederer, Ivo J., ed. *Russian Foreign Policy: Essays in Historical Perspective.* New Haven: Yale University Press, 1962.

Lee, Vladimir. "The National Liberation Movement Today." *International Affairs* (Moscow), December 1969.

Legum, Colin, ed. *Africa Contemporary Record: Annual Survey and Documents, 1974-1975*, vol. 7. New York: Africana Publishing Company, 1975.

_____ . "The USSR and Africa: The African Environment." *Problems of Communism,* January-February 1978.

_____ . "Angola and the Horn of Africa." In *Diplomacy of Power. Soviet Armed Forces as a Political Instrument,* edited by Stephen S. Kaplan. Washington, D.C.: The Brookings Institution, 1981.

Legum, Colin, and Tony Hodges. *After Angola: The War over Southern Africa.* New York: Africana Publishing Company, 1976.

Legvold, Robert. *Soviet Policy in West Africa.* Cambridge, Mass.: Harvard University Press, 1970.

_____ . "The Soviet Union's Strategic Stake in Africa." In *Africa and the United States: Vital Interests,* edited by Jennifer Seymour Whitaker. New York: New York University Press, 1978.

LeoGrande, William M. "The Revolution in Nicaragua: Another Cuba?" *Foreign Affairs,* Fall 1979.

Lescaze, Lee. "Castro Lists Soviet Strength in Cuba during 1962 Crisis." *Washington Post,* October 1, 1979.

Levkovskiy, A.I. "Specific Character and Limits of Capitalism in a Transitional Society of the 'Third World'." *Mirovaya ekonomika i mezhdunarodnyye otnosheniya,* no. 1 (1974).

_____ . "Practical Class Problems of the Developing Countries." *Rabochiy klass i sovremennyy mir,* no. 2 (March-April 1975).

_____ . *Tretiy mir v sovremennom mire* [The Third World in the Contemporary World]. Moscow: Izdatel'stvo Nauka, 1976.

Lewis, Flora. "Reports from Iraq Indicate Crisis in Its Leadership." *The New York Times,* July 28, 1979.

_____ . "Beyond the Havana Talks: Castro Sows Trouble for U.S." *The New York Times,* September 12, 1979.

_____ . "With Neto Gone, Angola Rebel Renews Plea for Talks to End Civil War." *The New York Times,* September 15, 1979.

Lowenthal, Abraham F. "Cuba's African Adventure." *International Security,* Summer 1977.

Luers, William H. "The U.S.S.R. and the Third World." In *The U.S.S.R. and the Sources of Soviet Policy.* Occasional Paper no. 34. Seminar sponsored by the Council on Foreign Relations and the Kennan Institute for Advanced Russian Studies, The Wilson Center, Washington, D.C., April-May 1978.

Mackintosh, J.M. *Strategy and Tactics of Soviet Foreign Policy.* London: Oxford University Press, 1962.

Mangold, Peter. "Shaba I and Shaba II." *Survival* (London) 21 (May-June 1979).

Manthorpe, Captain William H.J., Jr., U.S. Navy (Ret.). "The Soviet Navy in 1979: Part I." *U.S. Naval Institute Proceedings,* April 1980.

Marcum, John. *The Angolan Revolution: Exile Politics and Guerrilla Warfare (1962-1976),* vol. 2. Cambridge, Mass.: MIT Press, 1978.

Marder, Murrey. "Cubans Expand Role in Ethiopia, U.S. Says." *Washington Post,* April 1, 1978.

Markham, James M. "Alliances, Allegiances Switch Often in Western Sahara War." *The New York Times,* February 17, 1980.

Marquez, Gabriel Garcia. "Cuba and Its Intervention in Angola." *La Prensa* (Lima, in Spanish), January 10-16, 1977. Translated in Joint Publications Research Service, *Translations on Latin America,* no. 1613 (February 25, 1977a).

_____ . "Operation Carlota." *New Left Review* (London), February-April 1977b.

Maslennikov, Arkadiy. "Vain Attempts: Behind-the-Scenes Events." *Pravda,* December 23, 1979.

McBeth, John. "Bringing Down the High Fliers." *Far Eastern Economic Review* (Hong Kong) 107 (February 29, 1980).

MccGwire, Michael, ed. *Soviet Naval Developments: Capability and Context.* New York: Praeger Publishers, 1973.

McConnell, James M. "The Soviet Navy in the Indian Ocean." In *Soviet Naval Developments: Capability and Context,* edited by Michael MccGuire. New York: Praeger Publishers, 1973.

McConnell, James M., and Bradford Dismukes. "Soviet Diplomacy of Force in the Third World." *Problems of Communism,* January-February 1979.

McNamara, Robert S., and John Hughes. "Special Cuban Briefing." State Department Auditorium, Washington, D.C., February 6, 1963.

Meyer, Herbert E. "Why We Should Worry about the Soviet Energy Crunch." *Fortune,* February 25, 1980.

_____. "Russia's Sudden Search for Raw Materials." *Fortune,* July 28, 1980.

Middleton, Drew. "Airlift to Ethiopia Seen as Soviet Test." *The New York Times,* January 8, 1978.

_____. "Eritrean Situation Has NATO Worried." *The New York Times,* July 15, 1978.

_____. "Oman Wary of Soviet Buildup in Southern Yemen." *The New York Times,* June 4, 1979.

_____. "U.S. Seeks a Strategy to Employ Its Conventional Forces." *The New York Times,* July 9, 1979.

_____. "In Afghanistan, 2 Soviet Trends Now Emerging." *The New York Times,* October 30, 1979.

_____. "Soviet Display of Flexibility." *The New York Times, December 28, 1979.*

_____. "Soviet Said to Build Arms Caches in Libya, Syria, Persian Gulf Area." *The New York Times,* March 14, 1980.

_____. "Afghans May Confront New Soviet Tactics." *The New York Times,* April 21, 1980.

_____. "Soviet Troops Said to Test New Weapons in Afghanistan." *The New York Times,* July 10, 1980.

"A Mideast Buildup." *Newsweek,* March 19, 1979.

Miller, James Arnold; Daniel I. Fine; and R. Daniel McMichael, eds. *The Resource War in 3-D: Dependency, Diplomacy, Defense.* Pittsburgh, Pa. World Affairs Council of Pittsburgh, June 1980.

Mirskiy, G.I. *Armiya i politika v stranakh Azii i Afriki* [The Army and Politics in the Countries of Asia and Africa]. Moscow: Izdatel'stvo Nauka, 1970.

_____. *"Tretiy Mir": Obshchestvo, Vlast', Armiya* [The "Third World": Society, Power, Army]. Moscow: Izdatel'stvo Nauka, 1976.

Mitchell, R. Judson. "The Soviet Succession: Who, and What, Will Follow Brezhnev?" *Orbis,* Spring 1979.

Momyer, Gen. William W., USAF (Ret.). *Air Power in Three Wars (WWII, Korea, Vietnam).* Washington, D.C.: Department of the Air Force, 1978.

Moose, Richard M. "The United States and Angola." *Department of State Bulletin,* December 1980.

Morison, David. "USSR and Third World," *Mizan* (London) 12 (October 1970).

"Moscow Again Warns Washington over Use of Force in Iran Crisis." *The New York Times,* December 10, 1979.

"Moscow Is Said to Send New Units to Kabul."*The New York Times,* July 4, 1980.

"Moscow's Helping Hands." *Time,* February 20, 1978.

"Moscow Tilts toward Qum." Editorial. *The New York Times,* December 9, 1979.

Mosely, Philip E. "The Kremlin and the Third World." In *Soviet Policy in Developing Countries,* edited by W. Raymond Duncan. Waltham, Mass.: Ginn-Blaisdell, 1970.

Moss, Robert. Article on the MPLA (Angola). *Sunday Telegraph* (London), January 30, 1977.

———— . "Battle of Death Road." *Sunday Telegraph,* February 13, 1977.

Mozolev, Maj. Gen. V. "In Foreign Armies: The Role of the Army in the Developing Countries." *Voyenno-istoricheskiy zhurnal,* no. 4 (April 1980).

Murphy, Caryle. "S. African Guerrillas Gain New Vigor." *Washington Post,* August 19, 1980.

"Naval Base in Somalia—Exit Russia, Enter U.S." *U.S. News & World Report.* March 3, 1980.

"Nearing Victory, Eritrean Rebels Fear Division." *Baltimore Sun,* December 28, 1977.

Negaran, Hannah, pseudonym. "The Afghan Coup of April 1978: Revolution and International Security." *Orbis,* Spring 1979.

"New Afghan Leader, Taking Over, Promises a 'Better Socialist Order'." *The New York Times,* September 18, 1979.

Newell, Nancy Peabody, and Richard S. Newell. *The Struggle for Afghanistan.* Ithaca, N.Y.: Cornell University Press, 1981.

"New Regime Moving Afghanistan Deeper into Soviet Orbit." *The New York Times,* November 16, 1978.

Nickel, Herman. "The U.S. Gropes for a Mideast Strategy." *Fortune,* February 25, 1980.

Nixon, Richard. *The Memoirs of Richard Nixon.* New York: Grosset & Dunlap, 1978.

Nossiter, Bernard D. "Angola Rebel Leader Says His Forces Are Beating Cubans." *The New York Times,* November 8, 1979.

———— . "Angolan Rebels Report Capturing 2 Soviet Airmen." *The New York Times,* December 13, 1980.

O'Ballance, Edgar. *The War in the Yemen.* Hamden, Conn.: Archon Books, 1971.

Oberdorfer, Don. "The Superpowers and Africa's Horn." *Washington Post,* March 5, 1978.

_____ . *Washington Post,* May 29, 1978.

_____ . "The 'Brigade': An Unwelcome Sighting in Cuba." *Washington Post,* September 9, 1979.

_____ . "Asians Reject Soviet Ship Visits." *Washington Post,* September 19, 1979.

_____ . "U.S. Details 'Covert Activities' by Cubans in Latin America." *Washington Post,* December 2, 1981.

_____ . "Haig Asks Joint Action on Cuba." *Washington Post,* December 5, 1981.

_____ . "U.S. in Secret Dialogue, Sought Rapprochement with Nicaragua." *Washington Post,* December 10, 1981.

Oberdorfer, Don, and Walter Pincus. "Soviet Troops Talks Continue Amid a Swirl of Controversy." *Washington Post,* September 12, 1979.

"Only There for the Port," *Economist,* November 3-9, 1979.

Orestov, O., "Independent Africa in the Making." *International Affairs* (Moscow), November 1975.

Ottaway, David B. "Syrian Leader Assad Gambling in Attempt to Bolster Position." *Washington Post,* October 22, 1980.

_____ . "Iraq Hardens War Aims, Seeks to Dismember Iran." *Washington Post,* April 19, 1981.

_____ . "Soviets Move to Bolster Influence in Iraq." *Washington Post,* May 5, 1981.

Ottaway, Marina and David. *Ethiopia: Empire in Revolution.* New York: Africana Publishing Co., 1978.

Paige, Glenn D., *The Korean Decision.* New York: Free Press, 1968.

Pajak, Roger F. "Soviet Arms and Egypt." *Survival* (London), July/August 1975.

_____ . "The Effectiveness of Soviet Arms Aid Diplomacy in the Third World." In *The Soviet Union in the Third World: Successes and Failures,* edited by Robert H. Donaldson. Boulder, Colo.: Westview Press, 1981.

Pankratov, N.P. "V.I. Lenin on the International Character of the Armed Forces of a Socialist State." In *V.I. Lenin i voyennaya istoriya* [V.I. Lenin and Military History], edited by M.V. Zakharov. Moscow: Voyenizdat, 1970.

Papp, Daniel S. "The Soviet Union and Cuba in Ethiopia." *Current History,* March 1979.

Pentagon Papers, Senator Gravel ed., vol. 4. Boston: Beacon Press, undated.

Perlmutter, Amos. "The Yemen Strategy." *The New Republic,* July 5-12, 1980.

Petrov, A. "Rebuff to the Forces of Reaction and Imperialism." *Pravda,* March 21, 1979.

_____ . "Display Prudence and Restraint." *Pravda,* December 5, 1979.

Petrov, Vladimir. "New Dimensions of Soviet Foreign Policy." In *Evolving Strategic Realities: Implications for U.S. Policymakers,* edited by Franklin D. Margiotta. The National Security Affairs Institute 1979-1980 Seminar Series, Washington, D.C., 1980.

Pike, Douglas. "Vietnam in 1980: The Gathering Storm?" *Asian Survey* 21 (January 1981).

Pipes, Richard, ed. *Soviet Strategy in Europe.* New York: Crane, Russak & Company, Inc. 1976.

———. "Soviet Global Strategy." *Commentary,* April 1980.

Ponomarev, B. "Topical Problems of the Theory of the Revolutionary Process." *Kommunist,* no. 15 (October 1971).

Ponomarev, B.; A. Gromyko; and V. Khvostov, eds. *History of Soviet Foreign Policy, 1945-1970,* English ed. Moscow: Progress Publishers, 1974.

———. "Joint Struggle of the Worker and National-Liberation Movement against Imperialism and for Social Progress." *Kommunist,* no. 16 (November 1980).

Porter, Bruce D. "The USSR in Local Conflicts: Soviet Military Intervention in the Third World, 1917-1980." Manuscript, 1980.

"Press Conference of M. al-Shaer." *Pravda,* July 15, 1979.

Price, David Lynn. "Moscow and the Persian Gulf." *Problems of Communism,* March-April 1979.

Quandt, William B. *Soviet Policy in the October 1973 War,* R-1864-ISA. Santa Monica, Calif.: The Rand Corporation, May 1976.

———. *Decade of Decisions.* Berkeley: University of California Press, 1977.

Quester, George H. "Missiles in Cuba, 1970." *Foreign Affairs,* April 1971.

Ra'anan, Uri. "Moscow and the 'Third World'." *Problems of Communism,* January-February 1965.

———. *The USSR Arms the Third World.* Cambridge, Mass.: MIT Press, 1969.

Ra'anan, Uri; Robert L. Pfaltzgraff, Jr.; and Geoffrey Kemp, eds. *Arms Transfers to the Third World: The Military Buildup in Less Industrialized Countries.* Boulder, Colo.: Westview Press, 1978.

Rabin, Yitzhak. *The Rabin Memoirs.* Boston: Little, Brown and Company, 1979.

Rader, Ronald R. "The Russian Military and Afghanistan: An Historical Perspective." In *Soviet Armed Forces Review Annual,* vol. 4, edited by David R. Jones. Gulf Breeze, Fla.: Academic International Press, 1980.

Randal, Jonathan C. "Afghanistan: Moscow's Vietnam?" *Washington Post,* May 10, 1979a.

———. "Iranian Leftists Emerge from Isolation." *Washington Post,* December 3, 1979b.

"Red Stars over Africa." *Newsweek,* March 13, 1978.

Rees, David. *Soviet Strategic Penetration of Africa.* Conflict Studies no. 77. London: Institute for the Study of Conflict, November 1977.

———. *Afghanistan's Role in Soviet Strategy.* Conflict Studies no. 118. London: Institute for the Study of Conflict, May 1980.

Reisner, L.I. *Razvivayushchiyesya strany: Ocherk teorii ekonomicheskogo rosta* [The Developing Countries: An Outline Theory of Economic Growth]. Moscow: Izdatel'stvo Nauka, 1976.

Remington, Robin Alison. *The Warsaw Pact: Case Studies in Communist Conflict Resolution.* Cambridge, Mass.: MIT Press, 1971.

"Report of the Central Committee to the 20th Party Congress." In *Current Soviet Policies II: The Documentary Record of the 20th Communist Party Congress and Its Aftermath,* edited by Leo Gruliow. New York: Frederick A. Praeger, 1957.

Robinson, William F. *Eastern Europe's Presence in Black Africa.* RAD Background Report/142 (Eastern Europe). Radio Free Europe Research, June 21, 1979.

Rose, Leo E. "The Superpowers in South Asia: A Geostrategic Analysis." *Orbis* 22 (Summer 1978).

Rosen, Jane. "How the Third World Runs the U.N." *The New York Times Magazine,* December 16, 1979.

Roslavlev, A.V. "Once More about the 'Theory' of Multiple Elements in Countries of the 'Third World'." *Rabochiy klass i sovremennyy mir,* no. 1 (January-February 1977).

Ross, Jay. "High-Level Soviet Diplomat Expelled from Iran on Charges of Espionage." *Washington Post,* July 1, 1980.

Rosser, Richard. "The Soviets and Vietnam: A Tragic Miscalculation?" *South Atlantic Quarterly,* Summer 1973.

Rubinstein, Alvin Z. *The Foreign Policy of the Soviet Union.* New York: Random House, 1960.

———. "Air Support in the Arab East." In *Diplomacy of Power: Soviet Armed Forces as a Political Instrument,* edited by Stephen S. Kaplan. Washington, D.C.: The Brookings Institution, 1981.

"Russia in Afghanistan: The Tribesmen Who Took on a Titan." *Economist,* May 23-29, 1981.

"Russia Said to Send Copters to Ethiopia." *International Herald Tribune,* June 14-15, 1980.

Ruszkiewicz, Lt. Col. John J., USA (Ret.). "How the US Lost Its Footing in the Shifting Sands of the Persian Gulf—A Case History in the Yemen Arab Republic." *Armed Forces Journal International,* September 1980.

Sadat, Anwar el-. *In Search of Identity.* New York: Harper & Row, 1977.

Saivetz, Carol R. "The Soviet Perception of Military Intervention in Third World Countries." In *Soviet Policy in the Third World,* edited by W. Raymond Duncan. New York: Pergamon Press, 1980.

Samuels, Michael A., et al. *Implications of Soviet and Cuban Activities in Africa for U.S. Policy.* Washington, D.C.: Center for Strategic and International Studies, Georgetown University, 1979.

Saunders, Harold H. Statement before the Subcommittee on Asian and Pacific Affairs of the House Foreign Affairs Committee on September 26, 1979. *Department of State Bulletin* 79 (December 1979).

Schaufele, William E., Jr. *The African Dimension of the Angolan Conflict.* Washington, D.C.: Department of State, Bureau of Public Affairs, February 6, 1976.

———. "Testimony in U.S. Congress, *Angola,* Hearings before the Subcommittee on African Affairs of the Committee on Foreign Relations, U.S. Senate, 94th Cong., 2d sess., January 29 and February 3, 4, and 6, 1976.

Schlesinger, Arthur M., Jr. *A Thousand Days: John F. Kennedy in the White House.* Boston: Houghton Mifflin Company, 1965.

Schwartz, Morton. "The USSR and Leftist Regimes in Less Developed Countries." *Survey* 19 (Spring 1973).

Scott, William F., and Harriet Fast Scott. *A Review and Assessment of Soviet Policy and Concepts on the Projections of Military Presence and Power.* Volume 2 of *Soviet Projection of Military Presence and Power,* 1040-01-79-CR. McLean, Va.: General Research Corporation, January 1979.

Segal, Jerome M. "Scarcely a Soviet Shadow in Salvador White Paper." *Washington Star,* May 18, 1981.

Sergeyev, S. "The Formation of a New Ethiopia." *Mezhdunarodnaya zhizn',* no. 4 (1979).

Servortyan, R.E. *Armiya v politicheskom rezhime stran sovremennogo vostoka* [The Army in the Political Regime of Countries of the Contemporary East], Moscow: Izdatel'stvo Nauka, 1973.

Sharp, Adm. U.S. Grant, USN (Ret.). *Strategy for Defeat: Vietnam in Retrospect.* San Rafael, Calif.: Presidio Press, 1979.

Sherman, Richard F. "Marxism on the Horn of Africa." *Problems of Communism,* September-October 1980.

Shipler, David K. "Soviet Terse in Invasion Report, Implying No Decision on Action." *The New York Times,* February 18, 1979.

Shlaim, Avi, and Raymond Tanter. "Decision Process, Choice and Consequences: Israel's Deep-Penetration Bombing in Egypt, 1970." *World Politics* 30 (July 1978).

Shulman, Marshall D. *Tales of Afghanistan, Moscow Style.* Washington, D.C.: Current Policy no. 143. Department of State, Bureau of Public Affairs, March 1980.

Sidenko, V. "USSR-Ethiopia: Shoulder to Shoulder." *New Times* (Moscow), no. 48 (November 1978).

_____ . "Two Years of the Afghan Revolution." *New Times* (Moscow), no. 17 (April 1980).

Sim, Richard, and James Anderson. *The Caribbean Strategic Vacuum,* Conflict Studies no. 121. London: Institute for the Study of Conflict, August 1980.

Simes, Dimitri K. "Imperial Globalism in the Making: Soviet Involvement in the Horn of Africa." *Washington Review of Strategic and International Studies,* Special Supplement, May 1978.

_____ . "Those Soviet Bombshells." *Washington Star,* January 6, 1980.

_____ . "The Death of Detente?" *International Security* 5 (Summer 1980).

Simmons, Robert R. *The Strained Alliance: Peking, Pyongyang, Moscow and the Politics of the Korean Civil War.* Glencoe, Ill.: Free Press, 1975.

Simoniya, N.A. "On the Character of the National Liberation Revolutions." *Narody Azii i Afriki,* no. 6 (1966).

_____ . "Afro-Asian Concepts of Socialism." *World Marxist Review* (Toronto), December 1971.

"Sixth Conference of Heads of State or Government of Non-Aligned Countries, Havana, September 3-9, 1979." *Review of International Affairs* (Belgrade), September 20, 1979.

Smith, Hedrick. "Cuban Military and Advisory Presence in Africa." *The New York Times,* November 17, 1977.

_____ . "Russia's Power Strategy." *The New York Times Magazine,* January 27, 1980.

Smolansky, Oles. *The Soviet Union and the Arab East under Khrushchev.* Cranbury, N.J.: Associated University Presses, 1974.

Sobolev, A. "National Democracy: The Way to Social Progress." *World Marxist Review* (Toronto), February 1963.

"Socialism, Capitalism, and the Less Developed Countries." *Mirovaya ekonomika i mezhdunarodnyye otnosheniya,* nos. 4 and 6 (1964).

Sokolovskiy, V.D., ed. *Voyennaya Strategiya,* third ed. Moscow: Voyenizdat, 1968.

Solarz, Stephen J. "Arms for Morocco?" *Foreign Affairs,* Winter 1979/1980.

Solodovnikov, V. "Some Aspects of Non-Capitalist Development," *International Affairs* (Moscow), no. 6 (1973).

Solodovnikov, V., and N. Gavrilov. "Africa: Tendencies of Non-Capitalist Development." *Mezhdunarodnaya zhizn',* no. 2 (February 1976).

"Somalia Says Ethiopia Attacked Two Towns." *The New York Times,* September 22, 1980.

Sonnenfeldt, Helmut. "Linkage: A Strategy for Tempering Soviet Antagonism." *NATO Review,* no. 1 (February 1979).

————. "Implications of the Soviet Invasion of Afghanistan for East-West Relations." *NATO Review,* no. 2 (April 1980).

South African Defense Forces Headquarters. "Nature and Extent of the SADF's Involvement in the Angolan Conflict." Pretoria, February 3, 1977.

"South Yemen Replaces President." *The New York Times,* April 22, 1980.

"Soviet Asked to Explain Turkish Border Buildup." *Baltimore Sun,* August 27, 1980.

"Soviet Commander Appears in Charge in Afghan Capital." *The New York Times,* February 26, 1980.

"Soviet Military Said to Have Morale, Drinking Problems." *Baltimore Sun,* May 7, 1981.

"Soviet Naval Force Stages Show for Southern Yemenis." *The New York Times,* May 31, 1979.

"Soviet Naval Presence Doubles in Indian Ocean, Lacks Support." *Aviation Week & Space Technology,* April 6, 1981.

"Soviet Navy Accused of Shelling Eritreans." *The New York Times,* June 18, 1978.

Soviet Report, 1, no. 1. (Washington, D.C.: Center for Strategic and International Studies, Georgetown University, November 1979).

"Soviet Said to Cancel Syrian Debt." *The New York Times,* November 4, 1979.

"Soviet Said to Enter Yemen Conflict." *The New York Times,* March 9, 1979.

"Soviet Said to Propose African Confederation." *The New York Times,* May 16, 1977.

"Soviet Sent 3,000 Experts." *The New York Times,* December 15, 1968.

"Soviets Claim Troops to Repel 'Aggression'." *Washington Star,* December 31, 1979.

"Soviets Reportedly Take Afghan Allies' Heavy Arms." *Washington Post,* September 13, 1980.

Spector, Ivar. *The Soviet Union and the Muslim World, 1917-1958.* Seattle: University of Washington Press, 1959.

St.Jorre, John de. *The Brothers' War:Biafra and Nigeria.* Boston: Houghton Mifflin Co., 1972.

Starushenko, G.B. "The Struggle against Right and Left Opportunism in Africa." In *Leninizm i bor'ba protiv burzhuaznoy ideologii i anti-Kommunizma na sovremennon etape* [Leninism and the Struggle against Bourgeois Ideology and Anti-Communism at the Present Stage], ed. M.B. Mitin. Moscow, 1970.

"Statement by Spokesman of the Chinese Government: A Comment on Soviet Government Statement of August 21." *Peking Review,* no. 36 (September 6, 1963).

"Statement of Conference of Representatives of Communist and Workers' Parties." *Pravda,* December 6, 1960.

Sterba, James P. "Gunfire Said to Continue in Kabul As Strike Keeps Businesses Closed." *The New York Times,* February 25, 1980.

Stockholm International Peace Research Institute (SIPRI). *The Arms Trade with the Third World.* New York: Humanities Press, 1971.

Stockwell, John. *In Search of Enemies.* New York: W.W. Norton and Company, 1978.

Stoessel, Walter J., Jr. Statement before the Senate Foreign Relations Committee on March 8, 1982. *Department of State Bulletin,* April 1982.

"Strategy in Africa." *The Times* (London), May 27, 1980.

Sullivan, William H. "Dateline Iran: The Road Not Taken." *Foreign Policy,* Fall 1980.

Sumbatyan, Yu.G. "The Army in the Political System of National Democracy." *Narody Azii i Afriki,* no. 4 (1969).

"Syrian Arms Minister in Soviet: Rift on Weapons May Be Subject." *The New York Times,* January 5, 1979.

"A Tale of Two Yemens." *Newsweek,* July 10, 1978.

Tanham, George K. *Communist Revolutionary Warfare: The Vietminh in Indochina.* New York: Frederick A. Praeger, 1961.

Tarabrin, E. "Africa at a New Turn of the Liberation Struggle." *Mirovaya ekonomika i mezhdunarodnyye otnosheniya,* no. 2 (February 1979).

"Teheran Threat to Recall Envoy from Moscow." *The Times* (London), August 9, 1980.

Texier, Jorge. "General and Distinct Features of the Liberation Process." *World Marxist Review* (Toronto), April 1972.

Text of UN's Afghanistan Resolution. *The New York Times,* January 15, 1980.

Theberge, James D. *Russia in the Caribbean*, Part Two. Washington, D.C.: Center for Strategic and International Studies, Georgetown University, 1973.

Thomas, Hugh. *Suez.* New York: Harper & Row, 1967.

_____ . "Cuba's 'Civilizing Mission': Lessons of the African Adventures." *Encounter* (London), February 1978.

Tikhmenev, V. "Leninism and the Revolutionary Process in Latin America." *Kommunist,* no. 3 (February 1971).

Tingay, Michael. "Yemen War Stalemate as Iraq Neutralises Soviet Moves." *Financial Times* (London), March 29, 1979.

Toth, Robert C. "New Soviet Afghan Mission." *Washington Post*, September 5, 1979.

Treverton, Gregory F. "Cuba after Angola." *The World Today* (London), January 1977.

Trewhitt, Henry L. "Somalia-Ethiopia Conflict Continues Its Devastation." *Baltimore Sun*, August 4, 1980.

Trumbull, Robert. "Foes of Afghan Rulers Are Hoping Skirmishes Will Bring on Rebellion." *The New York Times*, February 5, 1979.

Tuchnin, R. "On International Themes: An Irreversible Process." *Izvestiya*, August 5, 1979.

Twining, Major David T. "Soviet Activities in the Third World: A New Pattern." *Military Review*, June 1980, p. 6.

Tyagunenko, V.L. "The Theory and Practice of the Non-Capitalist Way of Development." *International Affairs* (Moscow), November 1970.

Tyushkevich, S.A., ed. *Sovetskiye vooruzhennyye sily: istoriya stroitel'stva* [The Soviet Armed Forces: The History of Their Construction]. Moscow: Voyenizdat, 1978.

Ulam, Adam. *Expansion and Coexistence: The History of Soviet Foreign Policy, 1917-67*. New York: Frederick A. Praeger, 1968.

Ulyanovskiy, R. "Some Features of the Present Stage of the National Liberation Movement." *Pravda*, January 3, 1968.

———. "On the Unity of the Anti-Imperialist Front of Progressive Forces in the Newly Independent States." *Mirovaya ekonomika i mezhdunarodnyye otnosheniya*, no. 9 (September 1972).

———. "The 'Third World'—Problems of Socialist Orientation." *Mezhdunarodnaya zhizn'*, no. 8 (August 1977).

———. "Concerning the Countries of Socialist Orientation." *Kommunist*, no. 11 (July 1979).

U.S. Air Force. *The Tale of Two Bridges* and *The Battle for the Skies over North Vietnam*, vol. 1. USAF Southeast Asia Monograph Series, Monographs 1 and 2. Washington, D.C.: U.S. Government Printing Office, 1976.

U.S. Arms Control and Disarmament Agency. *World Military Expenditures 1966-67*. Washington, D.C., December 1968.

———. *World Military Expenditures 1971*. Washington, D.C., July 1972.

———. *World Military Expenditures and Arms Trade 1963-1973*. Washington, D.C., 1975.

———. *World Military Expenditures and Arms Transfers 1965-1974*. Washington, D.C., 1976.

———. *World Military Expenditures and Arms Transfers 1967-1976*. Washington, D.C., July 1978.

———. *World Military Expenditures and Arms Transfers 1968-1977*. Washington, D.C., October 1979.

_____ . *World Military Expenditures and Arms Transfers 1969-1978.* Washington, D.C., December 1980.

"U.S. Cites Cuba's Role in El Salvador." *Washington Post,* March 26, 1980.

U.S. Congress. House. Committee on Foreign Affairs. Subcommittee on Inter-American Affairs. *Impact of Cuban-Soviet Ties in the Western Hemisphere, Spring 1979.* 96th Cong., 1st sess., April 25 and 26, 1979.

_____ . House. Committee on International Relations. Subcommittee on Inter-American Affairs. *Impact of Cuban-Soviet Ties in the Western Hemisphere.* 95th Cong., 2d sess., March 14 and 15, April 5 and 12, 1978.

_____ . Joint Economic Committee. *Dimensions of Soviet Economic Power.* 87th Cong., 2d sess., December 10 and 11, 1962.

_____ . Joint Economic Committee. *Soviet Economic Performance: 1966-67.* May 1968.

_____ . Joint Economic Committee. *Soviet Economic Prospects for the Seventies.* Compendium of Papers. June 27, 1973.

_____ . Joint Economic Committee. *Soviet Economy in a New Perspective.* Compendium of Papers. October 14, 1976.

_____ . Senate. Committee on Foreign Relations. Subcommittee on African Affairs. *Angola.* 94th Cong., 2d sess., January 29 and February 3, 4, and 6, 1976.

_____ . Senate. Committee on Foreign Relations. Subcommittee on African Affairs. *U.S. Policy toward Africa.* 95th Cong., 2d sess., May 12, 1978.

_____ . Senate. Committee on Foreign Relations. "Report on U.S. Conventional Arms Transfer Policy." Draft. June 3, 1980.

U.S. Department of Defense. *Annual Report, Fiscal Year 1981.* Washington, D.C., January 29, 1980.

U.S. Department of State. *Department of State Bulletin,* August 11, 1975.

_____ . *Department of State Bulletin,* January 19, 1976.

_____ . *Department of State Bulletin,* December 12, 1977.

_____ . *Department of State Bulletin,* December 1979.

_____ . *Department of State Bulletin,* June 1980.

_____ . *Department of State Bulletin,* July 1980.

_____ . *Department of State Bulletin,* December 1980.

_____ . *Department of State Bulletin,* March 1981.

_____ . *Department of State Bulletin,* April 1982.

_____ . Bureau of Intelligence and Research. *Communist States and Developing Countries: Aid and Trade in 1969.* RECS-5. Washington, D.C., July 9, 1970.

_____ . *Communist States and Developing Countries: Aid and Trade in 1970.* RECS-15. Washington, D.C., September 22, 1971.

_____ . *Communist States and Developing Countries: Aid and Trade in 1971.* RECS-3. Washington, D.C., July 10, 1972.

——— . *Communist States and Developing Countries: Aid and Trade in 1972*. RECS-10. Washington, D.C., June 15, 1973.

——— . *Communist States and Developing Countries: Aid and Trade in 1973*. INR RS-20. Washington, D.C., October 10, 1974.

——— . *Communist States and Developing Countries: Aid and Trade in 1974*. Report no. 298. Washington, D.C., January 27, 1976.

——— . Bureau of Public Affairs. Press Release no. 627, December 23, 1975.

——— . *Secretary of State Vance, Press Conference: Soviet Troops in Cuba*. Current Policy no. 85. September 5, 1979.

——— . *President Carter, Broadcast: Soviet Troops in Cuba*. Current Policy no. 92. October 1, 1979.

——— . *Background on the Question of Soviet Troops in Cuba*. Current Policy no. 93. October 1, 1979.

——— . *Soviet Invasion of Afghanistan*. Special Rept. no. 70, April 1980.

——— . *Soviet Dilemmas in Afghanistan*. Special Rept. no. 72, June 1980.

——— . "Response to Stories Published in the *Wall Street Journal* and the *Washington Post* about Special Report No. 80," June 17, 1981.

——— . *Cuba's Renewed Support for Violence in Latin America*. Special Rept. no. 90, December 14, 1981.

——— . *Chemical Warfare in Southeast Asia and Afghanistan*. Special Rept. no. 98. Report to the Congress from Secretary of State Alexander M. Haig, Jr., March 22, 1982.

——— . *Communist Interference in El Salvador*. Special Rept. no. 80, February 23, 1981; and *Communist Interference in El Salvador*. Documents Demonstrating Communist Support of the Salvadoran Insurgency, February 23, 1981.

"U.S. Puts Advisers at 8,000." *The New York Times*, December 11, 1979.

"U.S. Says Soviet Buildup Continues in Afghanistan." *Washington Post*, December 16, 1979.

USSR. Ministry of Foreign Affairs. *Sbornik deystvuyushchikh dogovorov, soglasheniy i konventsiy, zaklyuchennykh SSSR s inostrannymi gosudarstvami* [Collection of Treaties, Agreements, and Conventions in Force, Concluded by the USSR with Foreign Governments], no. 12. Moscow: Izdatel'stvo Politicheskoy Literatury, 1956.

Valdes, Nelson P. "Revolutionary Solidarity in Angola." In *Cuba in the World*, edited by Cole Blaiser and Carmelo Mesa-Lago. Pittsburgh, Pa.: University of Pittsburgh Press, 1978.

Valenta, Jiri. "The Soviet-Cuban Intervention in Angola." *Studies in Comparative Communism*, Spring/Summer 1978.

——— . "The Soviet Invasion of Afghanistan: The Difficulty of Knowing Where to Stop." *Orbis*, Summer 1980a.

——— . "From Prague to Kabul: The Soviet Style of Invasion." *International Security* 5 (Fall 1980b).

Valkenier, Elizabeth K. "Recent Trends in Soviet Research on the Developing Countries." *World Politics*, July 1968.

————. "Sino-Soviet Rivalry in the Third World." *Current History*, October 1969.

Valkenier, Elizabeth Kridl. "Soviet Economic Relations with the Developing Nations." In *The Soviet Union and the Developing Nations*, edited by Roger E. Kanet. Baltimore: Johns Hopkins University Press, 1974.

————. "The USSR, the Third World and the Global Economy." *Problems of Communism*, July-August 1979.

————. "Development Issues in Recent Soviet Scholarship." *World Politics*, no. 4 (July 1980).

Vance, Cyrus. In U.S. Congress. Senate. Committee on Foreign Relations. Subcommittee on African Affairs. *U.S. Policy toward Africa*. 95th Cong., 2d sess., May 12, 1978.

Vance, Cyrus. *Soviet Troops in Cuba*, Current Policy no. 85. Washington, D.C., Department of State, Bureau of Public Affairs, September 5, 1979.

Van Hollen, Eliza. *Soviet Dilemmas in Afghanistan*. Special Report no. 72. Washington, D.C.: Department of State, Bureau of Public Affairs, June 1980.

————. "Afghanistan: A Year of Occupation." *Department of State Bulletin*, March 1981a.

————. "Afghanistan: 18 Months of Occupation." *Department of State Bulletin*, October 1981b.

————. "Afghanistan: 2 Years of Occupation. Special Report no. 91. Washington, D.C.: Department of State, Bureau of Public Affairs, December 1981c.

Vanneman, Peter, and Martin James. "The Soviet Intervention in Angola: Intentions and Implications." *Strategic Review*, Summer 1976.

————. "Soviet Thrust into the Horn of Africa: The Next Targets." *Strategic Review*, Spring 1978.

Verbin, U. "Defending the Gains of the Revolution." *Izvestiya*, March 20, 1979.

Volsky, George. "Cuba's Foreign Policies." *Current History*, February 1976.

Walker, Lannon. Statement before the Subcommittee on Africa of the House Foreign Affairs Committee on March 5, 1980. *Department of State Bulletin* 80 (August 1980).

"War in the Horn." *Newsweek*, February 13, 1978.

Weinland, Robert G. "Soviet Transits of the Turkish Straits: 1945-1970." In *Soviet Naval Developments: Capability and Context*, edited by Michael MccGwire. New York: Praeger Publishers, 1973.

————. "Land Support for Naval Forces: Egypt and the Soviet Escadra 1962-1976." *Survival* (London), March/April 1978.

Whetten, Lawrence L. "June 1967 to June 1971: Four Years of Canal War Reconsidered." *New Middle East*, June 1971.

_____ . *The Canal War: Four-Power Conflict in the Middle East*. Cambridge, Mass.: MIT Press, 1974.

Whitaker, Jennifer Seymour, ed. *Africa and the United States: Vital Interests*. New York: New York University Press, 1978.

Whiting, Allen S. *China Crosses the Yalu: The Decision to Enter the Korean War*. Stanford, Calif.: Stanford University Press, 1960.

Whiting, Kenneth R. *The Chinese Communist Armed Forces*. Air University Documentary Research Study, AU-11, Maxwell Air Force Base, Ala.: 1974.

Whitney, Craig R. "20-Year Treaty Brings Afghans Closer to Soviet." *The New York Times*, December 6, 1978.

_____ . "Moscow Says Drive into Cambodia Is by Vietnamese-Supported Rebels." *The New York Times*, January 5, 1979.

_____ . "Moscow Backs Iran on Hostages While Conceding Breach of Rules." *The New York Times*, December 6, 1979.

_____ . "U.S. Aides in Soviet Angered over Iran." *The New York Times*, December 7, 1979.

_____ . "Afghans Offer Way for Soviet Pullout." *The New York Times*, May 15, 1980.

_____ . "Soviet Seen Attempting to Sow Discord in West." *The New York Times*, June 23, 1980.

Willenson, Kim. "Red Stars over Africa." *Newsweek*, March 13, 1978, p. 39.

Wilson, George C. "Soviet Use of Cam Ranh Bay as Sub Base Arouses U.S. Concern." *Washington Post*, May 10, 1979.

_____ . "Departing Soviets Unneeded in Afghanistan War." *Washington Post*, June 26, 1980.

_____ . " 'Contingency Plans' for Caribbean Being Drafted, Pentagon Tells Hill," *Washington Post*, December 16, 1981.

Wimbush, S. Enders, and Alex Alexiev. *Soviet Central Asian Soldiers in Afghanistan*. N-1634-NA. Santa Monica, Calif.: The Rand Corporation, January 1981.

Wohlstetter, Roberta. *Cuba and Pearl Harbor: Hindsight and Foresight*. RM-4328-ISA. Santa Monica, Calif.: The Rand Corporation, April 1965.

Wolfe, Thomas W. *The Soviet Quest for More Globally Mobile Military Power*. RM-5554-PR. Santa Monica, Calif.: The Rand Corporation, December 1967.

_____ . *Soviet Power and Europe: 1945-1970*. Baltimore: Johns Hopkins University Press, 1970.

_____ . "Soviet Naval Interaction with the United States and Its Influence on Soviet Naval Developments." In *Soviet Naval Developments: Capability and Context*, edited by Michael MccGwire. New York: Praeger Publishers, 1973.

Wren, Christopher S. "Modern Soviet Arms on Way to Damascus." *The New York Times*, November 4, 1979.

_____ . "In Yemen, the East and West Do Meet." *The New York Times*, May 7, 1980.

_____ . "Forgotten War in Ethiopia's Ogaden Heats up Again." *The New York Times*, May 26, 1980.

_____ . "Big Power Rivalry Echoed in Latest Yemen Shake-Up." *The New York Times*, April 27, 1981.

Wyden, Peter. *Bay of Pigs: The Untold Story*. New York: Simon & Schuster, 1979.

Yelyanov, A. *Razvivayushchiyesya strany: Problemy ekonomicheskogo razvitiya i rynok* [The Developing Countries: Problems of Economic Development and the Market]. Moscow: Izdatel'stvo Mysl', 1976.

Zagoria, Donald S. *Vietnam Triangle: Moscow, Peking, Hanoi*. New York: Pegasus, 1967.

_____ . "Moscow's Friendship: Catalyst for Third World Aggression." Letter to the editor. *The New York Times*, January 19, 1979.

_____ . "Into the Breach: New Soviet Alliances in the Third World." *Foreign Affairs*, Spring 1979.

Zagorodnikov, Lt. Col. N. "The Military Might of the Socialist System and the World Revolutionary Process." *Kommunist vooruzhennykh sil*, no. 16 (August 1966).

Zarine, D. "Classes and Class Struggle in Developing Countries." *International Affairs* (Moscow), no. 4 (April 1968).

Zaytsev, Maj. Gen. A., and Col. V. Kondrashov. "The Downfall of Imperialism's Colonial System." *Kommunist vooruzhennykh sil*, March 1980.

Zhdanov, Andrey. "The International Situation." *For a Lasting Peace, For a People's Democracy* (Moscow), November 10, 1947.

Zhukov, E.M. "Problems of the National-Liberation Struggle after the Second World War." *Voprosy ekonomiki*, no. 9 (1949).

Zimmerman, William. "The Korean and Vietnam Wars." In *Diplomacy of Power. Soviet Armed Forces as a Political Instrument*, edited by Stephen S. Kaplan. Washington, D.C.: The Brookings Institution, 1981.

Zumwalt, Adm. Elmo R., Jr. *On Watch*. New York: Quadrangle/The New York Times Book Co., 1976.

Index

About the Authors

Stephen T. Hosmer is a senior staff member of The Rand Corporation in its Washington, D.C., office. He received his academic training at Yale University where he was a Ford Foundation and Overbrook Fellow and received the M.A. in Southeast Asia Studies and the Ph.D. in International Relations. Prior to joining Rand in 1961, Dr. Hosmer served in the U.S. Air Force as an Intelligence Staff Officer specializing in Asian affairs. At Rand, his research has focused primarily on national security issues relating to East and Southeast Asia, communist revolutionary warfare, and Third World conflicts. He is the author of *Viet Cong Repression and Its Implications for the Future* and the coauthor of *The Fall of South Vietnam: Statements by Vietnamese Military and Civilian Leaders.*

Thomas W. Wolfe is an internationally known authority on Soviet military affairs and foreign policy. Author of *Soviet Strategy at the Crossroads, Soviet Power and Europe: 1945-1970,* and *The SALT Experience,* he is also a contributing author to more than a dozen other books on Soviet matters, including *Prospects for Soviet Society, Soviet Naval Development, The Soviet Impact on World Politics,* and *The Soviet Empire: Expansion and Détente.*

Formerly a senior staff member of The Rand Corporation and a faculty member of the Institute for Sino-Soviet Studies, George Washington University, Dr. Wolfe is a retired regular U.S. Air Force colonel who served as U.S. Air Attaché in Moscow in the late 1950s. He subsequently traveled to the USSR as a visiting scholar on several occasions in the 1960s and 1970s. Dr. Wolfe is currently a consultant to The Rand Corporation. He received the B.A. degree from Hiram College, the M.A. from Columbia University, and the Ph.D. from Georgetown University.

Selected Rand Books

Brewer, Garry D., and Martin Shubik. *The War Game: A Critique of Military Problem Solving*. Cambridge, Mass.: Harvard University Press, 1979.

Dinerstein, H.S. *War and the Soviet Union: Nuclear Weapons and the Revolution in Soviet Military and Political Thinking*. New York: Frederick A. Praeger, Inc., 1959. Reprint Edition, Westport, Conn.: Greenwood Press, 1976.

Fainsod, Merle. *Smolensk under Soviet Rule*. Cambridge, Mass.: Harvard University Press, 1958.

Garthoff, Raymond L. *Soviet Military Doctrine*. Glencoe, Ill.: Free Press, 1953.

Goldhamer, Herbert. *The Soviet Soldier: Soviet Military Management at the Troop Level*. New York: Crane, Russak & Company, Inc., 1975.

Horelick, Arnold L., and Myron Rush. *Strategic Power and Soviet Foreign Policy*. Chicago, Ill.: University of Chicago Press, 1966.

Hosmer, Stephen T. *Viet Cong Repression and Its Implications for the Future*. Lexington, Mass.: D.C. Heath and Company, 1970.

Hosmer, Stephen T.; Konrad Kellen; and Brian M. Jenkins. *The Fall of South Vietnam: Statements by Vietnamese Military and Civilian Leaders*. New York: Crane, Russak & Company, Inc., 1980.

Hsieh, Alice Langley. *Communist China's Strategy in the Nuclear Era*. Englewood Cliffs, N.J.: Prentice-Hall, Inc., 1962. Reprint Edition, Westport, Conn.: Greenwood Press, 1976.

Johnson, A. Ross; Robert W. Dean; and Alexander Alexiev. *East European Military Establishments: The Warsaw Pact Northern Tier*. New York: Crane, Russak & Company, Inc., 1982.

Johnson, John J., ed. *The Role of the Military in Underdeveloped Countries*. Princeton, N.J.: Princeton University Press, 1962.

Kolkowicz, Roman. *The Soviet Military and the Communist Party*. Princeton, N.J.: Princeton University Press, 1967.

Leites, Nathan. *The Operational Code of the Politburo*. New York: McGraw-Hill Book Company, Inc., 1951. Reprint Edition, Westport, Conn.: Greenwood Press, 1972.

———. *Soviet Style in War*. New York: Crane, Russak & Company, Inc., 1982.

Leites, Nathan, and Charles Wolf, Jr. *Rebellion and Authority: An Analytic Essay on Insurgent Conflicts*. Chicago: Markham Publishing Company, 1970.

Rush, Myron. *The Rise of Khrushchev*. Washington, D.C.: Public Affairs Press, 1958.

_____ . *Political Succession in the USSR*. New York: Columbia University Press, 1965.

Sokolovskii, V.D., ed. *Soviet Military Strategy*. Englewood Cliffs, N.J.: Prentice-Hall, 1963.

Solomon, Richard H., ed. *Asian Security in the 1980s: Problems and Policies for a Time of Transition*. Cambridge, Mass.: Oelgeschlager, Gunn & Hain, Publishers, Inc., 1980.

Tanham, G.K. *Communist Revolutionary Warfare: The Vietminh in Indochina*. New York: Frederick A. Praeger, 1961.

Wolfe, Thomas W. *Soviet Strategy at the Crossroads*. Cambridge, Mass.: Harvard University Press, 1964.

_____ . *Soviet Power and Europe, 1945-1970*. Baltimore: Johns Hopkins University Press, 1970.

_____ . *The SALT Experience*. Cambridge, Mass.: Ballinger Publishing Company, 1979.